THIRSTY
DRAGON

THIRSTY DRAGON

China's Lust
for Bordeaux
and the Threat
to the World's
Best Wines

Suzanne Mustacich

Henry Holt and Company
New York

Henry Holt and Company, LLC
Publishers since 1866
175 Fifth Avenue
New York, New York 10010
www.henryholt.com

Henry Holt® and 🛡® are registered trademarks of Henry Holt and Company, LLC.

Library of Congress Cataloging-in-Publication Data

Mustacich, Suzanne, author.
  Thirsty dragon : China's lust for Bordeaux and the threat to the world's best wines / Suzanne Mustacich. — First edition.
    pages cm
  ISBN 978-1-62779-087-1 (hardback) — ISBN 978-1-62779-088-8 (e-book)   1. Wine industry—France—Bordeaux (Aquitaine)   2. Wine and wine making—France—Bordeaux (Aquitaine)
3. China—Commerce—France.   4. France—Commerce—China.   I. Title.
  HD9382.7.B6M87 2015
  338.4′766322309447144—dc23

                                                                                            2015015519

Henry Holt books are available for special promotions and premiums.
For details contact: Director, Special Markets.

First Edition 2015

Designed by Meryl Sussman Levavi

Map by Jeffrey Ward

Printed in the United States of America

1   3   5   7   9   10   8   6   4   2

Pétrus and Pétrus.
This story is for you.

Contents

....

1. First Growths   1

2. No Boundaries   23

3. Planting Vines   53

4. Lucky Red   81

5. Château Mania   104

6. All in a Name   130

7. Standoff   157

8. Shifting Winds   186

9. *Gan Bei*   215

10. Adjust Measures to Local Conditions   244

Epilogue: Shangri-La   270

Notes   283

Acknowledgments   323

Index   327

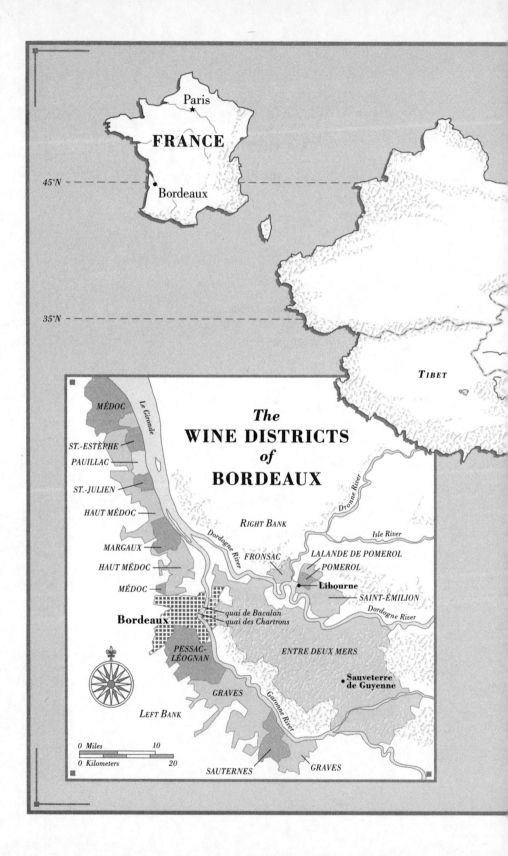

FRANCE

Paris

Bordeaux

45°N

35°N

TIBET

The
WINE DISTRICTS
of
BORDEAUX

MÉDOC

Le Gironde

ST.-ESTÈPHE

PAUILLAC

ST.-JULIEN

HAUT MÉDOC

RIGHT BANK

Dronne River

Isle River

MARGAUX

Dordogne River

FRONSAC

LALANDE DE POMEROL

POMEROL

HAUT MÉDOC

MÉDOC

Libourne

SAINT-ÉMILION

Dordogne River

Bordeaux

quai de Bacalan
quai des Chartrons

PESSAC-
LÉOGNAN

ENTRE DEUX MERS

Sauveterre
de Guyenne

GRAVES

Garonne River

LEFT BANK

0 Miles   10

0 Kilometers   20

SAUTERNES

GRAVES

45°N

INNER MONGOLIA

GOBI DESERT

Beijing ★   CHANGLI
                COUNTY

ANSU   Helan Mountains   Yinchuan   Tianjin   Dalian
                                          Bohai Sea
                                    Taiyuan   Penglai   Yellow
                                                   Yantai   Sea

NINGXIA HUI   SHANDONG   35°N
AUTONOMOUS   Qingdao
REGION   SHAANXI   Tai Shan Mountains

         SICHUAN   Yangtze River

Shangri-La   Shanghai
(Zhongdian)

ekong River
Yangtze River

CHINA

                                          Wenzhou

                                    Fuzhou

                                                 0 Miles   500
YUNNAN   0 Kilometers   500
                        GUANGDONG
             Guangzhou   Xiamen   TAIWAN
Pu'er   Shenzhen

                        Hong Kong
                  Macau

BORDEAUX
and the
WINE REGIONS
of
CHINA

THIRSTY
DRAGON

Author's Note

This is a true story, though some names and details have been changed or withheld.

1

First Growths

 Uncertainty hung over the Place de Bordeaux in the early spring of 2009.

Jean-Pierre Rousseau hoped the First Growth estates would release their prices early, setting the tone and tempo for that year's sales campaign. During a bullish year, the five most prestigious Bordeaux châteaux—known as the First Growths—sat back and waited, calculating exactly how high the prices for their wines might go, dragging out the campaign into late June, when everyone would rather be at the beach. During a bad year—and the campaign for the 2008 vintage was shaping up to be particularly bad—the merchants hoped the First Growths would release their prices early, because there was no campaign to speak of, and the pricing hierarchy for Bordeaux's wines was set from the top down. This year, however, banks were collapsing in the United States and Europe and the economy was in free fall; there was really no telling what the First Growths would do.

The Place de Bordeaux isn't a square or a leafy promenade or even a physical building; it is the virtual exchange through which Bordeaux's wines have been sold for centuries, and Rousseau was a *négociant*, which meant he was a wholesale wine merchant. As was the custom, he bought wine from the châteaux through a licensed intermediary, called a *courtier*, who brokered the deals. Courtiers were famously tight-lipped, taking 2 percent on every transaction for settling the price and amount of wine— called the *allocation*—granted by a winegrower to a négociant, and guaranteeing the quality and provenance of the wine. The arm's-length nature of the deals buffered some of the natural suspicion and animosity between growers and négociants. For as long as they had been trading, more than eight hundred years, the négociants tried to drive down prices, and the growers tried to push them up. The négociants needed lower prices to ensure that they could sell the wines to their clients around the world without losing money. Some vintages might be sold instantly, but others might not find a customer until they were in bottles and ready to ship, two years down the line. And some might not sell even then.

In the spring of 2009, the courtiers and négociants fervently hoped they were not going down in flames. For the past several months, the market for Bordeaux wine had been collapsing, a casualty of the global economic crisis. Importers couldn't place orders because their credit lines were frozen. Restaurants closed their doors for lack of customers. Collectors, hit hard for cash, emptied the contents of their cellars at firesale prices. And for the first time since the Asian banking crisis of the late 1990s, canceled orders were flooding into the Place de Bordeaux. In a matter of days, the châteaux would offer six hundred million bottles of their new vintage for sale, and customers were begging off. The mood on the Place de Bordeaux was morose.

Not a customer in front of us, thought Rousseau.

He knew how much he could spend, and he knew that many of the smaller négociants didn't have the cash reserves to buy wine they couldn't immediately resell.

When the market was like this, the larger négociants—Compagnie des Vins de Bordeaux et de la Gironde (CVBG), Maison Ginestet, Maison Joanne, Maison Schröder & Schÿler, and Rousseau's own firm, Diva— increased their allocations of certain wines, so that when the market turned, and it would turn eventually, they would control large quantities of the most sought-after labels. "There is always someone trying to replace you," said Rousseau. "It's so difficult to get allocations of the top châteaux that no one wants to leave the stage."

It was a crapshoot, but no one stepped onto the Place de Bordeaux if he didn't like to gamble.

Late on the afternoon of April 16, 2009, one of the five First Growth estates, Château Lafite Rothschild, released its 2008 vintage at €130 ($166) per bottle. For any négociant who still had money, this was a very good deal indeed: it was 30 percent cheaper than any other available Lafite vintage. Other châteaux followed suit, dropping their prices in the face of the weak market. But the gesture was not enough for the American distribution giant Château & Estate Wines. For the first time in thirty-five years, C&E refused its Bordeaux allocations, leaving a huge quantity of the world's finest wines unwanted and unsold. The betrayal reverberated across the region.

At Diva's offices at 34 quai de Bacalan, Rousseau looked on with a mix of resignation, satisfaction, and curiosity. It had been a predictably feeble campaign, but he had taken advantage of the lower prices and the weakness of certain of his competitors to increase his allocations. The wines would not be bottled for another eighteen months, but he felt he could hold on until the market turned. And he hadn't been forced to finance as much of his purchases out of his own pocket as he had feared. He had already resold some of the wine to regular customers who were weathering the banking crisis, which had helped to reduce his exposure. But it was his client in Hong Kong that had jumped in with both feet. The percentage of Rousseau's business with that client had doubled. It was extraordinary.

"I've sold 20 percent of the wine to Topsy Trading," he said with a combination of relief and astonishment.

The impact on Bordeaux would be immediate if slight, a rivulet sprung from a barrel.

✳

Topsy Trading is a Hong Kong–based wine importer owned by a legendary local merchant named Thomas Yip. Yip's family had fled Sichuan Province for Hong Kong shortly after the Communists took control of

China in 1949. The Yips were entrepreneurs, and by the time Thomas was in his twenties in the 1960s, he was running his own travel business. When his wife pressured him to find a more stable income, he took a job in the warehouse of Caldbeck MacGregor & Company, the leading wine and spirits importer in East Asia.

From its premises at 4 Foochow Road, just off the Bund in Shanghai, Caldbeck MacGregor had dominated the market for fine wine in that city's international settlement before the revolution. After 1949, the company's Hong Kong office slaked the thirst of the British colony's many diplomats and businessmen. Yip was quickly promoted to controller of the company's wine division, where he thrived, building a network of contacts in the cellars of Europe and in Hong Kong's hotels, restaurants, and duty-free shops.

Within a few years, the Hong Kong and Shanghai Hotels group, informally known as the Peninsula Hotels group, recruited Yip to supply wine to its hotels, and when he proved good at it, Peninsula branched out and started supplying wine to other hotels as well as restaurants. In 1976, the company created Lucullus, a wine and food outfit, putting Yip in charge.

Nothing symbolized the tangled history of China, Hong Kong, and commerce more than Peninsula. The hotel group was owned by the Kadoorie family, Sephardic Jews from Baghdad who had arrived in Shanghai via Bombay in the nineteenth century and had made a name for themselves as international merchants. As their influence and wealth grew, the Kadoories diversified into real estate and utilities, founding Hong Kong's first electricity company, China Light & Power Company Syndicate, in 1901. When the Japanese seized Hong Kong during the Second World War, the British surrendered to their conquerors at the Kadoories' Peninsula Hotel in Kowloon. Several family members were imprisoned during the war, and another heavy blow came after the Communist victory in 1949, when Mao Zedong's government forced the Kadoories to sell their stakes in their prized properties, including the Palace Hotel and the Astor House hotel, at a heavy loss. Despite this, the family decided to stay in Hong Kong, rebuilding and investing.

Three decades later, in 1979, the Kadoorie family agreed to manage the 528-room Jianguo Hotel, a five-star hotel in Beijing, the first hotel joint venture in the People's Republic of China. When Deng Xiaoping launched his policy of *gaige kaifang* in December 1978, opening China to the West, few believed Deng would achieve his goal of quadrupling China's gross domestic product within twenty years through a transition to state capitalism. But Deng did what his predecessors never dared: he admitted that his country could benefit from Western science, technology, manufacturing, banking, and commerce. China would import and absorb all that the West knew, and export all that it wanted to buy. To accelerate the process, Deng allowed the formation of joint ventures between Western corporations and Chinese state agencies, including the Jianguo Hotel.

At Jianguo, Thomas Yip was responsible for the first private contract to import wine into China. As he considered his orders for the hotel and its restaurant, Justine's—the first French restaurant in Communist China—Yip realized that he would be selecting a wine list for foreigners, who could afford to spend a night or a week in a luxury hotel, and not for Chinese workers, who drank a fiery grain alcohol called *baijiu*. There were no Chinese consumers yet for imported wine. The country was desperately poor and primarily agrarian; the Chinese did not have wineglasses, decanters, or corkscrews, and they did not dream of vineyard landscapes and First Growths aging quietly in the cellar. Per capita annual income was $182. A night at the Jianguo cost $90 to $120. Even a thimbleful of Bordeaux's most basic wine was well beyond the spending power of most government or military officials, let alone a typical Chinese family.

But Yip knew exactly what the first luxury hotel in the People's Republic of China needed on its wine list, and it was Bordeaux. Five-star hotels, watering holes for expats and tycoons, were Bordeaux's reliable clients all over the world. At the time, the entire Chinese trade for Bordeaux was worth just $10,000, a scanty 311 cases shipped directly to the diplomatic missions. But Bordeaux's commercial structure meant that famed wines such as Château Lafite were sold as commodities, making them available to anyone, anywhere.

From Yip's perspective, what made Bordeaux especially marketable was the 1855 Classification, which singled out sixty-one châteaux, mostly from the Médoc peninsula, as the leading wines from France's largest and wealthiest wine-growing region. It appealed to connoisseurs and novices alike. Everyone easily grasped the five rankings, and the classification made it easy to justify a hierarchy of prices. It read like a supply and price list, ratified by pomp and history—which was exactly what it was.

The classification was originally created for that year's Universal Exhibition in Paris. In the months leading up to the opening, the leading citizens of Bordeaux were arguing over which wines to send. The previous November, they had received a letter from Dijon stating that the winegrowers of Burgundy and Champagne were putting their wines on display for the world's visitors, but none of Bordeaux's elite had thought to send their wine to Paris. Wine was a traditional agricultural product, hardly an example of French industrial might. But the Bordeaux growers had heard that their competitors from Burgundy and Champagne were going to be represented at the exposition, and they wanted to be included as well.

This created a delicate situation. Both the growers and the négociants had a financial interest in how the wines were to be presented to the exposition's expected five million visitors, and they weren't completely aligned. At the time, nearly all wine was bottled by the négociants, who bought it in barrels from numerous châteaux, aged the wine in their cellars, and labeled the bottles for public consumption. Quality and quantity varied from vintage to vintage, and the system allowed the négociants to combine the harvest from more than one estate in the same commune, or village, in order to bottle enough of a distinct wine. Négociants gained recognition not only for their business acumen but also for their ability to blend and age wines. The négociant's name on the bottle's label was more important than the name of the estate or the location of the commune. Still, some estates managed to achieve renown for their wine, and these wines were sold as "château" wines. Several négociants might sell wine from the same château, and the bottles would carry the négociant's label. The négociants had all the power.

The exhibition presented an opportunity as well as a threat. Some growers thought they could use the limelight of the exhibition to achieve higher rankings on the courtiers' price lists. Others might even have hoped to cut out the négociants, circumventing the Place de Bordeaux and contacting buyers directly. The négociants could not countenance that; it would spell the end of their livelihood.

Tensions were heightened by the question of how to label and rank the wines. Everyone agreed that there were far too many Bordeaux wines for all of them to be presented physically, and that a selection of the best wines should represent the region. They also agreed that a lineup of uniform bottles did not make a good display; Bordeaux's wines would come across as ordinary rather than individual and magnificent. The selection of the wines and the design of the labels required diplomatic handling, so as not to give advantage to either side, nor allow a single château to stand out. In the end, the wines were labeled with the name of the château and the owner, and the display at the exhibition was illustrated with a large map of the entire region, promoting the different wine villages.

The task of ranking the wines was given to the courtiers, who kept meticulous notebooks listing the transactions for each vintage. Prices varied by vintage, of course, but the relative hierarchy of prices remained fairly stable. It was impractical and inefficient for the courtiers to renegotiate prices each year, especially as the reputations of many wines were well established. A few estates were known to the courtiers for consistently making higher quality wines, and these were sold under the name of the estate rather than the name of the commune. The practice inspired other growers to improve their wine, too.

The courtiers had started calling the most expensive wines *Premier Crus*, or First Growths. So when the Union of Courtiers was asked to rank the red wines of Bordeaux for the display, they quickly consulted their meticulous notebooks and selected sixty wines, placing them into five *crus*, or growths, according to their reputation and typical prices. All were produced on the Left Bank of the Gironde estuary as it flowed to the Atlantic Ocean. Within each growth, the names were listed alphabetically on the illustrative map, with the courtiers insisting that the estates of each category were of equal merit. They also published the price range for each growth to justify their rankings. Three red wines from the Médoc peninsula were placed in the Premier Cru: Château Lafite, Château Latour, Château Margaux. They were joined by one red wine from the Graves, Château Haut-Brion, the first estate to obtain higher prices than other wines from Bordeaux.

The 1855 Classification was never intended to be an official, perpetual guide to Bordeaux. Even as the courtiers submitted their list, they demurred from an "official list" as the classification was a "delicate thing & likely to arouse sensitivities." But the guide was such a success that it has been modified only twice since its inception. Not long before the exposition closed, Château Cantemerle was added to the list of Fifth Growths. Then nothing changed until 1973, when Château Mouton Rothschild rose from Second Growth to First Growth status, following decades of lobbying by its owner, Baron Philippe de Rothschild. What started as a courtiers' price list became an immutable promotional tool—a stamp of quality that transcended a single year's bad weather and a buying guide in shorthand, written by an ostensibly neutral authority. It frustrated the upwardly mobile aspirations of lower-ranked châteaux, but it made Bordeaux the envy of wine regions around the world. While later classifications were developed for other regions, the 1855 remained the calling card for Bordeaux, used by négociants to introduce the wines into new markets.

Thomas Yip saw that the 1855 Classification was perfect for the Chinese market because it satisfied a deep cultural itch: the need to save and display "face," particularly the forms of face known as *gei mianzi* and *liu mianzi*. Gei mianzi was the Chinese belief that you gave face or honored someone by showing him or her respect. The most frequent example was offering a gift appropriate to a person's status. Liu mianzi was the belief that you gained face by avoiding mistakes. Wise action reinforced your honor and reputation.

The classification had history, allure, and a precise ranking of status. It was a gift giver's dream.

❋

Just a short drive from the Chai Wan subway station on Hong Kong's Island Line, wedged between tire shops and mechanics, Thomas Yip had found space for his new firm's offices. The wide road was often two cars deep with repair jobs, and the door to the Yip Cheung Center at 10 Fung Yip Street was easy to miss. The name of the building and the name of the street had nothing to do with Yip or his family, but the coincidence seemed fortuitous. Befitting the surroundings, the building lobby was little more than a dingy entryway. To get to Yip's offices, visitors took the service elevator to the thirteenth floor, then climbed a final flight of stairs to the door marked TOPSY TRADING COMPANY, LTD.

Yip founded the company in 1982, building on the contacts he had made in supplying wine for the Peninsula Hotels group. He saw the potential for profit in buying wines that he thought would appreciate in value, and at the top of his list were the wines of Bordeaux. The quality was trustworthy and the international renown was unparalleled. And Bordeaux's method of distribution meant that he could buy dozens of different wines from a handful of négociants.

The greatest potential for capital appreciation came from buying wines *en primeur*, purchasing a quantity of wine two years before the vintage matured enough to be bottled, but which could then be sold at a healthy markup to wealthy customers in Hong Kong and China. For the first ten years, Yip didn't have the cash reserves to buy en primeur, but he did allow himself two exceptions: in the spring of 1983, just after he started Topsy, he ordered five cases of the 1982 Château Pétrus and ten cases of the 1982 Château La Fleur–Pétrus from the Mouiex family, old friends from his Peninsula days. He paid 180 French francs (about thirty-four dollars) for each bottle of Pétrus en primeur, he recalled. It was a beautiful price. The bottles arrived fifteen months later, with TOPSY TRAD-ING printed in English and Mandarin on the lower part of the front label—a landmark moment that stayed with him.

The first sign that things were changing came in 1994. The en primeur campaign in Bordeaux had been tepid, to say the least. Christophe Reboul Salze was a young wine merchant working for CVBG, one of the largest négociant firms. The fine wines Reboul Salze sold represented less than

5 percent of Bordeaux's volume, but they brought glamour to the region and wealth to those who made and traded them. Now they were piling up in cellars, contributing neither glamour nor wealth. Profits had disappeared. Reboul Salze had just sold the 1993 vintage from Château Pichon Longueville Comtesse de Lalande, a lovely Pauillac estate, for a paltry $13.71 a bottle. That gave him a 4 percent margin over his purchase price, not enough to earn his keep. And he wasn't alone on the Place de Bordeaux. The châteaux were as desperate to do deals as the négociants were.

Through a series of discreet phone calls, the courtiers arranged meetings between representatives of CVBG and the growers. The châteaux quietly admitted they were ready to sell large single lots of certain vintages to clear out their cellars. The deals were huge—a thousand cases here, five hundred cases there. CVBG hired seven trucks to haul away its windfall.

But the sell-off wasn't over. Christophe Salin, the president and CEO of Domaines Barons de Rothschild (Lafite), made contact with CVBG CEO Jean-Paul Jauffret, which placed a single-lot deal in front of Reboul Salze that there was no question of CVBG turning down: one thousand cases of 1982 Château Lafite, one of the great vintages of the century. It would be a beautiful coup for the wine merchant, so long as he could sell it. CVBG's export manager had built a network of Asian clients, and Thomas Yip figured on the list. Reboul Salze mentally thumbed through his Rolodex. *Whom do I call? Who has the money to take on a deal this size?*

When the phone rang and Yip heard that Reboul Salze was calling with an offer from Lafite, he gestured for his son Vincent to listen in. Vincent had just finished school and was now working for his father, and this was going to be one of his first lessons in how the Bordeaux wine trade worked.

"Thomas," Reboul Salze began, "I have a good deal here and I want to ask you what you think: 1982 Lafite, from the château's cellars, one thousand cases. You take half, I take half, split the margin."

The 1982 Lafite was arguably one of the finest wines ever produced in Bordeaux. The provenance was perfect, too—direct from the château.

"Let's do it," Thomas said without hesitation.

When he hung up the phone, he knew this was his big break. He could feel it.

China was a Lilliputian wine market in 1994, and no one imagined there were customers there to buy the wine piling up in Bordeaux's cellars. And surely Bordeaux didn't need China. It had its faithful followers across Europe and America, who would soon come rushing back when news spread of the excellent 1995 vintage, one of Bordeaux's finest, and the region started to boast about that year's record crop, a staggering 872 million bottles. Though Jean-Pierre Rousseau wasn't able to sell everything he bought en primeur, the remaining wine was gaining value for the first time in years. The business at the heart of Bordeaux— speculation—was paying off. The relief on the Place de Bordeaux was palpable.

Thomas Yip had known from the start that there was no demand on the mainland for his allocations of Bordeaux. He first had to convince the Chinese to drink it. He threw parties and hosted events, creating what he deemed to be an appropriate atmosphere for wine. When he served the wine, he explained that it was made from grape juice that had been fermented, so there was a little alcohol. He'd explain that it was good for one's health. He'd politely show people how to store and uncork a bottle, how to decant it, and how to pour a glass. He never suggested that anyone stop drinking traditional Chinese drinks, but he did intimate that they might find pleasure in widening their drinking habits. He was so knowledgeable about French wine that he was inevitably asked what he did for a living. Weeks, maybe months later, he'd get a call and an order for some of that wine he'd been talking about.

The Yips started getting requests from businesses dealing with the government as well as from a high-ranking Chinese government official who wanted wine in order to entertain important guests. The official didn't know anything about wine, and the Yips had a reputation for being discreet and professional. The client didn't know anyone with a wine cellar nor did he have one himself, so Thomas dispatched Vincent to Beijing to quietly oversee the construction of a small cellar. But the official's real concern was the quality of the wine. The government was trying to attract as much investment as possible from the West. There weren't many joint ventures in those days, and the message was invariably the same: "I need to impress them. I need them to come invest."

Yip reassured the official. He had just the wine for him, one with an impeccable pedigree: Château Lafite, a legendary wine, one of the four original First Growths. No one could fault such a gift. He happened to have some stock of Lafite's 1982 vintage, direct from the château's cellar. It wasn't too expensive, maybe two hundred Hong Kong dollars a bottle. The official bought them.

The five hundred cases of Lafite that Yip had bought from Reboul Salze were such a success that he returned to the Place de Bordeaux for more, albeit at a higher price. And he let other négociants know that he was open to making more big single-lot deals. When Reboul Salze offered a thousand cases of the 1989 Lafite at 485 French francs ($91) per bottle, Yip took it, even though he knew the price was going to be difficult for most of his customers. So now he was looking for something less expensive to round out his stocks.

Topsy Trading was already offering three wines that enjoyed some recognition in greater China: Châteaux Beychevelle, Talbot, and Lynch-Bages. Although it was a Fifth Growth, the Yips found it particularly easy to sell Château Lynch-Bages because it was served to first-class passengers on Cathay Pacific, Hong Kong's flagship airline.

In 1989, the owner of Château Lynch-Bages, Jean-Michel Cazes, had never heard of Cathay Pacific and he'd never been to Hong Kong, but he had inherited the management of an estate in need of major investment. So when he got a call from Jean-Claude Rouzaud, the head of his own family's Champagne Louis Roederer group, to say Cathay Pacific needed a large stock of classified growth red wine that would set them apart from their competitors, Cazes didn't hesitate. He wasn't going to ignore a potential client, even if he'd never heard of it. The negotiations over the order were marked by caution and suspicion. Cazes contacted the Banque de France de Commerce d'Extérieur to make sure his new client wasn't suspected of laundering money. Cathay Pacific insisted that its cases be stored in a segregated area in the château's cellar and that the vintages be verified by a notary, to ensure that it was indeed receiving the wine it had paid for.

Finally, Cazes signed the biggest sale in the history of the estate: twenty-three thousand cases of Château Lynch-Bages. Naturally, the Cathay Pacific buyer had only wanted the best vintages, such as the 1982. Instead, Cazes gently persuaded the airline to buy nine consecutive vintages, ranging from 1980 to 1988; otherwise, there would be no deal. He even got the buyer to pay the current price on the Place de Bordeaux for the older vintages. The total came to 35 million French francs. Cazes was staggered by the immensity of it. It was an incredible deal.

It was the kind of product placement that made the Yips' job easier. Unfortunately, not all of the Bordelais had been so lucky, and these days Vincent Yip needed to pick potential winners on his own. He looked over the price list Reboul Salze had sent by fax and noticed a wine called Carruades de Lafite, which carried the magic name of "Lafite." It was cheap—much cheaper than the 1982 vintage he had just bought. He'd never heard of it, so he decided to call Reboul Salze and ask him about it. Reboul Salze admitted that the price was right; the quality was only average. It was the second wine of Château Lafite, named after the Carruades plateau, which had been added to the estate in 1845. It had previously been called Moulin de Carruades, and the winemakers at Lafite hoped it would sell better under the new name.

Vincent was still new to the business, so he tried to imagine what his father would ask next. Was the wine exported anywhere? Yes, maybe ten cases to Germany each year. Then Vincent asked how many cases CVBG had in its warehouse. When he heard the answer—seven hundred cases—Vincent smiled. Somehow, he managed to keep his tone even as he told Reboul Salze that he'd take the entire lot.

"We bought it at sixty French francs a bottle," Thomas Yip recalled. At the equivalent of eleven dollars a bottle, Carruades de Lafite was cheap. In order to control a large quantity, the Yips began buying it en primeur, and eventually they locked in an allocation of one thousand cases by buying not just from Reboul Salze but also from other négociants.

In two short years, Topsy Trading had invested more than $2 million in Château Lafite. The importer put Lafite into duty-free shops at the border, into the hands of officials, and on the banquet tables where business deals got sealed. A bar opened in Hong Kong that served only Lafite from Topsy stock. Château Lafite gradually emerged as an approved official gift in Communist China.

But perhaps the pivotal event for Topsy came in March 1996, during the National People's Congress in Beijing, when the Ninth Five-Year Plan for turning China into an economic powerhouse was approved. From 1980 to 1990, Deng Xiaoping had aimed to double China's gross domestic product, so that the Chinese people would be able to afford food and clothes. By doubling GDP again over the next decade, Deng had said, the Chinese people would come to enjoy a more comfortable life. The reality was that the population was growing rapidly, and many still went hungry. By the mid-1990s, the Communist leadership was struggling to spread the message that Chinese families had no reason to fear a return of the Great Famine of Mao Zedong's time.

An easy target came in the form of a bottle of baijiu. To make the ubiquitous fiery liquor, China's spirits companies distilled rice, sorghum, and other grains—staple food crops. It took two kilograms of grain to distill one liter of baijiu; twenty-five billion kilograms of grain went into the alcohol each year. That was an appalling waste, but the leaders knew there was no point in ordering people to stop drinking. Worse, everyone had heard stories of government officials getting drunk on expensive Cognac and the high-end Moutai baijiu. There couldn't be a hint of a double standard. So, at the congress, Premier Li Peng stood up, criticized the negative impact of baijiu and other grain spirits on people's health, and extolled the benefits of red wine. China already had a huge crop of table grapes, he said. Grape vines were marvelous plants. They grew on hillsides and in poor soil, in places where very little else could thrive. Li further surprised his audience by toasting with red wine, and urging others to do so at future party banquets. It was an unmistakable signal to every official, state employee, and entrepreneur that red wine was approved by the Communist leadership. Deng had opened China to the West. Li had opened China to wine.

On the Place de Bordeaux, no one was quite sure how the Yips were selling the wine—or exactly to whom they were selling it. All they knew was that Topsy Trading seemed to be the first company to sell any volume of high-quality Bordeaux into the Chinese market. When Jean-Pierre Rousseau asked Thomas Yip where his wine was going, the normally chatty trader clammed up: "I have my way. It's not quick, but it works." Rousseau decided he didn't need to know more. For centuries, Bordeaux had built markets by supplying wine to reliable partners, and the Yips had proved themselves reliable.

Topsy Trading focused on classified growths, but Beijing's official approval of red wine created a mini-boom for cheap table wine. On the mainland as well as in Hong Kong and Taiwan, wealthier Chinese started ordering red wine in restaurants and karaoke night clubs, often drinking it mixed with soda to make the flavor more palatable. Usually, this was inexpensive table wine. Traders with no background in wine rapidly placed their orders, speculating that demand would continue to grow. "It was crazy," remembered Yannick Evenou, who succeeded Pierre Dourthe as export manager at CVBG. "We shipped about three hundred containers [about three million bottles] of French table wine between January and October in 1997." At a dollar a bottle, getting into the wine trade seemed easy.

Then the Asian financial crisis hit. Drastic currency devaluations, a credit crunch, and bankruptcies created panic. The speculators relying on cheap wine to break into the trade scattered. Some of Bordeaux's clients in Asia couldn't pay their bills when they came due. Containers of wine sat on the docks in the hot Asian sun, turning to vinegar.

Even CVBG's most faithful Hong Kong client was in trouble. When Evenou flew to Hong Kong to meet the legendary Thomas Yip for the first time, he knew it was going to be a tough conversation. "Topsy had bought a lot of the 1996 en primeur and a lot of the 1995 en primeur," said Evenou. Yip politely asked CVBG to buy back the wine, which they both knew had never left Bordeaux. "He was a good bargainer. It was difficult for him, he lost face, but it was the only way to survive." CVBG agreed to terms with Topsy and quietly resold the wine in Europe.

Despite the meltdown in Asia, a bigger problem loomed for Bordeaux in the United States. The 1997 vintage, overpriced and copious, weighed on the bloated market for three years like a bad meal no one could digest. America's discontent with Bordeaux's prices would leave the Place de Bordeaux particularly vulnerable to opportunists.

❋

Bordeaux was coming under increased pressure to deliver on its reputation. No other wine-producing region attracted as much attention in the press or among wine aficionados. But the constant scrutiny from critics, intensified by the immediacy of Internet reviews, meant that any time a château had a lousy vintage, it spelled disaster.

The First Growths were especially vulnerable. The Rothschilds had acquired Lafite in the 1860s and had coasted somewhat on the wine's reputation until the 1970s, when Baron Eric de Rothschild took over the reins and slowly began to recruit new staff. In 1984, he hired a Champagneois named Christophe Salin as an assistant, and later Charles Chevallier became the estate's winemaker. By the time the trio was in place, Lafite was widely considered to be the weakest of the First Growths, and their goal was to return Lafite to its former preeminence. The atmosphere at the estate reflected the three men—professional but relaxed, erudite without undue swagger—as they assiduously rebuilt Lafite's reputation: its brand, its distribution, its quality.

As Salin climbed up the leadership at Lafite, eventually becoming president and CEO of the Rothschilds' entire wine business, he chose to avoid animosity toward the négociants. Domaines Barons de Rothschild (Lafite) distributed its own brand wines made from bulk wine they bought from smaller growers and could have easily sold its château wines, including its flagship First Growth, directly to importers, but the baron and Salin adopted the opposite strategy. While other First Growths tried to control their distribution by limiting the number of négociants with whom they worked, Lafite granted allocations large and small to dozens of firms. It was like tossing a bag of golden coins onto the cobblestones of quai des Chartrons for any chancer to grab. This extensive network of négociants then worked their markets, selling wine in dozens of countries, to hundreds of clients, using their allocation of Lafite as leverage. The amount of goodwill the gesture created for Lafite could not be overestimated.

The rest of the châteaux responded to the pressure to improve the quality of their wines by reducing yields, sometimes drastically, and by adopting new techniques in an effort to snatch higher ratings from the critics. Due to an extraordinary combination of soil, climate, and savoir faire, Bordeaux's best wines have always aged beautifully, retaining a remarkable freshness even fifty years after harvest. By gaining a better understanding of soil and subsoil, vineyards could plant and harvest grapes plot by plot. In the cellars, vintners developed a variety of new vats to ferment the grapes plot by plot, too. They handled the grapes as delicately as possible, using gravity rather than pumps to move fruit and grape must from basket to sorting table to vat and finally into the barrel. The selection of the perfect fruit became an obsession. Costly optical sorters, used in the industrial food industry to separate vast volumes of produce by quality, arrived at the estates.

Lafite eschewed many of the technological advances embraced by its neighbors, staking its faith on the vines, the soil, and precision. It clung to its tradition of hand-sorting the grapes, even building its own barrels from French oak, which the winemakers thought would ensure a subtle play of aromas and tannins. Such traditions were part and parcel of the Lafite name.

Altogether, these changes were good for consumers. The wines had never been better.

Of course, no amount of technological wizardry or old-fashioned craftsmanship would have made any difference if it rained every year and the grapes rotted. Bordeaux was at the northern geographical limit for perfectly ripening its main red wine varieties, Cabernet Sauvignon, Cabernet Franc, Merlot, and Petit Verdot. Under the best conditions, the environment produced fine tannins and the sensual pleasure of fermented ripe fruit. Under the worst conditions, the wine was thin, herbaceous, and harsh. Usually the weather fell somewhere in between, but the Bordelais had learned how to manage the triple threat of rot, mildew, and odium. Harvests that would have been a disaster in the past were now passable, and harvests that were superior blossomed into something truly exceptional.

Savvy investors realized that the rising value of the wines could be captured in more sophisticated ways. Mutual funds were launched, their portfolio holdings based on critics' wine ratings. When possible, mutual fund managers purchased Bordeaux wines en primeur, shortly after the week of barrel tastings that were held before each year's sales campaign. The critics had grown so powerful that châteaux were loath to set prices for their wines until the ratings were released. The mutual funds snatched up the highest-rated classified growths, fueling speculation, which was now a constant presence in the market.

It was ironic that Bordeaux had gone to such lengths to improve the quality of its wines and yet, at the top, the wines were not being drunk but rather bartered like gold bars. This new breed of speculators secretly flattered the château owners, who no longer considered themselves to be mere agricultural tinkerers whose product was to be savored with a simply grilled entrecôte. They were purveyors of a luxury commodity, architects of a sound, long-term investment.

The jargon of Bordeaux changed. Mingling over their glasses at a wine tasting, a château owner and a "wine MBA" would worry in somber tones about the value of a "brand," something that would never have happened a decade earlier. While châteaux had long been conscious of their image, a brand implied standardized quality. A Hermès bag did not change from year to year, nor did a Rolex watch. A château wine, on the other hand, was a subtle alchemy of soil, climate, and skill, evolving over time, varying in quality—and price—from vintage to vintage. Now the word "brand" seemed to fall off everyone's lips as they sipped and swished and spat into buckets.

Brand building and courting speculators were the means to an end for the most ambitious classified growths. Nowhere was this more obvious than in the commune of Saint-Estèphe, where the Second Growth estate of Château Cos d'Estournel made its home. Cos is nestled on a hill overlooking the estuary; at its rear, across a small brook called the Breuil, is Château Lafite. It was the fervent ambition of every Second Growth to be a First Growth, but Cos, though it had one of the finest

terroirs in Bordeaux—a layer of Quaternary pebbles over limestone—
had not been able to break the ceiling imposed by the 1855 Classification. The frustration must have been intense. In 2000, Michel Reybier
had bought the château with a fortune derived from lunch meat and
luxury hotels, and hired the former owner's son Jean-Guillaume Prats
to manage the estate. Together, they undertook an extravagant renovation, including the installation of sumptuously designed reception rooms
and a multimillion-dollar cellar with an elevator for gently lifting grapes.
Some of the investments helped Prats in his quest for perfection, but the
cosmetic changes were meant to reinforce Cos's image as the Porsche
Cayenne of Bordeaux wines. It was a sexy wine for men with fast money.
Yet improving quality and image was not enough to make Cos the equivalent of a First Growth in the eyes of the trade and collectors; it would also
have to raise the price of its wine through year-after-year speculation.

Nature did its part to help out. First came the surprise 2000 vintage,
which had overcome a mildew-plagued start with a spectacular harvest.
Prices spiraled, stoked by "millennium madness." Then a heat wave in
2003 produced rich, jammy wines that seduced the critics' palates. Two
years later, a remarkable collection of conditions induced Bordeaux to
declare 2005 the vintage of the century just midway into the new century's first decade. The early growing season was exceptionally dry, bor-
dering on drought, followed by balmy days and cool nights as the fruit
turned purple. The small berries were rich with tannins, fresh aromas,
crisp acidity, and a stunning ripeness. The critics' enthusiasm for the
wine unleashed a buying mania.

On the Place de Bordeaux, the négociants grumbled that the market
was overheating, but they had little hope of reining in the châteaux.
The profits to be realized were immense, and the overwhelming share
of those profits was going to the growers. The pendulum of power was
swinging from the négociants to the estates, forcing the merchants to
sit through one obsequious lunch after another, powerless to do anything
but beg for bigger allocations. At the same time, new négociant firms
were being founded on the Place de Bordeaux. The competition for allocations grew ferocious.

In Hong Kong, Vincent Yip read the en primeur offers for the 2005 vintage and knew he had some hard decisions to make. His father had put together massive allocations of fine wines from a variety of négociants. For example, Topsy had been granted the right to purchase 2,500 cases of Carruades de Lafite every year. Looking over the offers, he saw that Bordeaux's price structure was losing its logic. The second wines of the First Growths, like Carruades, were now more expensive than the first wines of Second Growths, like Cos d'Estournel. He couldn't shake the feeling that the classified growths were turning their backs on their faithful customers in order to reap as much money as they could from the speculators. Prices had increased an average of 68 percent over the past ten years; some wines had doubled in price. The price of Château Lafite had shot up 900 percent from a decade earlier.

The vast majority of châteaux—those that never made it onto the 1855 Classification—attracted few speculators, so they allowed themselves just a modest uptick in price in this phenomenal year. Still, the classified growths, for better or worse, epitomized Bordeaux in the minds of long-standing consumers. And now those wine enthusiasts had to face the fact that they could no longer afford to drink First Growth Bordeaux. It was a wine for Wall Street bankers, dot-com millionaires, and third-world despots.

Vincent had no doubt that the wines were overpriced, but his instincts told him there was still an opportunity to make a profit. He reduced Topsy's exposure by declining allocations of some wines the company had carried for many years, all of which were made by people he genuinely liked. He had to place some limits somewhere. When he was done placing his order, he had spent $26 million.

On the warehouse floors at 10 Fung Yip Street, Topsy Trading had built walls of Lafite, Beychevelle, Pétrus, every famous Bordeaux château. Visiting négociants stood in awe of the Yips' stockpile. What they needed now were more customers.

❊

The astronomical prices of the 2005 vintage did not dissuade Americans from buying. True to their colors, they paid out for the acclaimed vintage, but they refused to swallow the more pedestrian 2006 and 2007.

By then, the wholesale price of Lafite had risen to over $500 a bottle. It was an extraordinary run. So extraordinary that it raised the question of whether the client who had bought a bottle at $40 ten years earlier would shell out that much more for the brand-name elixir. The answer came in the spring of 2009, when Château & Estate Wines refused its allocations.

C&E had been the brainchild of Abdallah "Ab" Simon, who built a uniquely effective distribution network for Bordeaux classified growths in the U.S. market. Simon had found his calling in the early 1950s while sampling a bottle of Château Latour 1929 aboard the lavish ocean liner *Queen Mary*. In 1974, he was hired to start C&E as the imported wine division of Seagram. By the late 1980s, he was credited with importing one of every five bottles of First Growths coming into America. The *New York Times* called him a "Superpower." The châteaux particularly liked to do business with Simon because he readily bought huge allocations en primeur, then stocked the wine until it was ready to drink years later, a vital supplier for restaurants and shops. C&E was a pivotal link to the world's biggest wine market, and the châteaux's biggest quasi-banker.

In the industrial docklands in the north of Bordeaux, C&E had set up a sister négociant firm, Vignobles Internationaux, to increase the company's access to wine. Unfortunately, things started to go sour for C&E in 2000. A year after taking delivery of the 1997 vintage and shipping some containers to the United States, C&E was shipping the wine back to Vignobles Internationaux in France to join cases that had never even left the warehouse. There had been no demand. Worse, the 1997 and 1998 vintages failed to gain value over time. You could buy both wines for close to their initial offer price almost anywhere around the Place de Bordeaux. This put C&E in a precarious position. It appeared that C&E's customers had stopped ordering Bordeaux. The wines were losing their spot on restaurant wine lists and store shelves. In the fiercely competitive American market, once a spot was lost, it was almost impossible to win it back.

With each new vintage, towering stacks of unsold wine grew in C&E's warehouses on both sides of the Atlantic, and C&E's parent company was troubled by that inventory. In 2000, the British conglomerate Diageo acquired Seagram, and both C&E and Vignobles Internationaux came under scrutiny. Diageo's accountants looked over the books and saw that due to a weak dollar, the 2001 vintage that had been purchased en primeur had lost 40 percent of its value by the time it was delivered. The two firms grew even less secure when the 2006 vintage finally sailed west in the fall of 2008. C&E contacted clients to confirm their reservations and arrange for delivery, and their clients responded by canceling their orders. C&E was once again stuck with a glut of overpriced wine. A new term was coined: "Bordeaux fatigue."

By the time the 2008 vintage was ready to be offered in the spring of 2009, C&E had reached its limit. With so much wine languishing in its warehouses, it refused its entire allocation. To the Bordelais, C&E's decision felt like a brutal betrayal. Decades of trust and handshake deals were nullified in an instant. And it came at the worst possible moment for the Place de Bordeaux, just as the global financial crisis was freezing commerce around the world.

When Jean-Pierre Rousseau contacted Topsy Trading, there were hardly any other buyers to call.

2

....

No Boundaries

In the gloomy early months of 2009, it was convenient for the négociants of the Place de Bordeaux to blame the lack of buyers on a bunch of irresponsible Wall Street bankers and the less-than-extraordinary 2008 vintage. The inconvenient truth, however, was that trouble had been brewing in Bordeaux for more than a decade. Just as winegrowers recalled the date of the bud break and the weather at harvest for every vintage of their lifetimes, négociants remembered the prices for each year's en primeur campaign and the huge single-lot sales of fine wine, defining their careers like fishermen bragging about their biggest catch or lamenting the one that got away.

Jean-Pierre Rousseau limited his laments to a shrug, revealing the confidence of a self-made man nearing retirement. Rousseau had started with nothing but a good education; he was a product, he liked to say, of the French meritocracy, having been born in the school where his mother taught in Sorde l'Abbaye, population five hundred, an hour from the Spanish border. He had grown into the role of the typical French businessman, helped by his sharp features and his dark hair, now flecked with gray. These days, he lived in a magnificent Art Deco mansion about twenty minutes from his négociant firm in the Chartrons wine district in the center of Bordeaux. He and his wife had rescued the estate from a developer's bulldozer and undertook a meticulous restoration.

By Bordeaux standards, Rousseau's company, Distribution Internationale de Vins et Alcools (Diva), was an upstart, having been established in 1979 by Pierre Beuchet in the offices of another investor's mail-order wine business. Beuchet focused on Burgundy, the Rhône valley, and Champagne, so, beginning in 1987, Rousseau took charge of Bordeaux and tried to carve out a spot for himself. As a newcomer, he brought with him none of the weighty expectations that came with a legacy on the Place, or, unfortunately, the allocations. But within two years, Diva was growing, and Rousseau had enough revenue to invest in a brick-and-limestone building on the quai de Bacalan that had been erected in the nineteenth century by a forgotten German négociant. The ground level had dirt floors and a cooperage for making and repairing barrels. It was one of the rare structures along the embankment that was wider than it was tall, likely due to its relatively late construction on a plot of cheap land.

Toward the city center, the quai de Bacalan becomes the quai des Chartrons, which gave the merchants' quarter its name. The Chartrons, the center of the wine trade, was named for the Carthusian monks who had originally settled the marshlands, though by this time the monks were long gone, replaced mostly by Protestant merchants. The quays stretched over a mile along the curve of the Garonne River that bisects the city of Bordeaux, and Rousseau's new office was a short, brisk walk from seven major courtiers and a dozen competing négociants.

For centuries, the négociants and courtiers had settled along or near the quays, primarily for logistical reasons. The quays were located at the point in the river where the flat-bottomed *gabare* boats, heavy with barrels of wine from the vineyards, could easily dock and roll their cargo along the flat embankment into the négociants' cellars. The narrow streets leaving the quays were paved with the cobblestones once used as ballast for the ships arriving without heavy barrels of wine, a permanent reminder that this was the heart of the Bordeaux trade. Only yards away, ships flying Dutch, German, Flemish, English, Danish, and American colors were moored in the Garonne, ready to carry the wine to distant ports once a price was determined.

In the early days, négociants dealt not only in wine but a variety of goods coming through the city. The merchants were usually foreigners who had arrived in Bordeaux looking for products to sell back home, but soon many began to trade in markets farther afield, including Imperial Russia, Africa, the Caribbean, and the Far East. Most lived and worked along the quay, with their homes and offices in rooms above vast ground-level warehouses.

The first building in the merchants' quarter, the Hôtel de Fenwick at 1 quai des Chartrons, had been built by Joseph Fenwick, a wine merchant and partner in an international shipping firm who was put in charge of the United States' first foreign consulate, which opened in Bordeaux in June 1790. Secretary of State Thomas Jefferson had personally charged Fenwick with the job of securing the new nation's interests in France's principal port, which had been a point of departure for the French arms used by the colonists in the Revolutionary War. Ships belonging to Fenwick and his partners had dominated American business in France since 1788, and the men were intimately involved in the negotiations over the sale of French goods to replace goods previously supplied by the British. Joseph Fenwick was an inspired choice: as a French-speaking wine merchant and established shipper in Bordeaux since 1787, he was already a full member of the local business community. One of President Washington's first requests for the new consul was 150 bottles of 1785 Château Margaux.

Fenwick chose the location of his home-cum-consulate with care. From the building's widow's walk, he had a fine view of the bustling trade on the quai des Chartrons. His neighbors were the Anglo-Irish Bartons and Lawtons, the English Sichels, the German Cruses, the Hanseatic Schröders and Schÿlers, the French-Swiss de Luzes, and the Scottish Johnstons. These families dominated the Place de Bordeaux, cementing alliances through marriage until, it was fair to say, virtually all of the leading négociant families were related in one way or another. Within a few generations, these dynasties could argue, with good reason, that the success of Bordeaux's fine wine was not a product of the fortuitous layering of pebbles, clay, and limestone through a succession of ice ages, or of the climate at forty-five degrees north latitude, but of the calculated, relentless striving of adventurous men who came to the port to make and lose fortunes. The hunt for the perfect terroir, the alchemy of soil, climate, and sunlight that bestow the grapes with a distinctive character, and the science of fine wine production came later. Commerce was the essence of Bordeaux.

Two hundred years later, Jean-Pierre Rousseau had an instinct for commerce that had not been satisfied by his first career managing cinemas during what he called his "hippie period." His solution was to work part-time for a year without pay as an export manager for a négociant in Libourne, in the eastern part of the Bordeaux region. A year later, in 1987, he launched a start-up négociant firm, Vignobles & Traditions, with the backing of Pierre Beuchet. The partnership flourished, and two years later Beuchet hired Rousseau as the managing director of Diva Bordeaux, awarding him a small stake in the company, while Beuchet focused on Diva's operation in Burgundy.

At the time, Diva Bordeaux was a small company and something of a sideline for Beuchet. "We had four customers. If you lost two, you were dead," Rousseau recalled.

Rousseau's first order of business was to win allocations for some of the most sought-after wines. He knew it was not an easy assignment. He was not connected to any of the old négociant families, and most of the châteaux had never heard of Beuchet. From the start, Rousseau had to offer something different. Historically, négociants did not tell châteaux who was buying their wine, and the châteaux did not care, as long as the wine sold. He decided to be more open about this information in order to get the châteaux to trust Diva as though they'd been doing business together for decades if not generations. "We were one of the first négociants to be transparent," Rousseau explained, "one of the first to bring customers to the châteaux when others were afraid of being bypassed."

At the same time, Rousseau knew that he needed to find a way to court the directors of the First Growths and other prestigious estates. One of the most important was Philippe Cottin, who led Château Mouton

Rothschild and was the gatekeeper to allocations for the entire range of Baron Philippe de Rothschild estate wines. "I tried to find a different angle through my artistic side," said Rousseau. Like many château directors, Cottin did a lot of his business over lunch. Rousseau surmised that Cottin and the directors of the other estates might be bored with the ritual, so he injected some excitement into the proceedings. "I invited them to private, sneak movie screenings at the UGC cinema and we served them Champagne," he recalled. "I brought Gérard Depardieu to Beychevelle, Mel Brooks to Figeac and Cheval Blanc. I was the young guy who had different ideas."

A turning point came when Cottin was looking for a distributor in Japan for his group's mass-market brand wine, Mouton Cadet. At the time, few négociants were selling to customers in Asia, but Diva was. The company had customers for Taittinger Champagne, Louis Latour Burgundy, and J. P. Moueix Bordeaux in Japan, Korea, and Hong Kong. Pierre Beuchet put the Mouton group in touch with the Japanese wine-trading company Enoteca. Cottin thanked Beuchet by giving Diva allocations of his First Growth wine, Château Mouton Rothschild.

Diva's growing network of contacts in Asia would prove invaluable. "It is the fundamental job of a négociant to build new markets," said Rousseau, and a newly minted négociant had to find markets that no one else was seeing. Beuchet told Rousseau that there were two men in Hong Kong he needed to know: Thomas Yip and David Webster. "Thomas was discreet, behind the scenes. Webster was the man out in front," Rousseau said.

While Thomas Yip was quietly putting Bordeaux and other fine wines into hotels and duty-free shops in China, David Webster was helping the Cognac giant Rémy Martin. By the time Rousseau met Webster, the outgoing Englishman was well known for his love of fine wine. No one in Hong Kong threw a party quite like Webster. Six years after joining Diva, Rousseau found himself at a dinner at the Hong Kong Hilton. The menu was the height of sophistication, but no one was there for the food; they were there because Webster was pouring a "vertical"—magnums and double magnums of Mouton Rothschild for every great vintage between 1914 to 1990, all supplied by Diva with the support of Philippe Cottin.

A year after that glorious evening, Rousseau received the call that confirmed he had finally established himself on the Place de Bordeaux. The Rothschilds were paving the way for the launch of Almaviva, a Chilean wine they were producing in collaboration with Concha y Toro, one of the oldest and biggest wineries in South America. Almaviva was going to be the first foreign wine sold on the Place, and Diva had been given one of the prized allocations. "We were one of ten négociants to receive allocations. It was a huge privilege to be counted among the top guys," said Rousseau.

But the business had changed dramatically in the past decade. As Rousseau arrived at his office on the quay in April 2009, the only river traffic was cruise ships and a bus-boat for tourists. The wine no longer arrived by barrel, and his fellow négociants were, for the most part, dispersed throughout the city. The vast warehouses that extended more than two football fields in length had disappeared. He watched as the latest batch of tourists stumbled along the cobbled road.

His turnover was €24 million—about $30 million—but he was worried about how he would continue to find customers. He'd recently been to America, where the dollar was weak, unemployment was high, and the market was slow. In Japan, his customers had backed away from classified growths in favor of more modestly priced wines. The mature markets were contracting, and there seemed to be no relief in sight. Rousseau ran a lean staff—only eleven people. *The lower the overhead, the better,* he thought.

He was also traveling more frequently to Asia. One of his key British clients, Farr Vintners, showed up for the en primeur tastings with eighteen people. He knew they had to be very interested in buying, but it wasn't clear whom they were buying for. Were their clients in London or Hong Kong? One never knew with the English.

The Yips at Topsy Trading were easier to read. They bought en primeur only in order to guarantee the provenance of the wine and lock in the best prices, and they bought a wide portfolio of classified growths, accounting for 10 percent of Rousseau's en primeur sales. The other traders selling in mainland China seemed to be interested in only a handful of estates—Lafite, Carruades, Margaux, Mouton, Haut-Brion,

Latour, Beychevelle, and Lynch-Bages. It was maddening. Rousseau had dozens of wonderful wines on offer, classified growths and their equivalents, but his customers wanted fewer than ten of them. He couldn't understand why.

❋

Just a month after Li Peng toasted the National People's Congress with a glass of red wine in April 1996, a Canadian-American father and son stood in Beijing awaiting the arrival of a freight container with 1,400 cases of California wine. They knew how to seize an opportunity when it landed in front of them.

The father, Don St. Pierre Sr., was an old China hand. He'd been doing business on the mainland since 1985 and was the former vice chairman of Jeep's Beijing division. Over the years, he had built a network of important contacts in the complex bureaucracy of Chinese government and state industry. But he was one of the few Westerners who were willing to rattle the Chinese leadership. He once sent a letter directly to Zhao Ziyang, then the premier, when it looked as though the joint venture between American Motors Corporation and Beijing Automobile Works was going to be derailed by financial issues. That letter had made him famous in the business world.

After leaving Jeep, Don Sr. continued his career in the automotive and defense industries for another five years, working in China, Taiwan, and Pakistan. In 1991, he started his first company with his son, Don Jr. The business, called Eagle Exim, imported ammunition from China to the United States. Don Sr. was based in China, while Don Jr. ran the operation in Santa Clara, California.

Within a few years, the St. Pierres ran into difficulty. In May 1994, President Bill Clinton placed an embargo on importation of Chinese arms. The St. Pierres had to get ammunition from new suppliers. Then the following May, agents from U.S. Customs and the Bureau of Alcohol, Tobacco, and Firearms raided Eagle Exim's Santa Clara premises. In an instant, the St. Pierres lost a year's worth of sales. One veteran ATF agent called it "the largest ammunition seizure I've ever seen."

The feds confiscated seventy-five million bullets—enough to fill ten tractor trailers—mostly large-caliber munitions used in semiautomatic weapons, which the agents claimed had been manufactured in China and thus were illegal. The St. Pierres could face charges of smuggling and receiving unlawful firearms, and possibly prison sentences as well.

The St. Pierres were outraged. "This is absolutely ridiculous," Don Jr. told the press. "All you have to do is look at the document and look at the product to realize that this is a Russian product. They don't make this in China."

The agents did not know that the St. Pierres had switched to a Russian supplier. Although father and son were eventually cleared of all charges, the seizure effectively put an end to their first joint business.

It was obviously time for a career change, and the St. Pierres were still drawn to China. Don Sr. had seen what it was like to work with a state company, and he suggested that they focus on launching a family business. Why invite the headaches of a joint venture? After the Eagle Exim debacle, they had $2 million in capital, and they used it to set up a "wholly foreign-owned enterprise," or WFOE, with a license to trade, import, and export. WFOEs were required to "benefit the development of the Chinese national economy," but they were free from most of the meddling of government officials.

The men shared an entrepreneur's faith that the Chinese would accumulate wealth, and that they would want things to buy. They hoped that this would be enough to ensure that they met the government's conditions for serving the public interest. "We saw a middle class coming—a middle class that was going to be buying cars and luxury bags," said Don Sr. They considered publishing, baby care products, and golf courses. But they eventually decided to go into the wine business.

Neither of the St. Pierres were connoisseurs, but Don Sr. got introductions to four prestigious brands through executives he knew in the automotive industry. They began importing Bollinger Champagne and choice wines from around the world, including Beringer from Napa Valley, Petaluma from Australia, and Col d'Orcia from Italy. Nor did either of them expect a surge of demand from the Chinese, but they knew from experience that businesses operating in China were looking for supplies of wine to entertain guests. Experience had also taught them how hard it was to find fine wine on the mainland. Only one small outfit on Tiananmen Square sold fine wine. There had to be room for another importer, especially one with these brands to sell.

Next, they had to set up a foreign company that would officially own the WFOE. "This had nothing to do with a handover to China," Don Jr. explained. "Rather, it is standard procedure for most foreigners that own a China company—in other words to have a holding company in Hong Kong." Asia Solutions Corporation (ASC) opened for business on April 26, 1996.

To announce ASC's entry into the Chinese wine scene, the St. Pierres threw a big party. Oddly, there wasn't any wine to drink at it. All the hours they'd spent waiting on the docks for those 1,400 cases of California wine were for nothing. Importing into China had its own headaches. It seemed that their American partner's Chinese wife's brother-in-law had heard about the shipment. He pulled some strings and when the wine arrived at the port, he received the delivery.

"He hijacked the wine!" recalled Don Jr. with a laugh.

❊

The St. Pierres had a sense of humor about doing business in China, but, more important, they were tenacious. In the first year of ASC's operations, they met a young Bordelais named Jean-Guillaume Prats, whose family owned Château Cos d'Estournel. Prats had been sent to China by his father to find someone who could serve as an importer for the family's wine. The St. Pierres didn't know much about Bordeaux, the estates, or the 1855 Classification, but they did understand that Bordeaux was a brand in the world of wine, a luxury product associated with quality, history, and wealth.

They hit it off with Prats, and when he returned home to Bordeaux, he mentioned his new contacts at ASC to Bertrand Carles, the export manager for the négociant Ginestet, which had some of the largest allocations of classified growth wines. Based on the tip from Prats, Carles flew to Beijing to meet the St. Pierres in the hope that they could help him build up Ginestet's base in the Asian market. The connection between ASC and the Place de Bordeaux was made.

The St. Pierres considered how they might get their wines in front of expatriates, leaders of Chinese state-run companies, and other government officials, who were busy wooing one another for favors—and might like to woo one another with fine wine. One idea was to organize an event at one of the newly built golf clubs that were popping up on the landscape. Golf was another Western import aimed at the Chinese business elite. The setting seemed perfect. When the day of the event arrived, the St. Pierres sent a few employees ahead to the club to show the staff how to open the wine bottles. When the St. Pierres arrived a short while later, they discovered that the corkscrews they'd provided had mysteriously disappeared, and the club staff were trying to uncork the wine with beer-bottle openers. They knew the learning curve was going to be steep, but not quite this steep. "Selling wine in China was one unexpected and implausible situation after another," Don Jr. said.

Starting up in China was also costly. More money poured out to establish a distribution network and to train staff than trickled in from sales. The expatriate and diplomatic community accounted for 80 percent of the St. Pierres' business, and it was clear they needed to find more customers. Cash flow was a never-ending stress. Bordeaux wines were sold *ex-cellar*, which meant that ASC took possession of the wine directly from the châteaux, and was thus responsible for paying for the wine and the transportation long before it arrived in China, and longer still before the wine was sold to customers. After such a promising start, the St. Pierres were facing bankruptcy, and they'd only been in business for two years.

Then they got lucky again. Standing outside the Beijing Hilton Hotel, Don Sr. met the billionaire Gernot Langes-Swarovski over a cigarette. Swarovski headed his family's cut-crystal empire and owned a winery in Argentina. Six months later, the St. Pierres sat down with Swarovski's representatives in Frankfurt and left with a $600,000 deal. Over the years, Swarovski would funnel $3 million into ASC in exchange for a 49 percent stake in the business.

It was easy enough to deliver wine from Hong Kong to Beijing or

Shanghai, but reaching other cities and more remote provinces was all but impossible. Wine is a fragile product, requiring careful, temperature-controlled handling and storage. The St. Pierres tried joint ventures with several multinationals distributing spirits and Chinese wine, but were disappointed in the results. "Existing wholesalers and distributors of alcoholic beverages, including wine, were not at all capable of selling or even providing logistics for imported wine. They were box movers at best and for something as complicated and new as imported wine, they could not do this well," said Don Jr.

The only way to expand was to open offices in the cities where they wanted to do more business. They trained their own sales, distribution, and warehouse staff in American business practices as well as the qualities and handling of wine. They opened offices in the city of Guangzhou, then in Shanghai, where Don Jr. moved in 1999. Gradually, the St. Pierres proved to Ginestet and other négociants that they understood China. Ginestet hired a man in Shanghai whose only job was to manage the relationship with ASC.

"Honestly, if we had come to China as wine people, we would never have survived," Don Jr. said. "In the early days, it was a bit of the Wild West, and it was not the place for people who were fairly focused on wine being the priority. We were pioneers. Usually the pioneers get shot. We got shot at a few times, but they didn't kill us. We kept on learning and kept on . . . building our understanding of how to do business in China."

❋

Half a world away, in London's diamond district, a competitor was eyeing Bordeaux's slow march into the Celestial Empire. The British had long held a dominant position in the China trade, and as far back as the eighteenth century the Bordelais had come to realize that it was easier and quicker to ship their wine to the Far East via England. For every four French ships sailing to Guangzhou, there were more than three hundred British ones.

The British extended their reach after the First Opium War (1839–42), when the British won Hong Kong as part of the peace settlement.

The small island didn't produce much of anything, but it had long been a trading hub, and the British transformed it into a commercial powerhouse with ready access to the coveted Chinese market. Much to the consternation of the French, the British traded in Bordeaux wine, and they did well by it. For the French, the main obstacle was that they did not have opium to sell, they did not drink tea, and the Chinese did not drink wine. It was a small consolation to the French that the large contingent of British and Americans who dominated the port of Hong Kong drank such copious amounts of Bordeaux that it almost made up for the lack of Chinese interest.

The London merchants had grown used to their dominant position in the Hong Kong wine trade. One of the more aggressive London merchants was a relative newcomer named Gary Boom. A South African, Boom had entered the business in 1997, when he founded a firm called Bordeaux Index. He had arrived in London ten years earlier to work as a foreign exchange trader in the City, and he enjoyed splashing out for the best wines. But he was irked by the haughtiness of the established London wine merchants, who acted as if they were doing him a favor when they sold him a bottle of Bordeaux classified growth. They seemed to be trading on reputation rather than skill since they offered little service, even when delivering a twelve-bottle order—nearly $8,000 worth of wine. "I once ordered a case of '85 Pétrus and they just left it in the rain round the back of my house. It's like shoving a Cartier watch through the mailbox," Boom said.

A decade later, he sensed there were probably a lot of people like him who didn't wear an Eton tie but liked Bordeaux First Growths. People like him who would appreciate customer service delivered without the snobbery. Collectors like him who would respond to fair and reasonable prices. In other words: he saw a business opportunity.

He and a partner started the company with £500,000 and rented office space on St. John Street in North London. Boom's goal was fairly simple: he wanted to make it easy for people with money to buy wine. It didn't matter to him if they thought of a bottle as something to drink or as an investment. From his trading post in London, he would sell and deliver fine wine to anyone, anywhere.

He might have focused on Burgundy, which he personally enjoyed drinking, but Burgundy was complicated. There could be as many as seventy owners attached to a single tiny appellation, each owning an acre, which made it difficult to explain the wine to consumers who were accustomed to buying wines based on estate names in addition to appellations. The minuscule size of Burgundy estates also meant that very little of each wine was produced; there was no chance of selling large volumes of one label. For instance, the Domaine de la Romanée-Conti produced only 5,600 bottles of its famous flagship wine per year, and that wasn't enough to support a trading business. Boom sold some wines from Burgundy and Champagne as well as from Tuscany, Alsace, and other renowned regions, but he had made a calculated commercial decision when he named his company and specialized in Bordeaux.

Bordeaux had volume. Every year, the First Growths alone produced about 100,000 cases, or 1.2 million bottles, of wine. The wine's quality depended in part on the soil, but because the estates rather than the land were classified, a classified growth could purchase plots from a nonclassified neighbor and add the output to its classified production line. When the châteaux realized the profits that could be gained through expansion, a land grab was created. The volumes produced by the classified estates ballooned. Boom could concentrate on selling large quantities of recognizable brands that négociants had been promoting around the globe for more than a century.

Yet his big advantage was having well-lined pockets. On the Place de Bordeaux, pragmatism ruled the day. "If you pitch up in Bordeaux without money, that's one thing," he said. "You pitch up and you're ready to buy, they take you seriously. So they took us seriously pretty quickly. They're merchants."

In the beginning, Bordeaux Index's six employees sat on wooden boxes as they made calls to potential buyers on mobile phones. His vision was to bring a new transparency to the fine wine market. On his retail website, Boom published his prices and the quantities available. One section of the website was devoted to trading, where he published his "buy" and "sell" prices.

His placed his first advertisement in *Decanter* magazine in March 1997. It marked him out from his competitors, particularly the renowned Berry Bros. & Rudd, which had set up shop next to St. James's Palace in 1698. His ad read: "You're not a customer with an account. You don't want to order a dozen cases of Pétrus. You didn't row for Cambridge. And you certainly weren't in The Horse Guards with 'Binky' Carmichael." His phone started ringing.

Within three months of opening, 40 percent of Bordeaux Index's sales were from clients based in Asia. On June 30, 1997, when British colonial rule of Hong Kong ended and Hong Kong became a special administrative region of the People's Republic of China, he saw an enormous opportunity. Boom and Berry Bros. had to buy Bordeaux from négociants like anyone else, and the négociants were themselves trying to break into the Chinese market. But few traders understood the history of the Hong Kong market better than the Londoners. So while Boom found himself competing with some of his suppliers, he knew his London address would be a useful calling card.

Like ASC Fine Wines, Bordeaux Index was known for being unstuffy and modern. Boom personalized the company's services and invited clients to exclusive tasting events and dinners at Michelin-starred restaurants. He focused on hiring talented employees, purchasing stocks of the best wines, using fluctuating currency exchange rates to his advantage, and enlisting full-time computer programmers to devise more advanced trading strategies. "You look at wines across vintages," he explained. "You find the ones whose price is out of line and buy it and you sell the overvalued ones."

He was a fast talker and put muscle into every word. His company had overcome the challenges facing a start-up—lack of capital, lack of customers, lack of suppliers, and fierce rivals. "Your competition absolutely trashes you, you get bad references from competitors, and you're facing a wall of prejudice from start to finish. But everything is measurable in small steps, and we just had to concentrate on providing a better standard of product."

His team grew to fifty and his client list to the thousands; eventually he was selling wine in 120 countries. He bought a five-story building in central London to serve as the company's headquarters. In 2008, he opened an office in Hong Kong.

❋

If you stuck a pin on a map to mark where people were buying wine in 2008, it would have been planted on Hong Kong, and that delighted traders like Boom. That February, the chief secretary of Hong Kong, Henry Tang, announced that he was eliminating the 40 percent duty on wine imports. Nearly everything entered Hong Kong duty-free, and now Tang, a tycoon politician who styled himself as a wine collector, had added wine to the nearly endless list. Hong Kong was set to become the main logistics hub for delivering fine wine throughout Asia.

Hong Kong was not an obvious choice for shipping wine. It was muggy and hot, subject to typhoons and heat waves. London, with its system of bonded warehouses and dismal weather, was the traditional way station for wine shipments. From October to May, British weather was cool but mild, ensuring safe storage. But Hong Kong was located on China's doorstep, and no one else in the world was buying these days. It was better to get the wine to where the buyers were.

The troubles in the American market made it ever more imperative to look to China. After it decided to abandon Bordeaux's classified growths, Diageo Château & Estate Wines started selling off their inventory of millions of dollars' worth of wine on the market. At the prestigious Sherry-Lehmann wine store in Manhattan, CEO Chris Adams received sales lists with prices slashed up to 70 percent. Top-of-the-line Bordeaux was selling at bargain-basement prices. "It's a bloodbath," said the importer Guillaume Touton. One château went so far as to buy back fifteen vintages from C&E, shipping the 2,700 cases back to Bordeaux, in order to protect its brand. The sell-off continued for months. Some estimated C&E's original stock to have been worth $200 million. There was little reason now to ship wine to New York. At least in Hong Kong and Beijing, there was a small but healthy market.

Boom read about Tang's zero duty on wine with concern. Zero duty made it cheaper to buy Bordeaux from Hong Kong than from London. If he wasn't already fighting to keep his customers from defecting to Hong Kong–based traders such as the Yips and the St. Pierres, he would be now. He'd also have to compete against them when buying the wine from négociants. With 350 négociants competing with one another, the wine often went to the person with ready cash. Bordeaux Index was grasping for a share of an increasingly slim margin.

But Boom also knew that Hong Kong was just the point of entry to bigger prospects. Decades of plying wine in China were finally paying off. The Chinese economy was breaking records for growth, and the real estate market was taking off, with new skyscrapers going up seemingly every day. Any way you wanted to measure it, China had cash; the Chinese were flush and confident. It didn't matter that most Chinese drank little wine and liked it even less—that didn't deter anyone. The previous year, China had imported only $184 million worth of wine—less than half of the $400 million sold in Hong Kong itself. Only eighteen million Chinese drank wine, but they lived in cities and earned enough money to buy Bordeaux; in fact, most of the imported wine they bought was from the region. If another 1 percent or so of the Chinese population started drinking wine, it would set off a wine boom. And Hong Kong was the obvious way to get to them, especially now that an importer didn't have to pay duties.

Within the year, hundreds of new wine companies opened for business in Hong Kong and on the mainland. Training courses for sommeliers and salespeople spread from Beijing and Shanghai to cities no one in Bordeaux had ever heard of, though they had populations in the millions. Wine imports increased 80 percent.

Like other négociants, Jean-Pierre Rousseau believed in the inherent charm of Bordeaux's wines. He was proud to sell it. No other wine region in the world offered the same quality in such large volumes. Now he sensed a promising shift in the market. Few Chinese were buying the 2008 vintages en primeur, but those who did were already making money on the investment. The Chinese needed somewhere safe to put their money, and Bordeaux's classified growths were being promoted as a good spot by Chinese banks, British merchants, mutual funds, and even négociants. The Chinese were extremely brand conscious, and there were few luxury brands as well known as Bordeaux. The rising prices immediately attracted the attention of Chinese traders, including some based in Hong Kong, none of whom had any previous interest in fine wine. It was this idiosyncratic system of distribution that made Bordeaux both attractive and vulnerable to Chinese speculation.

Bordeaux Index racked up sales of $111 million in 2009, and Boom expected his Hong Kong office would grow 50 percent year over year. The office sold an Imperial bottle—the equivalent of six and a half bottles of wine—of 1982 Pétrus for a record $67,000. As the classified growths took off, traders started seeing more demand for lower-end wines as well. There seemed to be no end to new customers. Profits soared.

❋

Hong Kong's zero duty on wine was a watershed in part because of the logistics involved in freight forwarding. Shipping anything directly to China was complicated. There were 40 ports of entry, from which goods were reshipped to some 150 destinations. New destinations kept appearing overnight. Local customs officials varied wildly when it came to which regulations were enforced and how efficiently freight moved on. Wine arriving in Shanghai might pass quickly to its final destination, but if it landed in Fuzhou, it could sit in the heat for weeks.

This was something that J. F. Hillebrand France, one of the world's largest forwarders for wine and spirits, knew all too well. One in three bottles of wine arriving in China was carried by Hillebrand containers. The company's Bordeaux warehouse moved millions of cases of wine a month. Hillebrand had been shipping wine to China since the 1980s, and its managers understood that the only way to ensure that the wine arrived at its final destination in a drinkable state was to ship it using a refrigerated container, called a "reefer" for short. Unfortunately, the Chinese importers almost unanimously refused to pay the extra cost for reefers.

All it took was one blistering hot day on the docks to severely damage the wine. The best-case scenario was "baked" wine; the worst, bulging, popped corks. The latter incensed the Chinese traders. Baked wine they could sell on to hapless consumers, who had no idea the wine was damaged, its unpleasant taste an aberration. But a damaged bottle was useless, and the Chinese traders blamed the winemakers for the damage, convinced that the Bordelais knowingly used cheap corks.

On the other end of the spectrum, the Chinese took special care of their most expensive purchases—especially First and Second Growths. They asked that the finest wines be packed in the middle of a regular container with the cheap wine stacked around it. The cheap wine would insulate the expensive wine from any temperature shocks. Sometimes this "buffer" wine took a circuitous journey around the world. When one container eventually made its way to the United States, the customer removed a single row of cases to discover the interior filled with bags of sand. The rest of the inventory had been offloaded long beforehand.

But using cheap wine as insulation was a sly logistical solution for other reasons. The Chinese government calculated customs duty on the value of the wine, rather than on the volume, as was the rule in the United States and other countries. The cargo was often worth more than a million dollars, once the quality of the wines was considered, and China applied a crippling 48 percent duty on imported wine. Many customs officials, peering into a container, only saw the outer stack of cases of cheap wine, saving importers a lot of money.

In the early years, Beijing's high, value-based duty probably seemed like a smart way to protect domestic, state-owned wineries from having to compete head-to-head with foreign imports. Until 2000, the biggest volumes of wine coming into China had been bulk wine from Chile that was swiftly bottled and labeled as "Chinese" wine to be sold to the masses. The volume was substantial, but the wine was cheap. However, such imports had tapered off in recent years. Now it wasn't just wealthy Chinese who were getting a taste for expensive wine, it was the officials at the state-owned food conglomerates. They were buying expensive wine from négociants to distribute in China, and they wanted to eke out as much in profits as they could—their future in the government bureaucracy depended on it. So, when a container of classified growth wines arrived in China, paperwork would be attached to the cargo, undervaluing the wines and reducing the duties owed. An insulating layer of cheap wine was the perfect cover. The result was that as the Chinese thirst for classified growths grew, so did the demand for table wine, cheap wine, wine with obscure appellations, even bad wine. Much of it must have been camouflage for getting classified growths through customs at a lower price.

Hong Kong's new zero duty offered another option. Each day, near the stairs leading to the Sheung Shui subway station, the last stop before the border crossing between Hong Kong and the city of Shenzhen in Guangdong Province, hundreds of beat-up wheeled carryalls got locked to a garden railing. A few feet away, beyond the dying plants and trash of the garden, a thin Chinese woman in her forties held her bag steady for a young Chinese man. They treated each other with courtesy, working methodically, without haste and in plain sight. The young man removed from a wooden case two bottles of Château Pichon Longueville Comtesse de Lalande, a Second Growth wine from Bordeaux, and packed them in the woman's carryall, tucking the bottles neatly alongside cans of baby formula. She was one of an army of small-time couriers who rode the subway back and forth between Hong Kong and Shenzhen, importing pricey goods such as Bordeaux to Chinese living on the mainland.

Smuggling was often a matter of perspective. Under the personal consumption allowances, a person could bring two bottles of Bordeaux into China at any one time without paying the 48 percent duty. Walking, driving, or carrying wine out of Hong Kong was not technically illegal. Hong Kong was a free port, and fiercely proud of its history of trading. The island had made its name importing products and reexporting them, particularly after Deng's reforms in the 1970s. When British colonial control ended, China instituted a policy of "one country, two systems." As Don St. Pierre Jr. observed, "The reality is that Hong Kong has become an important wine hub, but if you dig deeper, it has also become a huge smuggling hub into China."

The Hong Kong authorities regarded the couriers with something like a benign pride. If someone had a job that needed doing, there was someone in Hong Kong who would do it. These "ants," as the couriers were nicknamed, provided an essential service. If Hong Kong–based traders managed to avoid duties while bringing wine into China by employing ants, it was because the Chinese market was too big and too dysfunctional to police itself.

Chinese customs officials had a different view. Wine imports were a source of revenue—whether in the form of duties to be collected for Beijing or as bribes to enrich the officer working that day. The ants were annoying because they had a legal right to those two bottles and thus little to fear from the customs police; they weren't breaking the law. But the customs officers knew that the system was being cheated, and increased their scrutiny of larger quantities coming across the border. There were reports of trucks going across, moving hundreds of thousands of cases. This put the St. Pierres and other big importers at the mercy of the customs officials, who were under pressure to bring in revenue for the government.

The customs officials also faced a gargantuan task in policing wine imports. There was no set price for a Bordeaux wine. Depending on when and where it was purchased, the price could include layers of fees to intermediaries, as well as fluctuations in the market value and currencies. The same wine could legitimately have different values on back-to-back days; sometimes different values were quoted on the same day from competing sources. Take a bottle of 2008 Château Lafite purchased in France for around $180: a customs official in Shenzhen might look up the value online and discover that the vintage was selling in Shanghai that day for 7,800 yuan, roughly $1,200—when that wasn't necessarily where the wine was heading, or how much it would sell for once it reached its destination. There was also the risk that an official would slap a completely arbitrary value onto a bottle to raise his daily customs intake, whether on the government books or as a personal kickback. "Maybe that was the day they had been told to collect more taxes, and you're the one," said a Hong Kong wine seller. "Every shipment, every time, it's the same thing."

To further complicate matters, the health and hygiene department required samples of every wine in every shipment. An importer might suddenly be informed that the wine had been confiscated.

A successful shipment was one part bribe, one part timing, one part luck. And sometimes luck ran out.

❃

Don St. Pierre Jr. was sitting in the gilded nineteenth-century salon of Jean-Guillaume Prats's mansion in downtown Bordeaux. During ASC's first year, he and his father had sold twenty-seven thousand bottles of wine worth $3.4 million. A decade later, ASC was selling three million bottles and bringing in $70 million. The company had grown 46 percent on average per year between 2000 and 2007. Don Sr. had retired and Don Jr. had taken the helm. He had 1,200 employees and offices all over China. The company offered tasting classes and private cellaring to clients throughout the mainland.

Don Jr. was settling into middle age with the air of success. He was on the stocky side, kept his blond hair cut short and his suits expertly tailored, and he didn't wear his emotions on his sleeve. There was barely any hint of the eager young student who had first come to China under his father's wing. He was now a seasoned executive, himself an old China hand. While Don Sr. had been renowned for his hard-living, flamboyant, confrontational style, Don Jr. cultivated a low profile marked by discretion. He spoke with quiet intensity and flashes of humor. It seemed a good fit for a wine trader in China, where the main customers—government officials—preferred to keep their dealings shielded from public scrutiny. But his low profile was about to be shot.

In March 2008, he flew to Bordeaux in advance of the annual barrel tastings, the event at which the previous year's vintage is first introduced to the wine trade. While critics and wine buyers gauge the vintage for quality, the châteaux, courtiers, négociants, merchants, and importers use the meetings to wrangle over allocations and prices.

Don Jr. was making the rounds. On March 6, he was finishing a lunch meeting at Café Lavinal, a bistro owned by the winemaker Jean-Michel Cazes that was tucked behind his estate, Château Lynch-Bages, which, after its deal with Cathay Pacific, had become one of the best-known French wines in China. Visiting was always a pleasure, but as St. Pierre left the restaurant, his cell phone rang. It was his father, and the news was bad.

The Smuggling Prevention Department of the Chinese Customs Service had raided ASC's office in Shanghai. On its own, this was nothing out of the ordinary. Government departments made unannounced visits every six months or so—it was said they were looking for handouts or wine. The authorities had the right to seize what they wanted, when they wanted, without need for a search warrant. Every importer faced the same harassment. It was simply one of the challenges of operating as a wholly foreign-owned enterprise in China, without the protection of a Chinese partner.

As usual, the officers seized piles of documents, but something about the raid seemed ominous to Don Sr. A handful of other wine importers had been hit during the same period. The authorities appeared to be on a hunt. They had also taken two of ASC's employees into custody.

Don Jr. assured his father that he'd catch the next plane back to China to help sort out everything. When he phoned his Chinese-born wife, Monica Xu, however, she begged him not to come home. Fortunes changed quickly in China, and perhaps ASC had gotten on the wrong side of someone important. While it was tempting to sit tight in Bordeaux, two issues weighed heavily in Don Jr.'s mind. First, since his father's retirement, he was now the person legally responsible for the company, and he needed to be in China to have any hope of arguing effectively on behalf of his employees and his company. Second, he knew there was a good chance they'd arrest his father in his absence.

"I wasn't going to let them take my father," he recalled, the turmoil of emotions cracking his normally relaxed countenance. "Jesus, he was sixty-eight years old. I had to go back."

He got the first plane out of Mérignac airport, eventually arriving in China on March 9, 2008. On his long-haul flights, he had plenty of time to think about what awaited him in Shanghai. From what his father had told him, it seemed as though the customs police had acted on a tip, as though they'd been told exactly where to look, what to seize, which employees to pull in. There were quite a few Chinese and foreign-owned companies that would have loved to see the St. Pierres put out of business. Did he have an enemy?

The morning after he got back to China, Don Jr. went straight to the customs building for a sit-down with the investigators. He assumed full responsibility for the company's operations, then answered the officers' questions dutifully for three hours. The investigators were interested in

ASC's imports, which they noticed were invoiced through the firm's Hong Kong office. Don Jr. agreed—it was how many businesses operated. And now Hong Kong was poised to become a major duty-free logistics hub.

The session seemed to go well, and the officials let him leave for a lunch break. When he returned he was feeling optimistic, but the mood of the interrogation turned hostile. At the end of the day, he was locked up in a cell half the size of his office in Shanghai's Detention Center. Carrie Xuan, ASC's vice president of logistics, purchasing, and private client business, was also held in custody.

St. Pierre shared the small cell with five men: three from China, one from Nigeria, and one from Hong Kong. Two were charged with murder, two with theft, and one with real estate fraud. Everyone slept on the floor on quilts; there were no beds. There was one open toilet and one sink. The food budget for each detainee was five yuan per day, which provided a diet of rice, vegetables, and an occasional scrap of meat.

The detainees' daily routine was rigidly controlled. Each morning, they attended a class where they were educated about the rules of detention. There was a forced midday nap, during which talking and reading were forbidden. An afternoon class required them to provide a written group answer to a question, checked by a guard. Five times a day they walked in circles for exercise. They went to bed at 9:30 P.M., but St. Pierre's nights were mostly sleepless. He was too anxious to sleep; plus, the lights in the cell were never turned off.

Don Sr. scrambled to get his son released from jail. He appealed to the U.S. ambassador in China, Clark Randt, but nothing came of it. The U.S. embassy was able to get one of their staff in to see Don Jr., but they told him they had no leverage. Several Chinese authorities warned Don Sr. that if he involved the American government, he risked never seeing his son again. Relying on the American diplomats might actually make the situation worse.

Days passed. Don Jr. was allowed out of the cell just five times, and two of those occasions were to let guards check the cell. He met with a lawyer his father managed to send to the prison in order to check that he was okay, but the lawyer was not allowed to discuss the case with him. All the lawyer could say was that the laws did not seem to be in his favor. Don Jr. was frightened. He could be stuck in this cell for years, perhaps for the rest of his life.

"I had to make peace with it," he said.

As he sat in the cell, he considered the charges made by the Smuggling Prevention Department. He began to see that the problem was ASC's practice of hedging currency values when it bought and sold wine. When the St. Pierres bought wine from Europe or South Africa or the United States, they issued purchase orders from their original Hong Kong company. On the books, they converted the invoiced currencies to Hong Kong dollars, based on a hedge rate. Then the wine was invoiced to ASC's China WFOE, converting Hong Kong dollars to Chinese renminbi. Many wine importers did this; it made paperwork much easier when it came time to declare the value of the wine to Chinese customs.

Because import duties were based on value, not volume, everyone understood that companies had a motivation to lowball the value of the wine whenever they could. It dawned on St. Pierre that the Chinese officials most likely suspected that ASC was using the variations in exchange rates to declare, for example, that a $100 bottle of wine was worth the renminbi equivalent of $80. In actuality, the declared value of the wine was usually open to discussion between the importer and the customs agent at the border, since the value of the wine was constantly changing. Conducting the currency conversions in Hong Kong might be convenient, and often profitable, but it had the appearance of a shell game. Given everything he knew about China, it was, St. Pierre realized as he sat in his cell, a really stupid thing to do.

The currency conversions meant that, in the view of Chinese customs, ASC had overdeclared the value of inexpensive wines and underdeclared the value of expensive wines in the previous year. The discrepancy between the declared value of the goods and the real value was about 2.38 million yuan, or $350,000. The St. Pierres could have readily paid the money owed. It was only 1 percent of the total value of duties they had paid between March 2006 and March 2007. But the customs officials weren't listening. Any time a discrepancy added up to over 250,000 yuan, they had the right to detain the head of the company while an investigation was conducted, and they were going to keep Don Jr. in custody.

By now, Don Sr. had abandoned his attempts to engage the U.S. embassy. What this problem required was *guanxi*, the benefit of his personal connections in Chinese society. In China, business deals got done and government projects got approved based on a person's ability to cultivate a personal network of influential partners and officials who would happily provide a favor when needed—often because the person was providing favors in return. Mastering guanxi was central to navigating Chinese bureaucracy. Don Sr. thought about his connections. He had a friend, Zhang Hao, who for the past twelve years had been the vice general manager of Bacardi Greater China. Zhang was also a former government official who had deep connections and an intimate understanding of how Chinese officials functioned. Don Sr. appealed to Zhang for help, as well as for discretion.

Unfortunately, any hope Zhang had of keeping Don Jr.'s detention quiet died a few days later. On March 17, Don Sr. sent a letter to ASC's customers and suppliers to quell rumors about the investigation and to play down the seriousness of his son's situation. That same day, an influential wine educator in Hong Kong named Simon Tam contacted him about the detention, presumably having heard the news from someone who had received the letter. Don Sr. stuck to the company line: this was merely a routine investigation and would soon be wrapped up.

Tam didn't believe him. He published an article on the website of the British wine critic Jancis Robinson, all but condemning the St. Pierres for gaming the system on purpose. "It appears to have been common practice by a number of wine importers to systematically undervalue the declared value of wine by upwards of 50%, thus reducing the total cost of a bottle of wine by nearly 25%," wrote Tam. "The subtle manipulation of declared wine value has the potential to have an enormous impact on a company's profitability by lowering the sale price, increasing margins and driving business away from the smaller companies who don't have the luxury of generating the volume of sales needed to thrive in this cut-throat emerging wine market." For many readers, including Don Sr., that was as good as accusing ASC of fraud while his son was being held in Chinese custody.

This time, Don Sr. wasn't in a position to write directly to the premier to protest unfair treatment, so he launched a fiery one-man public relations campaign in defense of his son.

On March 20, 2008, Robinson published Don Sr.'s retort, which lambasted Tam for being "irresponsible" and said that he had relied "almost solely on rumor and innuendo" in writing his report. He denounced Tam's article as an "industry hit job." Tam, he said, was out to take down a rival business, since Tam had tried and failed to compete with ASC's wine education program in China, even attempting to poach some ASC staff members while Don Jr. was in jail.

He also scoffed at Tam's lack of understanding of how business worked in China. In the article, Tam had suggested that ASC owed $6.8 million in fines and that both father and son would likely be deported. Don Sr. sneered that businessmen were only deported from China when they dealt in drugs or very serious smuggling, and that the Chinese government would never impose a fine that would bankrupt a company, thereby denying themselves a nice, ongoing stream of customs revenue.

Tam didn't respond until April 1, after an article in the *International Herald Tribune* confirmed Don Jr.'s arrest. "What this story ends up being is something so much bigger than fines and elaborate schemes of shell companies, falsified documents, and missing millions in imports," Tam wrote. But Tam wanted to make a bigger point. The St. Pierres and their ilk had reached the end of their era in China:

> This is no longer the wild west of wine countries. The maverick tactics of smuggling, bribing with cases of first growths and buying off exclusivity of wine lists for tens of thousands of RMB are all bound to bite the dust along with the falsified customs documents. . . . The Chinese wine industry is coming of age. Customs is wising up. Loopholes are closing up. We will remember this moment as a watershed period in the growth of China's wine industry. Not for fines or detentions or for how many companies end up being taken

to task, but for how this one moment will forever be emblematic of changes long since started, yet still just gaining steam.

A week later, on April 8, 2008, Don Jr.'s cell door swung open and he was free without any explanation. He had been in jail for twenty-eight days; on his thirtieth day in custody, the authorities would have had to formally charge him with a crime. Carrie Xuan was also freed. ASC agreed to admit that the firm had undervalued its imports, and the St. Pierres paid a fine as well as back fees based on the difference between the hedged currency exchange rate and the real rate at the time of the import. The total bill came to 1.8 million yuan, about $220,000—less than a single day of sales at ASC.

"In plain American talk that's called 'peanuts,'" declared Don Sr. in his final, ferocious public defense of his son and their company.

"Stepping back, I've been living and doing business in China for 22 years now and have gone through lots of these kinds of things and survived," said Don Sr. "China is not for the weak hearted."

The Chinese authorities seemed satisfied. The next year, Don Jr. could boast that he had bought more Château Latour than anyone else in the world. But he was looking for a way to maintain control over ASC while sharing some of the risk of doing business in China. Near the end of 2009, after Gernot Langes-Swarovski suffered a stroke, St. Pierre out-maneuvered attempts by the Swarovski management team to wrest ASC from him, and he sold a substantial stake in the company to Suntory, the Japanese beverage giant. Perhaps the move would help to insulate him from Chinese customs in the future.

❀

Stephan Delaux, the president of Bordeaux's Tourism Bureau and of Bordeaux Grands Evénements, was gazing out on the crowd that had gathered along Hong Kong's West Kowloon waterfront, with the city's dramatic skyline behind them. To his left was Hong Kong's financial secretary, John Tsang, who was eager to join him in christening the first Hong Kong Wine and Dine Festival, which began on October 29, 2009. The event was the first time Bordeaux had exported its popular festival, which gives winegrowers the chance to introduce their wines by the glass to the general public. It had taken months of planning and cross-cultural collaboration.

Delaux, who also served as Bordeaux's deputy mayor, felt a sense of vindication as he scanned the crowd. In his heart, he believed Bordeaux to be one of the most beautiful cities on earth. Over the past fifteen years, he'd spent many an hour talking to Philippine de Rothschild of Château Mouton Rothschild, Jean-Michel Cazes of Château Lynch-Bages, and other esteemed winegrowers about how they might turn Bordeaux into a wine tourism capital. This week he had succeeded in transporting the spirit of the city he loved to the front door of the fastest growing economy in the world. If he couldn't yet entice the Chinese to come to Bordeaux, he would deliver a glass of Bordeaux wine to them.

Though Hong Kong's zero duty was part of the appeal, as was the two-bottle consumption allowance, there were other attractions for the main-land Chinese. The strange language and culture, the cost of travel, and visa restrictions made it difficult for the average Chinese family to travel to France. Hong Kong was already a regular tourist destination for China's growing middle class. Holding a version of the festival in Hong Kong created common ground for Old World winemakers and merchants to meet China's budding wine consumers.

Tsang began with a review of the dividends of Hong Kong's zero-duty policy. "Since eliminating duties on wine in my budget last year, our wine trade has provided some welcome economic fizz during the global financial crisis," he reported.

> "The value of wine imports increased by 80 percent year-on-year in 2008; it further increased by another 42 percent in the first eight months of 2009, amounting to $2.3 billion. A number of wine-related businesses have expanded their operations or launched new enterprises here. These include retail outlets, storage facilities, trading companies, and more. We even have a winery now in Hong Kong, which is quite special considering we don't produce any grapes. The industry forecasts that Hong Kong is overtaking

NO BOUNDARIES | 51

London . . . to become the world's second largest wine auction center, just behind New York."

On that note, the party got started, lasting well into the night.

However, on the second morning of the festival, the Frenchman who represented the Bordeaux Wine Council in Asia faced a crisis. Thomas Jullien lived in Hong Kong, so he was accustomed to China's hyper-charged pace. Still, he couldn't believe that the festival's organizers, himself included, had so dramatically underestimated attendance. There was still another day and a half to go, and Bordeaux had not sent enough wine. Jullien and the other organizers called every importer they could reach in an urgent effort to buy back stock and satisfy festivalgoers.

The Chinese visitors' voracious demand was difficult for many in Bordeaux to understand, and most didn't try. It was a gift to be cele-brated. In Bordeaux, they had to beat back the anti-alcohol lobby; they had to constantly worry about inebriated festivalgoers falling into the Garonne and drowning. Here, they were giddy with profits. Thanks to China, Bordeaux would soon be back on its feet. When the 2009 vin-tage came on the market in the spring, everyone expected that the Chi-nese would buy, and that they would buy big.

❋

People were still gossiping about Don Jr.'s arrest more than a year later, but none of the theories about how the family had gotten on the wrong side of the Smuggling Prevention Department were as mundane or as accurate as hedged currency values. Most of the whispers involved plots hatched by the central government in Beijing.

As the rumors spread, Don Jr. gained a certain mystique: this was the man who'd faced life in a Chinese gulag and come out on top of a pile of classified growths—and profits. His opinions on wine and China carried authority. So when, in the early months of 2010, he said he was worried that Bordeaux might lose its special appeal in the Chinese wine market, people listened.

St. Pierre couldn't stop thinking about a new trend he had noticed on his monthly customs reports: the price per liter for imported French wine was dropping. Bordeaux dominated the supply of wine from France, so this statistic could only mean that the demand for the dregs of Bordeaux's cellars was increasing. It didn't bother him if cheap appellation wine from Bordeaux was competing with local Chinese wine, and there weren't, as far as he knew, any vineyards in China that could compete with the classified growth estates. But he wasn't convinced that the masses had started drinking cheap wine.

The fact was that Bordeaux had a glut of bad wine, and some unscrupulous, opportunistic négociants assumed they could take advantage of Chinese naïveté to get rid of millions of unwanted bottles of it. But the Chinese were learning, and events such as the Hong Kong Wine and Dine Festival were educating them about wine. It wouldn't be long before they, too, refused to buy the plonk no one else wanted.

"Bordeaux is definitely a brand in China—it is by far the most well-known wine-producing region in China," St. Pierre explained. "They are buying something they believe is better quality, something with history. The danger for Bordeaux is that there are a lot of low-quality wines being shipped into China, and this will, over time, erode the quality of the brand."

He was worried that all the years he'd spent building Bordeaux's reputation for fine wine might dissolve in a flood of thin, bitter Cabernet.

3

....

Planting Vines

Since 2009, Emma Gao Yuan's blend of Cabernet Sauvignon, Cabernet Franc, and Carmenère had been on the menu at the five-star Aman boutique resorts in China. Yet Gao didn't exude the brash confidence typical of a trailblazer, especially one who had come of age in the early days of Chinese capitalism. Her winery in northern China was a tiny outfit, producing only eight hundred cases a year, she said with a shy grin. She was strong but slight, dressed neatly, her voice low but confident.

Emma's father, Gao Lin, had introduced her to the wine business. Until 1990, he had been the general manager of a state-owned clothing factory in the dusty city of Yinchuan, the capital of the inhospitable, remote Ningxia Hui Autonomous Region, some 550 miles west of Beijing on the frontier of Inner Mongolia. After the factory was suddenly closed, Gao found himself unemployed. He formed an export company with his two brothers and in 1992 set out for Saint Petersburg, taking his eldest daughter, Emma, with him, and leaving his wife and youngest daughter in Yinchuan. He traded in cashmere and wool—any clothes made back home that he could sell to the Russians—while Emma studied economics at Saint Petersburg University. It was an amazing time to be in Russia, so soon after the collapse of the Soviet Union. For five years, father and daughter reveled in their life as "overseas Chinese."

The openness of post-Soviet Russia was a relief. Gao Lin was all too aware of the difficulties of negotiating the shifting winds of Chinese politics. His own father had been the director of a middle school in Shaanxi Province when the Communists began to organize into an underground movement in the 1930s. He decided to join them and march north to Ningxia. "My [paternal] grandfather arrived with a horse, two soldiers, and a pistol," said Emma Gao. Despite this humble start, he was soon a prominent leader in the local Communist Party. On her mother's side, her Tatar peasant grandfather joined the People's Liberation Army as it swept through the northwest territories, seizing control of the country. At the time, 95 percent of the population in Ningxia was illiterate, and there were no institutions of higher learning. But her maternal grandfather taught himself to read, and he, too, rose up through the ranks and joined the local party committee. Both families were loyal Communists with influence over political affairs in Ningxia. They were important and trusted.

Then, in 1966, at the outset of the Cultural Revolution, their luck changed. Both of Emma's grandfathers were betrayed by an unnamed party leader and banished to the countryside. Gao Lin's father, renounced as a member of the educated class, spent ten years peeling vegetables in a remote commune kitchen. They had been targeted under the directives of Mao's "Down to the Countryside" policy. Eventually, the two men managed to make their way back to Ningxia and their families, grateful to have survived when millions of others had perished. They had lost everything, including their most valuable asset: guanxi. It would take decades—and the deliverance of the exit visas to live and work in Russia—for the Gaos to overcome this tarnished political biography.

In 1997, when Emma finished her studies, Gao Lin was called back to China and assigned to work at a Shizuishan chemical factory, north of Yinchuan. Hot and dry in the summer and frozen in the winter, Ningxia had largely remained undeveloped; the chemical factory was a powerful employer in the area. The company owned coal mines and manufactured electronic goods in addition to producing vast quantities of chemicals. There was none of the excitement of the new Russia, but he was fortunate to have the job.

The following year, he was put in charge of an 823-acre state farm in Luhuatai. The land was arid, surrounded by the Gobi Desert in every direction. The only break in the landscape was the Yellow River, running along the east side of Shizuishan and Yinchuan, with the Helan Mountains to the north and west providing natural protection from the desert sands.

Only a slim fraction of Ningxia's twenty-five thousand square miles of land was covered with plant life. The surrounding sands were on the verge of claiming the region as their own, sapping it of water, vegetation, and wildlife. Every acre planted was a victory.

Ningxia was not alone in facing desertification, which affected four hundred million people and more than a quarter of China's land. "Land desertification is the most important ecological problem in China," said Zhang Yongli, the deputy director of China's State Forestry Administration. "It causes erosion to the available space for people's existence and development, provokes natural disasters like sandstorms and endangers agricultural production by degrading the land." In the 1990s, 1,326 square miles of the countryside were lost every year. More recently, land was slowly being reclaimed, and Beijing had plans to reclaim 77,000 square miles for agricultural projects by 2020.

In Ningxia, leaders were required to develop the area's agriculture in accordance with the latest Five-Year Plan. Understandably, Ningxia encouraged projects such as Guangxia Industry, a joint venture with Pernod Ricard that reclaimed 5,400 acres of desert, removing 450 million cubic feet of sand in the process. The company planted 2 million trees, 1,500 acres of medicinal plants, and 2,640 acres of vineyards. Another project used air seeding to plant millions of trees. Two other crops, dates and goji berries, also took root in the region.

At the state farm where Gao Lin worked, the managers had another idea. They wanted to plant grape vines, and they placed Gao Lin in charge of the vineyard. Grape vines were a calculated choice.

In the mid-1990s, Yinchuan had hosted a wine conference at which assorted party and local officials could hear presentations on where grapes might be planted in China. One of the presentations featured Dr. Li Hua, who had recently founded the College of Enology at Northwest Agriculture and Forestry University in Yangling, in Shaanxi Province. It was the first program of its kind in Asia, and Li was on a mission to bring fine winemaking to China. He had earned a PhD from the prestigious Faculté d'Oenologie at Bordeaux University, publishing a dissertation on downy mildew, the great plague of any aspiring vintner. After his studies in Bordeaux, he had toured China, investigating the capacity for making fine wine in different regions.

Ningxia had the benefit of a dry climate, with average rainfall just shy of eight inches, and cool nights and warm days, which would lend the grapes a fresh, attractive aroma. The dry climate also meant that there would be less of a threat of mildew and rot during the critical window when the grapes developed a balance between sugar and acid. The high desert at the foot of the Helan Mountains was generally sandy, but there were some sections with clay and pebbles. The combination of soil and climate pointed to a terroir that could produce fresh wines with complex aromas. Poor, remote, underpopulated Ningxia, Li said, had real potential.

Li made his presentation when Chinese officials were beginning to see the value in growing wine grapes rather than table grapes. In 1995, there had been just 240 wineries in China, but between 1996 and 1997, after Li Peng's toast with wine at the National People's Congress, 200 more wineries had sprouted up. In 1997, Vice Premier Wen Jiabao returned from a tour of France with a mission to establish a model vineyard on Beijing's doorstep. The next year, the Chinese government signed a joint venture with the French government for a Sino-French Demonstration Vineyard and hired a Bordeaux winemaker, Nicolas Billot-Grima, as the consultant. In 1998 alone, the new Chinese state wineries imported 4.5 million vine cuttings from France.

Gao Lin had been told that it would take three years for his vines to go into production. He also understood that the road to success was volume. Every vineyard manager had heard the story of Dynasty Fine Wines, the triumph of Tianjin, and wanted to duplicate it.

❋

In November 1979, François Hériard-Dubreuil, the thirty-one-year-old scion of the Rémy Martin Cognac family, left Hong Kong to cross the border at Shenzhen, China's newly designated special economic zone, to catch a plane north. From the window, all he could see were rice paddies. But earlier that year, at the annual World Economic Forum in Davos, Switzerland, China had sent a delegation for the first time, and four officials in Mao-style suits had approached Hériard-Dubreuil to say that Beijing was keen on a joint venture. The idea gained momentum when an Indonesian-born trader named Benny Cheung contacted Rémy's office in Hong Kong and offered to act as a go-between. A message soon arrived from Beijing that the joint venture could happen in Tianjin, a municipality directly under the control of the central government. Hériard-Dubreuil had never heard of Tianjin, a city of some seven million at the time, but nothing could quell the thrill of finding himself at this turning point in history.

Tianjin was the closest port to Beijing, an hour away by train, situated on the Bohai, the innermost bay of the Yellow Sea. After the Second Opium War, the port had been opened to trade with the British and other foreigners. The international settlements flourished until the civil war between the Nationalists and the Communists stymied their commercial operations; after the Japanese invaded in 1937, most Europeans left. Under Deng Xiaoping, Tianjin was once again open for business with the West, and it wielded the influence to make deals happen. The Communist party chief of Tianjin sat on the Central Politburo. Like other Chinese cities, Tianjin was hungry for foreign currency, jobs, training, and industrial expertise. The city boasted a fruit wine company, owned by Tianjin Yiqing Group, and a vineyard.

The "Friendship Vineyard of Bulgaria and China" belonged to the state-controlled Tianjin Agribusiness Group. Fifty acres of Muscat grape vines had been planted by the Bulgarian government after the People's Liberation Army marshal Nie Rongzhen fell in love with the fragrant white wine during an official trip to Eastern Europe in 1958. Few vineyards existed in Communist China at the time. The Changyu winery, set up in 1892 by an extravagantly rich overseas Chinese named Zhang Bishi, had won four gold medals at the 1915 Panama-Pacific International

Exposition in San Francisco, but after the winery was nationalized in 1949, it produced disappointing wines that no peasant wanted to drink, let alone a top Red Army commander. A churchyard winery established in 1910 by a French priest not far from Beijing's Summer Palace had also been nationalized, then razed.

In the absence of local winemaking know-how, the Bulgarian experiment in Tianjin faltered, too. The vineyard was a mix of grape varieties, Muscat of Hamburg, Dimyat, Carignan, and Chinese varieties like Longyan, known as Dragon's Eye, and Baiyu, called White Feather. As was the case at the other nationalized wineries, the drink that was sold as wine was a strange hybrid product. Not quite a wine, not quite a spirit, it was on occasion a toxic mix of colorants and chemicals. When it was made with grapes, table grapes were typically used, but grapes were not the primary ingredient; apple juice was more common. It also didn't help that the climate on the edge of the North China Plain was inhospitable to wine grapes. It rained during the growing season, all but guaranteeing a constant losing battle against rot and mildew. What little wine was produced wasn't 100 percent grape, and it did little to recommend itself to even the most parched consumer. Most of the vineyard's harvest was sold as table grapes.

The officials lodged Hériard-Dubreuil in a colonial-era hotel, in which all of the doors, including those for cupboards, had been removed. Communist officials entered his room at night to keep an eye on him.

"The next day they took me outside the city to an old school made of red clay, which was where Dynasty started," said Hériard-Dubreuil. A section of a wall had been painted black, and the Frenchman used chalk to outline his plans. He had arrived in Tianjin expecting to produce whiskey or brandy, but the vineyard gave him the idea of making wine. This required transferring the venture from the ministry of light industry, which oversaw distillation, to the Tianjin Farm Bureau, managed by a man named Bai Yin.

Bai kept the talks brief. He knew that the Frenchman across the table from them could help Tianjin transform these pathetic vines into a real wine. Three months later, in January 1980, Hériard-Dubreuil shook hands on the deal with the Tianjin officials. Bai Yin became the chairman of the joint venture, the second in all of China.

Tianjin would supply the electricity, water, and workers, and Rémy Martin would supply the equipment and expertise, overseeing the winemaking. The French would also be in charge of sales and distribution. The deal gave Tianjin 62 percent and Rémy 38 percent ownership in the joint venture. The initial investment from Rémy Martin was relatively small—a million dollars. "The results were satisfactory," one of the Chinese executives recalled, "since Rémy Martin was eager to gain a firm foothold in China, and we needed to study French advanced wine-making techniques. Dynasty's strategy was to produce first, negotiate later."

By August, however, there was trouble in Tianjin. The first winemaker Rémy Martin had sent to Tianjin had come and gone, and the replacement, the French winemaker Pierre Delair, rejected half of the grape harvest as either green or rotten. The verdict triggered angry demonstrations by the grape-growing farmers. The Chinese manager mollified the peasants by offering to pay a premium—around 1.3 yuan, or twenty-one cents, per pound—for any grapes that he judged ripe and healthy. That first year, the company produced a test batch, and then in 1981 produced enough wine to fill one hundred thousand bottles.

When it came time to bottle and ship the wine, the joint venture hit more roadblocks. It was impossible to use the bottles that had been supplied by the Chinese manufacturer. They had arrived in sacks, filthy, and they broke easily. Rémy scrambled to order replacement bottles from Australia and France. It was also impossible to ship the wine directly from Tianjin. At the time, China did not have the logistics industry to export wine anywhere, so the wine had to be forwarded to the British colony of Hong Kong for export.

Finally, some samples were shipped to Rémy Martin's Hong Kong–based marketing team, headed by David Webster. Webster's father had been a Caldbeck Macgregor veteran, and after attending school in England, the son had returned to Hong Kong and obtained an entry-level position in the wine and spirits section of the retailer A. S. Watson. When Watson's wine and spirits business was sold to Rémy Martin, Webster remained, working for the Cognac group. He had the palate of an Englishman raised in the trade. Now it was his job to come up with a blend of Chinese wine that would appeal to Western consumers.

Webster had never visited the operation in Tianjin, but the wine spoke for itself. It was a thin, medium-dry white wine, barely hitting 11 percent alcohol content, fruity and aromatic, the result of a mix of Muscat of Hamburg, Dimyat, Dragon's Eye, White Feather, Carignan and any other vines that Delair could coax into producing ripe grapes. German white wines were all the rage in the United States, and Webster thought there was no reason why it wouldn't sell. But the wine needed a name that would appeal to Chinese immigrants living in the West. In Tianjin, the Chinese chose the name "Shen Zhou," which translated as "the Divine Land of China." Unfortunately, however, the name was already trademarked. Webster and the Rémy Martin marketing team in Hong Kong put forward an inspired alternative: "Dynasty." "The TV show was the most popular, the biggest hit on television," he recalled. "There were obvious Chinese links to the word. And it was easy for everyone to pronounce." The Chinese managers back in Tianjin seemed pleased enough.

As the enterprise grew, Dynasty needed more grapes, and it was a constant challenge for Delair to find ripe grapes. Grapes were the only fruit grown locally that were ripe in time for the Chinese Mid-Autumn Festival, or Moon Festival, and farmers got a higher price selling them as table grapes for the holidays. But the communes weren't the only option for sourcing. The joint venture could also buy grapes from the nearby Qinghe, Banjiao, or Tuanhe Farms. When the Chinese manager took Delair to visit Tuanhe, the Frenchman wasn't surprised to see the workers in uniforms and the police at the reception. That was how peasants dressed and everyday life was heavily monitored. He needed official permission just to drive from Tianjin to the winery. What he did notice right away was that the grapes were ripe—the best he'd seen yet in China, and he told the Tianjin manager he wanted them. What he didn't know was that Tuanhe was not an ordinary farm.

Tuanhe Farm was, in fact, a death camp. Also known as Beijing RTL—RTL stood for "reform through labor"—the *laogai* was part of

China's shadowy network of forced-labor prison camps. Conditions were brutal. The Laogai Research Foundation estimated that around twenty-five million people had died in the Chinese gulags. During Mao's time, the camps had focused on forced labor, torture, and starvation to suppress dissent, while using the prisoners for massive construction projects. Since opening to the West, China had identified the potential of exploiting prison labor to boost the country's export economy, giving the camps innocuous names for their enterprises while keeping the official penal system name secret. Grapes weren't the only subcontracted labor. Prisoners at another RTL, the Tianjin Municipal Banqiao RTL, also known as Banqiao Farm Machinery Parts Factory, fabricated boxes for the Rémy Martin–Tianjin joint venture.

Tuanhe had 824 acres of vineyards, where fifteen thousand men, women, and children worked for up to fifteen hours each day, earning ten dollars a year. Some had been convicted of crimes, but most had disappeared into the gulag without trial—political prisoners, such as Harry Wu Hongda, who spent nineteen years in a series of forced labor camps after criticizing the Soviet invasion of Hungary during the "Hundred Flowers" free-speech campaign in 1957. Wu, the son of a Shanghai banker, was imprisoned at Tuanhe from 1962 to 1968. As a punishment for low productivity, he said, prisoners were tied up naked in the vineyard and left overnight to be feasted on by insects. Although there was no barbed wire, there was no chance of slipping away unnoticed. Wardens marked out the fields with flags, and any vineyard workers who moved past the flags would be shot and killed. Many inmates succumbed to disease, malnutrition, or torture. Others were executed.

It may have been revolting to use forced labor, but it was not illegal, unless the wine was exported to the United States or a handful of other countries. Nor was it clear whether the Tianjin managers knew at the time that they were buying grapes cultivated by prisoners. In 1990, Rémy's northeast Asia zone manager, John Wong, told a *Financial Times* reporter that they had bought grapes from Tuanhe, and he had been to the Tuanhe farm a few years earlier, but had only visited the reception area. A year later, in an award-winning story by *BusinessWeek*, an official at Rémy Martin told investigating journalists that from 1982 to

1985 some grapes used in Dynasty wines were harvested by prisoners. At any rate, it was a short-lived relationship: the prison officials had found they could sell the grapes for more elsewhere. But the winemakers would not have been the first to unwittingly employ gulag labor. A delegation of American lawyers visiting Shanghai Prison No. 1 stumbled upon packaging for Seagram's wine coolers, produced by inmates, for a joint venture. "Without our knowledge, subcontracting was done at the prison the ABA visited," said Seagram spokesperson Robert Kasmire. "When Seagram found out, we ended that relationship."

Rémy's French winemaker Pierre Delair drew the same line.

"In 1986, they brought a truck of grapes from the concentration camps—the laogai, it's true, but Pierre had a second sense. He asked where it was coming from," said Hériard-Dubreuil. "He knew the place was a laogai. He refused."

By 1987, Hériard-Dubreuil sensed that Delair needed a respite from China, and offered him and his family a stint in Brazil. Delair left Tianjin, exhausted but confident of the team he'd trained.

Several other joint ventures followed. The Great Wall Wine Company was founded in 1983, its winery built on the site of a notorious laogai camp, the vineyard's plots leased to farmers who were required to sell their grapes to the joint venture. Four years later, when the French liqueur company Pernod Ricard teamed up with the Beijing Friendship Winery, a young Languedoc winemaker was put in charge. Like Rémy Martin before it, Pernod Ricard wanted a name for the resulting wine to resonate with Chinese consumers. The Chinese considered themselves descendants of the dragon; the wine was named "Dragon Seal." The first vintage was sold in 1988, the Year of the Dragon, as a marketing ploy.

Even if China's emerging middle class didn't quite like the taste of wine, they liked the *idea* of it—how it conveyed personal success and an end to the deprivations common during the Great Famine and the Cultural Revolution. Sure, sometimes they might mix wine with soft drinks in an attempt to make the tannins more palatable, but even so, it was glamorous, sophisticated. In the evening soap operas, a prop bottle of wine was used as a cue to the audience that a seduction was under way. Doctors prescribed nighttime wine "tonics." At a luxury shopping plaza in Shanghai, one of the busiest restaurants was the Häagen-Dazs café, where two scoops cost nearly a full day's typical salary. The menu helpfully suggested pairings of fine wine and ice cream.

Over the years, the Dynasty Winery found customers, both at home and abroad. The company sold fifty-seven million bottles of wine a year in China, making it the country's fourth largest domestic wine producer, and its wines were served at official state banquets and Chinese embassy events. As China's per capita income increased, Dynasty's managers hiked up the prices. Chinese wine had rarely sold for more than five dollars a bottle, but now Dynasty's wines often cost twenty-five dollars a bottle, or more.

In less than a quarter century, it had become one of Tianjin's biggest businesses and a leading tourist attraction. At the company's headquarters twelve miles north of the city, most visitors were ushered through the elaborate *paifang*, or archway, to an enormous three-story restaurant, which became a regular spot for business and government banquets. A 118,000-square-foot castle was planned, its spires, battlements, marble statues, tapestries, medieval suits of armor, and eighteenth-century furniture modeled on the Château de Versailles. On completion, the castle would have twenty-two guest rooms, several banquet halls, a spa, and an armchair that had once been owned by the philosopher Michel de Montaigne, who hailed from Bordeaux. Inexplicably, a glass pyramid, a replica of the I. M. Pei–designed entrance to the Louvre in Paris, would stand in front of the castle. Like the original, Dynasty's pyramid would sit atop an art gallery.

It was odd that Dynasty chose to build a replica château rather than a distinctly Chinese palace that would showcase the wine's origins. Bai Zhisheng, Dynasty's chairman and the executive director of Tianjin Development Holdings, explained the choice: "This was a humble decision, because we believe and we know that all wine actually originates from Europe and is very much related to the culture in Europe. The château is one that we can relate to. If Dynasty produced spirits that were made in China, then we would definitely have built something Chinese in structure, to represent Chinese spirits." He had not said the words, but the ideal wine in China was still a French red.

At Tianjin and in Ningxia, big state-owned enterprises were making wine. Yet, for the most part, the Chinese had no idea what they were drinking. Enthusiasm for wine outpaced knowledge. Most Chinese consumers had little ability to determine the value of a wine from its label— unless it was a classified growth.

✻

There was nothing romantic about the industrialization of wine in China, but that didn't keep Gao Lin from being intoxicated by the quest to produce a uniquely authentic Chinese fine wine.

The turning point came in 1999, when he was selected to join the official Ningxia delegation on a two-week trip to France and Germany in preparation for running the Luhuatai state farm. The junket was intended to be a crash course in grape growing, winemaking, wine tasting, tourism, and commerce, but two weeks was only enough time to gain a glancing knowledge of enology and viticulture. Still, it took far less time for Gao to fall in love with the vineyard landscapes of Europe, and the lifestyle. When he returned to Ningxia, he called Emma, who was working for an electronics company in another city and trying not to think too hard about her dismal future. He asked if she wanted to go to France to study. She didn't even ask where in France she would be going, or what she would be studying. Yes, she said without pause. He dispatched her to Orange in Provence to learn French and get an introduction to the technical aspects of winemaking. Months later, she was in Paris, contemplating how she might delay her return to dusty Ningxia, when she struck up a conversation with a Chinese man at a nearby table in a bistro. He introduced himself as an expatriate working in exports for Dynasty. If she wanted to learn how to make wine, he told her, the best place to go was Bordeaux's prestigious Faculté d'Oenologie.

Now she knew her goal; she simply needed to find a way of making it a reality. She made her first trip to Bordeaux working as a translator for Ningxia's newly formed wine industry association. The next step was becoming an official student of enology. In 2000, with the support of her father, Emma applied and was accepted to Bordeaux's renowned three-year course, one of thirty to win a place from a pool of three hundred candidates.

With his eldest daughter studying in Bordeaux, Gao Lin turned his attention to studying the soil and climate of Ningxia, trying to identify the perfect vines to grow there. He sought the advice of experts from Australia and France, seeking to understand the many parameters involved in creating a successful winery from the ground up. At the Luhuatai state farm, he planted Riesling and Chardonnay vines for white wine, and Bordeaux varieties—Merlot, Cabernet Franc, and Cabernet Sauvignon—and a vine the Chinese called Cabernet Gernischt, for red. But he dreamed of having his own wine, his own family vineyard, with Emma at his side, where he could truly experiment. On the outskirts of Yinchuan, along a concrete-lined canal, past a strip of mechanics' shacks and junk dealers, he found an apple orchard. It was only 10 *mǔ*—about 1.6 acres—but the elderly owner agreed to sell him the leasehold in the land. Gao ordered 2,500 Cabernet Sauvignon, Cabernet Franc, and Cabernet Gernischt grape vines from a Chinese nursery. It was a start.

Three years was a long time to wait for his eldest daughter to return home. Gao Lin was nearing retirement and the state farm was on the verge of abandoning its winemaking venture, preferring to restrict its operation to growing grapes. In his spare time, he and his wife tended the family's tiny vineyard.

In Ningxia, like elsewhere in northern China, the rows of vines were widely spaced, so the vines could be covered with dirt. Grape vines are dormant in the winter, preparing for the next crop so long as temperatures stay above fourteen degrees Fahrenheit. But when Siberian winds sweep down from the north, temperatures could drop to seventeen degrees below zero in Ningxia. This was yet another reason why the common cultivated grape vine *Vitis vinifera* had not, historically, caught on in China. But modern China was determined to overcome this obstacle.

Gao Lin and his wife carefully buried each vine for the winter to protect it from Ningxia's bitter cold, unburying each vine and the new shoots in the spring and reshaping them into a workable canopy. It was arduous work, but these vines were the promise of a better future for their family.

To Gao Lin's amazement, Emma was thriving in France. She had landed a one-month internship at a famous estate called Château Calon-Ségur, which, she'd informed her father proudly, was a Third Growth and one of the first three vineyards set up in the commune of Saint-Estèphe. There seemed to be no end to the things she could learn from the winemakers there. She was eager to do everything, even the physically difficult, dirty work of cleaning out tanks. Thierry Courtade, the cellar master of Calon-Ségur, was an engaging Frenchman of local Médoc stock. When her internship ended, he and another Thierry working at the estate drove Emma back to the city of Bordeaux. "At first there were two Thierrys. They would come every weekend to visit me. And then there was only one Thierry who came," Emma recalled with a smile. The couple was married in Bordeaux in 2003.

Gao Lin could not believe his good fortune. His wife had wisely hoarded their savings, his youngest daughter had a successful restaurant, his eldest daughter was a trained enologist, and now he had a Bordeaux winemaker as a son-in-law. The Gaos might not have political guanxi, but they had within their small family almost everything necessary to make the best wine in China.

They were well aware that learning to grow vines and making wine was only one part of the wine business. Distributing and marketing the wine without the support of the Chinese government would be challenging. And it was scarcely easier even with the support of the government.

❀

Back in 1988, David Henderson, an American engineer, and Carl Crook, the Beijing-born son of a missionary, had opened Montrose Food & Wine in Beijing. Located six hundred feet from Mao's tomb on Tiananmen Square, Montrose had the first direct license to import wine into China. From the start, the partners found themselves in a tricky business environment. There were few rules, and what rules there were, the government changed frequently and without warning. There was no tax code, so the officials simply taxed everything coming into the country. Arbitrarily, the government levied a 365 percent duty on imported wine. (The 48 percent duty of later years was a relief.)

Like most Americans in China in those days, Henderson had come to work on a joint venture, in this case producing orange- and lemon-colored soda bottles. He didn't stick with the bottle factory, but he fell in love with the country and culture. It was a magical time, especially for someone with an eye for opportunity. People in the West were going crazy over the Terracotta Army recently discovered in Shaanxi Province, and he flew around China picking up artifacts that could be copied in factories and exported for sale. Carl Crook—known as Ke Lu in Chinese—had spent several years as a teenager during the Cultural Revolution working in a metal factory, making joints for the four-inch pipe that ran the length of the Ho Chi Minh trail. Bill Hinton, a longtime American expatriate living in China, had put Henderson and Crook together. Crook didn't know wine, but he knew China.

They started by importing containers of basket-bottled Chianti for their fellow expatriates and something sweeter targeted for the Chinese. Henderson believed that the Chinese market would develop in similar ways to the American market of the 1970s, with most customers flocking to sweet white wines, perhaps with a touch of fizz. He settled on a red sparkling Italian wine from Riunite, a Lambrusco "with a little spritzer, a little fruitiness," and packaged it in the colored soda bottles. It was a complete disaster. The Chinese would drink whatever he gave them, but no one was willing to pay for a comparatively expensive drink that they found sour. "I was losing money. I couldn't keep giving away Lambrusco," he said.

Henderson asked around for advice about what to try next. He was told to try Bordeaux, where the négociants always offered an open door to entrepreneurs in new markets. By the time Henderson left France, Montrose was the exclusive distributor in China for DBR Lafite's and Calvet's brand wines. Both Calvet and DBR Lafite produced large-volume, standardized wines, made from bulk wine sourced from wine-growers, which sold well because of their association with prestigious brands. Henderson also imported DBR Lafite's classified growths, and Christophe Salin flew to China to host lively winemaker dinners. Then a savvy négociant named Bernard Magrez supplied Montrose with more classified growths.

Everyone who knew Magrez knew he was one tough businessman. Born to an affluent Bordelais family, he was not afraid of anything, certainly not failure. His father had pulled him out of the local school at the age of thirteen and sent him to the Pyrenees to apprentice as a carpenter, where he was forced to wear wood clogs and fought with the other apprentices for his share of food rations. There he met another boy, François Pinault, who would one day own Château Latour. When Magrez was sixteen he returned to Bordeaux to work as a runner for his uncle Jean Cordier, a charismatic négociant. In 1964, at twenty-one, with his uncle's backing, Magrez bought a little-known firm called Greloud that had been founded by Henri Greloud, once owner of Château Lafleur. Magrez didn't want to keep someone else's name for his company, and he wanted something that sounded classy. He settled on a fictional name, William Pitters. By 1997, his company had a turnover of $180 million.

Magrez hired and fired employees often enough that a revolving door would not have been out of place, but he was also known for sparing no expense in his quest for excellence. When he sold off his spirits business and moved into wine, his goal was to find the best expression of the local terroir. At harvest, he would hire more than a hundred people to sort every grape by hand. He would send his employees to auction house after auction house, hunting for religious art to accentuate the papal theme of his estate, Château Pape Clément, in Graves.

At heart, Magrez was not a vintner; he was a marketer. He personally created all of his own brand names, and had made a fortune from three in particular: Malesan wines, William Pitters port, and William Peel whiskey. At one time, Malesan had been the second-largest Bordeaux brand in the world, selling twelve million bottles annually. When the luxury car industry moved into China, he felt the urge to follow, setting up meetings with David Henderson and other established Westerners. Magrez wanted to get into the Chinese market early and build a distribution network that he would control.

At the wine exhibition Vinexpo in Bordeaux in the early 1990s, he met a Chinese businessman representing the local government of Qingdao, a major city in Shandong Province, who suggested that they form a joint venture. With Beijing endorsing wine as the drink of celebration,

Qingdao's officials had decided to capitalize on their existing local infrastructure. A state-owned liquor company with 1,200 employees already
produced spirits, and the city had access to vineyards and more farm-
land. It needed someone to provide the cash and the talent to expand into
wine production. The city offered Magrez a 75 percent stake in the company, but he wavered: he had owned 100 percent of William Pitters, and
he liked it that way. Still, giving Qingdao a 25 percent stake seemed like
a small price to pay. An old hand in China could have told him that even
with 25 percent, the Chinese were in control.

He signed the joint venture in 1995, and the partners began construction of a château-like tower at Jiaonan, facing the Yellow Sea. "To build
in China was magnificent," he recalled. It was a relatively small winery
with a few stainless steel vats and a small bottling line. For grapes, they
had access to the crops of local farmers, mostly Italian Riesling and
Chardonnay for white wine, and a Russian Muscat for red wine. Magrez
wasn't convinced these were the best grape varieties or the best clones
of the varieties for the region, so he planted a twenty-acre experimental
vineyard with Chardonnay, Sémillon, Italian Riesling, Cabernet Sauvignon, and Merlot. He was in China for the long haul, and so he made
plans to expand production by planting seventy-four acres in 1998,
another seventy-four acres in 1999, and ninety-nine acres in 2000. "The
objective is to produce wines ready to drink quickly and at a reasonable
price," he said.

Next, he put his marketing talents to work. He considered names for
the Chinese wine, and settled on La Pagode de l'Amitié, or the Pagoda of
Friendship. "It was a remarkable wine, which sold well," he said, and he
got his sales team to expand distribution into France, Germany, and the
United Kingdom. In China, a thirty-person sales force was scattered
around Qingdao, Beijing, and Shanghai to promote the new wine as well
as Magrez's Bordeaux wines and whiskey, which would be imported.

On the surface, his relationship with the local power brokers appeared
solid. In recognition of his investments in the local economy, the mayor
of Jiaonan and the general secretary of the Communist Party had named
him the "twelfth economic counselor" for the city. But from the start,
there was a healthy level of distrust. Soon after the deal was struck, the

Qingdao government sold its share to a state-owned spirits producer, which soon insisted on using its own accountant. As far as Magrez knew, it was the first time the foreigner in a Chinese joint venture had received a 75 percent stake, and so it probably should not have come as a surprise that the company was audited frequently. Magrez countered by hiring an American accounting firm to check the numbers to be sure that the Chinese accountant wasn't on the take. "All you have to do is give the guy three RMB and he falsifies the numbers," Magrez said years later, by way of explanation.

Regardless of who did the accounting, the profits were more than good. One day, the Chinese side of the partnership called for a meeting. The businessman congratulated Magrez on the excellent results, and then remarked that the Frenchman had only a lease on the land. Magrez didn't argue. No one in China had the right to buy land for the long term. All land was owned by the government.

"Under the vine roots, it is China," said his partner, pushing the point.

"I think so, even the stones are Chinese," Magrez responded.

"In that case, you need to share the profits," his partner said.

Magrez argued there was no law that said he had to share more of the profits. Funnily enough, there was, said his partner. It was a new law, just three months old. Magrez had no choice but to hand over the money.

He could see that the Chinese partner wanted him out. The French employees were being harassed. Workers continuously went on strike, seemingly with the support—possibly even the encouragement—of local officials. Endless rounds of conflict held up production. The situation grew untenable. In April 2000, less than two years after he'd first sent his winemaking team from Bordeaux, he pulled his employees out of the project, and by 2002, it was all over. "We left with nothing, but we left standing up," said Magrez.

Magrez was not alone. Pernod Ricard had pulled out of Dragon Seal in the late 1990s when it realized that as the foreign partner, it would never own the brand itself. "It was like any other major company. They'd decided they'd had enough and just closed down," said David

Henderson. At Dynasty, Rémy Martin had pulled its employees out of Tianjin, adopting the position of silent partner. Indeed, most of the early wine joint ventures became 100 percent Chinese owned or controlled.

Henderson, however, was undeterred. By the turn of the millennium, he had decided to try his own hand at winemaking. He had spotted the potential in Ningxia in the 1990s, when he'd hosted Jess Jackson of Kendall-Jackson during a trip to scout for places to make wine. "When the jet landed in Ningxia, our search for the ideal location to grow grapes in China was over," he said.

While others were discouraged by the endless stretches of uninhabited desert, Henderson saw the potential to replicate the success of Australia and California, planting French varieties and producing international-quality wines. With support from the central government, the leases on the land were free for people planting vines. "It was a huge reclamation project—not just the reclamation of the desert but the reclamation of jobs, too," said Henderson.

Henderson convinced some farmers to plant a vineyard of Cabernet Sauvignon, insisting on wide spacing between the rows. The farmers thought he was crazy to plant a crop that would begin to make money only after three years. When he left, they planted the Chinese table grape Dragon's Eye in the spaces between the rows. "It was so invasive it destroyed the entire Cabernet vineyard," said Henderson.

At the same time, the government invested in a winemaking facility, later called Helan Mountain. Henderson used the facility, producing his first vintage of a wine called Xi Xia in 2000. It was an inauspicious start.

"It was awful," said Henderson.

The only way for his venture—and Ningxia—to succeed was to impose quality standards in the vineyards and in the winemaking. Henderson began a relentless push to create an officially designated vineyard area similar to an appellation, which he could use on his label to reassure wary American consumers of the quality. Officials in Ningxia had no idea what he meant by an appellation or quality, so he took his cause to the state-owned food conglomerate in Beijing where he had good connections from his early days importing wine.

Meanwhile, he changed the name of his wine to "Dragon's Hollow." The Chinese name for the wine translated as "Proud Dragon in the Cloudy Valley," evoking the beauty of the Helan Mountains. The first vintage debuted in 2005.

Finally, in 2008, after five years of phone calls and meetings with the Washington, D.C., representative of the Chinese Ministry of Agriculture as well as officials in Beijing, Henderson succeeded. He received the official document from Chinese representatives in Washington, which led to the Ningxia government creating an official national standard for wine originating in the designated Helan Mountain area. "We were the ones directly responsible for creating the Eastern Foot of Helan Mountain appellation," he recalled. "I believe it was the first appellation in China, and we were only able to get this done [through] a combination of Beijing and Washington."

Henderson felt exultant, but he couldn't help noticing the distinct lack of enthusiasm from Chinese officials. "It basically went silent," he said. "They never pounded their chests and said, this is really important."

❋

Gao Lin was eager for his daughter Emma to help him at the vineyard. The vines were seven years old, he told her, mature enough to produce a good wine. But Emma didn't have the luxury of concentrating full-time on her family's tiny vineyard. Thierry kept his job in the Médoc, caring for their baby daughter, while Emma worked as a consultant for wineries in the Xinjiang Uygur Autonomous Region, in China's northwest, and in Shandong Province, on the coast south of Beijing, to make ends meet. That same year, in November 2007, Emma got a job in Shanghai with Alberto Fernández, the managing partner of Torres China, a distributor belonging to the Spanish wine company Torres and Baron Philippe de Rothschild SA. It represented a number of prestigious family-owned wines, including Opus One and Taittinger. Emma's title was training manager, which meant she taught hotel and restaurant staff members about Torres-distributed wine. It was a terrific opportunity for her to learn about marketing and distribution.

She noticed early on that the only Chinese wine distributed by Torres was Grace Vineyard, called Yi Yuan, or "Elegant and Beautiful Vineyard" in Mandarin, and she knew there were some lessons to be learned from its history. The vineyard was founded in 1997, the year that Emma and her father had left Russia, by a Hong Kong tycoon named Chun-Keung Chan, and it was regarded as the darling of the Chinese wine industry, one of the few Chinese wines that Westerners said they liked to drink. Grace's 2008 Chairman's Reserve, a barrel-aged Bordeaux blend, had won critical praise. Grace ran completely counter to the Dynasty model of wine production: Grace was about quality, not quantity.

Emma knew that she and her father couldn't wield the sort of guanxi and material fortune that Grace Vineyard had at its disposal. C. K. Chan's father had left his home in Fujian Province at the age of thirteen for Indonesia because his parents didn't have enough money to feed him. He had beat the odds against poverty and disease, earned a fortune as a trader, and started his own family. When a military coup in Indonesia fomented anti-Chinese sentiment, the Chan clan retreated to Beijing. Overseas Chinese like the Chans had been invited home with a patriotic appeal to help build the New China.

It was 1965, C.K. was fourteen and studying in Beijing, his family followed, and the Cultural Revolution was about to unfold. Despite promises of a warm welcome from the government, overseas Chinese were objects of suspicion and scorn. At seventeen, C.K. was sent to Inner Mongolia to work on a sheep farm for four years, and then to a steel mill in Hohhot, the regional capital. It was a chance encounter with an official from a college in Shanxi Province, to the south of Inner Mongolia, that got him a place as a student at the Taiyuan Institute of Technology, where he received a degree in wastewater treatment.

After school, Chan courted the daughter of another overseas Chinese from Fujian who had climbed from poverty to wealth in Indonesia. His future in-laws had also answered the call to build a New China, and although her family had lost most of its wealth, her father's position as an official representative of the overseas Chinese had allowed them to maintain a comparatively comfortable lifestyle. Though Chan's family had not been so fortunate, he charmed his future wife by taking her out for bike rides.

"My mother said that when she first started dating my father it was very romantic, cycle around Beijing, see this and that," recounted Judy Chan. "My father's side of the story is: 'When I first met your mother, her one day's pocket money was more than my salary for a month. So the only thing I could do was go on bike rides.'"

Rather than accept the family's diminished status, C. K. Chan's father exercised his right as an overseas Chinese to request exit visas for himself and his family. In 1975, he succeeded, moving the family to Hong Kong. There, C. K. Chan did what he knew: he became a trader, working for his father, scouring China for items that could be sold to Indonesia in what was known as the "98" trade. His 2 percent sales commission on containers of ink brushes, locks, and gongfu shoes was not enough to support his family, however, so in 1984, he took a job as the Chinese agent for a South African mining company, buying raw materials such as manganese and coal from mineral-rich Shanxi. His earnings allowed him to set up his own minerals firm, Eastern Century, trading and manufacturing coke, feral alloy, and other minerals. He chose to return to Taiyuan, where he had gone to college and had good contacts.

Like many self-made men, Chan had a hard time relaxing. Every time he went to France to negotiate a new contract for mineral exports, his French colleagues invited him to have a long dinner with lots of wine, when all he wanted to do was complete the deal and get back to "real" work. One of his close associates, Sylvain Janvier, who came from Burgundy, especially loved wine, and he insisted that Chan take part in French customs. As his ventures with the French businessman made Chan rich, the habits of the French started to annoy him less and less. "The more I was with my business associates in Europe, the more I enjoyed having a glass of wine with them. Wine represented to me a symbol of the 'beautiful life' that I believed many Chinese were looking for," he explained.

Eastern Century went public in 1992. Two years later, Chan sold his shares for $80 million. At first he contemplated buying a château in

France with his windfall, but then he and Janvier resolved to use the money to bring the "beautiful life" to China.

Shanxi was the obvious choice for location. As part of their work for Eastern Century, Chan and Janvier had spent years building guanxi with local party leaders and officials. With an initial investment of roughly $5 million, they hired a French enologist, Denis Boubals, known as the "apostle of Cabernet Sauvignon," to study the province's soil, and he recommended that they acquire a fifty-year lease on 247 acres in the Yellow River basin. It was an arid, fertile land 2,600 feet above sea level with a temperate, continental climate. The sandy soil was well drained and ran deep. The vine roots could stretch ten, twenty, a hundred, or a thousand feet into the earth, drawing up the nutrients needed to grow a top-quality fruit. Looking around, Chan and Janvier noticed that the farmers grew apples, corn, and dates. Obviously, the area supported crops, but this didn't offer any clues as to which grape varieties to plant. They hedged their bets, planting 370 acres with eleven different grape varieties from France.

They had soil, climate, and vines; all they lacked was a winemaker. In 2000, they hired a Bordelais named Gérard Colin to oversee the first vintage. Colin was an experienced enologist in his late fifties, admired for having revitalized Château Clarke in the Médoc for Edmond de Rothschild. He had arrived in Hong Kong a few years earlier, hired by a Chinese man who loved wine but didn't care for the high import duties slapped on each bottle. Colin's boss had discovered a loophole: grape concentrate was not taxed. Colin was thus hired to make table wine out of concentrate. It was not the proudest moment for the enologist, but the wine he produced wasn't half bad. Everything depended on the quality of the grape must. While it was possible to make bad wine from good grape must, it was impossible to make good wine from bad must. That one rule has never changed in the world of wine.

At Grace Vineyard, Colin immediately realized that the biggest obstacle to creating a world-class Chinese wine was getting ripe grapes. He sourced much of the harvest from about five hundred local farmers, each of whom worked a small plot of land. But just like Grace Vineyard itself, none of the farmers owned the land; it was leased to them by the local collective. This meant they were particularly dependent on the market value of each year's crop. Colin convinced the farmers to forget about dates and apples, and to replant their land with wine grapes, by promising to pay four times the going rate for the grapes. To assure the quality of the vines, Grace supplied the farmers with the plants as well as the poles, the price of which was to be repaid over ten years by deducting the cost from what the farmers earned by selling fruit. This kind of long-term commitment appealed to Chan. He knew from experience the grueling work of farmers, and understood they wanted a stable income to feed their families.

Time also taught Colin about the land itself. He eliminated the low-quality plots, reduced the vineyard to 173 acres, and focused on six grape varieties—Cabernet Sauvignon, Cabernet Franc, Merlot, Chardonnay, Riesling, and Chenin Blanc. To make a fine wine, he simply had to persuade the farmers to reduce their yields.

Extra clusters had to be pruned from the vine, so that the plant concentrated its efforts on ripening a small quantity of fruit. Every winemaker knew that this method produced the best wines. But the farmers had always sold their fruit by the kilogram, and those were the only terms they would accept. For them, more fruit meant more money. The farmers would not cut away the extra bunches, and they would not wait to harvest the grapes late in the season, when the sugar levels were higher and better balanced with the acidity, because they feared the threat of rain and rot, which would leave them with no fruit to sell at all. Grace's cellars would be plagued by the telltale green-pepper aroma of unripe Cabernet until Colin could find a solution.

✹

Emma Gao also saw that Grace Vineyard wasn't just a fellow family winery, it was a father-daughter business. By 2002, Chan's daughter, Judy, a petite twenty-four-year-old who had recently graduated with a bachelor's degree from the University of Michigan, had been put in charge of Grace Vineyard. By Judy's own account, she knew nothing about wine, but she was thrilled by her father's proposal that she become the vineyard's president. In a family where her grandfather did not allow his wife to drive a car, her father had supported her choice to study psychology and women's studies, and now he was showing his belief in her management skills. Just as important, Judy was not afraid of hard work. She remembered the hours she had spent as a child gluing decorations on small items to be resold in Indonesia. Yet her youth and inexperience were conspicuous: people commonly mistook her driver for the head of the vineyard, assuming she was the boss's secretary.

The year that Judy Chan took the reins, Grace released its first vintage, the 2001. It was not a success. When most Chinese consumers thought of Shanxi, they pictured coal mines and pollution, not an Italianate villa surrounded by row after row of grape vines. The labels were ugly, the packaging better suited to selling soy sauce. Out of half a million bottles, Grace sold ten thousand. The company gave away another ten thousand, hoping for some good publicity, and they redesigned the bottles and labels to offer a more upscale image. Local village leaders were invited to banquets, where Grace's vintages were served in place of traditional baijiu in hopes of gaining them as allies in fostering farming practices that produced better fruit for winemaking.

Yet when presenting clever, well-thought-out long-term business plans to local officials, Chan was met with disinterest. She quickly realized that she needed to find a different approach if she wanted the vineyard to succeed. Her deputy general manager, a Chinese man with a degree in mathematics, explained that the officials were interested only in short-term results that would help them fulfill government quotas for revenue and employment, and would lead to their promotion.

Chan persevered. The reason to start a family-run winery was to make great wine. The government might not be interested in long-term growth, but she was, and so was her father. The biggest difference between Grace Vineyard and the state-owned wineries was that Grace was privately owned. They might need to maintain guanxi, but they did not have to satisfy government quotas on productivity so long as they continued to provide jobs and tax revenues—or payments of what seemed like arbitrary fines when tax revenues appeared to be running low.

With each vintage, Chan's confidence grew, as did her knowledge of the wine market. Grace needed to extend its clientele beyond state-owned companies, wealthy entrepreneurs, and government officials, and it needed to find a way to entice the emerging Chinese middle class to start drinking Chinese wine. The state-owned beverage companies, which had lavish advertising budgets, dominated the main distribution networks, and Chan knew she wouldn't be able to compete with them, even with her family fortune. So she adopted a more personal approach, opening a series of small but stylish retail shops and wine bars. She wanted to create a relationship and a feeling of trust between Grace Vineyard and its consumers.

In the early days, Chan was intrigued when she noticed that the only people wandering in off the street to buy a bottle were foreigners looking to try a Chinese wine. It dawned on her that Chinese consumers, so new to wine, were afraid of displaying their ignorance. She revamped the shops to have a separate, intimate sitting area where a customer could discreetly learn more about wine and place an order. Her self-assured expatriate customers bought wine by the bottle, while her new Chinese customers usually bought several cases at a time.

In 2005, Gérard Colin was lured away by a call from Bordeaux. Christophe Salin, the chairman of DBR Lafite, told him he wanted to build a vineyard in China. Was he interested? After five years at Grace, Colin was ready for his next adventure. He was replaced by a tall, robust Australian named Ken Murchison, who immediately faced headaches over sourcing ripe grapes—and not just green or rotten fruit. One day during harvest, he arrived at a local vineyard, ready to check the grapes for ripeness, and found every row empty. He had a contract with the farmers, but that had not stopped them from picking the grapes the night before and selling them to someone else.

By this time, Grace was producing a substantial amount of wine by Western standards, but it was positively minuscule compared to the population of China. The local officials and villagers started complaining that the Chans were "holding back." Why didn't they buy more grapes and bottle more wine? Why didn't Grace import wine, like the state-owned wineries did, until they got more vines in production?

Yet, despite making trips to Bordeaux, Judy Chan had no plans to import wine to mix with her own stocks. She went to Bordeaux to hone her palate and observe how the Bordelais did business. Her customers could just as easily buy a classified growth; price and brand were what mattered most to them—that and a little discretion. Until the Chinese acquired a palate for wine and started to understand grape varieties and vintages, they would never be independent enough to choose a wine based solely on taste. Every wine she tasted helped teach her the standard by which her wines would be judged by the people that mattered—Westerners.

❁

The Gaos did not have a billion yuan, or party connections. That much was clear to Emma. They could not simply follow in the footsteps of C. K. Chan and his daughter. Even so, Emma's and Judy's paths were destined to cross; there were just too few family-run vineyards in China.

In January 2008, less than a year after Emma had joined Torres China, Alberto Fernández put her on a special project team. Torres was making a white wine called Symphony with Grace Vineyard, and a meeting had been scheduled at the vineyard in Shanxi between Ken Murchison and the Torres winemakers. This was a chance to see Grace's operation close up, and she jumped at it.

But Emma had other, personal ambitions for the trip as well. When she arrived at Grace, she brought with her a bottle of wine. It was naked—no label, no capsule, just a cork. It was the first vintage of a wine she and her family had made, she explained. They had a small lot—just over two acres; it was barely a start-up. Fernández didn't know what to think. He was surprised to learn that Emma's family was growing grape vines. But he gamely uncorked the bottle for a tasting.

"We were quite impressed," Fernández recalled later. In a way, the discovery of Emma's hidden talents came as a huge relief to the Spaniard. "She didn't have a future in marketing—we'd started hearing that she was telling people to be quiet during her presentations as a training manager—but she definitely had a future as a winemaker."

In April, Fernández flew to the city of Yinchuan to visit the Gaos' land. Emma had not been joking when she said the vineyard was tiny. A large, sandy garden near a river, a ramshackle series of buildings, and then a plot near the eastern foot of the Helan Mountains with a stony soil of schist. Her sister did the accounting, her father tended the vines, and her mother helped with lab work when Emma was away consulting. A menagerie of ponies and farm animals roamed the enclosed vineyard; they were a gift from Gao Lin to his French granddaughter who occasionally visited. The project was ridiculously small, but Fernández was taken by Gao Lin's passion for quality. The guiding ethos at Torres was family-owned vineyards of extraordinary quality. That's why he'd added Grace Vineyard to the roster. He decided to support the Gaos, too.

Back in Shanghai, Fernández worked with the marketing team to create a name, label, and packaging. "We created it from scratch," he said. Emma left her job at Torres in October 2008, and in April 2009, Torres launched the sale of two wines from what he decided to call Silver Heights—the Summit, made from the Helan Mountain vineyards, and the Family Reserve, from the sandy garden plot—with production of two thousand bottles for each. Fernández carefully meted out allocations to five-star hotels. "So little, so good," he said. It was the first "garage" wine of China—and an overnight success.

Later that year, Emma brought Fernández another sample. It was a new wine, she said, made of 100 percent Cabernet Sauvignon she had sourced from a special single plot. Fernández was immediately convinced of the quality. Torres's general manager advised Emma to bottle the wine in magnums to allow it more time and freedom to age.

Two years later, an unmarked magnum arrived at the Torres offices in Shanghai.

It was from Emma. A magnum, she reminded him, of the Cabernet Sauvignon, aged in a new French oak barrel. Just one barrel of wine. The Torres team was stunned.

"It's really the best Chinese wine I have ever tasted," said Fernández. He knew the demand would be intense for the limited line of 150 magnums of "Emma's Reserve." He wasn't disappointed.

The Gaos were ready to stand beside Grace Vineyard, leading China into a new beginning with fine wine.

4

....

Lucky Red

Château Lafite Rothschild had become a symbol of wealth, status, and sophistication among the Chinese elite. Cases were presented as gifts, bartered for favors, hoarded as investments, sold and resold. Bottles were served at banquets; on rare occasions, they were uncorked and savored at home. China loved Lafite. But it was an infatuation—reckless, unpredictable, unreasonable.

Christophe Reboul Salze, now the head of his own négociant firm, The Wine Merchant, didn't have any illusions about why the Chinese traders were interested in the fine wine business. China's newly rich might dream of Western wine and all that it symbolized, he reasoned, but the Chinese traders were pragmatic: they had witnessed how quickly Bordeaux's First Growths had risen in value despite the Lehman Brothers bankruptcy and the ensuing financial crisis. The châteaux had released their wines in 2009 at €90 to €110 a bottle and the négociants, including Reboul Salze, had resold them for €130. Months later, the wines were selling for €230 to €290 each. "It was absolutely madness," he said, shaking his head. "We bought 2008 Lafite at €13,500 [per case]. They were thirsty and thirsty, more, more, more."

But the Place de Bordeaux measured its health by the price at which generic Bordeaux, rather than the classified growths, was sold. Each

Tuesday the local paper published the going rate, with prices quoted by the *tonneau,* a measurement dating from the Middle Ages that is equivalent to nine hundred liters (238 gallons), or 1,200 bottles. Before the financial crisis the going price was €959 per tonneau, but many small growers worried that the price would not hold.

Bordeaux had more than seven thousand winegrowers, and several hundred of the smaller vineyards were teetering on the edge of bankruptcy. The small growers were struggling to sell their wines. It was popular among the Bordelais to blame the vineyards for overplanting in the 1990s, but world wine consumption had steadily grown over the past two decades, so it wasn't simply that too much wine was being made. The hard truth was that French wines were losing market share to rivals from Spain, Italy, and the New World, where the growers made friendly, fruity wines with cheerful labels in a successful move to target women buying wines to drink with friends or serve with a weeknight dinner. The consumer profile in the United States and the United Kingdom had changed dramatically.

Yet the promotional machine in Bordeaux continued to focus its efforts on fewer than two hundred châteaux, many of which were more interested in collectors than people browsing supermarket wine shelves. The small growers, who might have been able to go up against the competition for entry-level and middle-range wines, were left to market their wines on their own, and they were angry about it. They pruned their own vines and sprayed their own pesticides. They didn't speak second or third languages. They didn't have frequent-flier numbers or tasting rooms. In fact, many didn't bottle their own wine. They sold their stock in bulk to the négociants, who used the wine to create a *vin de négoce*— a brand wine—and the négociants had them under their thumb. There was more wine in the cellars than buyers wanted, so most of that wine was sold on the cheap, and it was ending up in the Chinese market, the only market that was more interested in the Bordeaux name than in a drinkable wine.

Many négociants shared Don St. Pierre Jr.'s concern that the bottom of Bordeaux's barrel was spilling into China, but they rarely admitted it outside of a private, chatty lunch. In public pronouncements, the market was always great. At a press conference in September 2009, Bordeaux Wine Council spokesperson Laurent Gapenne announced that the price of generic Bordeaux was holding firm at €950 per tonneau, a very slight dip from the precrisis price of €959. Gapenne was a small-time grower as well as a négociant, tasked with presenting a confident face to the outside world despite the desperate circumstances of many fellow growers. In reality, a great deal of Bordeaux's generic wine was selling for €650 per tonneau, about half what the smaller growers needed to earn a living wage from their vines.

This glut of cheap wine attracted the canniest traders.

❀

The Hong Kong Wine and Dine Festival and its Bordeaux original were used to promote wines to consumers, but the most significant event for Bordeaux's winegrowers was the annual barrel tastings, which were hosted over the course of a week each spring by the Union des Grands Crus de Bordeaux (UGC), an association of châteaux. Many of the 133 members of the UGC were classified growths, and all were high-profile players.

During the week, the UGC designated eight châteaux to hold tastings for importers, retailers, sommeliers, journalists, and others in the wine trade. Every day of the week was packed with lunches, dinners, and parties meant to woo VIPs. Only the grandest estates could accommodate such crowds. Tents interrupted the pastoral landscape, and parked cars lined the narrow vineyard lanes. Few small growers were invited to participate, but many estates had realized that they could not afford to sit by and watch as Bordeaux's best wines of the year were crowned around them. Over the past decade, some of these châteaux had banded together to host tastings, too. All together, more than six thousand professionals descended on the region to sample the year's vintages. Moving from château to château, tent to tent, visitors might sample two hundred wines a day. Tasting at the First Growths like Lafite or Margaux was even more exclusive, requiring an appointment. But even with a carefully vetted guest list, the First Growths could expect 1,800 people over the course of a few days.

Despite all the pomp, the barrel tastings were a natural part of the process of making wine. In the winter, the previous fall's harvest was blended and poured into barrels to age for eighteen months. Each morning of the tastings week, the cellar masters pulled fresh samples of the blended wine from their barrels, even though the wines were far from ready for table consumption. The tannins from the oak seemed to suck the moisture from the gums, and the wine stained the teeth and lips so that everyone sported a ghoulish, deep purple grimace by the end of the day. It took experience to imagine how a barrel sample might evolve over time to become a bottle with a 90-plus rating. And though the vintners denied they blended special barrels for the tastings, it was assumed that they put their best foot forward. No one goes to the dance in her second-best dress.

In March 2010, as visitors got a preview of the 2009 vintage, the Bordelais couldn't help but be elated by the number of Chinese visitors. It seemed that word had spread in Hong Kong and on the mainland that those who had been savvy enough to buy the 2008 vintage were making money. Prices had been rising steadily, as much as 10 percent a month. The investment was paying off. The Wing Lung Bank offered to lend as much as HK$5 million—about $650,000—to buy fine wine; the loan could be used to pay for up to 50 percent of the purchase price. If the borrower defaulted, the bank took the wine. It seemed impossible to lose.

Still, few expected the Chinese traders to buy the new vintage en primeur. The Chinese appeared to be cautious about investments, and everyone knew that the en primeur game was inherently risky for everyone but the château. That was part of the appeal of Bordeaux from the start. An en primeur purchase was, legally speaking, no more than a loan from a négociant to a château in advance of paying the full price and receiving the wine. If the négociant went bust between placing the order and receiving delivery, any of its customers who had advanced money for the wine were out of luck. The château still owned the wine and was under no obligation to deliver it to the négociant's customer. The Chinese would never shell out money for a product they didn't own and wouldn't see for another eighteen months. Too much could happen in eighteen months, especially in China. But now it seemed as though the négociants had vastly underestimated—or understated—the demand for Bordeaux in China.

Given the international origins of most négociant families, Bordeaux was particularly well prepared to welcome the Chinese visitors. Xenophobia was unacceptable on the Place de Bordeaux. Some négociants still held passports from their ancestors' homeland, generations or centuries after they had settled in Bordeaux; others were consuls for those countries of origin. The Bordelais swiftly adapted to Chinese culture. Château managers and négociants memorized Mandarin greetings. Menus were tailored to Chinese palates, and chopsticks were requisitioned. The Chinese New Year and Mid-Autumn harvest moon festival were marked on the calendar, so that wines could be shipped to China in time for these holidays. Soon, no one was batting an eye at the public spitting, belching, and farting that were accepted behavior on the mainland but not to French etiquette.

Yet China presented an uncommon challenge to the Place de Bordeaux. The Chinese didn't understand why they couldn't negotiate directly with a château. Négociants and courtiers were a short-term inconvenience. Most of the time, the négociants were cutting deals with companies worth more than the entire Place. A midsized négociant was happy with revenues of $40 million to $65 million a year; a handful of firms boasted of having sales over $100 million. But most négociants had sales that barely hit $25 million. Moreover, the Chinese had made their fortunes in the last fifteen years to twenty years, and they paid attention to centuries of family history for only two reasons: the value of a venerable brand like Lafite and the potential for grafting onto the French version of guanxi. And history wasn't of much interest, even then. What mattered in China was neither the past nor the future, but the present moment, your opportunity *right now.* The Chinese buyers had one common objective: buy as much wine as possible, so that they could control the brand and charge even higher prices for it back home. They wanted a quick, guaranteed profit, a sure thing.

Of course, the Bordelais also had to overcome the daunting and potentially treacherous language barrier. Négociants were often multilingual, but Mandarin was rare, Cantonese even more so. There was an urgent need for translators. Almost immediately, hundreds of Chinese immigrants descended on Bordeaux, most traveling on student visas and claiming to be enrolled in French schools, some of which were unfamiliar to the Bordelais. However, almost all were on the hunt for a job at a château or négociant firm. Many were women in their early to mid-twenties who already held an advanced degree from a university in China, though few looked like the studious type. As a whole, the women spurned the staid, local style—a Hermès scarf and driving moccasins—preferring a tiny miniskirt paired with six-inch stiletto heels. The outfit was a ludicrous choice in the eyes of the local establishment, especially when it came time for a translator to tour a vineyard's uneven terrain with her boss. But négociants had seen businessmen with female assistants dressed just like this on their trips to scout for new customers in China. It was the custom. Indeed, some Chinese tycoons arrived in Bordeaux with a coterie of young women, at least one of whom was widely assumed to be the man's mistress. The French understood that.

And the négociants had a sneaking suspicion that they might be misjudging the miniskirt brigade. While the négociants might take a minute to make a point in French, the translator would take five minutes to explain it in Chinese to the prospective client. It seemed unlikely that direct translations were taking place. More and more, the translators were adopting the role of gatekeeper to Chinese buyers and demanding a sales commission, often from both sides. Such commissions, thought to be split with the managers of the Chinese company, were growing common—another hit to the négociant's margin. But the stereotype of the corrupt Chinese businessman was so strong that few Bordelais protested it. This was just a cost of doing business in this new and ever-growing market. Sales volume would more than make up for it.

❋

Since Beijing had announced the decision to shift Chinese alcohol consumption from baijiu to wine, the local governments had been mobilized in a way that was only possible in China. The 1996 National People's Congress had approved the country's Ninth Five-Year-Plan, which called for a rapid increase in domestic wine grape production. New vineyards

like the one Gao Lin managed in Ningxia had been planted. Because sala-
ries and careers in state-controlled businesses and regional governments
were determined by annual production results, the winery managers
needed wine, and they needed it immediately. To meet these quotas,
China's industrial wineries, including Dynasty, Changyu, and Great
Wall, imported Chilean and Australian bulk wine and bottled and sold
it as being domestically produced. However, as Chinese families
earned more, they were no longer satisfied with less than the best. For
nearly the same price as a bottle of Great Wall's premium wine, they
could buy wine imported from France. If they were willing to spend a
bit more, they could buy a Bordeaux wine, possibly a classified growth.
Rather than watch their revenues siphoned off to foreign companies,
some of the state-owned wineries decided to get into Bordeaux. That was
why Lu Ming, Dynasty's general manager and wine buyer, was in Bordeaux for the barrel tastings in the spring of 2010.

Lu had placed Dynasty's first order from Bordeaux the previous
year—six shipping containers of cheap wines from Grands Chais de
France, one of the biggest wine producers in France—and now he planned
to expand into classified growths. That meant he had to make nice
with the négociants, at least for the time being. He had quickly gleaned
that the people who made the most profit bought wine en primeur at the
first *tranche*. The tranche system was yet another peculiar institution
of the Place de Bordeaux. Each spring, not long after the annual barrel
tastings, the First Growths released a small quantity of wine at a set
price. This price was quoted in the press, and a château used it to test
the waters. How much demand was to be expected? As the sales campaign progressed, the château released another batch of the wine at a
higher price, called the second tranche. Sometimes, when demand was
very high, a third tranche was released at an even higher price. The first
tranche set a floor; the price from the château never went lower than that.
Thus, the négociants and clients who bought the first tranche stood to
reap the most in profits.

When the Chinese started buying the 2008 vintage in September 2009, they had bought it at second- and third-tranche prices. Lu,
like other traders, had come for the barrel tastings in order to land a

first-tranche deal. He was confident he could get the wines he wanted. He had the cash. How could he fail?

Unfortunately for Lu, he had competition from another large Chinese company: Xiamen C&D of Fujian Province. Launched in the 1990s with capital from Southeast Asia, Xiamen C&D's supply-chain and real estate business was worth $115 billion, making it the 127th largest company in China and the largest company in Fujian. The city of Xiamen had prospered as a special economic zone, taking a foothold among about fifteen provincial capitals and economic powerhouses that made up China's emerging "second tier." Like most big companies in China, it was state-owned.

The chairman of C&D's wine division was Yang Wenhua. In his forties, fit and reserved, and with a better understanding of English than he let on, Yang had forged a career in the spirits business. He had studied chemistry at school but took work in import-exports. When C&D's parent company diversified into spirits in 1998, he got the job of running the division. At first he was hawking baijiu and beer, but as the Chinese market for wine expanded, he forged a distribution agreement between C&D and Castel Frères, France's largest wine company. The deal was finalized in 2006. After C&D started selling Castel's brands, Yang watched as his profits—and his profile in Xiamen—took off.

The following year, Yang met Baron Frédéric de Luze, the scion of an aristocratic Bordelais lineage and the owner of Château Paveil de Luze. He was also a sixth-generation négociant and was related, as usual, to nearly every other old wine family in Bordeaux. Yang asked de Luze if he might be interested in helping C&D set up mutually beneficial deals with well-regarded châteaux in Bordeaux. Yang mentioned C&D's experience working with Castel; he could provide reliable distribution to de Luze's friends and associates.

From the start, de Luze recognized that working with such a powerful buyer was going to be tricky. C&D was a state-owned company, and it had amassed wealth by controlling the distribution and price of a product in its market. There were no exceptions. Yang made it plain that he did not want another distributor competing with C&D. He promised to buy a huge amount of a vintage, and, in exchange, he wanted an "exclusivity." On the Place de Bordeaux, an exclusivity was theoretically attractive but practically impossible. Bordeaux's wines were sold as commodities. The same wine was sold by a dozen or more négociants, who, in turn, sold to dozens of clients. No one could guarantee that wine sold to a merchant in Bristol wouldn't end up in a store in Chengdu.

Yang's terms presented a conundrum, but de Luze was a resourceful and creative thinker. He was not new to doing business in China; his négociant firm, LD Vins, had been selling wine there for a few years. He considered what his Chinese buyer really wanted: an exclusive right to sell a Bordeaux brand. He then approached a handful of châteaux, all classified growths, and asked if the estates would be willing to let C&D sell a wine under a name that would be used only in China. The trademark would be jointly owned by the châteaux and C&D. Since few Chinese consumers knew the names of wines beyond Lafite and Margaux, the new wine would not be at a disadvantage in the market. And while it wasn't common, it wasn't unheard of for a classified growth to have a second "second wine" as a way of making a deal with a special client who ordered regular, large quantities.

It was an ingenious solution and ideal for C&D. Yang would have complete control over the price at which the wine was sold. Unlike in France or the United States, Chinese customers couldn't compare the price of a wine around the country. Few realized that they could look up the price of a wine outside of China, or that there might be a reason to do so, unless they were buying the wine as an investment. Yang's customers weren't speculators; they were China's new middle class.

The châteaux agreed to de Luze's offer on the condition that Yang placed a large en primeur order each year. Yang readily agreed. He needed as much of each wine as possible. He dealt in millions of bottles of alcoholic drinks a year. Bordeaux's classified growths might be expensive, but the volumes were laughably small. Soon a few other négociants, including Christophe Reboul Salze, proposed additional "private-label" classified growth wines to Chinese buyers. Later in the year, Yang would announce that C&D had been named as the exclusive Chinese distributor for thirteen classified growths. None were First

Growths, of course, but the chosen few gloated about their special status while their neighbors quietly seethed with jealousy.

China was the hottest market on the planet. If you weren't selling in China, you were no one. The châteaux chosen by C&D had it made.

❂

Not every Chinese buyer at the barrel tastings worked for a state-owned conglomerate. Many were independent traders looking for a commodity in which they might turn an easy profit. Some sold carpets or clothes, electronics or pork. Some had speculated on real estate or tourism. Wine was just another money-making scheme.

Companies such as Xiamen C&D and Dynasty could point to their experience distributing products in China, sometimes with a French partner such as Rémy Cointreau. But dozens of Chinese buyers had arrived for the barrel tastings, and many of them were completely unknown outside of the mainland, and they didn't boast such credentials. For the most part, very little of their business profile in China could be verified. The buyers came from cities the négociants had never heard of, where they had no contacts. The Chinese companies often did not have a website. A few had a website written entirely in Chinese. When they did have a website, there was no mention of wine.

Among the private Chinese buyers at the tastings were a Mr. and Mrs. Jin. The Jins were in their midforties and said they came from Wenzhou, a third-tier city in Zhejiang Province. They explained to the Bordelais that they had made their first million dollars by importing scrap leather from the European automobile industry. The leather was turned into powder, shipped to China, then reconstituted into leather for making shoes, coats, and handbags. The resulting material had a strange, plastic appearance, but the shoes were sturdy and sold well. On one of their trips to Paris for the leather business, they were encouraged by a restaurant sommelier to try a bottle of Bordeaux. It was intoxicating on many levels—and presented a heady new opportunity for them.

The Jins did business with a number of state-owned and privately held companies, and in the past few years their contacts had started asking the Jins how to get their hands on imported wine. Government officials and entrepreneurs routinely attended something on the order of eighteen banquets a week. Wine was the government-sanctioned drink for celebrating partnerships. After a while, it was obvious to the Jins that they should just buy wine to sell to them.

They had taken the high-speed train from Paris to Libourne, near the legendary vineyards of Saint-Émilion, in order to spend their first day in business as wine importers at the barrel tastings. As they got off the train they were greeted by the owner of a local château and his Chinese intern, one of the miniskirt brigade. The winemaker had anticipated that there might be quite a few Chinese buyers coming to the tastings this year, and he had decided not to depend on the négociants to get an introduction. The first step was to court the Jins and impress them.

As he escorted them to the entrance to his estate's eighteenth-century castle, the Jins could barely contain their awe. The four medieval towers, which once belonged to Henry IV, were the definition of impressive. Next they toured the park and the vineyards, enchanted by the winemaker's description of the estate's history and terroir. They were far from the sweatshops of Wenzhou.

The Jins turned to the Chinese intern and began to speak. When the intern translated for the Saint-Émilion winemaker, he got the bad news: the Jins wanted an exclusivity. He'd heard this before from other Chinese traders, and he knew it was something he could not promise, not truthfully. Nor was it in his interest if they had a lock on distribution of his wine in China. The Jins were small operators. He needed other customers in the market. Back and forth, the haggling went, until finally the Jins ordered three hundred cases of an older, ready-to-ship vintage—3,600 bottles. It was a small order, just something to test the market, they had told him. The winemaker smiled. One of his oldest, dearest clients in America ordered only fifty cases in a typical year. He was thrilled.

To thank his new VIP clients, he secured one of the most coveted invitations of the week for them: two tickets to the Wednesday evening party hosted by Château d'Yquem at Bordeaux's opera house, the Grand Théâtre. There were waiting lists to get into the best parties, and only 350 people were on the Yquem guest list.

Château d'Yquem was celebrated for its Sauternes, a sweet white wine often served with foie gras or with dessert. In the 1855 Classification, Château d'Yquem alone had achieved the lofty rank of *Premier Cru Superieur*. The wine was made in the Sauternes region southeast of Bordeaux along a stretch of the Garonne River, where each fall (misty weather permitting) *Botrytis cinerea*, or noble rot, transformed Sauvignon Blanc and Sémillon grapes into a sweet and complex elixir. It was said that when Grand Duke Konstantin Nikolayevich, a brother of Czar Alexander II, visited the estate in 1859, he paid twenty thousand gold francs to secure one tonneau of the 1847 vintage. In comparison, Château Margaux sold its 1847 vintage at 2,100 francs per tonneau. The intricate and costly process of producing Sauternes required that the grapes be handpicked at the ideal stage of noble rot. It took a full vine to produce a single glass of wine.

Bernard Arnault, the French billionaire and chairman of the luxury-goods firm LVMH, had taken a majority stake of Château d'Yquem after a family feud, but the man everyone in Bordeaux associated with the modern estate was its general manager, Pierre Lurton. Lurton owned a château in the Entre-Deux-Mers region and was himself a member of the wine elite, an heir to his own family wine dynasty. He was also one of the most well-liked men in Bordeaux, respected for the quality of his wines and his debonair style. When the Jins handed over their invitations in the eighteenth-century marble lobby of the Grand Théâtre, they could feel the excitement. Everyone around them believed the 2009 vintage was destined to be legendary, as good or better than the 2005. By the time they reached the salon, the mood was euphoric. Chandelier light popped off the room's gilt frames and mirrors to illuminate frescoes as people nibbled on hors d'oeuvres designed by a three-star Michelin chef. They were surrounded by the most important négociants in Bordeaux, drinking one of the rarest wines in the world.

As they sipped the lovely sweet wine, the Jins considered their prospects. As much as they enjoyed the taste and the experience, they were pragmatic: they decided not to chase after allocations of Château d'Yquem. Yquem was without doubt prestigious, but they didn't think they could sell it.

Among the Chinese, white wine did not have an association with good health, as red wine did. Their clients were not in Shanghai or Beijing; they did not have sophisticated tastes. They cared about familiar brands and logos—the Lafite name, or the five arrows that graced the labels of every wine produced by DBR Lafite. In fact, they could probably do better selling Saga, one of Lafite's "brand" wines—a wine sourced from many different growers and blended in large quantities. Saga did not have the pedigree of Lafite's First Growth, let alone Yquem's unique, superior status, but it carried the five-arrow symbol that Chinese customers recognized.

❀

The hectic schedule of tastings and parties continued apace, and tensions mounted as the wine critics began to publish their scores for the wines. Many wines scored the magical 100, which inspired a collective groan. Just how high could prices climb? The London merchants lobbied for prices in line with the 2005 vintage, which was the most expensive in history. They argued that even by holding prices steady, the wine would be 25 percent more expensive in London due to the weak British pound. No one in Bordeaux really believed that the wine was going to London. The only currencies that mattered were the Hong Kong dollar and the renminbi.

Ninety minutes and a world away from the frenzy of the barrel tastings was the medieval walled town of Sauveterre-de-Guyenne, population 1,800, in Aquitaine. Built in the thirteenth century, Sauveterre-de-Guyenne had changed hands ten times during the Hundred Years' War, though its strategic importance had diminished considerably since then. The town was located in the triangular region called the Entre-Deux-Mers, for "between two seas," north of the Garonne River and south of the Dordogne; in between were limestone valleys, knolls dotted with pine forests, and acres and acres of vineyards that produced inexpensive wine that had never attracted the sort of speculation that made Bordeaux famous. Businesses in the quiet town closed their shutters by dusk, sometimes earlier. Magnificent, crumbling manors lingered on the market for years without any takers.

Not far from the center of town stood a hodgepodge of late twentieth-century concrete and twenty-first-century prefabricated buildings, all belonging to La Guyennoise Propriétaires et Négociants. La Guyennoise was owned by the Martin family, who had been in the area for as long as anyone could remember. They were winegrowers as well as négociants; until very recently, they had been producing prunes. Unfortunately, the prune business had failed. Naturally, the sign outside the family offices still read LA GUYENNOISE LES PRUNEAUX DE GUYENNE. No one had bothered to change it. That was how it was in Sauveterre-de-Guyenne.

The Martins sold wines where the profits were counted in cents. Every week, sometimes daily, the father and founder of La Guyennoise, Michel Martin, tallied expenses and revenue. A short, aging man who dressed in the simple clothing typical of an occupation where clothes often got dirty, Michel spent his days in a glass-walled office that allowed him to watch over his employees as he did the accounting. Michel's son, Emmanuel, ran the company's day-to-day operations. Unlike his father, Emmanuel dressed sharply, though in an unpretentious manner. He was proud of how he had honed the business of selling wine so that every cellar, warehouse, and stage of production was arranged to shave off cents and add value.

On any given day, La Guyennoise's vats held the equivalent of 3.8 million bottles of wine. Emmanuel had one cellar for wines grown and produced at the Martin family estates, and another for wine they bought in bulk from various sources. The estate wine came from nearly one thousand acres of vines on the outskirts of Sauveterre-de-Guyenne that produced 3 million bottles of wine a year. Some of the bulk wine they blended to make brand wine was bought through Bordeaux's courtiers, who, to say the least, appreciated timely payments, but most of the wine in the vats had come from Spain. There was not a huge demand for Spanish wine, so Spanish growers sold their wine on the cheap. By adding a small portion of French wine to the vats, it became "European wine," which the Martins could sell for much more than the wine they were buying from Spain. It was a cunning approach to a tough market.

But, more than anything, it was the labeling department that set La Guyennoise apart. Rather than creating one or two brand wines from their blends of French and Spanish wines and putting those wines up for sale, the Martins let their customers pick a brand for themselves. A team of Chinese interns were set to work designing wine labels that were stored in rows and rows of shelves in the two-story label room. Prospective buyers thumbed through binders of these labels and procured the one they found most promising. If none of the existing labels appealed to them, they were free to dream up the elements of an entirely new label that would be designed for them. Images of châteaux were a popular choice, as were names that played on a similarity to a well-known estate. In both cases, the trademark was included in the deal. After customers selected the wine, label, cork, and capsule, it took three weeks to ship the wine to China. The Martins had set up a one-stop shop for establishing an exclusive wine brand. Most important to the Martins' financial outlook, the door of La Guyennoise was open to anyone who had the money to pay up front.

From their customers' point of view, the family was simply leveling the playing field. Few Chinese buyers had the deep pockets and blue-chip connections of Yang Wenhua at C&D or Lu Ming at Dynasty, but many shrewd upstart traders were seeking an exclusivity. There wasn't enough classified growth, let alone enough Lafite, for everyone, but an intrepid buyer could get something that looked an awful lot like it.

❂

Most of the Chinese clamoring after the 2009 vintage did not like what they tasted from the barrels—and vintage, legendary or not, held little or no significance in the Chinese market. Despite the Jins' certainty, it was anyone's guess which wine would suit China's dozens of regional cuisines. As much as wine experts enjoyed recommending wine and food pairings, it would be many years before a billion Chinese palates were ready to assert themselves.

Some resourceful entrepreneurs were trying to jump-start the process. Slim and fashionable, with heavy black-framed, lenseless glasses, Ma Lin had carved out a niche for herself in the budding Chinese wine scene, first by opening a Beijing branch for the Bordeaux sommelier school, Cafa Formations. She organized conferences in Beijing in conjunction with the Conseil des Vins du Médoc, an association that hosted training sessions, tastings, and meet and greets with winemakers. She hosted classes in second- and third-tier cities all over China—in Tianjin, Wenzhou, Wuhan, and Zhengzhou. However, the demand for sommeliers was still quite small, so she had branched out to train importers and VIP clients from banks and other companies. At the grand opening of the school, held at the Beijing Hilton, two hundred importers and fifty journalists had showed up. Sixty importers had attended a class in Nanjing. All were new to the wine business, with previous professions in many sectors, none of which had anything to do with beverages. But everyone hoped to earn a good living from wine. In the months since she'd opened the school in July 2009, she had trained three hundred people.

Ma introduced some of her students to château owners and négociants in Bordeaux who were looking for translators and assistants. But even though hundreds of Chinese students were arriving in Bordeaux to join the miniskirt brigade, they were a tiny percentage of the people in need of a wine education. While the Jins had not signed up for one of Ma's classes, they were exactly the sort of New Chinese that she was targeting. They still had much to learn.

The barrel tastings were proving to be a trial for the Jins. They were operating mostly by instinct, relying on external markers such as the splendor of a château or the familiarity of a brand name. On the last day of the tastings, the Jins took their seats in a dark-paneled tasting room at Château La Mission Haut-Brion, and readied themselves to get a preview of its sister property Château Haut-Brion, the venerable First Growth. The château's technical director stood in the middle of the room, the tables for the tasters arranged in a square around the perimeter. No one spoke; the mood was serious. Most of the tasters were taking meticulous notes as they sipped the wines, rating the qualities that might make each one mature into something special. Around the third wine, Mrs. Jin stopped tasting and thumbed through messages on her iPhone. Even at a First Growth, the tannins were astringent at this stage in the fermentation process. She couldn't taste which ones were worth buying and which ones should be skipped over.

Mr. Jin, however, closely followed the rituals of the tasting room. Without gaining experiences like this, it would be impossible for him to judge the quality of a wine—or the potential for profit. He mimicked the movements of his neighbor, the swirling of the wine in the glass, the careful tilt of the rim toward the nostrils, the sip and slurp to aerate the wine in the mouth, then the discreet spit into the small bucket. After going through the motions, he nodded and gave the wine a thumbs-up.

Later that day, the caterers served their last meals, the tents came down, and the exodus to the airport and train station began. Exhaustion set in. Even the most humble estates could say they had succeeded in producing an elegant wine, round and juicy with the aroma of ripe berries, cherries, and plums and a touch of vanilla and spices, as well as a backbone of tannins that guaranteed the wine would only get better over the coming years. They had customers. The Americans and the British loved the wine; that was obvious. Better yet, the châteaux and négociants could finally put faces to the growing demand from China, and it was intensely satisfying.

❁

Bordeaux Index had sent its entire team of salespeople to the barrel tasting of the 2009 vintage, but the boss, Gary Boom, didn't arrive until the following week. Boom preferred to sample the wines in a relaxed atmosphere. He liked having time to talk to the estate owners over a quiet meal about the plans for selling a wine. He had placed phone calls a month earlier, pushing for bigger allocations of the wines he was working extra hard to promote. The Bordelais already had his wish list. He sent only his staff to the tastings so they could honestly discuss the wines they were selling to his customers. When he tasted samples from the barrels, it was mostly to participate in every stage of the winemaking process.

Of course, this year one of the topics that he raised over lunches and dinners was the huge number of Chinese buyers at the tastings who were essentially his competitors. He was glad that the market was growing, but he'd been selling wine out of Hong Kong for long enough to advise the châteaux and négociants to be cautious. Fine wine required special handling, not only in terms of temperature and humidity, but in terms of sales pitch. Boom had a staff educated in wine who, in turn, educated consumers and advised collectors. His business was transparent. They could trust him. Could they say the same about the Chinese buyers with whom they communicated through an intern? But it was easy to dismiss his complaints as those of a jilted lover.

Not long after the tastings finished, however, Boom found good reason to sound the alarm. His sales director in Hong Kong, Sam Gleave, had learned that rogue traders on the mainland were allegedly selling bogus Bordeaux futures. One website, Jiuhang, was offering Carruades de Lafite 2009 at a price of 580 yuan. This was dubious. There was no way the price could be 580 yuan, because the wine was not yet on sale to anyone.

The Chinese fraudsters behind Jiuhang had invented nothing. It was an old scam: sell shares in Bordeaux en primeur wines, collect the money, then disappear before the wine was scheduled for delivery two years later. This sometimes happened even in France and Britain. Recently, a French retailer had absconded with millions of dollars by selling nonexistent en primeur allocations. In the United Kingdom, the managers of an investment firm that had sold wine funds were facing trial, accused of taking money for fictitious en primeur orders and using the money to buy cars and cocaine instead. The French company was eventually forced into liquidation, and the British men were convicted of fraud and sentenced to jail.

Boom worried that the en primeur system would be tainted in the eyes of the Chinese, who were already suspicious of a system that required them to put down money on a product they could not touch for more than a year. Several Chinese banks had withheld approval of outbound wire transfers for en primeur orders. Ironically, no sooner had the specter of en primeur fraud raised its head in China than the London wine merchants faced the same trickery in their own backyard. It wasn't exactly the sort of news that would calm the Chinese banks.

The Internet-based trading platform London International Vintners Exchange, or Liv-ex, operated out of the Battersea district of London. In May 2010, as the excitement around the 2009 vintage began to boil over, Liv-ex allowed traders to buy and sell en primeur, though the châ-teaux had not officially priced or released the wines for sale. On Wall Street, this was normal short selling, but the London merchants were out-raged. One case of Château Lafite 2009 sold for £10,000—roughly $15,600. Traders were listing Château Cos d'Estournel for £3,000 a case. Château Latour was at £4,275, Château Margaux at £3,330, Château Mouton Rothschild at £3,200, and Château Haut-Brion at £2,525. Liv-ex defended the sales, arguing that most of its en primeur supply was backed by bank guarantees. Boom roundly condemned the sales as reckless and disgraceful.

On the Place de Bordeaux, the short selling was dismissed as another sad example of the shenanigans created by Chinese demand. As Laurent Ehrmann, the chief executive officer of the négociant Barrière Frères, commented: "The whole circus surrounding Lafite and Carruades has become so crazy, and this is just another sign of it." Worse, the Liv-ex trades encouraged many châteaux to increase their prices. More than two months had passed since the barrel tastings, and the biggest names had yet to release their wines. The châteaux were eager to see just how high the market might go.

In mid-June 2010, the annoyingly drawn-out waltz finally came to an end. Haut-Brion and Latour released their first tranche at €500 a bottle wholesale, while Lafite, Margaux, and Mouton came out at €450 a bot-tle. Lafite had raised its price 323 percent over the previous year and 53 percent over the 2005 vintage. Latour had raised its price 85 percent relative to the 2005 vintage. Bordeaux watchers were horrified. This was only the first tranche. Subsequent tranches were destined to be set even higher. When Lafite offered Carruades de Lafite at 89 percent over the price of the 2005 vintage, Ehrmann complained loudly that the price of Lafite's second wine had been pushed to an unsustainable level. Reputable merchants, he said, could not honorably recommend its purchase. Yet they did, and the wines sold in a frenzy. In Hong Kong, stores sold out of their entire stock of Pontet-Canet in less than two hours.

In Europe, the retailers' anger was palpable. "If they aim to give their customers a return on their purchase, they have failed miserably. Of my top twenty customers, seventeen have bought nothing. Nor will they. Apply that nationally and Bordeaux is digging a vast hole for itself," said one European merchant. "Unless it plans to relocate to Asia, that is."

❋

In New York, Sherry-Lehmann, among the largest retail buyers of classified growths in the United States, had started the new year with a Bordeaux "blowout sale," but the sad reality was that even the well-heeled customers of Manhattan's Upper East Side were struggling in the challenging economy. Credit was hard to come by and the real estate market was unstable. The extravagantly priced 2005 vintage—widely hailed as the "vintage of the century"—had landed when America was riding high. Now Bordeaux had another vintage of the century, but no one seemed capable of moving the wine. There was a growing fear among merchants and négociants that the châteaux had priced themselves out of the U.S. market.

Elsewhere, the customers weren't faring any better. Europe was experiencing a deep recession, with the southern countries nearing default and desperately awaiting word of a bailout from the European Union or the International Monetary Fund. Greece was poised to receive its first aid package, and Spain and Portugal faced bankruptcy. Businesses closed, housing prices dropped, and unemployment mushroomed. The French economy was stagnating. In China, there was talk of a real estate bubble, and many feared that the heavily leveraged black economy would collapse. As the prices for Bordeaux continued to rise, the Chinese government reined in lending from the banks and tightened credit lines.

The precarious economic conditions provided an opportunity for those with ready cash to change the terms of sale. The Jins told the winemaker in Saint-Émilion that they were buying Bordeaux at one euro a bottle. The grower expressed dismay. At first, the Jins thought he was protesting because they weren't buying the wine through him. That was not the issue, he explained through his Chinese intern, whose translation, as usual, took much longer than his explanation. In an average year, generic Bordeaux sold for €959 per tonneau, or 80 cents for 750 milliliters of the wine alone—no bottle, no label, no cork or capsule. He pressed to know who had agreed to the deal, but the Jins refused to reveal their seller.

Worse, they were not the only Chinese buyers snatching up wine in Bordeaux at that price. Négociants across the Place de Bordeaux were getting the same demand. At Vignobles Internationaux, Edith Tirlemont-Imbert was struggling to keep the allocations she had previously bought for Château & Estates, and rebuild the business. The Chinese traders gave her pause, though they were the only game in town. "You don't have Bordeaux in the bottle for one euro," Tirlemont-Imbert insisted.

Nor was the request restricted to Bordeaux. In Burgundy, the export director for a highly respected Beaune négociant was fielding numerous requests from Chinese clients for wine at one euro a bottle. "I told him I don't sell wine at one euro a bottle, no one does in Burgundy," she said. "They told me to source it from somewhere else." This was worrying.

As they enjoyed the relative calm of the luxury townhouse they had recently purchased in the sprawling suburbs of Shanghai, the Jins were proud that they had not wagered their property investments on en primeur and instead had succeeded in making good deals for wines that were in the bottle and ready to sell today. Buying en primeur was not a gamble they were willing to take. They were not backed by a state-owned company. They did not hold a monopoly on oil or coal rights. They were not related to anyone of any power whatsoever. The only futures they dealt in concerned their children, and securing an education for them in America.

The Jins had chosen the location of their townhouse with care. It was near Shanghai's domestic airport, which allowed them to pick up clients and bring them to the townhouse, which served as a showroom for wine as well as for the many products they manufactured from reconstituted leather. The townhouse also provided a private venue for advising clients on which wines made the most appropriate gifts, helping them gain liu mianzi by avoiding embarrassing mistakes. Most of their clients were entrepreneurs who gave the wine to officials in hopes of banking some goodwill for future projects requiring government support and approvals.

In fact, the Jins did not import even half the wine they were selling.

There was no need. Government officials received so many cases of wine each week, they couldn't possibly drink all of it. With great discretion, Mrs. Jin bought wine from government officials who had received the wine as gifts, for less than the market value. In this way, she could stockpile competitively priced classified growths while lining the pockets of important officials with pure profit. Later, she resold the wine, often to the very people who had given the wine as gifts. It was a brilliant, low-risk business plan that could evaporate overnight, but Mrs. Jin enjoyed the gamble.

❋

In the Paris offices of DBR Lafite, Christophe Salin, the company's silver-haired and seductive chairman, was considering how to take fuller advantage of the demand in China for Lafite wine. Serena Sutcliffe, the worldwide head of wine for the auction house Sotheby's, had been cajoling him for years to hold an "ex-cellar" auction, in which the wine would come directly from Lafite's cellar in Pauillac rather than being cobbled together from various collectors. An ex-cellar auction ensured an impeccable provenance for the wine—and higher prices. Salin decided that it was time to call Sutcliffe and set a date. He had a vintage of the century and the market was hot.

In the spring of 2010, and with Baron Eric de Rothschild's approval, Salin carefully selected nearly two thousand bottles from 139 vintages of the family's personal stock. The wine was kept behind a heavy iron gate in the château's dark, cobwebbed underground cellar, and many of the bottles had been there for decades if not a century.

The wine had been under lock and key, but that did not guarantee it was in fine condition. Wine, while not precisely alive, was in a constant state of evolution. The tannins, polyphenols, and aromatic molecules that give wine its structure, body, color, and aroma change over time, and with exposure to temperature, light, humidity, and air. So, in the late summer, a team of experts from Sotheby's London came to inspect the level of wine in each bottle and the integrity of the corks and capsules. The team had to determine as certainly as possible that the bottles chosen by Salin had not turned to vinegar.

Once the painstaking work was completed and the bottles approved for sale, a special label with DBR's five-arrow logo and the tagline SOTHEBY'S HONG KONG OCTOBER 2010 was affixed to them; the bottoms of the bottles were laser engraved with the marker HONG KONG 2010. The bottles were then packed into boxes stamped with a Sotheby's case number and loaded into a climate-controlled container that imitated, as closely as possible, the conditions of Lafite's cellar. Every box was fixed with a Sotheby's seal to help identify any tampering during transit. Then, the wine began its five-week voyage to China.

These 139 historic vintages were the big event, but Salin also planned to use the Hong Kong auction to sell cases of the 2008 vintage. Only the cellar staff and the Sotheby's team had seen a special embellishment on the vintage's bottles that they were hoping would increase demand for the wine: a red 八, the Chinese character for the number eight, had been added to the shoulder.

Salin knew that eight is an auspicious number in Chinese culture because it sounds similar to the word for "wealth." Surely, China's good fortune was now also Bordeaux's.

5

....

Château Mania

In early September 2010, Robert Sleigh, Sotheby's head of wine for Asia, told his team it was time to pick up the phones. The Sotheby's staff was to call each of the little emperors and high rollers to get the buzz going. The first day of the October Hong Kong auction would feature a once-in-a-lifetime chance to buy Lafite directly from the château's cellars. On the second day, a full-range of classified growths would be on sale. Even Sleigh's boss at Sotheby's Wine, CEO and president Jamie Ritchie, worked the phones. Ritchie had been instrumental in building the auction house's wine department over the previous three decades. He had posted Sleigh to Hong Kong. Both men shared the conviction that the global wine market was now driven by Asia, with the former British colony at its hub.

Sleigh had first learned about wine by working for négociants in Burgundy, and then found his calling as an auctioneer, spending thirteen years working for Sotheby's in New York. He'd felt the rush of pounding the hammer at the end of numerous record-breaking auctions, including a 2007 Bordeaux ex-cellar auction for Château Mouton Rothschild that had netted $2.2 million. By the time he arrived in Hong Kong, he had sold more than $230 million in wine for the auction house. He could feel an undercurrent of tension around the Hong Kong event, but he wasn't worried about falling short of the printed estimates. The desire for Bordeaux was fierce.

There had never been a question of holding the auction in London or New York. Sotheby's had opened an office in Hong Kong back in 1973, catering to the growing wealth of Asian countries, led by Japan. Now, the most acquisitive wine collectors were in greater China. Cases of Lafite were the most coveted prize in Beijing, often traded ten times, sometimes more, before they reached their final consumer. Personal cellars worth $100 million were not uncommon. These Chinese collectors were new to wealth, they were new to wine, and they were obsessed with Lafite.

Still, every arrangement for the sale had been made with great care. Weeks earlier, Lafite's wine had been shipped to Tuen Mun in Hong Kong's New Territories, where it was stored in a high-security warehouse owned by a company called Crown Cellars, which kept the environment at a constant fifty-five degrees Fahrenheit with 65 percent humidity— as close as possible to the conditions in Bordeaux's cellars. The auction itself would be held in the Connaught Room of the legendary Mandarin Oriental Hotel in the Central District of Hong Kong. It had the feeling of a five-star gala, with the guests seated in small groups at round white-clothed tables set for a gourmet meal. The rarefied atmosphere, Sotheby's hoped, would push up the bidding.

Following the telephone campaign, Ritchie and Sleigh realized that they could not accommodate everyone who was interested. They had to limit the guest list to serious buyers only. Each guest was issued an admittance ticket carefully vetted to weed out sightseers and to create an aura of exclusivity. It was the first time Sotheby's had issued tickets for an auction, and it was a mark of wealth and status to be awarded a seat. In the end, 140 tycoons, mainly Chinese, all proven buyers of Bordeaux First Growths, made the cut.

At six P.M. on October 30, 2010, the first day of the auction, every seat was full. Lafite's director, Christophe Salin, had flown from France the week before to promote the sale on the mainland and to witness the event itself.

The wine on the block was especially attractive to the Chinese collectors in attendance. There were wine fairs being held all over China, but the top buyers were smart to assume that the wine for sale was often not genuine. At one wine fair held in the second-tier city of Chengdu, sellers openly peddled twelve-packs of blatantly fake Lafite, packaged with fake labels, filled with bitter wine, in obviously fake wooden cases that were stacked up like walls to ensure no one missed them. A year later at the same Chengdu fair, at eight A.M. on the first day of the event, DBR Lafite and their lawyer had organized a raid led by the police, and seized the fake wine. But counterfeiters continued to plague the market. Now Sotheby's was offering the chance to buy 190 lots of the first of the Firsts, direct from the winemaker's cellars.

Ritchie was presiding over the sale of a number of the lots, communicating prestige to the audience. When he stepped to the podium, however, he knew that much of his work was already done for him: Sotheby's had received more than one thousand write-in bids before the first hammer. But as he scanned the banquet room's tables, he could tell that the ticket holders fully intended to buy some wine that evening. It was his job to give them the opportunity.

He opened the auction with a case (twelve bottles) of Lafite 2009. The wine was still in barrels in Pauillac and would be delivered by the château in one year's time to Crown Cellars in Hong Kong. The lot had been estimated at a value of $10,000 to $15,000; three days earlier, an en primeur order for a dozen bottles of the vintage, with equally impeccable provenance, had sold for $17,066 on Liv-ex. There was good reason for the Sotheby's team to feel confident about their estimate. Two minutes later, the hammer price was HK$532,400, or $68,632. The rest of the 2009 lots sold at similarly astonishing premiums.

In the audience, Salin was considering what these high prices meant. Perhaps Chinese skittishness about buying en primeur was no longer an issue, if it was obtained directly from the château.

Next, Ritchie turned to nine lots of Lafite 2008, each of which was estimated at $6,000 to $8,000. Two of the lots sold for $34,316. Applause erupted after each hammer fell. The auction had been organized so that the vintages got older and older as the evening progressed. This was a well-established method for ensuring that anticipation continued to mount throughout an auction. By lot 167, the 1959 vintage was on sale. Ritchie presented a double magnum, called a jeroboam, estimated at between $30,000 and $50,000. It sold for $171,579.

At first glance it seemed as though Sotheby's had grossly underestimated the value of the wines. Had the house gamed the system in order to guarantee yet another super-performing record auction? But Jamie Ritchie, Robert Sleigh, and Christophe Salin were honestly stunned by the fierce bidding. Yes, they understood that demand in China was on the rise, but they'd never imagined that it was so pent-up that the estimates in the catalog had been woefully out of date the moment it was printed. When it came time to auction the storied 1869 vintage, no one—least of all, Salin—knew what to expect.

Three bottles of Lafite 1869 were on the block separately, each estimated at $5,000 to $8,000. That was a fair sum for a bottle of wine, but the 1869 vintage was significant for several reasons. It was the first vintage wholly made by the Rothschilds following the acquisition of Lafite by Baron James de Rothschild in August 1868. Only 60,000 bottles of the vintage had been produced, compared to the 240,000 bottles of the first wine and 360,000 of the second wine typical of modern vintages. It had been produced at a time when very little wine was being bottled at the estate, since in the nineteenth century most wine, including First Growths, was sold by the barrel and bottled by négociants or wine merchants. The 1869 also predated the arrival of grape phylloxera, the insect that decimated Europe's vineyards in the late nineteenth century. The oldest vines currently at Lafite had been planted in 1886. The 1869 vintage was unique.

Ritchie began the auction for the first bottle with a sense that something extraordinary was about to happen. The bidding was as aggressive as ever, but in the end, a telephone bid beat out the paddles in the room. A mysterious Chinese buyer paid HK$1,815,000—$233,972—for the bottle. It was the most expensive bottle of wine ever sold in the world. Then the same mysterious buyer exercised his right to forgo competition and buy the other two bottles at the same price. The room thundered with applause and Ritchie smiled, elated as well as relieved.

Christophe Salin was in a state of shock. There were still ninety-three lots to sell from the Rothschilds' cellars. Lafite's second wine, Les Carruades de Lafite, was on offer, as was Duhart-Milon, l'Évangile, and Rieussec, the other estates owned by DBR Lafite. All of these wines carried the famous five-arrow symbol of Lafite on the label, and Salin had been told it was one of the few marks that Chinese customers instantly recognized. What prices might these lots get? They'd clearly underestimated the demand. The Chinese, flush with cash and voracious in their quest to show off their newfound success and sophistication, were rewriting the rules of the fine wine market.

At this point, Robert Sleigh took over the hammer. A seasoned pro, he brought the sale to a striking close, selling three magnums of Château Rieussec 1967, a Sauternes, for an outrageous $17,166. The estimate had been $1,200 to $2,000 per bottle, and the Sotheby's team had deemed that price to be more than reasonable. The Rothschilds had purchased Rieussec in 1984, so the vintage's link to the family was tenuous at best. In Bordeaux, négociants sold Rieussec by twisting arms. Yet, that evening, all that mattered to the assembled tycoons was that Rieussec belonged to Lafite today. The last bid brought the sale for the day to a total of $8.4 million. The presale estimate had been $2.5 million. It was a new record for wine auctions.

The next morning at ten A.M., when the second day of the auction got to a start, many of the people in the room were visibly frustrated that they had gone home empty-handed the night before. They wielded their paddles with heated determination. But the auction that day wasn't all about Lafite. There were 624 lots of Bordeaux classified growths from the London warehouse of a company called SK Networks on sale. The wine had been purchased through a Bordeaux-based négociant named Philippe Papillon, but it did not have ex-cellar provenance. This sale was a litmus test of sorts.

Within ninety minutes, Ritchie had sold every lot. The auction had moved so swiftly that there had been no time to pass the hammer to Sleigh midway through, as planned. The sale broke the previous day's record, with the bids coming to $10 million. The total for the two-day auction was $18.4 million.

All of the wines had sold for more than their published value in New York, London, and Bordeaux. There was no logic to the prices.

A bubble was forming in China. Who knew how big it could swell before it popped?

❋

It was a sunny Saturday morning at the Bordeaux Chamber of Commerce, and the room was unusually full for a weekend. But today, no auctions were planned; instead, the auditorium was hosting a delegation of dark-suited politicians, officials, and executives from Dalian, a port city in Liaoning Province, with a population of seven million. One of Dalian's most successful companies, the Haichang Group, wanted to turn the city into a wine mecca. Haichang's ambitious founder had noticed the success of the Hong Kong Wine and Dine Festival and wanted to import a version from Bordeaux to Liaoning's "second city," which had been named a national economic and technological development zone, or special economic zone (SEZ), by the National People's Congress in 1984.

SEZ status was a tool concocted by Beijing to attract foreign investors. Not only were joint ventures allowed, so, too, were wholly foreign-owned enterprises. Construction was encouraged, all the more so if it brought in foreign capital. Market forces were embraced; a commodities exchange—the only one in China—was established. In the years since Dalian became an SEZ, the city had grown to include a free trade zone and a high-tech zone. Many Western companies, including Accenture, Citibank, Dell, HP, IBM, and Oracle, had offices there.

As part of the city's development, Dalian's beaches had been promoted as a tourist destination, and in 2001, Haichang Group, originally founded to work in the oil trade, started building theme parks. Haichang's first park, Dalian Tiger Beach (Laohutan) Ocean Park, opened the next year. Nearly three hundred acres in size, the park featured thirteen thousand feet of beaches, a polar animal exhibit and aquarium, a sculpture park, theaters, and a shopping center. The company had built several more theme parks, including Dalian's premier amusement park, Discoveryland, complete with roller coasters, a "magic forest," and a "legend castle." Haichang's executives had noticed that Dalian's beer festival attracted about six million visitors from across the north-eastern provinces of China each year, and they wanted to expand their entertainment empire into wine.

About an hour's drive from Dalian, the Haichang Group had a property development project called Jin Shi Tan, the centerpiece of which was to be focused on wine tourism. A luxury housing development named Château de Bordeaux offered villas, townhouses, apartments, shops, and restaurants featuring French architecture, their limestone facades meant to resemble the historic quays and mansions of Bordeaux. The project called for a plantation of four hundred acres of Bordeaux vines and a two-million-bottle cellar. Haichang's executives had proposed a wine museum in partnership with Bordeaux's avant-garde Cité des Civilisations du Vin, itself an $82 million sparkling glass building being erected on the banks of the Garonne River and set to open in 2016. Every year they would host a Dalian Wine & Dine Festival modeled on Bordeaux's popular event. When this didn't prove to be enough, Haichang promised to plant an additional five thousand acres of vines at Jin Shi Tan and buy one hundred bottles of wine from 1,200 châteaux to test the market for distribution—a purchase that would allow many winemakers to gain a foothold in China. That offer cemented the deal.

And so, on June 18, 2011, the Dalian contingent and the chamber had convened a press conference to announce the details and encourage négociants and appellations to book stands at the festival and lease retail space in the wine village. In the second row of Chinese delegates sat a man who did not speak but nonetheless exuded confidence and power. He was not introduced to the audience, and journalists were ordered not to photograph him. He was Qu Naijie, the founder, controlling shareholder, and non-executive director of Dalian Haichang.

Qu was a familiar face to the inner circle at the Bordeaux Chamber of Commerce. During the wine trade show, Vinexpo, which was owned primarily by the chamber and held in Hong Kong in May 2010, Qu had invited the chamber's president to visit Dalian. Normally, the chamber did business only with other public organizations, but Qu had been very persuasive. In addition to his theme parks, Qu owned one of China's largest oil shipping firms; in recent years he had diversified into real estate and golf courses. He was ranked by *Forbes* as holding one of the top three hundred personal fortunes in China. To many in China, and increasingly in Bordeaux, he was "Mr. Dalian."

If anyone else in Bordeaux recognized Qu, which was rare, they referred to him as Qu Cheng, his son's name, which suited him just fine. That was because Qu Cheng was the only name that had ever been attached to Qu during his more public dealings in France—those involving real estate. In November 2010, for $4.3 million, Qu had bought ninety-nine acres and a sprawling château badly in need of repair in the Côtes de Bourg, north of Bordeaux, and listed the property's ownership in his son's name. The vineyards in the region were the least profitable in Bordeaux, and growers there struggled to sell their wine and maintain their homes. The bank had effectively forced the owner to sell by freezing the château's line of credit. There was no apparent reason for Qu to spend $4.3 million on a struggling vineyard, let alone a crumbling house. But the seller had something of value: the unused but trademarked wine name Château Chenu-Lafitte.

"Lafitte" was a common name in Bordeaux, used as a surname as well as a place-name. In the old local dialect, spelled "Lafite" or "Lafitte," it meant "little hill," and had been a way to indicate the lie of the land on which a family lived. Much to the aggravation of Château Lafite Rothschild, whose wines had once used the "Lafitte" spelling, there was more than one château bearing the name "Lafitte"—including one in current operation. Château Lafitte had been producing wine since the eighteenth century, when a négociant named Lafitte set himself up on an estate on the other side of Bordeaux. DBR Lafite had successfully sued this Château Lafitte in 2003, and won on appeal, but in 2010, France's highest appeals court sided with Château Lafitte. Nevertheless, DBR Lafite considered the modest estate to be a usurper, riding the tails of its fame as a First Growth. Now DBR Lafite might also have to contend with Chenu-Lafitte, owned by a Chinese billionaire.

For now, Qu was focused on the Château de Bordeaux back in Dalian. After a year of meetings with the chamber, he'd finally won over the French. "First, the English, Dutch, Irish came. The Japanese came twenty years ago. It's logical that the Chinese arrive today," Georges

Haushalter, the president of the Bordeaux Wine Council, said of the partnership. "Bordeaux has always welcomed foreign investment."

A few Bordelais had been skittish about the partnership with Dalian. It was odd that the man who seemed to be driving everything on the Chinese side barely spoke in meetings and held press conferences where no one was allowed to acknowledge his presence. After the trip to Dalian, the Bordeaux Chamber of Commerce's leaders had looked into Haichang by employing the services of a French firm called Compagnie Française d'Assurance pour le Commerce Extérieur, or Coface. Coface specialized in export credit insurance, protecting against the risk of nonpayment by companies based in other countries, and it was the place to go for advice on the legitimacy of foreign entities. Everyone at the chamber sighed with relief when the Coface analysts said they had come up with nothing. Then again, when they said they had come up with nothing, they meant that they couldn't tell the chamber anything about Qu or the Haichang Group. That wasn't unusual when doing business with China.

The chamber considered the options, and the terms of the partnership were simply too good to pass up. Perhaps if one of their own was closely involved in Qu's business in Bordeaux, it would smooth any lingering misgivings. The involvement of Christian Delpeuch, the retired chief executive of the négociant firm Ginestet and a former president of the Bordeaux Wine Council, had helped to reassure those with doubts. When the chamber suggested that Delpeuch would be an invaluable adviser for Qu, Qu hired him as his managing director in France. Soon it became clear that the theme-park mogul wasn't content to simply replicate Bordeaux in Dalian and enjoy a lone château. He wanted more of Bordeaux. And he wasn't alone.

❋

On February 16, 2011, Philippe Raoux walked into La Winery, the wine tourism complex he owned in the Médoc, considering his prospects. Outside the $27 million sixty-four-acre site, an orange six-ton sculpture called *Tree of the Sun* waved at the cars speeding by on the roundabout. The hulk seemed cheerier than usual. It reflected Raoux's sunny disposition.

Raoux had opened La Winery in 2007, but it had never really taken off. Two years earlier, he'd received a call from a mergers and acquisitions firm in Paris, which said it had an offer for the business he would be foolish to refuse. A series of lengthy, frustrating negotiations had ensued, and he stopped believing that the deal would ever be inked. Then, out of nowhere, another bidder made an overture, and it was very enticing. This time, he felt certain it meant he was going to end the day considerably richer than he had started it.

Inside La Winery, Raoux sat down at the long conference room table next to the party that had made the counteroffer. A bank of photographers and television cameras were lined up, ready to record every move as the two men signed some routine paperwork. What wasn't routine about the day was that Raoux had agreed to sell his estate in Lalande-de-Pomerol to a Tianjin-based company called COFCO for $11 million. The man next to him, Wu Fei, was the head of COFCO's wine and spirits division.

COFCO had been founded in 1949 as the North China Foreign Trade Company after the Communists booted out foreign interests and nationalized the country's industries. Before then, foreigners, mainly British companies, had controlled imports and exports, and their expulsion left China drained not only of cash but expertise in international trade. The Communist leadership was worried that foreign companies would undermine the workers' welfare. It became illegal for any Chinese business to deal directly with a foreign company, and direct imports and exports were forbidden. In their place, nationalized companies were set up as trading monopolies.

The North China Foreign Trade Company and other trading companies acted as distributors, and they never imported anything for which they didn't already have a buyer. Within six months, as the newly installed government officials running the enterprise came to understand the overwhelming volume of goods that needed to be imported or exported in China, the company was split into six divisions, each with a specialty. The six units exposed the rough-and-ready state of China's economy after the war: cereals; oils and oil seeds; eggs; pig bristles; leather and fur; and tea and other native products. As the Communists adopted Five-

Year Plan after Five-Year Plan and plowed resources into various industries in an effort to catch up with the West, the trading company was split and restructured again and again, with the food and beverage unit eventually spun off into the China National Cereals, Oils and Foodstuffs Corporation, or COFCO. Regardless, the essential operations remained the same: find a buyer for a good and then import it, providing the government with guaranteed revenue.

Over the decades, COFCO had grown into a powerful, state-controlled conglomerate in its own right. When China opened up to the West under Deng Xiaoping, it was through COFCO that Coca-Cola and the Seagram Company first gained access to the market. During the late 1980s and the '90s, COFCO had expanded exponentially, developing the wine and spirits division and producing one of China's biggest domestic wine brands, Great Wall Wines, which sold 120 million bottles each year and had annual sales of $460 million. When it was all accounted for, COFCO's aggregated revenues were said to be in the neighborhood of $60 billion.

The wine division had built fake châteaux around China to impress its customers. Recently, with a $10 billion war chest at its disposal, it had started buying soybeans, grain, and other food resources overseas. Now, COFCO had turned its sights on foreign vineyards.

Philippe Raoux's estate, Château de Viaud, was COFCO's first purchase in Bordeaux. It was a smart way for the company to plant its roots. Château de Viaud was one of the oldest estates in Lalande-de-Pomerol, an appellation renowned for the Merlot and Cabernet varieties that thrived in its sandy, gravelly soil. More important, Lalande-de-Pomerol was separated from the Pomerol appellation by a stream, called La Barbanne, which made a significant difference for a savvy investor. Two and a half acres of vines in Pomerol, famous for iconic wines such as Pétrus, started at $1.2 million. The same size of vineyard in Lalande-de-Pomerol cost $184,000.

At the official signing, COFCO's vice chairman, Chi Jingtao, addressed the media. Chi said the acquisition was part of a global strategy, stretching from production to distribution, that would build on COFCO's success with Great Wall. He mentioned that his government's interest in securing a direct supply of Bordeaux wine was partly provoked by worries that fake wine was entering the Chinese market. "We have a strategy for constructing a complete chain from production to consumption to guard against forgeries and to reassure our clients," Chi said. "Being involved from the vineyard upward in Bordeaux helps to strengthen this commitment, and investing in vineyards internationally is part of the fight against fraud." He was toeing Beijing's line that a state-run company must work in the people's interest, even if it was trading in a product that interested only a small fraction of the Chinese public.

COFCO had paid $11 million for the privilege of buying Philippe Raoux's estate, but a much bigger deal was in the works. Behind the scenes, COFCO executives were promising Raoux that COFCO would work with him to develop a négociant business dedicated to distributing Bordeaux wines in China. The conglomerate imported $10 million of wine annually, and Raoux was ecstatic. COFCO's goal was to blend and package wines that would appeal specifically to Chinese consumers. Restricting a wine to one market, particularly an undeveloped market, meant it would not be tasted by influential critics or featured on wine lists in fashionable restaurants. But he could see the labels, elaborate with gilding, and taste the wines—soft, round, easy to drink. He thought the plan would work.

At the same time, COFCO's enormous size gave Raoux some pause. The conglomerate could drain Bordeaux of all its low-end wine to produce a single mega-brand. He had heard a lot of grumbling about how much the Chinese resisted going through négociants except when it was absolutely necessary—as with classified growths. The Chinese did not understand the need for intermediaries; they wanted to deal directly with the châteaux. And COFCO was already indicating that it wanted to bypass the courtiers, too.

Raoux assumed that his partnership with COFCO wouldn't become expendable, though it seemed that's how COFCO viewed the terms of business that Bordeaux had established centuries ago.

✳

COFCO wasn't the only Chinese investor looking to reinvent the very system that had created Bordeaux's reputation for producing the finest of fine wines. Among the mavericks was Shen Dongjun. Shen liked to make the point that he wasn't some rube from western China who had stumbled into Bordeaux. As the chief executive officer of a chain of jewelry stores called Tesiro, which had the exclusive right in China to distribute gems from Eurostar Diamond Traders, supplier to Tiffany and Cartier, he regularly conducted business in Europe. He also kept his eyes on how his own country was changing. "I've been thinking about the same question: What industries are going to develop quickly in China?" said Shen. "My answer is always the same: the wine industry."

In 2010, Shen began to import Bordeaux wine into China. He was an expert at marketing, and Bordeaux obviously had brand value. "Increasing numbers of Chinese consumers are learning to drink French wine and are falling in love with it," he noted. "The wine market is one of the biggest opportunities. And what wine lover doesn't dream of owning a château?"

For six years, he had been scouting for the perfect winery to buy. He visited forty châteaux before choosing one to purchase—Château de Viaud. His effort to buy his top choice had been thwarted when Philippe Raoux accepted COFCO's offer, which Shen claimed had "beat us by two weeks." Instead, Shen settled on Château Laulan Ducos, near Saint-Estèphe, in early 2011.

There wasn't much of a château, just a humble ranch-style house, some farm buildings, and fifty-four acres of vines. But the modesty of the estate didn't dampen Shen's enthusiasm. The day the deal closed, he celebrated by throwing a party in the gilded reception hall of the Bordeaux opera house, making the acquaintance of the city's glitterati where Château d'Yquem celebrated the barrel tastings each year. He then hired the previous owner of Laulan Ducos to run the vineyard. On the very day that the property changed hands, Shen told him to order new barrels and harvesting equipment.

Shen was experienced at turning a rough stone into a gem that dazzled. In the case of Laulan Ducos, his goal was to sell what had been a $10 bottle of wine for $240 in China. He was a quick study. His neighbors watched as he seemed to flip the fortunes of the estate overnight. Château Laulan Ducos was uncorked for the Belgian royal family at an event to introduce a new diamond cut, and it was served at the Berlin International Film Festival, of which Tesiro was a sponsor. Shen secured the actress Zhang Ziyi, the star of *House of Flying Daggers* and *Memoirs of a Geisha* and a judge on China's version of *The X Factor*, as the "face" of his wines. He established a wine company, called Laulan French Wine, to import his estate-bottled wine as well as brand wines into China for sale in Tesiro stores. Sales were strong, and he had a list of VIP clients. One of the first things he'd done to ensure his success, he said, was to take his wine off the Place de Bordeaux, shipping the entire production directly to China.

A year later, Shen invited his new contacts in Bordeaux to an evening event at Château Paveil de Luze in Margaux. Château Paveil de Luze was owned by Frédéric de Luze, the négociant who had arranged the exclusivities for Xiamen C&D. Baron de Luze was as blue-blooded as one could get. His Protestant ancestors had signed the Edict of Nantes. Although the family had fled to Switzerland during the worst persecution of the Huguenots, they returned to Bordeaux in the eighteenth century to establish themselves as wine merchants and château owners.

De Luze was a champion of the so-called *cru bourgeois* estates of the Médoc, the estates that had been left out of the 1855 Classification yet were generally believed to be of a decent quality. In 1932, the Bordeaux Chamber of Commerce had chosen 444 estates for cru bourgeois status, but an attempt to ratify the classification in 2003 had fallen apart when a group of châteaux were disqualified and launched a bitter lawsuit. The 2003 classification was banned by the courts in 2007. Somehow, a new association of vineyards, led by de Luze, had risen from the ashes of the old scheme, and de Luze had managed to get them all on board for a plan to woo Chinese into buying wines with a "cru bourgeois" label, which would be awarded every year based on the wine's quality. For months, de Luze had traveled from city to city in China, hoping to convince customers that cru bourgeois represented a standard of quality that could rival the classified growths, especially when price was factored in. Now the cru bourgeois had their first Chinese château owner in Shen Dongjun.

February in the Médoc is gray and cold, and on the evening of Shen's induction into the Commanderie du Bontemps, a select association of 350 négociants and winegrowers in the Médoc, Graves, and Sauternes, frost covered the soil and dormant vines. Shen donned a long purple velvet robe and a purple and white velvet cap, a nod to the *bontemps*, a wood bowl for beating the egg whites traditionally used in fining, the delicate process of removing sediment from the wine. The white velvet on top of the cap represented the frothed-up eggs. Shen grinned when he spotted his reflection, then stepped into the crowded room, where he was given a blind tasting and a quiz, both conducted in Mandarin through a translator. After he passed, he contentedly took an oath swearing his devotion to the Médoc.

Shen was part of a vanguard of Chinese who were gaining acceptance among the Bordeaux establishment while also insisting on a new way of doing business. His approach was quite simple: buy the resource, eliminate the courtiers, ignore the négociants, bypass the importers, and ship the wine to China, where he could sell it himself. Like COFCO, he was getting rid of the middlemen.

From the perspective of many Bordelais, this was folly. "There are loads of examples of foreigners coming to Bordeaux and investing in châteaux and export business, but they've almost always adopted the Bordeaux model of exporting to multiple markets," said a négociant. "Very few take the entire production for their home market." Bordeaux had made its name by being the most sought-after wine around the globe, not the most popular wine in Lyon or New York, let alone Xi'an. But the message was unmistakable: the Chinese intended to buy up and cut off the Place whenever feasible.

At Vintex et Les Vignobles Grégoire, Philippe Larché lost allocations of three wines he'd previously sold in several markets when Qu Naijie took over the estates and their wines. A château in Saint-Émilion came off the Place when a Chinese movie star bought it. Three châteaux were sold to a Chinese architect. The rate of acquisition was speeding up.

Christine Guillard, a spokesperson for the Union des Maisons de Bordeaux, a négociants' association, tried to make light of the threat. The Chinese were buying only minor châteaux, most of which cost less than $9 million. "The Chinese owners represent an extremely small part of the market and even if the phenomenon continues, we don't see them getting their hands on a *Grand Cru*," she said. "So, for the moment, there's no problem."

It didn't take long for the real estate brokers to realize that they could make far more money if they added China specialists to their staff. Over the following two years, Chinese investors purchased at least thirty estates in Bordeaux. More would have been sold, but several negotiations broke down due to miscommunication on both sides. For many of the Chinese buyers, this was a first foray out of their homeland. Some wanted the impossible, such as having a contract written in Chinese and governed by Chinese law—as was the case when a Dalian-based company called Zhongai bought the Château de la Salle, near Blaye. It took many days of negotiation before the company's managers agreed that a transaction in France had to be conducted under French law. Once the contract was finally signed, the new owners failed to show up for weeks, leaving two full-time employees unpaid while they did their best to prune the estate's forty-six acres of vines without the usual seasonal help.

The French, for their part, had a habit of asking for just a bit more as a negotiating tactic—a classic example was the line, "Oh, we didn't include the tractor in the deal." Several Chinese buyers walked out of sales, convinced they were about to be cheated.

Zhou Linjun, a Tesiro executive who helped manage Shen's purchase of Château Laulan Ducos, said that their negotiations had proceeded smoothly. She had lived and worked in France for some time, and Shen himself did deals with Belgian business partners on something like a weekly basis. They were used to navigating cultural differences that often led to failed deals. "The biggest difference is that, in China, we do not have so many laws and we will do anything for money. In Bordeaux, people take care of their land and they do anything for good business."

Both sides at the negotiating table were convinced they were in the right. But only one side had the money.

❋

At a nondescript office park near Bordeaux's only lake, about half a mile from the quai de Bacalan, Hervé Olivier was keeping tabs on the influx of Chinese businessmen touring the vineyards and châteaux with real estate brokers. Olivier was the regional director of the Sociétés d'Aménagement Foncier et d'Établissement Rural (Safer), a French agency that acts as guardian of the rural landscape. Olivier had the power to block plans to turn a farm into an asphalt parking lot. He could nudge the fate of a transaction in favor of a hardworking young farmer over a status-grabbing tycoon.

Olivier knew there were many vineyards in Bordeaux on the brink of going bankrupt or being abandoned, because the local growers came to Safer for help. Too often, the owners couldn't sell their wine for enough to cover the cost of equipment or payroll. In nearly every case, the local estates had little hope of generating enough income to ensure that the next generation could pay France's crippling inheritance taxes, which ran as high as 60 percent of the estate's value.

Sometimes, Safer agents would line up a buyer for a vineyard when the owner decided it was time to throw in the towel. Insurance companies and luxury groups were buying the most prestigious estates, transforming much of the Médoc and Saint-Émilion into corporate retreats with no families in sight. But those investors weren't interested in the humble appellations, like those in the Entre-Deux-Mers region, where the Martins and La Guyennoise were located.

A number of Bordeaux and Bordeaux Supérieur estates in the Entre-Deux-Mers region had been on the market for years, Olivier said with resignation. A stunning château and vineyard could be had for $9 million, but no buyer could anticipate making back that investment because the estate's wine typically sold for five dollars a bottle. All it took was one hailstorm or early frost, and the buyer would be coming to Safer to talk about filing for bankruptcy or selling. There were few winning business plans for the area; Olivier had a tough time assisting the owners. Over the past year, he'd watched with curiosity as Chinese buyers started to acquire châteaux in the Entre-Deux-Mers. He assumed they were attracted by the low real estate costs and that they were convinced they could sell the wine in China for more than a French grower could get away with.

It wasn't as though foreigners hadn't been buying châteaux for some time. Some of the châteaux that had been turned into corporate retreats were owned by multinational companies. Wealthy British, American, and Japanese businessmen had invested in Bordeaux real estate, and back in 1997 Peter Kwok, a Saigon-born banker based in Hong Kong and Taiwan, had bought Château Haut-Brisson, a little known estate in the flats of Saint-Émilion near the Dordogne, as a retreat where his children could learn French. Kwok didn't himself drink wine, but he was a self-proclaimed Francophile. As the market for French wine grew in Asia, he made some good money and decided to buy two more châteaux so that his three children would each have one to inherit.

Then, in 2008, Chinese buyers started to show an interest in the Entre-Deux-Mers. First, an heiress from Qingdao named Daisy Cheng Haiyan bought the 150-acre Château Latour-Laguens, which featured a sixteenth-century castle that might have served as the model for the Walt Disney logo, given its ostentatious turrets. Latour-Laguens was spread over seventy-four acres of vineyard and produced 160,000 bottles of wine, most of it generic AOC Bordeaux. The land itself had been a steal at $27,000 for two and a half acres; three years earlier, the price had been $59,000. Although Château Latour was an hour and a half away by car, Cheng seemed pleased to have bought some form of association with the $500-a-bottle First Growth. Cheng's family owned Longhai Investment Group, a property development company founded in the early 1990s, and she ran Longhai's wine division. The château fit into bigger plans: to create a subsidiary for importing and selling wines under the Latour-Laguens brand, starting at around $40 a bottle and climbing to $500, in a chain of Latour-Laguens shops. These were ludicrous prices for a generic Bordeaux—unless you were selling in China.

With so much money to be made from selling the land, more French winegrowers began to reconsider their long-term prospects, just as Philippe Raoux had. For example, Michel Rolland and his wife, Dany, had built a mini wine empire, owning vineyards in several countries as well as an enology laboratory. The charismatic Rolland was renowned for his palate and his talent for making the final blend of a wine. He was called the "first flying winemaker" since he had clients around the globe and spent a great deal of time abroad, but his roots were in Pomerol. Despite all his success, he still could not persuade his brother to hold on to the family vineyard, Château Le Bon Pasteur.

"I knew for years that I was going to have to sell the property because my brother wanted to get his share of the money out," Rolland said. "While the value of the property is quite high, the income you get from it is almost zero, so my brother wanted out and we had to sell. Of course it was sad to sell it as it's been in our family since the twenties, but we're not the first family in Bordeaux to sell and we won't be the last."

Rolland had, in fact, fought to hold on to the estate in the hope that the land value might improve. He held off the sale for five years, looking for an opportunity that felt right. Then, on one of his far-flung business trips, consulting for Sloan Estate in Napa Valley, he met Pan Sutong, the chairman of Hong Kong–based Goldin Group. Pan had spent $40 million to buy Sloan Estate, and he was interested in hiring the very best. That caught Rolland's attention. He had found his buyer.

At Le Bon Pasteur, Pan agreed to let Rolland stay on as consulting winemaker and keep a minor ownership stake in the vineyard. He might no longer own the family estate, but it was his legacy.

❋

A transformation of Bordeaux's centuries-old practices was under way.

For several years, Yang Wenhua had carefully managed Xiamen C&D's partnership with the French winemaker Castel. C&D was opening a chain of wine stores, named Roche Mazet after Castel's brand wine, which would sell Castel's brand wines and other wines imported by C&D. To solidify his position, Yang had set up exclusivities with twenty-three Bordeaux châteaux, and he used those deals to form a marketing category he had branded the "C&D Grand Cru Union." Now he was aggressively buying up as much of the négociants' allocations of Lafite's second wine, Carruades de Lafite, as possible in order to completely control the wine in the global market. As a result, the price of Carruades had risen so high that no one but the Chinese would pay the price. C&D was willing to buy huge quantities and charge high prices for all of their exclusivities, and both C&D and the châteaux stood to make a massive profit from it. Because of the power of its retail arm, C&D was as close to a guarantee of fame and fortune as a château could get in China.

C&D was the perfect partner for an upwardly mobile estate such as Château Angélus in Saint-Émilion. Château Angélus was a candidate for the First Growth crown. The winery did not possess the famed terroir of its neighbor, Château Ausone, but its owners had waged a thirty-year campaign to get it listed in the highest category, *Premier Grand Cru Classé* (A), in the Classification of Saint-Émilion wines, which was created in 1955 in an effort to promote the appellation as an attractive rival to the Médoc. The Saint-Émilion classification had three rankings: *Grand Cru Classé*, *Premier Grand Cru Classé (B)*, and *Premier Grand Cru Classé (A)*, the last two also known as "First Growth." For many connoisseurs, a First Growth (A) from Saint-Émilion was the equal of a First Growth from the Médoc. But unlike the 1855 Classification, the Saint-Émilion rankings periodically came up for review. The next ranking was scheduled for 2012.

For decades, Angélus had been ranked as Grand Cru Classé, a category that covered a wide spectrum in quality and reputation, and hung below the two First Growth categories. In 1990, the estate's co-owner, Hubert de Boüard, had famously changed the name from L'Angélus to Angélus so that the château would appear first on the alphabetical list of Saint-Émilion's classified growths. In 1996, Angélus was named to the second tier in the rankings, Premier Grand Cru Classé (B).

De Boüard was a tireless promoter of his wines. Through a connection in product placement, he arranged for his wine to appear in a scene in the remake of the James Bond film *Casino Royale*, but a subsequent appearance in *Quantum of Solace* reportedly got cut. According to de Boüard, 007 fans had been put off by the editors' decision.

Yang was on a visit to Saint-Émilion with his négociant, Christophe Reboul Salze, who was now operating his own company, The Wine Merchant, when Hubert de Boüard let it drop that his wine had a cameo in the upcoming 007 movie *Skyfall*. Some of the film had been shot in

China, de Boüard mentioned. Yang wasn't so stupid as to spend millions on a wine that may or may not appear in a movie, but he knew that if C&D could corner the market for Angélus in China, he would be able to name his own price to consumers.

When châteaux sold their wines en primeur, the offers from the négociants came to them through a courtier. There were two prices on the Place: the *ex-cellar* price, which was the price at which the château sold the wine to the négociant; and the *ex-négoce*, or ex-Bordeaux price, which was the suggested resale price. Traditionally, the ex-négoce price included a firm 2 percent commission for the courtier and a percentage for the négociant. The négociant's profit fluctuated with the price of wine on the resale market.

In most industries, manufacturers set a suggested resale price but resellers have a great deal of leeway in setting the price to consumers. Usually, a reseller aims to make some profit by setting the price above the wholesale price at which the good was bought from the manufacturer. Sometimes, demand falls so precipitously that a reseller has to take a loss, but it can still recoup some of the money it had spent on the good by selling it for less than the wholesale price. If demand far outpaces supply, a cunning reseller might be able to charge more than the suggested retail price, but that would likely result in a backlash from consumers—and the risk of losing sales to less avaricious competitors.

In Bordeaux, the suggested resale price of the wine wasn't suggested; it was strictly imposed by the châteaux. Négociants could sell the wine for more than the suggested price, but not for less. For centuries, the châteaux arrived at prices via three powerful influences: the demand as perceived through the various layers of intermediaries, their neighbors' prices, and their dreams of grandeur. Problems arose when the wines could not be resold at the dictated price, but until the age of the Internet, the négociants could quietly unload the wine without the châteaux being any the wiser. The château managers were not sympathetic to any complaints from négociants that they had miscalculated the price of a vintage. One veteran négociant was candid about how the system worked: "They don't care if we sell it. They don't care if we are stuck with it." The négociants absorbed all the risk.

25

The stakes for the négociants were increased still further because, unlike in some industries, the wine could not be returned to the château if it didn't sell through. For the négociants, the higher the prices, the greater the exposure. The obvious solution was for négociants to cut their margin and pass along any overpriced wine as quickly as possible when demand seemed to be drying up. Unfortunately for the négociants, the Internet had brought a startling degree of transparency, and news of "discounting" spread quickly via blogs and trade websites. "Discounting" was a nasty word on the Place de Bordeaux. It was rewarded with vitriolic letters from the châteaux and no allocations the next year. A négociant who tried to stay afloat by discounting wine would be put out of business by his suppliers.

The rules of the system meant that the châteaux had a huge incentive to raise prices in a strong market. And for the last year or so, the market had been very strong. The Chinese were happy to pay high prices. In fact, they seemed more willing to buy as the price got higher. Hubert de Boüard at Angélus knew this. He had set the ex-négoce price for his 2010 vintage at €225 ($276) per bottle. Yang Wenhua didn't blink. Reboul Salze closed a sale for more than four thousand cases. It was another lucrative deal in a bull market.

Vincent Yip at Topsy Trading couldn't shake his pessimism, despite what he was hearing from Bordeaux. As much as he liked the de Boüard family, he'd stopped buying Angélus a few years earlier. The prices set by the estate didn't make any sense—they seemed to be mostly about positioning Angélus as a top wine in the next Saint-Émilion classification rather than meeting market expectations. There was no question that the top Bordeaux brands were still selling, but Yip was worried. His long-standing clients had stopped buying, which signaled to him that the consumer market was made up almost entirely of speculators. Speculation had always been part of the business of Bordeaux, but never before had it overwhelmed traditional distribution and consumption. He could see that wine drinking was becoming more common in China, yet it was nowhere near the levels suggested by the quantities that state-controlled enterprises such as C&D and COFCO were trying to place in the consumer market. In fact, a recent study had put the number of potential imported-wine drinkers in China at just eighteen million. This was not news any château wanted to hear.

Yip thought about the 2009 vintage. Everyone said it was a phenomenal success, but Yip was having trouble moving his stock. Even the famous wines had not gained in value since he'd bought them, and he wasn't earning any interest on his investment. The same was true of the 2010 vintage. A wine that doubled and tripled in value within days of their purchase—like the 2008—seemed to be history. If this continued, the speculators were going to get twitchy.

Increasingly, the London wine merchants such as Gary Boom were reporting that the market had peaked. Nothing could match the heights of the Sotheby's auction in Hong Kong. If the châteaux tried to match the prices for the 2009 vintage when the 2010 was ready for release, there was no question that the wine would be discounted, whether or not the châteaux approved of it. The négociants would be desperate to move their allocations. "They're nervous," commented Simon Staples, the outspoken sales director of London merchant Berry Bros. & Rudd. They'd sacrifice their own profits rather than hold on to a wine that was steadily losing value.

Then, in early July 2011, the alarm bells sounded. The Liv-ex Index that tracked the prices of one hundred investment-grade wines declined in value. Ninety-five percent of the wines in the index were from Bordeaux. The Liv-ex website also displayed the most recent wine sales on the secondary market. Close students of wine—particularly collectors—monitored these sales in order to gauge when they stood to make the most profit, and what they were seeing was troubling. Not only had the 2010 vintage, sold en primeur just a few weeks earlier, gained no value on the secondary market, but it was possible to buy the First Growths at the suggested ex-négoce price—and occasionally for less. The négociants were cutting their losses. Equally troubling was an abundance of supply. People who had bought the 2010 had no confidence that the wines would hold or increase in value. They were reselling the wine as swiftly as they could. The tumbling prices were having an effect on the value of older vintages, too. In their inimitable manner, the Bordelais called it a "price adjustment." It was a glutted market.

Panic set in. The prices being offered by various négociant firms were posted on websites. Some were tweeted. The négociants who weren't discounting reported those who were to the châteaux.

One of the estates that was hardest hit was Château Cos d'Estournel. More than anything, Cos's owner, Michel Reybier, and its managing director, Jean-Guillaume Prats, wanted to break through the gilded ceiling of the 1855 Classification. They knew that after years of improving the wine's quality and investing in its image, the best option was to keep raising the price until it approached that of the First Growths. But no one could sell the 2010 at inflated prices, and Cos was one of the wines being heavily discounted. A steadfast négociant who had chosen to stick with the pricing system had given him the bad news. Furious, Prats fired off an email to the négociants on the Place, threatening a nuclear reaction if his wine continued to be sold at discount. But a Gallic flash of anger was the least of their worries.

The bubble that had formed in China was losing air. The question was whether it would gently deflate or burst.

In August, Christie Ling Zhijun, a professional money manager at Pacific Asset Management in Shanghai, got approval from China's Department of Investment Fund Supervision for the Dinghong Fund, a 1 billion renminbi ($150 million) wine fund. Zhijun projected a 15 percent return on her investments.

Zhijun made a lot of noise about the Dinghong Fund's blue-chip credentials. The fund would source its wines from Philippe Larché at Vintex, and Zhang Yanzhi, a Chinese-born rep for another négociant, Jean-Pierre Moueix. Chinese investors were required to lock their money—with an ante of 1 million yuan for individuals and 10 million yuan for institutions—for a minimum of five years. She predicted that China would bypass France in total wine consumption by the end of 2015, to become the third largest wine market in the world right after the United States and the United Kingdom.

The Dinghong Fund would buy its first stock of wine, worth 200 million yuan, in September. Sixty percent of the monies she had to spend would be earmarked for older vintages. The rest would be used to buy wine en primeur the following spring.

"One challenge will be to temper Chinese investors who think that twenty-two million euros to start is too small an amount, but we have to explain that it is better to spread out spending to reduce risk," said Philippe Larché of Vintex. Larché sensed the fund had the potential to become one of the most influential investment vehicles for wine—if only they could temper speculation.

❂

Exhausted by the events of the day, Zhang Jinshan, a forty-eight-year-old goji berry–liquor magnate from Ningxia, poured tea in his newly purchased château in February 2012. The band of journalists attending the press conference had left, and now he could reflect on his daring purchase: the 420-acre Château du Grand Moueys. The estate's Gothic Revival château was in desperate need of a $5 million face-lift, but the vineyards produced 1.2 million bottles of wine, which wasn't bad.

The main appeal for Zhang was the potential for development. He planned to convert 270 acres of the estate into a resort for Chinese tourists. There'd be a nine-hole golf course, tennis courts, spa, health retreat, and jogging trails. He had enlisted a good friend who owned eight restaurants across Ningxia to help him install a Chinese restaurant at the château. The very best Chinese ingredients would be imported. The menu would include Peking duck roasted over fragrant jujube and pear tree wood.

Zhang believed he would have ten thousand Chinese tourists visiting Grand Moueys within a couple of years. He just hoped his guests would not be too disappointed by the lack of a swimming pool. "There is already too much water. A pool would be bad feng shui," said Li Lijuan, the young woman who served as Zhang's translator and aspired to manage the estate. The decision to buy a château "between two rivers" restricted his options.

The development did have some complications. Zhang, whose company Ningxiahong produced 30 million bottles of alcoholic goji berry drinks annually, had trademarked the brands of many of the winegrowers in Yinchuan and several of his rivals were out for blood. "We're all worried what will happen to him," said one grower whose brand had been "squatted" by Zhang. "Maybe he'll commit suicide, maybe something else will happen." Zhang had less to worry about in France. Nearby, at the Château de Grand Branet, he had a Chinese neighbor, a fellow tycoon, who understood him. His name was Qu Naijie—not that they were in the same league.

In recent months, Qu had gone on a shopping spree. Christian Delpeuch had been given a secret mandate from Qu to buy more than two dozen châteaux for him. Many transactions did not make the news, but each time a château publicly came under Chinese ownership, the Bordelais reasoned that the Chinese investment was a good sign. These businessmen now had a vested interest in promoting and protecting Bordeaux wines in China.

The only problem was that some Chinese entrepreneurs had a very different business plan in mind.

6

....

All in a Name

It was supposed to be his last job.

Nick Bartman had just wrapped up an eight-month undercover criminal investigation in the textile sector that had taken him from Thailand to Malaysia to Indonesia to central China. He was exhausted after twenty-five years of protecting consumers and businesses by chasing down counterfeiters. To do his work, Bartman sometimes had to engage in some falsification of his own; he often presented himself using one of a number of alternative identities, aided by an average build and features that adapted easily to a variety of nationalities. His work had taken him into the underworld in twenty-five different countries. "Throughout all these experiences, and raiding many hundreds of companies with police, my body compass was forever pointing to China, the de facto center of counterfeits," he said. This last assignment had been no different.

It had seemed like a good idea to stop off at his Hong Kong office and decompress before heading home to Europe. Once there, he shook off his undercover persona effortlessly, and it hadn't take much persuasion from a friend to convince him to delay his flight and attend the 2009 Hong Kong International Wine and Spirits Fair. He had never done any work for the wine industry, but ever since Hong Kong had eliminated its import duties on wine, the wine scene there had been hot.

Within thirty minutes of snapping on his visitor's badge and beginning his stroll of the exposition hall, Bartman noticed a Chinese man scrutinizing the booths and snapping photos of the wines on display. He looked around. The staff at the booths did not seem bothered by him, as though taking photos of their bottles was standard practice. In industries with more experience holding trade fairs in Hong Kong, it would have been a red flag.

He glanced from booth to booth, trying to gauge the atmosphere. None of the booths had posted a NO PHOTOGRAPHS sign, normally standard issue in Hong Kong. It was as though the winegrowers had no idea that the port had a history as a gateway for counterfeiting.

The Chinese man was ready to move on, and Bartman followed him at a discreet distance. Soon, two women joined the man. At one booth, the women asked the staff for business cards and brochures, distracting attention so that the man could take more photos. Bartman sidled close enough to hear their conversation in Mandarin. They were talking about wine sales in China, about copying labels, about the money to be made in counterfeiting. Careless chatter, but they had not suspected that anyone around them could understand what they were saying—the staff at the fair spoke Cantonese, and it was unlikely that any of the Europeans spoke Mandarin.

As Bartman absorbed what he had heard, he noticed several other Chinese visitors kitted out with camera gear, systematically taking pictures of the bottles at the booths. They seemed to be carrying copies of the fair's layout, with the wines that they wanted to photograph preselected and marked.

After he returned to Europe, Bartman began to notice the headlines about wine. Exports to China were booming. He knew that the counterfeiters wouldn't pass up such a juicy opportunity in a fresh, naive market, especially when the wine exporters—at least based on what he'd seen in Hong Kong—were so trusting. In February 2010, Bartman made a self-financed trip to China to assess the extent of the problem. He didn't know wine, but he knew to start with suppliers and traders, so he targeted wine-growing areas and the cities where he figured the sales would be strongest, starting with Beijing. He visited supermarkets, small liquor shops, and warehouses, taking his own photographs to examine later. His pictures were of bottles that he suspected were counterfeit.

A short plane ride took him to Shandong Province, on the east coast of China, which had grown into one of the principal wine-producing regions, ever since Zhang Bishi had decided to start his winery, Changyu, there. Several giant state-owned wineries—not just Changyu, but COFCO, Château Junding, and more—were based in Shandong, in a belt of valleys not far inland from the Bohai Sea ports of Penglai and Yantai, as were dozens more small- and medium-sized wineries, also with fake châteaux, typically a facade attached to the winery's factory or bottling plant. Over the years, Bartman had found that, due to the size of China and poor transportation links, counterfeiters tended to cluster together. Shandong was no different. He visited fifteen of the area's wineries and bottling plants, and the evidence was alarming. He saw counterfeit labels with brands and appellations that were obviously false. The wine itself appeared to be either local Chinese wine or a chemical concoction.

Bartman then drove south through eastern China, visiting around a hundred shops as he traveled from Qingdao to Shanghai to Ningbo to Wenzhou to Xiamen and, finally, to Guangzhou, the capital of Guangdong Province, about seventy-miles from Hong Kong. "It could be said the further from Beijing, the more likely downside issues raise their ugly heads. Living proof are the very southerly cities which can depressingly be a law unto themselves," he observed.

One thing became clear: the greatest problem was in the second- and third-tier Chinese cities. Disposable income was increasing everywhere, and people wanted to buy French wine, but consumers outside Beijing and Shanghai knew next to nothing about it, making them a perfect target for fakes. Counterfeit Château Lafite and Carruades de Lafite were sold out of the same retail shops and wholesale outlets as the authentic items. The Chinese could not read the French-language labels. They might have a general grasp of European geography, but they did not know the location or names of French wine regions or appellations. They were also willing to overpay as a way of showing off their good fortune. A typical bottle of French wine might be priced at 152 yuan, the equivalent of $25, when a good monthly salary in Beijing was $800.

In Qingdao, Bartman discovered that the enterprising local mayor had changed the name of Yan'an Road to Red Wine Street, and twenty-five wine stores had opened their doors in the past couple years. The staff of these stores had no idea if they were selling fake or real Lafite, even though most of the Lafite for sale cost far less than the astronomical prices garnered on the legitimate market. For better or worse, the clerks didn't seem to be in on the scam.

To an experienced Western eye such as Bartman's, the fakes were easy to spot. Bordeaux did not produce port or Syrah, and it was geographically ludicrous to claim that a Languedoc red had been produced in Alsace. There was also more 1998 Bordeaux in China than had ever been exported. The vintage wasn't special—in fact, it was average in quality—but vintage didn't mean anything to the Chinese. Even the bottles were poor quality. Bartman speculated that the counterfeiters were betting on the attraction of the number 8 as a symbol of wealth and the number 9 as a symbol of harmony.

He was content to see that the counterfeiters' work was sloppy. Back when fake Rolexes first started appearing in shops, the second hands jerked and the name was often misspelled. The lack of sophistication on the labels was a sign that wine counterfeiting was still in its infancy. But in his estimation, at least 60 percent of the wine, maybe 70 percent, was fake in one way or another.

At the same time, this job felt urgent to him. Unlike a single, giant corporate client protecting a luxury trademark, French wine was produced by thousands of small growers. In the case of Bordeaux, it was then sold by intermediaries, distancing the producer still further from the market in China. These small companies didn't have a hope of stopping the counterfeiting on their own. The best solution was to form a coalition of brand owners or regions to pool resources and make the investigation feel important in the eyes of Beijing. Collective action would also put some fear in the counterfeiters. One angry winegrower from a distant country wasn't going to cause any worry. Hundreds of angry winegrowers would. But to be truly effective, Bartman knew a client needed Beijing on its side. "If the full force of Beijing's will is provoked, there are few places to run or hide," he said.

Based on experience, Bartman knew that China's central government would crack down on the counterfeiting if given support, but the officials in Beijing themselves knew next to nothing about wine, and they would need to be prodded into action as well. Counterfeiters were preying on Chinese consumers, who were still so new to wine. In Yantai and Penglai, a few wineries bragged about nonexistent joint ventures with foreign wine producers. They created documents confirming the right to import wines into the country. Elaborate brochures rhapsodized about how lucky aristocratic French families were to be doing business with grubby bottling lines in Yantai. It was extraordinary and bold, and no one was doing anything to stop it.

Bartman told his story to the traders in Hong Kong, and then to anyone who would listen at the London International Wine Fair. He contacted wine organizations at the national, regional, and appellation levels in France. He reached out directly to the big brands. He had been sure that the intelligence he'd gathered would sound an alarm. Instead, he met with apathy, boredom, or, worse, amusement.

By April 2010, he was stewing about the lack of concern in Bordeaux and in France's other top wine-producing regions. Some Bordelais believed that counterfeiting was so ingrained in China that there was nothing to be done about it. Others suggested that the fakes would drive Chinese consumers to buy more imported wine from closer to the source of production, which would serve to increase prices. Still others brushed off the worries, blinded by the money to be made in a bull market.

An American winemaker denied any knowledge of counterfeits in China, despite the multitude of photographs provided. Unbelievably, the producers of Niagara Icewine, one of the most copied wines in China, also denied any problem with counterfeiting. Lafite, he knew, had influence, but when he tried to get in touch he was informed that they were well aware of the problem.

He couldn't find a client to hire him.

Bartman feared the winemakers were going to lose complete control of their most valuable asset, their names. He'd seen it before. Initially, the international brand owners in the textile and watch industries had failed to band together and fight, and their trademarks had been plagued by counterfeits ever since. "The administration authority cannot control all things everywhere at all times, and in any event they prioritize. But where they have support from different industries pushing them to focus on particular problems, then things happen," he observed. "It is absolutely, positively, and hopelessly useless for any one wine brand, all the way through to country of wine origin, to beat their own path to sort this out. The problems are too big and widespread. Only a group approach will properly work."

Bartman's persistence eventually paid off. In May, the British wine journalist Jancis Robinson wrote a series of stories based on her conversations with Bartman. The stories caught the eye of the Bordeaux Wine Council. They wanted a meeting. On the way, Bartman made a detour.

Before wrapping up his initial investigation of counterfeit wine in China, Bartman had stopped over in Shenzhen, the city immediately over the border from Hong Kong that was China's very first special economic zone. One of the wine traders there had stupidly given him copies of labels and shipping documents to prove that the French wine he was selling was really from Bordeaux. The address on the shipping document was in Bayonne, France. He decided to pay it a visit.

When he got to the address, he found it was a négociant called Duprat Frères. Pulling out his photographs and documents, Bartman persuaded the managers to search the records for the wine in question. It turned out that some wine had indeed been shipped to the trader. But it was from the Languedoc, not Bordeaux. The trader's documents also listed quantities of wine far greater than what Duprat Frères had shipped to Shenzhen.

Bartman remembered a huge stock of inexpensive Chilean wine sitting in the Shenzhen warehouse. He realized that the most likely explanation was that it was being relabeled as Bordeaux so that it would sell for a much higher price.

The négociant said the deal had been organized by a Chinese broker living in France.

The pieces of the puzzle were falling into place. Past investigations had led Bartman to overseas Chinese communities, hubs for fencing fake goods and laundering money. This case merited a cross-border investigation.

The next day, Bartman finally got a paying client: the Bordeaux Wine Council, or CIVB. There was one caveat: they did not want the investigation to target anyone operating in France, whether or not they were French.

※

Several long months passed before Bartman was told in January 2011 that he could assemble a team of operatives and head back to China. Strangely, he was not authorized to investigate counterfeiters. He was told to limit his activities to buying wine in shops.

He suspected that the counterfeiters would have changed their tactics in the intervening months. He had his eye out for the next evolution in fake wine. His team of four investigators, three men and one woman, hit twelve cities in two weeks, buying suspicious bottles. "I had a rental car that was on its knees, with one hundred bottles of wine wedged into any spare space that could be found," Bartman said.

At night, in the privacy of their hotel rooms, the team photographed the bottles and logged data about the sale. The paper trail that had led Bartman to Bayonne was paying off. A pattern was emerging. Many southern traders, not just the one in Shenzhen, were apparently relabeling cheap imported wine and selling it as premium Bordeaux. More recently, they had concentrated on putting fake French labels on Chinese wine in Chinese bottles, rather than go through the trouble of importing wine from Chile or elsewhere. This provided even more profits for the fraudsters, as they no longer had to pay import duties or taxes of 48 percent. Chinese wine was readily available from the vineyards near the state-owned wineries. The only things they needed to supply for the con were some decent labels, bar codes, and paperwork that authenticated the wine as French.

Most of the paperwork was genuine in some aspect. "It's a myth that counterfeiters fake paperwork. It's actually pretty difficult to fake official paperwork with all the stamps," Bartman said. "It's much easier to make a small order and get original documents." The documents would be used again and again, until they seemed out of date, and then another order would be placed. The small influx of imported wine also lent some legitimacy to the business.

In Bartman's opinion, a small order that came every six to eight months should be a red flag to Bordeaux's winegrowers and négociants. It probably meant counterfeiting was going on, he told them.

Every instinct from his years investigating counterfeiters in China told Bartman to head to the source—the wineries and bottling plants. But he had to wait until his client gave him the green light.

Frustrated, Bartman dispersed his team. Months passed. Finally, he got word: he was allowed to investigate counterfeiting. In the meantime, thousands of fake bottles of wine had flooded into the market.

❋

In May 2011, the CIVB instructed Bartman to limit his investigation to the south, which was unfortunate, since most of China's wine production was located in the north. With yet another restriction hampering his work, Bartman targeted wine-trading companies, shippers, and warehouses.

The warehouses were a disappointment. The counterfeiters didn't keep much stock, because the wine could be ordered, bottled, labeled, and delivered in five days from the wineries in the north to the clients in the south. Even more frustrating, everything pointed to the northern regions surrounding Yantai and Penglai in Shandong and a county on the Bohai Sea in Hebei Province called Changli, as being the hubs of illicit wine production. Traders let it slip that more than 80 percent of the fake wine in China came from one of these three places.

From years of raiding and shutting down counterfeiters, Bartman thought it would be a mistake to target the southern traders, raiding the warehouses and shippers, without hitting the suppliers at the same time. They had only one shot. The criminals would scatter, companies would hide evidence, and his cover and those of his operatives would be blown. As a rule, counterfeiters never returned to their old terrain; the danger of discovery was too great. The penalty for producing fake, potentially fatal, food items under Chinese consumer-protection laws was imprisonment; severe infringers of public safety were punished with execution. Consequently, the stakes were high for Bartman and his operatives.

"I try to make sure my photo is never taken, but I'm there for the raid, and people have phones with cameras," said Bartman. He worried that his photo would be posted on QQ, a Chinese microblogging, instant messaging, and online chat service that had more than eighty million users, most of them in China. Counterfeiters kept their employees in line with threats and reprisals. They wouldn't hesitate to send thugs after spies trying to put them out of business.

Bartman grew increasingly irritated that the operation was being compromised by micromanagement from Bordeaux. The way he saw it, they paid for his experience and intuition, which trumped their inexperience and misguided instincts. His gut told him to head north. He disobeyed his client and took his operatives to Changli, 185 miles east of Beijing. About one hundred wineries were located in the vicinity. The city had been nicknamed "China's Bordeaux" by the national media, but the wine from Changli, fake or real, had a funny taste, and it was generally considered to be of bad quality. There was little to recommend Changli for wine tourists, but the local counterfeiters seemed to be doing a brisk trade.

Bartman had a list of twenty-five suspect suppliers. None of them were returning his calls. He imagined they were too busy panicking. The police had begun a second wave of raids following the airing of a documentary about Changli's wine wholesale market that had aired on the state-owned China Central Television (CCTV) just before Christmas in 2010. For maximum shock value, the CCTV program had shown footage of a sales manager admitting that some wines made in Qingdao contained only 20 percent fermented grape juice, the remainder sugar water and an alarming concoction of chemicals. Some of the additives had been linked to headaches, irregular heartbeat, and cancer. When the video went viral after its broadcast in December, the local authorities had Beijing on their back, and thus had no choice but to act. The police raided the area's wineries.

The counterfeiters' big mistake was producing fake bottles of Great Wall wine, which was owned by COFCO. The managers at Great Wall Wine Company grew increasingly angry about the forgeries. They suspected that the Changli police might be protecting local companies, so they appealed directly to Beijing. It was widely believed that the CCTV documentary was the result of that appeal. Bartman admired this kind of maneuvering. It got the job done while letting the local authorities save face.

In the months that followed the documentary, according to Chinese state-controlled media, three wineries in Changli—Jiahua, Yeli, and Genghao—were shut down. Authorities froze corporate accounts worth $427,000 and seized 5,114 cases of falsely labeled wine and nineteen templates for forging labels. One receipt showed that Jiahua had sold eight thousand bottles of fake wine to a buyer in Beijing. The company sold 2.4 million bottles of wine a year, according to CCTV.

Five individuals were sentenced to prison terms ranging from seven to fifteen years. A sixth, a former wine company deputy manager named Wang Chunping, was sentenced to life in prison and forfeited all of his personal property. Wang had been one of the earliest wine counterfeiters in China, as far as the authorities could tell, and he had been tampering with wine since at least 1998. He began by ordering his staff to take the grape pulp and skins left over from the winemaking process and add water, sugar, alcohol, and yeast to them. He sold half of the subsequent production to two winemakers in Changli. According to company documents, between March 2008 and December 2010, Wang and the winemakers had earned more than 28 million yuan from bottling and selling the mixture as real wine.

From Bartman's perspective, the Changli scandal was an exercise in applying the right laws for maximum effect. Had Great Wall pressed for charges of intellectual-property infringement, little would have happened. Chinese authorities rarely gave culprits for these crimes more than a slap on the wrist, because businesses were supposed to take care of their own brands. Fraud, deception of the public, and endangering consumer health and safety were another matter entirely.

The raids and the documentary were the direct result of a campaign code-named Bright Sword launched by the Ministry of Public Security in November 2010 to halt the production and sale of fake goods, targeting a range of culprits from organized crime to wine counterfeiters. Across the country, the police had so far confiscated more than 30 tons of bulk wines and 13.5 million fake bottles, caps, and labels worth 2 billion yuan, or $306 million. Another crackdown happened to coincide with Bartman's arrival in Changli.

He quickly discovered that the police had raided forty businesses, detaining thirty senior managers—so many that they could not all be accommodated in the local jail. The spillover was put under guard in a hotel. According to Bartman, the police had forced the senior managers to pay for their rooms and food on their own credit cards.

He decided to put his efforts into helping the local government authorities. After a few phone calls, he arranged an evening gathering for eleven officials. He provided them with his list of targets, in case they were not already among the businesses set to be raided by the police, and gave a forty-five-minute crash course on French wine—what to look for on the label and bottle to determine if the wine was fake. He explained what happened in Bordeaux, how prices were set, and what an appellation was. He even pulled out a map to show them where France's wine-producing regions were located. It was information the officials desperately needed, and he could see their spirits rising. At one point, he realized that he'd given them evidence for charging the managers they had in custody with additional crimes. The Chinese officials had focused on counterfeit Chinese wine with labels they could read. Now they had evidence of forged Bordeaux.

At dinner, Bartman and the officials unanimously agreed that the local wine was to be avoided. Beer was the beverage of choice.

The next day, Bartman gave the same presentation to the powerful health and safety office, pressing Bordeaux's case and gaining a commitment from the officials that they would clean up the local wine trade.

A ten-hour drive took Bartman to Penglai, "where wine was grown rather than made," as Bartman put it. Penglai marketed itself as one of the great coastal wine regions of the world, a sister to Bordeaux, the Napa Valley, and Cape Town. A sign on the highway pointed the way to "Nava Valley."

Presenting themselves as a European businessman and his Chinese assistants, Bartman's team quickly found evidence of wine fraud. One factory hid a bottling line for counterfeit wine behind a false wall that could be accessed only from a neighboring business that manufactured metal components. Another operation was hidden in an apartment behind a retail shop. When Bartman walked through a hidden door in a wardrobe in the apartment, he found "a Heidelberg printing machine churning out reels of poor-quality counterfeit labels."

The most disturbing revelation came from a wine factory boss. The boss was new to the wine business, so he'd found a Chinese partner in France who arranged a deal to import bottled and bulk wine from one of the estates. He had registered the estate's trademark in China in anticipation of their joint business, but it hadn't worked out with the château and he'd ripped up their contract. He claimed he had since found another château to work with and was bottling its wine under the other château's brand. To make it look legitimate, he had counterfeited French bar codes.

That was bad enough, but Bartman doubted that there was a new French partner. There was no sign of imported wine in the factory, but there was plenty of Chinese wine nearby. With a registered French brand, a French label, and a French bar code, he had a lucrative business.

But unlike in Changli County, Beijing was not pressing down on the local police. In fact, the police were downright hostile. They allowed the local wine board to obstruct every move taken by the investigators. It was the familiar stench of protection, bribery, and corruption. Bartman and his operatives soon packed up and left.

✳

As the Bordelais emptied their cellars into China by the container load, the CIVB had asked the châteaux to register their brands. Few took the advice. But counterfeiters weren't the only threat to a wine brand's intellectual property. There were also brand squatters.

Canny entrepreneurs realized that China was a first-to-file nation. The China Patent Trademark Office granted the rights to a trademark to the first person to register it. Prior use meant nothing. In September 2011, American Grenada Holdings, a shadowy holding company domiciled in the British Virgin Islands and doing business as Megara, had registered the trademarks for a slew of wine brands. Megara now owned the right in China to the names of several brands and second wines from famous châteaux, including Les Brulières de Beychevelle, Connétable Talbot, Domaine de Baron'arques, Lafleur Chevalier, Terra Burdigala, and several of the first labels, including Châteaux Certan de May de Certan, Latour à Pomerol, Les Carmes Haut-Brion, and Château Pavie, a Saint-Émilion First Growth. It didn't matter that many of these wines had been sold in China for years, or that they were available for purchase in most wine-drinking markets. The only way to trump first registration was to prove a preponderant presence in China, and in such a young market, few French wines could hope to do that.

That same month, the Beijing Intellectual Property Management agency registered seventy-nine wine brands on behalf of a single client. In addition to the name, all of the Bordeaux appellations, so vital to selling wine to consumers, were registered. Even the 1855 Classification itself was trademarked. Other Bordeaux properties were falling left and right. Several companies had registered versions of "Médoc," including Mido Trading, based in Zhejiang Province. A wine company in Inner Mongolia registered "Pomerol." It was nothing less than a full-on brand attack.

Brand squatting was a low-risk, low-energy occupation compared to counterfeiting. Trademarking a brand from Bordeaux was a business opportunity requiring an investment of about $700, but it paid good dividends and attracted its own variety of crooks. An entry-level brand squatter might hold trademarks on a few products, not all related to wine, and some of which were legitimate. Often the name would be slightly misspelled or would combine two well-known brand names, as in the case of "Mouton Latour."

The next level of brand squatter displayed more professionalism, focusing exclusively on wine brands, sometimes trademarking everything on the label. In one extreme case, a company in Yantai registered not only the name of the estate but the owner's name. More often, they trademarked symbols. The back label of wine sold in China usually contained an easily pronounceable Chinese name for customers who could not read the wine's language of origin. The Chinese name might be a transliteration of the wine's original name, but more often it was a character or a word with a symbolic connection.

For instance, Château Angélus was known as "Kin Chung," or "Golden Bell," for the bell on the front label and the name of the estate's second wine, Le Carillon de l'Angélus. China had become such a big market for Angélus that the bell was taking over as the château's identity. Hubert de Boüard sold 50 percent of his 7,500 cases to China each year, so he was distressed to find that trademark number 9105485, held by a man named Li Daozhi, was for "Ka Si Te Jin Zhong," which roughly translated as "Castel's Angélus." Similarly, Dongguan R&O Sovilong Trading Company held the trademark for Aubertangelusbouardlaforest; Megara had registered La Fleur de Boüard; and the Tianjin Food Import and Export Stock Company had the trademark for brands and images featuring gold bells. Château Angélus's deputy managing director, Stéphanie de Boüard-Rivoal, was perplexed. "We're not even sure what they're doing with the trademarks," she said.

❊

Nearly a year later, in July 2012, Bartman briefly returned again to China on the trail of wine fraud. This time his targets were the printers in Shenzhen. If you needed a fake label, any kind of fake label, Shenzhen was your place. It wasn't that the printers in Shenzhen didn't print legitimate labels, but many would be out of business if they depended solely on legitimate orders.

Shenzhen, a major city located immediately north of the Hong Kong Special Administrative Region, was China's most porous border crossing. Whether through "ants" or more sophisticated smuggling operations, thousands of cases of expensive wine came illegally into the mainland via Shenzhen. Cheap wine also came across the border, usually through legal routes. If you did not have scruples, it made commercial sense to slap a fake French label, particularly one claiming an origin in Bordeaux, on some of the bottles.

Each day, Bartman and his team visited the printing shops to look through their work. Everyone seemed to have some version of the Château Lafite label. Counterfeiters were often nervous about using exact copies, so they designed labels and created names that were similar but just a little different. Some were ridiculous, like a label for

"Lafite Gooditem" produced in the "Minervois." But to a consumer whose only language was Chinese, the label was convincing. It had a picture of a castle and listed the year of vintage, the appellation, and the alcohol content. The counterfeiters also included a bar code in the label's design. They'd search the GS1 identification system website, where all bar codes are listed, and find the bar code of the wine they were copying. For instance, the bar code 3296332007108 belongs to Château Lafite. The counterfeiters changed the last number from 8 to 9, for which there was no registration. Any customer who discovered that the label was wrong would most likely be lulled into thinking that there had been a design mistake, and that the wine was real. The printers also had what looked to be official customs documents giving them the right to print labels. If inspectors arrived—which seemed unlikely—they were covered.

Bartman suspected that the labels were designed by people back in France or some of the spies he'd spotted at the Hong Kong Wine and Dine Festival. As it happened, he got to meet one of the forgers. The manager of a public relations agency in Shenzhen proudly explained to him how her company provided exemplary customer service to Chinese wine importers. She personally visited the wineries in the north of China to get the specifications for the wine labels. Then her employees surfed the Internet looking for names, logos, appellations, and images that could be used to cobble together the artwork. "She told us it was a simple formula, low risk, basic work, and easy money," Bartman said. He noticed that the woman drove a BMW worth $100,000, so he figured she was telling the truth about the easy money.

The next link was transportation. The counterfeiters couldn't operate without truckers to transport the labeled wine. A haul from Shenzhen to the wine-growing regions crossed five provinces and took more than twelve hours. The chances of getting caught were not negligible, but the trucking companies weren't likely to let a European man investigate the merchandise they were carrying. Bartman lucked out. A bored truck driver waiting outside one of the label-printing outfits for his delivery was happy to chat with him.

Like the U.S. states, each province in China has its own license plate. Truckers are less likely to get pulled over for inspections if their truck has a local plate. So the company supplied the driver with plates for each province, paying the drivers extra to switch them along the way and keep silent. The rolls and rolls of wine labels were hidden among legitimate consignments on the drive north. On his return, his truck was packed with fake wine to be delivered to customers. The turnaround time from order to delivery was usually five days.

Bartman could feel that this was his big break. A well-orchestrated raid could knock a serious hole in the counterfeit wine trade. Many wine-growers in France had no idea that their names and pictures of their homes had been stolen and were being used to sell fake wine to unwit-ting Chinese customers. But the investigation went belly-up.

Back in Bordeaux, the CIVB was troubled. The council represented 7,000 winegrowers, 300 négociants, and 95 courtiers. Budgets and strat-egies were approved by committee, and the cost of the investigation had mounted. At the same time, the CIVB leadership was facing decisions about an investigation whose objectives it didn't completely grasp. Wine fraud was not new to Bordeaux, but the Bordelais had difficulty com-prehending the complexity of fraud on this scale. Illicit print shops in Shenzhen seemed a long way from fake bottles of Bordeaux on store shelves. The CIVB leadership grew nervous and indecisive. Then the board made the decision: it was time to pull the plug.

Bartman and his team had spent three weeks building covers and reeling in the fraudsters. All of that effort had been wasted, and he was furious.

Then in November, the CIVB approached him to restart the investi-gation. They had decided on a more aggressive approach that included securing the trademarks of Bordeaux's appellations, and they needed to show Beijing they were serious. Bartman was still smoldering, but he agreed. He wanted to nail the counterfeiters. Finally, the CIVB was giv-ing him the green light to focus on the bottling businesses in Changli and Penglai.

He wasn't entirely surprised to discover that the wine counterfeiters were still open for business—even in Changli. The police raids had ended. The bottling companies were so comfortable about what they were doing that they were happy to have a Western man and Chinese woman take a look around as they decided what wine to buy. When he quizzed the counterfeiters, they claimed that they had a direct relationship with a French supplier, which had been set up by a Chinese intermediary living in France. Bartman knew in his gut that he had to get on the ground in France if there was to be any hope of stopping the counterfeiting before it spiraled completely out of control. It was standard for counterfeiting rings to have operations in several countries. He believed that the counterfeiters had people in France ordering legitimate wine and getting authentic documents as cover for their illicit operations. And, most likely, they were living in Bordeaux.

❃

Bartman pulled into the parking lot of the Shandong Yantai Mingyang Wine Company near the center of Penglai. Bartman had dangled some lines, and the owner of Mingyang, a man named Zhang Quang Ming, had taken the bait. The winery, Bartman noted, was prominently located and built to impress. At the entrance was a guest drop on a ramp, with a classy canopy overhead, and the door slid open automatically as Bartman walked in. In the reception area he noticed the photographs of French vineyards adorning the walls and the antique winemaking equipment set up to look like a mini museum. There was a sweeping staircase that led to Zhang's office. Bartman and his operatives climbed the stairs in anticipation.

They weren't disappointed. The office had space for fifty workers but held just four enormous sofas and a coffee table decorated with wine books. Zhang was finishing a meeting with a customer, a fashionably dressed woman adorned with expensive jewelry, who had just placed an order for fake wine to supply to supermarkets in northern China. With that deal done, Zhang turned his attention to Bartman, whom he believed to be another potential client.

The wines Zhang had to offer were lined up on a long sideboard. His talented in-house winemaker had earned her enology degree from a leading Chinese university. She wore a white lab coat, and showed Bartman her most recent attempts at faking Bordeaux.

Bartman could see that many of the wines were variations on wines produced by a company named Michel Gonet et Fils. Zhang had registered the Michel Gonet trademarks in China, and the label design and shape was a copy of the design used by the Gonets, right down to the drawing of their home. Zhang had taken particular care to copy Michel Gonet's legitimate bar codes so that any check would take the searcher back to Michel Gonet in France. But Michel Gonet was only one of Zhang's targets. He also produced fake Rothschild brands as well as the wines of Maison Bouey, a Bordeaux négociant he had visited, and other estates.

In the role of a hardened crook, Bartman expressed skepticism at Zhang's outfit. He didn't want to get caught, after all. To reassure him, Zhang produced fake paperwork that "proved" he was using imported French wine. In reality, Zhang filled the bottles with Chinese plonk. It was so simple. He eagerly led Bartman to see the rest of his operation.

In a separate building on the same lot, Zhang showed him the areas used for winemaking, bottling, and storage. It was a sleek operation, using the latest equipment. It was here that his enologist made wine from fruit that Zhang bought from subsistence farmers working patches of land squeezed between the shacks they called home. There was no attempt to produce quality fruit, and the grape varieties grown had no relation to the grape varieties on the label. It wouldn't have passed a taste test against the real thing, but it seemed clear that few Chinese consumers had experience drinking real Bordeaux.

When Zhang invited him to lunch, Bartman accepted without hesitation.

The restaurant was dingy, and they drank bad wine from dirty, chipped water glasses. Zhang had the habit of grimacing in a manly way when he drank wine, as if he were tossing back baijiu. Zhang admitted to Bartman that he didn't know anything about wine, except that it was profitable. As they threw back glass after glass, he proudly revealed the linchpin in his operation: his son, Zhang Taiyang. Like many Chinese with money and connections, he'd been able to get a passport for his son, then a visa to study in France, where he was enrolled in a

Bordeaux wine school. While his son studied, Zhang had busied himself setting up a winery and a bottling line. Then he had considered their options. In the end, he decided that the most money could be made from fake Bordeaux.

In France, Zhang Taiyang wheedled introductions to châteaux and négociants through his sommelier school. Like many of the Chinese "students," he offered to help them export their wine to China. He targeted wines that had promising names. He particularly liked "Gonet," or "Gounai" in pinyin. Like Lafite, it was easy to pronounce.

Zhang Taiyang spent a number of months in Bordeaux, easily blending into the swarm of Chinese students in the city. He introduced himself on the Place de Bordeaux, and pitched himself as an agent for négociants including LD Vins, Maison Bouey, and Producta. He imported wine and offered consulting services, and presented himself in China as a "French Bordeaux chief sommelier CIVB." Not surprisingly, that impressive title didn't exist. The CIVB had a school that offered short courses on Bordeaux wine, but they did not certify sommeliers. The CIVB denied that Zhang Taiyang had attended its courses, but it turned out he had attended classes at another school, Cafa Formations.

While Zhang Quang Ming waited for the Bordeaux wine bought by his son to arrive in China, he filled his bottles with Chinese wine kitted out with fake labels, capsules, corks, and bar codes for the copied French brand. He registered the trademark for the Bordeaux wine as a coup de grâce. That way, even if he no longer had a legitimate supply, a winegrower couldn't come after him for intellectual property infringement. He was selling only a brand he owned. As usual, the official documents from the imports from Bordeaux were the only proof he needed to show to customers and officials that his wine was genuine. And sales were booming.

"The whole package was one big plausible scam with each and every element thought through and planned over some considerable time," said Bartman. "Customers would be easily duped due to the prominence, quality, and layout of the place."

Bartman figured Zhang had revealed his con because Bartman had posed as a Westerner living in China with the ability to check out Zhang's story in France. And Bartman had perfected the role of corrupt businessman.

"He thought we were as big of criminals as him," said Bartman.

When Zhang Taiyang returned to China, his father rewarded him with a white Porsche Cayenne. The son then set up his own business in Qingdao, through which he served as a consultant to local enforcement agencies. He helped the police identify fake French wine but charged nothing for his services. He was clearly up to something.

Bartman convinced Zhang Quang Ming to introduce him to his son. They drove four hours to Qingdao, and, over a meal in an expensive restaurant one night, Bartman tried to lead Zhang Taiyang into selling him fake wine, but the young man was too clever. "He shuddered at the very mention of counterfeits," Bartman remembered. "If I hadn't known the true story, I might even have believed him." Zhang Taiyang wouldn't even be drawn into drinking wine. All the young man would say was that he could help Bartman make more money than could be dreamed of.

Several clues led Bartman to believe that a counterfeiter was shipping wine via a Chinese-run company in Paris that shared an address with a Chinese Evangelical Baptist church and an agency offering accommodation addresses—mail drops for individuals and businesses that do not have a residence or an office where they can receive mail and other deliveries.

Bartman had seen this before: it was probably a "black bank" in China's so-called shadow-banking sector, which included everything from posh wealth management firms to pawnshops. Small- and medium-sized businesses couldn't always get loans from regular banks, so people with extra cash offered it to an informal lending network, earning interest on top. The first black banks had appeared under Mao, but they were still thriving in China and other places with a significant Chinese diaspora. Black banks allowed for convenient cash transfers from one currency to another. A deposit could be made in Shanghai in renminbi and withdrawn in Paris in euros. Some analysts feared that black banks carried so much debt that if their loans defaulted, they could bring down the Chinese economy.

The black banks operated from outwardly innocuous businesses so that their clients could come and go unnoticed. Bartman knew about one black bank in Dubai that was run out of a hotel. It was a clever front, as clients could check in with empty suitcases and check out with their luggage full of cash. Although ultimately Bartman never had an opportunity to definitively confirm this, instinct and experience told him that Zhang and his son might be caught up in a larger crime ring.

Bartman began to consider how he might definitively identify the Chinese operators in France who were facilitating counterfeiting and brand squatting. They had to be set up in a way similar to how Zhang had set up his son in Bordeaux, though it wouldn't necessarily be a family member who sent an agent to France. His thoughts kept returning to the Chinese Evangelical Baptist church in Paris. He wondered if, in addition to making Chinese students feel at home, it was laundering money.

Chinese students were typically contacted by strangers soon after their arrival in France: Would they be interested in making a couple hundred euros to go shopping? The shopping list included luxury goods, usually small items—watches, for instance—that could be shipped back to China and resold for three to five times the price in Paris. In this way, money was laundered at a profit.

Illegal immigration was also a thriving side business. It could cost $10,000 to $15,000 to get someone with false papers into France. "They say a Chinese person never dies," said Bartman. Instead, someone assumes the identity of the recently departed.

A Chinese person living in France could also register a French company using an accommodation address. They could provide the local mail drop to register trademarks and apply for product bar codes.

"All of this could be uplifted as a package and transmitted to China to provide the perfect front," Bartman explained. "Wine carrying all this information would, for all intents and purposes, quite wrongly appear to be French."

❋

It wasn't long before Bartman noticed hostility when he contacted some of the Chinese targets whose names he'd been compiling. They had been warned. The obstructionist, state-controlled wine board had been busy, telling people that the Westerner who was visiting too many wineries probably wasn't a potential client.

That meant the investigation would have to wind down soon. "Nobody had yet connected us with our real work, but it would surely only be a matter of time before doors were locked behind us in preparation for another sort of interrogation," Bartman explained.

Before he left China, however, he had one more opportunity to gather vital proof of counterfeiting. It was December, and he was sure it would be a lucky month for finding trucks carrying fake wine. The Chinese New Year was only a few weeks away. People were placing their orders for gifts for government officials and business partners and for parties. He would put good money on the trucks being full.

In reality, he needed at least two to three months more on the ground to nail all the counterfeiting operations on his list, but the CIVB's budget couldn't take it. He decided to focus on a few hot spots. With eight days of legwork, he had put together a list of confirmed targets. Five of them were subsidiaries of counterfeiters in Yantai and in the Penglai region. In all, his list of targets included bottling factories, wineries, label printers, transporters, and warehouses. He estimated that the total value of the targeted counterfeits was $37 million. Closing these businesses would not be easy. Doing so would result in unemployment and reduced tax receipts. Some serious guanxi was involved. His only hope was a coordinated sweep from Beijing.

Conscious that the crime sweep could have political implications, the CIVB asked the French embassy in Beijing to get involved. Bartman hunkered down with French police and customs agents to prepare a dossier for the central government. His team put together detailed reports on every target, including a list of its customers, label suppliers, and transporters.

Days later, the French and the Chinese officials sat down on either side of a massive table in the offices of the enforcement division of the powerful General Administration of Quality Supervision, Inspection and Quarantine. Four French officials had come with Bartman to the meeting; the Chinese had sent a taciturn group of fourteen.

For the next two hours, Bartman presented his evidence. The

astonished Chinese officers explained that they had sent officers to Penglai and Yantai to investigate shady wine dealings, but they'd come back with nothing more than suspicion. They now offered full support for the necessary raids.

A task force was assembled. Local and regional government authorities were to be told to clear their calendars but given no further information. On the day of the raids, the cell phones and radios of the local and regional police were to be confiscated. Only one senior officer in each squad car would be given the destination the squadron was raiding. The teams quickly closed down their targets, rounding up employees, sealing doors, and seizing paperwork and wine bottles. Mingyang, the company owned by Zhang Quang Ming, was among the companies hit. It would take months to wade through all the evidence.

Bartman was satisfied with how the sweep had gone, but he couldn't quell the frustration of knowing how many people were walking free. The warehouses, label-printing shops, and shipping companies had not been touched.

Disappointed, he and his team began the tiresome work of examining every confiscated bottle, cataloging the telltale signs of trickery. The contents were determined to be wine if they left sediment on tissue. Many bottles contained no wine at all, only an alcoholic concoction. Meanwhile, the managers, directors, and owners of the raided companies were brought in for questioning by the police. Bartman and his team tried to stay out of sight, but it was impossible. Outside the bureau, they sensed they were being followed. Many suspected their phones were being hacked. They knew their cover had been blown when bribes and threats of physical harm started to arrive. And these arrived regularly.

To strengthen the state's evidence against the suspected criminals, it was agreed that a selection of full wine bottles would be shipped to France to be tested in a lab. Chinese scientists did not have the knowledge of wine to determine if the wine was fake Bordeaux. The bottles were given to the CIVB for shipment with the promise that the results would be available in twenty-eight days.

A few days later, word came that three bottles had been broken, the evidence destroyed. The CIVB informed the Chinese that it would take longer to get the results. The Chinese were furious. The timeline for the trial was not very flexible. But it got worse: "When the results did eventually come back, they were written in French and were nothing more than a string of descriptive laboratory terms, numbers, and percentages that meant nothing to the Chinese authorities," said Bartman. "There was no summary confirming the wine was fake"—even though Bartman considered that it all was.

For Bartman, it was the end of his investigation into wine fraud. His cover was blown.

He was appalled by the outcome. "What started out to be the perfect storm resulted in nothing more than mediocrity, with lost opportunities in France as well as China. Our long-term damage to counterfeiters was estimated at €30 million, but this was low compared with what could have been achieved," he said. "Worse still, the Chinese government's legal actions against counterfeiters were hampered by the shenanigans in France."

Just as amazingly, Bartman learned, his prime suspect, Zhang Tai-yang, was still working with the Bordeaux négociants from his base in Qingdao. He and his father were selling "Lesparre" wines, including a special cuvée purporting to originate in the Médoc and a Merlot from the Périgord. Grudgingly, the CIVB had admitted to Bartman that Zhang Tiyang was most likely a counterfeiter, but the botched sting and the desire to control bad press meant that they had not definitively proved or publicized the allegations. There was no rogue's gallery of counterfeiters. Dozens of négociants and hundreds of châteaux thus remained vulnerable to suspected rogue operators.

✵

When the Gonet family discovered that the Shandong Yantai Mingyang Wine Company, sometimes translated as Yantai Eagle or Yantai Ming, held the trademark in China for their company's name "Michel Gonet," named for the father, as well as "Lesparre," the name of one of their estates, their first instinct was to negotiate. The Gonets produced more than a million bottles of wine from their land in Bordeaux and Champagne. They distributed their wines themselves, dealing primarily with supermarkets, so they were accustomed to tough deals. But every time they tried to buy back their brand from Zhang's company, the price went up. In a round of offers and counteroffers in early 2013, the Gonets were quoted a price of $300,000. This didn't feel like a negotiation. It felt like a ransom demand. Yantai Mingyang had even trademarked the first name of the owner's son, the wine company's export director Charles-Henri Gonet.

When he heard the news, Charles-Henri was reduced to inarticulate anger. After a few minutes, however, he quieted and recovered some of his normal equilibrium. The Chinese could have his first name. All he wanted was his father's name back.

A European trademark lawyer named Celine Baillet said she had once dealt with a Chinese man who had registered nearly three hundred Bordeaux château names. "He just needed to sell back two or three of them to make it worthwhile. He had no intention of physically producing the wines; it was little more than a hobby."

As a convenience, the same Chinese agencies that registered trademarks also offered negotiation services for "recovering" a brand—although they didn't call it that. Instead, the agencies allowed you to ask that a registration be canceled if it wasn't used for three years. The charge for the basic service was $450, not including hourly staff fees. It cost another $550—again, before hourly staff fees—to file a request with administrative authorities, and a $650 minimum to launch legal proceedings against a trademark infringer.

The problem of brand squatting had grown as the négociants tried to get more brands into the Chinese market. Wary of potential lawsuits, distributors started checking the Chinese trademark database before agreeing to order a wine. They refused to import anything for which a trademark was held by a different party in China. They didn't want to waste time and money promoting a wine that would get hung up in a trademark fight. A brand squatter could thus effectively keep a wine-grower out of the Chinese market at a time when China was the only customer with money.

Brand squatting had become a big enough issue that in March 2011 the Bordeaux Chamber of Commerce had offered a seminar on how to register a brand in China. Among those who attended was Bruno Finance, the export manager in Asia for the négociant Yvon Mau. He had spent enough time in China to have seen how serious the threat was. The problem was that the people who found potential buyers, made the endless sales pitches, negotiated the prices, developed distribution, and chased down payments were the négociants, not the châteaux. But the négociants could not register the trademarks for the wines; only the winegrowers could do that. And too many of the producers assumed they could defend their brands in China—they'd been in business for centuries, after all. Finance hoped he could light a fire under Yvon Mau's suppliers, but he wasn't optimistic.

A few days later, his mood brightened. DBR Lafite's chairman, Christophe Salin, had filed a bunch of trademark lawsuits against Chinese companies in China and had just won his first victory against Lafite counterfeiters.

The previous November, the Changsha Intermediate People's Court had posted on the Internet a live video feed, broadcast on China Court Network, of a trial featuring DBR Lafite. In the trial, Lafite's lawyer Li Yongbo attacked the Shenzhen trade company Jinghongde Corporation for using the trademark "Lafite Family" and a version of Lafite's distinctive five-arrow graphic to sell wine. Li explained that Lafite had registered its brand in China in 1996 and its five-arrow graphic in 2001. He also took the time for a primer on Bordeaux, including the essentials of the 1855 Classification. But he admitted that one source of Lafite's problem was that it had not trademarked the popular transliteration of its name, "La Fei Te." Predators had swarmed, hawking wines with names such as "Lafite Empire," "Lafite Field," and "Lafite Legend." The great Bordeaux First Growth, Li argued, had had no choice but to defend itself. On February 28, 2011, the court decided in Lafite's favor, and awarded Lafite 300,000 yuan ($48,000) in compensation. Li was jubilant. The case, he said, laid a sound legal basis for safeguarding the winemaker's civil rights.

But a month after the decision, the China Central Television network ran an exposé on its program *Focus* revealing that unscrupulous traders were blatantly selling fake Lafite at the hugely popular China Sugar and Wine Fair in Chengdu. The network reported that in one year Zhejiang Province alone consumed thirty thousand bottles of "Lafite." Christophe Salin would file more than 160 trademark lawsuits against Chinese companies in China that year, as police seized five thousand bottles of the fake Lafite. The First Growth had gone on the attack, and soon it would be known that the company would defend itself.

"If things go well, with the cooperation of the Chinese government, fake Lafite will be eradicated within two years," Salin told the Shanghai media.

There were an untold number of Lafite look-alikes on the Chinese market, and only one came from Pauillac.

❀

Months later, the half-finished job still nagged at Bartman. Sitting in a pub in Europe, he said there were loose ends that he would like to see tied up. He had been frustrated that the CIVB, however good their intentions, had not accepted rational advice. Bartman was sure he could find Chinese operators in Bordeaux and Paris, if he were just given the chance to run a cross-border investigation. He'd been conducting anti-counterfeiting cases for twenty-five years, but this one was different. "This was the one capable of making a difference to so many more individuals than the normal international corporate client," Bartman said, thinking of the thousands of family-run châteaux that lacked the large pockets of a multinational corporation.

Over the length of his career, Bartman estimated that he had done at least $300 million in damage to counterfeiters. He knew it was essential for the French vintners to form a coalition and make it so difficult, expensive, and dangerous to fake Bordeaux that the counterfeiters would move on to easier targets.

"Counterfeit control is a mental game with the bad guys," he said.

7

....

Standoff

By the middle of 2011, fake wine was not the only threat to Bordeaux's commerce in China. Demand was slipping. A crackdown on smuggling across the notoriously porous Hong Kong and Macau borders had cooled the interest of black market speculators in classified growths. And prices had risen so high that even the most loyal and passionate customers worried for Bordeaux's future.

"I believe the high price of Bordeaux wines may eventually hurt the image of Bordeaux," said George Tong, a respected observer. "A fine bottle of Bordeaux has become a luxury good fewer and fewer people can enjoy. It might not turn out to be such a good investment as the release price is so high, and there is not a lot of room for the price to appreciate."

Tong had a reputation for only buying wines he liked to drink, which set him apart from most Chinese newcomers to the wine scene. He was vice president of his family's toy manufacturing company, Wong Hau Plastic Works & Trading Company, which operated quite profitably under the distinctly Chinese slogan "You Name It, We Make It"— profitably enough to land him on *Asia Tatler*'s "500 List" of Hong Kong's power elite. In 2003, he and his wife, Kathy, had started buying Bordeaux classified growths en primeur, then added fine wines from

Burgundy, gradually experimenting with cult labels from California. The quiet, elegant couple were regulars on the black-tie wine circuit, and had educated themselves on the nuances of vintage and terroir until they could knowledgeably discuss the merits of a 1953 Château Margaux or a rare tawny port from 1855.

As the 2010 vintage landed on the market, Tong noticed that Chinese customers were showing the true nature of their interest in the wine. The potential for profit was all that mattered, and that meant buyers were easily influenced by price—but not in the usual manner. "Berry Bros. & Rudd had six hundred cases, first tranche, of 2010 Château Pontet-Canet for Hong Kong. It sold out in less than twenty minutes, even though prices had increased compared to 2009," Tong said. "For Cos d'Estournel, although prices were lower by 10 percent . . . merchants had difficulty selling it."

The quality of the wine—pristine, sophisticated, powerful—was beside the point. Investors feared that Cos d'Estournel, which had tripled its release price with the 2009 vintage, left them no room for profit. And what mattered most was whether the estate name was grand enough to be used to open a Chinese banquet—and if it wasn't a First Growth, then the determining factor was the wine's price tag and image. If the guests didn't marvel at the money spent on the wine, the wine was worthless as a gift. It didn't convey the appropriate gei mianzi, or respect.

Other, far greater forces were also at work, however. The Communist Party in large part maintained its monopoly on power by delivering rapid economic growth every year, and it appeared that even China's double-digit growth rate was not immune to the aftershocks of the global financial crisis. Much of China's recent economic expansion had been tied to real estate development, and many China watchers feared a bubble had formed. Quite a few of the tycoons who were buying classified growths had significant assets in real estate. If a Chinese real estate bubble popped, billions of yuan would disappear overnight. And it wasn't just some wealthy entrepreneurs who would be affected. A 2010 audit revealed that approximately ten thousand financial platforms used by local authorities to access money for development projects carried 10.7 trillion yuan in debt, an amount China watchers believed to be an underestimate.

Analysts at the ratings agency Moody's had found an additional 3.5 trillion yuan ($540 billion) in poorly documented, local government debt after scrutinizing figures provided by Chinese authorities. Eleven provinces had racked up debts of 759 billion yuan building toll roads no one used, and only the central government in Beijing had turned a profit. As the central bank raised interest rates and ordered the banks to pull back credit, local authorities and businesses turned to the unregulated "shadow banking" sector.

Tight credit and increased interest rates in 2011 meant that wealthy Hong Kong Chinese such as George Tong were feeling the pinch. They were forced to transfer money from Hong Kong to China to repay loans that were being called in by the banks, leaving them short on cash. In this context, no one wanted to get stuck with overpriced wine.

"There is a panic among the speculators who have been holding these wines. They are selling, bringing down prices," commented Don St. Pierre Jr. of ASC Fine Wines. Fortunately, wine was a relatively easy investment to liquidate. But some of the biggest Chinese traders—those who had decided to gamble by buying vast quantities of First Growths en primeur—chose another course of action.

❂

Back in 2005, Philippe Papillon had seemed to arrive out of nowhere on the Place de Bordeaux. He had set up his company, Ipso Facto, on one of Bordeaux's side streets in a modest two-story building whose stonework was pocked and scratched with wear, with two arched windows on either side of the main door. In an effort to minimize the sunk costs of business, Papillon's wife, Nathalie Castagnon, had set up the offices for her law practice upstairs. But it wasn't fair to say the business was a small, family affair.

From the beginning, Ipso Facto had been the sole agent and fiscal representative in France for the SK Group, South Korea's third largest company, a *chaebol* with seventy thousand employees and tentacles in everything from telecommunications to construction to energy. In fact, SK had been Papillon's only major client then—his calling card on the Place as a specialist selling wine in the Asian market—and, typical of a "tiger economy" conglomerate, SK's executives had told him that they intended to buy aggressively. Big was never big enough; fast was never fast enough.

At the time, Papillon didn't have allocations of classified growths of his own, so he played the role of intermediary, escorting SK's sourcing managers to meetings with the châteaux and the most powerful négociants on the Place. Papillon explained that SK planned to sell wine through its network of retail stores, but it would also hold some of its inventory in an investment fund domiciled in the British Virgin Islands, which did not tax capital gains, profits, sales, gifts, or inheritance. The arrangement was bound to appeal to speculators. As the Chinese started to show interest in classified growths, SK expanded its horizons, opening fine wine subsidiaries in London and Hong Kong, and a distributorship in Shenzhen.

In 2007, SK first tested the waters in Bordeaux's en primeur market, buying a small amount of the 2006 vintage. Then the following year, when the négociants' traditional American and European customers turned down their allocations of the overpriced 2007 vintage, SK seized the opportunity, as Papillon and Ipso Facto effectively gained allocations of First Growth and Second Growth wine that had previously been in the hands of more established négociants. It was an accepted truth on the Place de Bordeaux that someone was always ready to take your place. Papillon himself took significant stakes in several highly speculative vintages—the 2000, 2003, and 2005—with the foresight that any wine with a good brand name attached might pay off very soon. "This is the time when the machine started working," he later said with obvious nostalgia.

By 2010, SK had invested something on the order of $100 million in Bordeaux wine, but the company's relationship with Papillon was souring, at least from his perspective. Whenever he took SK executives to visit a château, he was appalled by the grandiose promises they trotted out. "They always added or subtracted a few zeroes," he remembered. Such flippancy endangered his reputation on the Place de Bordeaux. If SK broke its word, it would be as if he had broken his word—and his career as a négociant would effectively be over.

Just before the barrel tastings in the spring of 2010, Papillon cut his ties with SK. It was a prescient move. Six months later, on the day after Sotheby's record-breaking Hong Kong sale of Château Lafite wines, the auction house had sold a record $10 million of classified growths on behalf of SK Networks, one of the chaebol's subsidiaries. All of that wine had been bought by Papillon for the company. Fickle, they were exiting the market as quickly as they had entered, whatever the cost.

"They invested too much on crazy vintages at the top of their prices," recalled Papillon. "They tried, they failed, they stopped."

Now they were dumping the wine.

Papillon had done well in his first five years, but now he needed another fat client. In January 2011, he was introduced to Yu Kelong.

❋

Papillon could sense from the moment he met Yu Kelong that he would never learn anything about the man's business interests. Yu was urbane and cultivated, but that meant nothing. He could be a respected manufacturer or a shady operator, for all Papillon knew. Yu was from the coastal city of Ruian, south of Wenzhou, in Zhejiang Province; he kept a yacht in Hong Kong and ran a holding company called USA Piilii Jepen International Group. Piilii, as Papillon called the company, controlled a myriad of unknown businesses owned by numerous anonymous shareholders. There was no trace of Piilii on the Internet, beyond a few necessary listings with the authorities in Hong Kong. It was the definition of shadowy.

Papillon's entrée to Yu came through a vivacious young trader from Shanghai named Jenny Chen, whom everyone called "Jenny C." and whom he had met in 2008. The amiable Frenchman felt a kinship with Jenny C. from the start. She was smart, sincere, and hardworking, and she had a sharp instinct for the business side of wine. Papillon agreed to pay Jenny C. a commission on his sales to Piilii, which wanted to invest in Bordeaux classified growths—as much as possible, as fast as possible.

Papillon could deliver fast. The quickest option was to buy older vintages that were ready to drink. He picked up the phone and dialed one of his courtier contacts to see what might be available directly from the châteaux or other négociants. In a few short months, the total value of the four contracts he entered with Piilii topped €17 million—roughly $25 million. Papillon then entered into contracts with the châteaux to buy the wine. In order to meet his obligations, Papillon scheduled eight payments from Piilii, with the first payment of $4 million due on March 31, 2011. Since Yu was such an unknown, Papillon insisted that he receive payment up front rather than follow the usual custom of paying in installments, with part of the total bill paid at the time of the order and the rest paid on delivery. The first installments from Piilii were late and only partial payments, but the money arrived in sufficient quantities to reassure Papillon that he had found the perfect client to replace SK on his books.

Unfortunately, Papillon could not keep Piilii for himself. Yu wanted to get his hands on far more Bordeaux, both older vintages and en primeur, than tiny Ipso Facto could supply. With Papillon's knowledge, Jenny C. set up deals with twelve other négociants. Piilii bought between 500 and 1,000 cases of Second Growth wines from Margaux, Saint-Julien, and Saint-Estèphe. It bought between 100 and 300 cases of Third, Fourth, and Fifth Growths in the Médoc. It bought 100 cases of every First Growth in the Médoc and their equivalents in Saint-Émilion. Piilii's en primeur tab ran to approximately $30 million for the 2010 vintage, according to Papillon. "At that time, it was crazy in Bordeaux," he said.

But in the first week of July, Papillon began to get nervous. On July 5, 2011, €1 million from Piilii cleared Papillon's account in France, which fell far short of what was owed. Piilii and Jenny C. blamed their difficulties on Chinese bureaucracy and promised the money was on its way. They insisted that Papillon ship the next container of wine. Conveniently for Papillon, everything in Bordeaux slowed to a crawl in the months of July and August during the summer holidays, and he was able to buy time, effectively suspending shipments, without becoming immediately confrontational. On July 23, Piilii promised the money would arrive within eight days, but by August 15, a national holiday in France, Papillon faced a mounting catastrophe, as Piilii now owed him $10.4 million in late payments.

So when Papillon received a request for a meeting on Saturday, September 10, to discuss Piilii's business, he got himself ready for a challenging conversation.

It was always a bad sign, thought Papillon, when people told you what good friends you were, so he was put immediately on edge when he was greeted as such at the start of his sit-down with Piilii. While he tried to maintain a countenance of relaxed confidence, his mind scrutinized the situation for danger. Yu Kelong had not shown up for the meeting at Ipso Facto. Instead, seated on the other side of the conference room table, were three so-called emissaries: Yu Kelong's younger brother, another man who was supposedly Yu's right-hand man at Piilii, and Jenny C. Papillon could see that Jenny C., who was acting as translator, was quite nervous. This served to only tighten the knot forming at the back of Papillon's neck.

The meeting got under way. Yu's brother announced that Piilii was canceling its order of the 2010 vintage en primeur. Papillon froze with shock. The order was worth $8.5 million. He didn't have that kind of money. Nothing like it. Négociants generally paid châteaux in two installments, with the first due between July and September, and he always timed it so that his clients paid him enough in advance to meet these obligations. Papillon owed the châteaux €2 million on September 15, and now his client was backing out.

Papillon explained that cancellation was not an option. He had arranged to purchase the wines on behalf of Piilii; more to the point, he was contractually obligated to purchase them, and had only made the order on behalf of his client. His tone was urgent, on the point of pleading. If Piilii did not pay, he was facing bankruptcy. Had Jenny C. made it clear that the contract had to be honored?

Yu's brother was unmoved. They were good friends, he said again, and they were canceling their orders of en primeurs and older vintages. With that, the business of the day was done, and it was time for him to leave.

Papillon fought back his panic as he walked upstairs to discuss the turn of events with his wife. From the earliest days of Papillon's business, Nathalie Castagnon had made sure that her husband and Ipso Facto were protected from unscrupulous speculators who might agree to a deal and then look for a better price in London or elsewhere. She had insisted that all new clients sign contracts, and she had not relented when it came to Piilii. This was unusual on the Place de Bordeaux, where most transactions were agreed with a phone call or an email, the legal equivalent of a handshake. Only when dealing with the Russians, who had become notorious as nonpayers since the collapse of the Soviet Union, or other unstable markets did most négociants require payment before delivery. It was the ironclad wording in Castagnon's contracts that had thus far ensured that Papillon was not required to deliver in advance of full payment.

Castagnon had the weekend to consider the options, beginning with a review of the paperwork her husband had for Piilii's orders. Papillon had agreements with the châteaux via the courtiers, and he had signed contracts with Piilii. That was a good start. But it wouldn't get them very far if they had only a company name, registration number, and address in Hong Kong. Then she asked her husband what assets Piilii had in France that might be seized by the courts as payment on the contract. He knew that Piilii consolidated the wine it purchased from various négociants in a bonded warehouse in Bruges, a suburb to the north of Bordeaux. By Papillon's reckoning, that pile of wine had to include more than twenty thousand cases of older vintage Second Growths that he and a handful of other négociants had sold to Piilii. They were worth roughly $8.5 million—perhaps just enough to save his skin, thought Papillon.

On Tuesday, September 13, 2011, Piilii brazenly emailed Papillon and insisted that the deliveries recommence. That same day, Castagnon took their battle to Bordeaux's Tribunal de Commerce, located on the grand crescent at the Place de la Bourse on the quai de la Douane. The building had been erected on the Garonne River in the eighteenth century for King Louis XV as a royal square to welcome visitors to the bustling port, its wings containing the stock exchange, customs house, and agricultural hall—the lifeblood of the old city. The Place de la Bourse had retained much of its original purpose, serving as home to Bordeaux's offices for the French customs service, a customs service museum, and the Bordeaux

Chamber of Commerce. Castagnon had carefully drafted the documents she sent to the tribunal: the official demand to sequester the wine owned by Piilii that remained on French soil in the Bruges warehouse. The judges on the tribunal were business leaders, and Castagnon and Papillon were wagering on their sympathy as well as French law.

Papillon wasn't the only négociant to receive a visit from the USA Piilii Jepen contingent that September. Over the next three days, Yu's brother and Jenny C. canceled Piilii's en primeur orders with each of Yu's "good friends" on the Place de Bordeaux. Papillon calculated that the damage to the Place de Bordeaux was in the neighborhood of $30 million. In some of the meetings, Yu's brother complained that Piilii had been accused by the authorities in Beijing of being a money-laundering operation. The problems had supposedly started when a heavyweight négociant firm on the Place had sold Piilii more wine than it could deliver.

According to the story told by Yu's brother, the négociant had informed Piilii in June that it could deliver only five hundred of the one thousand cases of Les Pagodes de Cos, the second wine of Château Cos d'Estournel that Piilii had ordered and paid for. According to Piilii, the négociant was happy to send a revised invoice for the smaller order, but rather than refund the money already paid, he offered to supply Piilii with other wines to make up the difference. This was standard practice on the Place de Bordeaux, but Piilii did not want "substitute" wine, and when the Chinese authorities noted that the amount on the revised invoice did not match Piilii's wire transfer, an investigation had been triggered. Many négociants accepted the story at face value and blamed the bigger négociant for their troubles. That was simpler and cheerier than imagining that other Chinese customers might start canceling their orders, too.

Had there been any demand for the wines that Piilii had ordered, the négociants could have quietly resold their allocations. But that was not the case.

❋

Five days after their previous visit, Philippe Papillon again entertained his three visitors from Piilii. He had barely slept since the last meeting, and he did not know how much more bad news he could withstand.

Translating a direct order from Yu's brother, Jenny C. tried to convince Papillon to agree to cancel the orders. They were tired of receiving his demands for payment, and wanted to find a resolution since they were, as Papillon had heard before, such good friends. Throughout, Yu's "right-hand man" stared glassily at Papillon from across the conference table, saying nothing. From what Papillon could tell, they had no inkling of his wife's petition to the tribunal for the right to sequester Piilii's stocks of wine. They were still planning to walk away from the orders, but they wanted a document from him to keep everything aboveboard.

Papillon had not yet heard from the court, and until he did, he knew he had to refuse any accommodations. He also had to keep the plan secret; otherwise Piilii could make arrangements to quickly and legally export the wine, and he'd be left with nothing. He was a wreck. Finally, when he thought he couldn't stonewall the trio much longer, he was called out of the meeting. He felt physical relief as he excused himself from the grilling of the once-delightful Jenny C. If only he didn't have to return to the conference room.

Upstairs, his wife delivered good news: she had just received authorization from the Tribunal de Commerce to seize Piilii's stock in Bruges. While his wife called the bailiff to execute the court's decision, Papillon returned downstairs and ordered his visitors off the premises without explanation. Jenny C. broke down weeping. He couldn't tell if she had buckled from the stress of the confrontation or was worried about her livelihood. Either way, it made him worry about the blowback he should expect from Yu Kelong and his brother.

Within the hour, he had his first evidence that he could not trust anyone associated with Piilii, not even Jenny C. Immediately after Papillon had expelled them from Ipso Facto, Yu's brother, Jenny C., and the right-hand man had gone to Bruges hoping to move the wine out of reach of the French authorities. One possibility was to transfer the ownership of the wine to an Italian shoe manufacturer owned by Yu Kelong. But the Piilii representatives arrived too late. The bailiff had already secured the wine.

A friendly informant alerted Papillon to the warehouse visit, so he wasn't surprised when the trio returned to his office that afternoon displaying considerably less poise and considerably fewer mentions of their friendship.

"You little piece of shit," Yu's brother began.

Despite the insults and threats that followed, Papillon held his ground, buoyed by the confidence that twenty thousand cases of classified growths can give a man. He tried not to make eye contact with Jenny C. She was beside herself. That's when he remembered that she had invested her personal profits in the wine she'd come to know so well, stockpiling her own purchases with Piilii's inventory. There was no paperwork indicating which wine was hers and which was Piilii's. She'd lost her wine in the seizure, too.

As word of the court's action spread through the Place de Bordeaux, other négociants caught up with Piilii approached Papillon. Could they get a share of the seized stock in order to help pay their own overdue bills to the châteaux? Papillon considered each of these entreaties seriously. He realized that many of the négociants were facing ruin. If the request had come from a good friend, maybe he would have said yes, but to be honest, he didn't have any friends on the Place de Bordeaux. He was part of the 25 percent of the Place branded as *arriviste*, an outsider among the wine-trading aristocrats. Some part of him couldn't shake the feeling that maybe a powerful hand in Bordeaux had wanted to put him in his place. Maybe he had tried to reach too high, too fast.

He also realized that his first priority was in paying his own bills to the châteaux. The estate managers could have called in his debts, but they hadn't. "The châteaux, they are my brothers. They have stuck with me through this," said Papillon. Each had agreed to extended payment terms to give him time to raise the money he owed. Sure, some were charging an onerous interest rate, but none had forced him into bankruptcy. "If you cancel your order with the châteaux, you lose your credibility. It's finished for you. You're out of the system," he continued. "It's a question of money and honor."

Papillon understood that he was in no position to celebrate his victory in court. The tribunal's decision held the twenty thousand cases of wine out of Piilii's reach, but it did not authorize Papillon to take them in hand or sell them off. He would have to repay his debts to the châteaux somehow—but not today with Piilii's wine. There was no easy way forward.

Papillon had not given up hope of reasoning with Yu Kelong, so he flew to Hong Kong to meet with the man—twice. But Yu would not be moved. He had no intention of paying for his en primeur order or any other money owed.

From where Papillon stood, the fiasco was made more complicated by the sudden lack of interest in classified growths—at least, that is, the lack of interest for the wine at the prices set by the estates. The 2010 vintage, still resting in barrels, could not currently be sold at anything but a heavy discount. Dumping Piilii's cases of Second Growths on the market would further depress prices. Though they did not openly admit it, the château managers were well aware that they might not get another chance to sell their wines at such an inflated price for many years to come. They were addicted to the fervor that had ignited the Chinese market, and they weren't yet ready to admit that demand had evaporated.

❂

Ipso Facto and the twelve other négociants stung by Yu Kelong's cancellations would soon have company. In early 2012, Christophe Reboul Salze stared at an email from Lu Ming, the director of fine wines at Dynasty, and cursed. Like Xiamen C&D, Dynasty had asked for exclusivities on Bordeaux wines, and Reboul Salze had toiled to pull the deal together, which had required the creation of a new second label for an estate wine and unique back labels that featured a Chinese name and Chinese text to satisfy Lu's requirements. In return for procuring these exclusive brand names in the Chinese market, Lu had promised to buy a pile of the wine every year.

This was not Reboul Salze's first deal in Asia. Soon after founding his négociant firm, The Wine Merchant, in 1998, he supplied wine to China's duty-free shops. Over the years, his company had sales of $50 million, 80 percent of that figure coming from exports. He sold wine in roughly fifty countries. In June 2010, he'd opened offices in Hong Kong and Guangzhou, working both sides of the border in an effort to beat his many rivals in the Chinese market.

Reboul Salze had modeled his business on the structure embraced for generations by old négociant families, which meant he spread his risk between inexpensive brand wines, petits châteaux, and classified growths. He didn't sell everything he bought. He held some inventory back, waiting for the wine to gain value, and now he had a stash of one million bottles in his temperature-controlled warehouse. Like many of the most successful négociants, he also owned his own vines, in his case two vineyards near Blaye, a modest winegrowing region north of the Médoc and the Gironde estuary. He understood the longing to find a guaranteed customer for an estate's wine, especially the second wine.

Back in the spring of 2011, Lu Ming had collected half of Dynasty's order of wine from Reboul Salze, but for the past several months Lu had been dillydallying about the arrangements for the remainder. Reboul Salze hadn't been overly concerned. At times, Lu had come across as an unpleasant character, but Dynasty was one of China's largest state-owned companies. It was listed on the main board of the Hong Kong Stock Exchange, and Rémy Cointreau remained the company's second largest shareholder. The company's chairman, Bai Zhisheng, had announced in a 2010 interview that for the next few years Dynasty planned to spend between 100 million and 200 million yuan (around $15 million to $30 million) annually on investments. Lu was good for the money. But what was his word worth?

Not much, as it turned out. The message from Lu was succinct. Dynasty would not be paying for the rest of the wine.

Reboul Salze was fuming. If Lu had taken all of the order according to the original schedule, the wine would have been paid for and gone weeks before. Instead, Lu had stalled, as his boss, Dynasty's chairman Bai Zhisheng, watched the market and his career prospects. Dynasty's domestic sales were dropping. The company's share price had fallen, and now Bordeaux prices were falling, too. Even though Dynasty's foray into fine wine was a small line on the company's balance sheet, neither Bai nor Lu could afford to take the order at a loss; their board of directors would consider this unacceptable. And so Lu was walking away from the deal.

As was always the case in Bordeaux, the château's contract for the wine was not with the end client, Dynasty, but with Reboul Salze's firm, which put him on the spot. Like Papillon, he had to find a way to pay the bill for the wine. He instinctively explored options for getting Lu to cover the bill instead. He knew that Lu regularly bought container loads of plonk from Grands Chais de France, which, in its ongoing quest to become France's largest winemaker, offered a range of "supermarket wines" from Bordeaux and other regions. Lu shipped that wine back to China and resold it as though it were cru bourgeois. Why not offer Lu a similar deal, drawing on his own stocks of low-priced Bordeaux? Reboul Salze could use his profits to help pay for the canceled orders, and Lu would make the hefty margin he had expected. As Reboul Salze put it, "We wanted to find a negotiation."

Yet, when he offered Lu a cheap wine that could be resold for nearly the same price as the private-label wine, Lu refused.

"I bought the wine for you!" the Frenchman exploded.

Lu's response, sent by email: *I don't care.* He was canceling the order. He had to be pragmatic. In a state-controlled company, performance and profits determined your job today and your career trajectory in the future. Forget the Five-Year Plan; evaluations were made in the short term. Lu had promised fat profits that had turned into fat losses. It was better to cauterize the loss right now than hope that the market would heal on its own next year or the year after. He could be pushed out of Dynasty before that happened.

Bad news traveled fast in Bordeaux, and the two fastest pieces of news were reports of hailstorms and the inability to pay. Reboul Salze had worked on the Place for three decades. He had been forced to collect many a debt and face many an unpleasant client over the years. But one thing he had never considered was telling a château he couldn't take the wine he had ordered. "The day I cannot honor a commitment, I prefer to disappear from Earth," he said. He leaned forward, flushed and intense. "We can't *not* pay. We just can't. We would not exist anymore. We have to pay the château."

One of the wines for which the orders had been canceled was a second label for Château Clément-Fayat, now managed by Yannick Evenou, the former CVBG export manager. When Reboul Salze alerted Eve-nou to the problem, Evenou tracked down Lu at Vinexpo Asia-Pacific in Hong Kong in May 2012 and didn't mince words. Soon the two men cut a deal. Evenou agreed to buy back the stock of Lu's wine that remained in Bordeaux, and Reboul Salze agreed to pay to have the Chinese back labels stripped off. "It was my job to protect the wine," said Evenou.

Strictly speaking, canceling orders was not a new behavior for the Chinese, not even when Yu Kelong's posse showed up at Ipso Facto's offices. The disregard the Chinese had for contracts and handshake agreements was well known on the Place de Bordeaux. However, in the past, the impact of these lost deals had been offset by the scrum of traders eager to grab the nervous buyer's orders. "For every canceled order, we had fifty more," said Philippe Larché, a partner at the négociant Vintex.

Larché held on to his faith that the market would turn, but what had begun as a few isolated, unfortunate events metastasized into a full-blown systemic syndrome that threatened the very existence of the Place de Bordeaux. Not only were Chinese buyers backing out of their 2010 orders, they were openly scoffing at the prospect of being hood-winked a second time. "Our mainland Chinese customers say they feel desperately cheated by the 2010 primeurs, and have no intention of buy-ing the 2011," reported Simon Staples of Berry Bros. & Rudd.

It was a falling market. Chinese customers began canceling their en primeur orders and their orders for older vintages that were losing value, just as Piilii had done. Typically, the delay between the order and the shipment of older vintages rarely stretched beyond a month, the amount of time it took for a négociant to gather additional cases to fulfill the order from various châteaux and other traders.

As the reports of canceled orders arrived in Shanghai, Don St. Pierre Jr. didn't bother to hide his frustration. He had warned his customers that buying Bordeaux en primeur was a risky business. "There were a lot of unprofessional brokers promising unrealistically high returns," he complained. "So they backed out of their primeurs orders. No one explained to these people that you can't just back out or it affects your

ability to buy in the future. Nor did they understand the risk of investing in primeurs."

Nor was Vincent Yip at Topsy Trading surprised when he heard that
Chinese clients were canceling big orders. He had tried to explain to his
friends in Bordeaux that the Chinese government held two principles
dear when it came to business development: contribution and control.
Every decision made by the managers of a state-run enterprise had to
show a contribution to the economic development of China, and that
included decisions about which luxury wines to buy. Further, no business was allowed to spin out of control, whether because of volatile prices
or rickety business practices. Bordeaux might insist that it was unique
in the wine world, but China's central government did not care: it was
treated the same as any other trading partner. Topsy Trading had spent
decades building a slow, steady business that generated profits. Now
uncontrolled greed and capricious traders threatened to upend that
hard work.

"The fundamental of business is that there is no future. You make
the money, it's cash in your pocket, you're happy. So the Chinese don't
care," explained Vincent Yip. He was exasperated with the Bordelais'
incomprehension of Chinese business culture. "Of course they canceled
their orders. They say 'au revoir.' "

The Chinese were canceling their orders because they refused to lose
money. The Bordelais honored their orders with the châteaux because
they refused to lose face.

❂

How a négociant responded to a canceled order depended on the depth
of his or her pockets. Some négociants were backed by larger companies
and could foot the bill for the 2010 vintage in the hope that it might regain
value and be sold to another customer in the future. One such négociant
who had a pile of unpaid contracts with Chinese clients, including Piilii, simply tossed the contracts in the trash. He would never see the
money, and the idea of suing for nonpayment seemed quixotic, even
laughable. Another Chinese company had informed him that the
employee who had ordered the wine was not officially authorized to make

the purchase, so the contract was not valid. How could he verify the facts one way or the other? Plus, the costs of the legal battle with a company on the other side of the globe would quickly mount up, possibly dwarfing the price of the wine itself. It was better to pay the châteaux and wait for a brighter day—unless you were a small, independent négociant like Philippe Papillon, in which case you didn't have the cash reserve to wait.

One spark of optimism flickered on the horizon. Courtiers on the Place de Bordeaux confirmed that shipments of modest Bordeaux wines had increased more than 100 percent every month of the previous year. China was turning its back on pricey classified growths, but it hadn't turned its back on Bordeaux as a whole. Nor had the Chinese lost their love of luxury gifts.

Gary Boom of Bordeaux Index rationalized that the demand for First Growths was one part of a much larger market, because other wines were selling well. "Our turnover is up almost a third on last year in spite of buyers turning away from established favorites like Château Lafite and instead seeking wines that are offering better value for money," he said.

In particular, the thirst for Burgundy was growing, and Boom had seen a massive rise in sales of the rarest Burgundy wines. People who had never heard of the limestone ridge called the Côte de Nuits or its patchwork of terroirs were now vying for Pinot Noir wine made from the tiny *monopole* Domaine de la Romanée-Conti. "We've seen a whole host of various DRC wines in all formats being snapped up like there's no tomorrow," Boom said. "If this level of demand continues, DRC may end up becoming the new Lafite in China."

There was no question in Boom's mind, or anyone else's, that attention from Asia was guiding the ebbs and flows in the market. Asia was still the place to be, and Hong Kong was still the hub.

At Wine Future Hong Kong in November 2011, open to anyone who could pay the $2,500 entry fee, Bordeaux was still the big-ticket draw, despite the setbacks of the previous few months. On the third day of the event, a seated tasting hosted by the famous wine critic Robert Parker was restricted to one thousand guests. The tasting, called "Parker's Magical 20," showcased his twenty picks to be the future stars of Bordeaux—wines that could rival the First Growths, though they did not have that ranking in the 1855 Classification. Among the wines to be sampled were Château Lynch-Bages, Château Angélus, and Château Cos d'Estournel.

In the months prior to the tasting, Pancho Campo, at the time a Master of Wine and the president of the Wine Academy of Spain, approached several companies to serve as corporate sponsors. One of the executives he approached was Li Daozhi, and Li had immediately accepted the offer to gain an audience with movers and shakers in the wine industry. In the end, he was the only Chinese sponsor at the event, standing onstage with Robert Parker's arm draped over his shoulders as though they were old buddies. Li's smile was radiant. He had arrived.

However, some of the Chinese speakers in the room were wincing silently at the spectacle before them. Emblazoned on the backdrop behind the men was the name of Li's company, CavesMaître France. In pinyin, the company name was rendered as "Ka Si Te," and many at this tasting were well aware that "Kasite" was the pinyin name used by Castel Frères, by far the biggest wine company based in Bordeaux, possibly all of France. It appeared that Li had hijacked the brand's name and chosen a very visible platform for displaying his defiance.

A native of Wenzhou who had emigrated with his family to Spain, then returned to the mainland, Li had started his career at the state-owned Wenzhou Hardware and Electric Material Chemical Corporation, where he became the manager of the wine division in 1998. That year, the company applied for the Kasite trademark and obtained the registration in 2000. It was a Class 33 registration, meaning that the trademark had to be used for a wine or spirit, but the company didn't produce anything under the mark. In 2002, when the company was restructured, Li left to start two of his own companies, Panati Wine and Shanghai Castel Wine Company, taking the unused Kasite trademark with him. He was standing on a gold mine.

That gold mine was called Castel. Founded in Bordeaux in 1949, Castel Frères had made a fortune in table wine, eventually expanding its production lines into beer and soft drinks. The company produced 4.6 billion bottled beverages each year. Wine was a small but prestigious part of the business, accounting for 640 million bottles. While the négociants used the 1855 Classification and Bordeaux's iconic châteaux to sell wine in the lofty world of luxury goods, Castel battled in the trenches with New World brand-wine groups over shelf space in supermarkets, where profit margins were counted in cents rather than hundreds of dollars.

After the Second World War, Castel had invested in global distribution, focusing initially on Africa, and in the 1990s it decided to break into the Chinese market. In 1999, Castel's first Chinese bottling plant—called Langfang Winery Château Rouge, or Red Castle—opened under the auspices of a Chinese subsidiary, VASF. The plan was to import bulk wine from France and bottle it for sale in China. In its annual report, Red Castle listed its owner as "Faguo Kasite Jituan," which translated to "France Castel Group." The venture floundered, but the experiment marked the first time Castel officially referred to itself as "Kasite" in China.

Castel regrouped and in 2001 entered into a joint venture with Changyu, the state-controlled winery set up in the late nineteenth century by Zhang Bishi. The name came from the founder's surname, Zhang (Chang), and *Yu*, the Chinese character for prosperity, and over the decades, the Changyu Pioneer Wine Company had prospered, in its way. It had survived the Communist Revolution and then the Cultural Revolution, though the quality of the wine in those years was marginal. Since Deng's "opening up," Changyu had snatched a quarter of the domestic consumer market for wine, rivaling Dynasty, Great Wall, and other state-owned enterprises for the mantle of biggest winemaker in China. With a healthy infusion of cash from its partnership with Castel, Changyu built a 333-acre vineyard capped by the Château Changyu-Castel, an extensive complex located in the Penglai-Yantai wine belt on the Shandong peninsula. Two years later, in 2003, Castel opened an office in Shanghai with the name "Faguo Kasite Xiongdi Gufen Youxian Gongsi Shanghai Daibiao Chu," or "France Castel Frères S.A. Shanghai Representative Office." Several Chinese names had been concocted for Castel in a short span, but "Kasite" was the name that stuck.

Around this time, Castel learned that it had a problem in Wenzhou called Li Daozhi. The year that Castel opened its Shanghai office, Li offered to sell the Kasite trademark to the company for 1 million yuan, or roughly €118,000. Castel might have paid the ransom, but Li over-played his hand and increased his demand to €1 million. Talks broke down.

Li was counting on several things. He bet that the local magistrate would rule in favor of a Wenzhou native over a foreigner. And because China was a first-to-file nation, it didn't matter that Castel had traded for years under the name, whether in France or in China. The first per-son to file the trademark in China owned it there. Li thought he had an open-and-shut case.

There was one loophole in Chinese trademark law that could work to Castel's advantage, however: if the trademark holder didn't bring a prod-uct to market under the brand name for three years, the mark could be challenged for nonuse. Although Li owned several wine companies—including Wenzhou Panati, Shanghai Panati, Shenzhen Panati, Shang-hai Castel Wine Company, and Jacubs International—he was not commercializing wine under the Kasite label. The best way to beat Li at his game was to follow the letter of Chinese law and let the clock run out. In 2005, when Li still hadn't produced a wine using Kasite, Castel petitioned the China Patent Trademark Office to cancel Li's trademark, and Castel won.

But Li was a wily adversary. He appealed the decision, claiming that he had not received the notices about Castel's challenge because they had been mailed to an out-of-date address. To Castel's utter astonishment, the Wenzhou court reinstated Li's ownership of the Kasite name. He had another three years to establish his use of the mark.

The staff in Castel's Shanghai office refused to go down without a fight. They continued to build the company's distribution network in China, partnering with Yang Wenhua at Xiamen C&D. They opened the Roche Mazet chain of retail stores together. They shipped millions of bottles of French wine to China. Though the wine was officially being sold under the French name "Castel," the Chinese labels on the wine also included the Chinese simplified characters for Kasite. Castel's mar-keters realized that Chinese customers could not read "Castel" any more than most Westerners could read Chinese logograms. The name "Kasite" was essential for communicating the wine's source to the Chinese public.

Even though Li's demand for €1 million was an outrageous amount, Yang Wenhua, Castel's partner at C&D, knew a quiet payment to purchase the trademark was the only way to resolve the problem. But he could see that the Frenchmen were too proud to let what they considered to be a two-bit villain from Wenzhou best them.

In 2008, with the clock on his trademark running out, Li cleverly created a new company, Kasite, which he transliterated as CavesMaître. In Mandarin, CavesMaître had a more direct translation, "Jiu Jiao Dashi," for "wine cellar master," but Li insisted that Kasite was more accurate. He also registered "Faguo Kasite," which meant "French Kasite," to avoid any unnecessary legal complications on his side. CavesMaître started importing French wine, buying quite a lot of it from Castel's biggest competitor in the supermarket-wine trade, Grands Chais de France. Soon after setting up the company, he moved his headquarters from Wenzhou to Shanghai. Then, in a bold offensive move, he countersued Castel. Before the friendly Wenzhou Intermediate People's Court, Li argued that Castel had been infringing on *his* Kasite trademark since 2001. Castel, he said, had sold millions of bottles by taking advantage of his famous brand. He demanded 40 million yuan in damages.

As Castel's lawyers pulled together the company's defense, they discovered that Li had filed for sixty-three separate trademarks with the Chinese authorities, none of which were associated with his own companies. Many were Chinese transliterations of Bordeaux château or international brand names, such as Penfolds. In January 2011, he had registered "Kasite Jin Zhong," roughly meaning "Castle Angel Bell," in what seemed a clear attempt to grab Château Angélus's most fitting Chinese name. He had even registered generic names like "Château Le Vin."

Not all of Li's predatory trademarking panned out. He had tried to register Château Mouton as "Mu Tong" and "Mu Tong Jiu Zhuang," both of which were refused. For Château Lafite, he tried registering "Lafei" and "Li Zi Laei," which were also refused. But Li would never fail for lack of trying. He and another man named Li Shen had registered the trademark for the Chinese name of Penfolds, a wine brand owned by the Australian powerhouse Treasury Wine Estates. The trademark was

"Ben Fu," which roughly translates as "dashing towards wealth," which seemed to be the direction Li was headed.

Despite this clear pattern of brand squatting, Castel's lawyers could not convince the Wenzhou court that Li had hijacked Kasite out from under the French company, and in March 2012 Li was declared the rightful owner of the trademark. The State Intellectual Property Office was unequivocal: "The court held that Castel Frères took advantage of the Kasite's reputation to sell its products in China." The court even went so far as to condemn Castel for producing and selling wines under the brand name without Li's permission. Even though CavesMaître had seldom used the mark, the court attributed all of Castel's profits in China to intellectual property infringement. The court ordered Castel to pay damages to Li and his company in the amount of 33,734,546.26 yuan— about $5.6 million. It was the largest compensation ever awarded in the history of wine infringement in the People's Republic of China.

Yin Kai, Castel's China area director, was outraged. "Would anyone in the wine industry believe that Castel, a European industry leader founded in 1949, hopes consumers would mistake its products for products from a Chinese company or a Chinese merchant Li Daozhi?" he implored. But even as he argued against Li's right to the brand, he tried to mitigate Castel's potential losses, by arguing that Castel had never actually used Kasite as an official brand. It only appeared as the Chinese translation of the company's trading name, Castel.

Later that same year, Li quietly bought three châteaux in Bordeaux for $6 million. One of the estates was Château Lamour, an obscure nine-acre vineyard a short walk from Castel's vineyard in Saint-Émilion.

❋

Vincent Yip sat in Topsy Trading's offices on Fung Yip Street and typed up his annual business report. Every March, before the barrel tastings, well before the prices for the wines were set by the châteaux, he sent a report to his friends in Bordeaux to give them a sense for the market in Asia. The Yips were the biggest en primeur buyers in Hong Kong, but they never went to the barrel tastings. Instead, they handled most of their business affairs by phone and email, and timed a discreet, yearly pilgrimage to Bordeaux for the fall, at harvest time. In recent years, they had noticed that some of their clients had attended the barrel tastings, in what the Yips assumed was an attempt to cut them out of the distribution chain. For this reason, it was important that Vincent Yip got a chance to communicate directly with his suppliers before the tastings, or they might be tempted to reduce his allocations in favor of a direct deal.

The consensus was that the market was in trouble—Yip didn't need to tell them that. As of the start of 2012, the Liv-ex Index had dropped 15 percent over the past year, and 21 percent since the first signs of weakness in July 2011. The price of the 2009 Château Lafite had fallen 27 percent in six months; those of the other First Growths, such as Château Haut-Brion and Château Mouton Rothschild, had fallen 16 to 17 percent. Even the famous 2008 Lafite had lost its appeal, its price plummeting 43 percent.

Vincent Yip chose his words carefully, weighing every sentence. Wine consumption was still growing in China and Hong Kong. That was the good news. Still, he was seeing a significant shift in demand. Consumers wanted wines that cost between $25 and $50, making for a fiercely competitive, price-sensitive market. The people buying wine in China were no longer speculators but consumers, he emphasized.

The second paragraph of Yip's report was devoted to the supply of Grands Crus. He allowed himself to remind the Bordelais that classified growths should not only improve with age but their value should increase with time. He asked that the people who buy and drink these wines be treated with respect, no matter the knowledge they demonstrated or the sophistication of their palates. For the past twenty months or so, speculators and châteaux had been driving the prices up, but this could not go on endlessly, as the cancellations of the past few months had proved. Like many traders, he was constantly being told that Bordeaux's prices were "working," yet his most loyal and long-standing clients had stopped buying altogether.

The financial prospects for the coming year were sobering. The 2010 vintage en primeur was impossible to sell, and people who had bought the 2010, 2007, and 2006 vintages would likely take a loss. He wasn't complaining, he said, but he was concerned.

As more Chinese buyers explored opportunities to buy directly from négociants or châteaux, the Bordelais also risked losing sight of the role of importers in gauging the reliability of the market—and of specific customers. "More and more producers try to eliminate us," Yip wrote with unease. Topsy Trading's goal was to build a long-term business with négociants as well as with its own end customers. He wanted both sides to be happy and confident buying and selling Bordeaux wine. Wasn't that what the Bordelais wanted, too?

At Diva, Jean-Pierre Rousseau read Vincent Yip's report with interest. The Yips could be counted on to be professional, insightful, and cautious. Sixty percent of Diva's sales came from Asia, most of them from mainland China. He agreed that Bordeaux now depended on China, and that the Chinese were not beholden to the customs of Bordeaux. Many of his fellow négociants had been forced to pay for the overpriced 2010 vintage out of their own pockets when Chinese buyers canceled their orders. Those négociants who had managed to squeeze a merchant into buying the stock were discovering that, in the process, they had lost a regular customer. Like the other négociants, he worried that the châteaux would not lower their prices on the 2011 vintage enough to seduce traditional customers back to the en primeur sale. In all likelihood, the négociants would buy their allocations and yet again finance all but a few of the most popular wines themselves. The classified growths were so expensive that this required a mountain of cash. Many took out loans. The effect was to reduce the number of négociants who could stay in the en primeur game, and the amount of wine the négociants could buy when they did.

The week of barrel tastings in March 2012 came and went with less than the usual pomp, as the 2011 vintage received a cool reception. The crop had weathered hail, drought, and heat waves, and the wine was ordinary. Some British buyers came, mostly to complain about prices. Though French wine exports to the United States had hit an all-time high in 2011, a number of longtime American buyers stayed home. They were fed up with how Bordeaux pandered to the Chinese market while taking America for granted.

"I'm not saying the system is broken, but I can't keep putting up money for two years to buy 'okay' wines," said Barbara Hermann, the fine wine buyer for Binny's, a retail chain based in the Midwest. She was among those who decided not to attend the barrel tastings that year. "It didn't seem like a good use of my company's money to taste the 2011 when there is only a very slight chance I'll buy any." Hermann didn't mince words: if Bordeaux wanted to reconquer America, it would need to lower the price of its wines to fit the budgets of middle managers in Chicago rather than tycoons in Chengdu.

The châteaux and négociants may not have taken much notice of Hermann except for the fact that fewer Chinese buyers had shown up at the barrel tastings compared to the year before. The Bordelais had always assumed that the Chinese wouldn't buy en primeur, and had been pleasantly surprised to be proved wrong. Now they were sorely disappointed to be proved right.

Shortly after the barrel tastings, the French billionaire François Pinault's First Growth Château Latour decided that it was the system for selling wine that was broken, rather than the prices at which the wine was being sold. On the morning of April 13, 2012, each of the négociants with allocations of Latour received a letter from the estate's director, Frédéric Engerer. The letter, dated the day before, gave one year's notice that Latour was withdrawing its wine from the en primeur system. The 2011 vintage was the last to be sold en primeur.

In recent years, Latour had winnowed down the number of négociants it dealt with, and the amount of wine it sold en primeur was already a drip. Instead of releasing the wine to merchants, the château amassed a colossal stock in its cellars in Pauillac. As that inventory built up, Engerer had begun to ask the select group of négociants with allocations of Latour to reveal the names of their clients. "It started out with him asking for the country where the wine was being shipped, then it was the company, finally it got to be that every case had to be accounted for," said one négociant. Engerer claimed he wasn't going to bypass the négociants; he simply wanted to be sure the wines were well distributed and to give Latour's best customers some personal attention.

The négociants were suspicious. The most obvious reason for demanding the identities of their customers was to sell directly to them. With some sleuthing, they found proof of Engerer's disloyalty: French customs figures showed that Latour was operating a clandestine sales channel that circumvented the Place de Bordeaux, and the value of that trade made it one of Bordeaux's leading wine exporters. While the good citizens of the Place had been busy hustling Latour's wines all over the planet, the château had been selling behind their back, cutting out not just the négociants but also the courtiers, long-trusted advisers to the estate managers. It wasn't as though Latour could claim that they were simply trying to find a way to align prices with demand. The wines had not been priced to be less expensive to the consumer or investor. The château had decided to pocket all of the available profit.

When Château Latour announced it was quitting the en primeur system, the move was widely interpreted as a play for a larger share of the Chinese market. The Chinese wanted wines that they could drink, give, or trade, and they wanted reassurance that the wine was not fake. In place of en primeur, Frédéric Engerer proposed to offer older vintages twice a year—not on any particular schedule, simply when he felt the wines were ready to drink, and only through twenty-nine négociants. Buyers would not have to wait eighteen months for delivery, and Latour would guarantee the provenance with a special label and traceability.

Privately, the négociants prayed that Latour's gambit would fail. The particular relish with which they considered the many ways in which Latour could fall from grace was in no small part due to Frédéric Engerer's reputation on the Place de Bordeaux. He was a polarizing figure, a pal to wine critics but an irritant to négociants, many of whom chafed under his arrogance and plotted his comeuppance.

Bordeaux's commercial and social network depended on the hierarchy of the 1855 Classification, and relationships and loyalty still counted. The en primeur system was a microcosm of those alliances. For centuries, the châteaux had relied on the négociants to create new markets for their wines, and the négociants had served as the châteaux's bankers, getting a percentage commission on the châteaux's prices as their reward. The négociants had worked with distributors around the globe to build up

Bordeaux's brand. Regardless of the vintage or the market, the barrel tastings and en primeur sales focused buyers, critics, and journalists on Bordeaux wine. Even when people lamented Bordeaux's prices, they were still talking about Bordeaux. No one spent much time debating the prices in the Languedoc.

For négociants such as Diva, Millésima, and Duclot Export, a line had been crossed, and they reacted by refusing to sell Latour unless the estate returned to the en primeur system. Most négociants continued to sell Latour, whether as one of those chosen by Engerer or by trading with other négociants. Still, many agreed with Yann Schÿler, the head of his family's firm, Maison Schröder & Schÿler, founded in 1739, who considered what Latour's decision meant for Bordeaux and for the distribution of Latour itself. "It might work in some markets—emerging markets like China, who don't buy en primeur," he said, "but it could also destroy the work in other markets done by négociants over centuries to give Latour the best possible distribution."

Schÿler's family had held allocations of First Growths since the eighteenth century, and they owned a Third Growth estate, Château Kirwan. An opened crate of old bottles still packed in the original straw sat in his tasting room, awaiting a gentle uncorking. In his office were labels and bottles of Yquem and Margaux, sold under his family's name, dating back to the nineteenth century. Under his guidance, Schröder-Schÿler had sold its vast cellar, as well as his childhood home above the company offices, on the quai des Chartrons, moving a block inland to the cours du Médoc. Christophe Salin's Bordeaux office at DBR Lafite was across the street, and he was within eyesight of four other négociants.

Many of the négociants were apprehensive about the possibility that other châteaux, particularly other First Growths and the Second Growths, would be inspired by Latour's bold move and abandon the en primeur system in order to sell directly in China. Such an exodus would destroy the Place de Bordeaux. A First Growth had certain duties. It needed to create an aura of admiration and respect, while not always being within reach. But most important, a First Growth was an invaluable ambassador and a linchpin on the Place de Bordeaux. In a year like 2011, the

First Growths and their second wines represented €420 million in en primeur sales for the négociants, about $500 million to $600 million. The courtiers earned 2 percent, the négociants took 10 to 12 percent, but the lion's share was pure profit for the châteaux. In seconds, the wines were sold to buyers around the world. The reputation of the First Growths helped sell hundreds of wines from a region where one in six jobs was tied to the wine industry. It was not uncommon for a négociant to require a client to buy a selection of other wines in order to secure a few precious cases of a First Growth. Already many journalists and wine buyers were scathing in their criticism of the en primeur system, which seemed designed to encourage manic speculation. Latour had just validated that position, and it was undermining the apparatus of Bordeaux by squeezing out the middlemen. To the négociants it was nothing short of infuriating.

❋

The following Monday morning, Latour's defection hit the headlines, but it did not signal the demise of the en primeur campaign as many had feared. Instead, attention was focused on Château Lafite. Christophe Salin had released the 2011 vintage for sale, dropping the price from the previous year by 30 percent to €350, or around $459. The decision was widely hailed as a demonstration of solidarity with the Place de Bordeaux, all the more so since Lafite spread the wealth, divvying up its allocations across more than seventy négociants.

As it happened, the timing was pure coincidence: Salin had set the date and the price for the release weeks in advance. He had determined the price for Lafite's first tranche by reviewing the current price of the five most readily available vintages, taking particular note of vintages similar in quality to the 2011.

"It's great, they came out early, which was essential this year and the price shows they are making an effort," said Lilian Barton-Sartorius, an Anglo-Irish négociant whose family owned the Second Growth Château Léoville-Barton and the Third Growth Château Langoa-Barton. She was equally excited when two more First Growths, Château Mouton Rothschild and Château Margaux, each released at around $460.

She and her father, Anthony Barton, had set the price of their own wines cautiously, offering Léoville-Barton for €45, nearly 40 percent cheaper than Second Growth rivals Pichon Longueville Comtesse de Lalande and Pichon Baron. The orders came as fast as her clients could hit "reply." "There's been a huge demand with people calling to make sure they get their allocations. It's basically sold," she reported.

The conquest of the Chinese market had turned into a four-way wrestling match between China's state-run conglomerates, entrepreneurial Chinese charlatans, the Bordelais establishment, and maverick wineries looking for a chance to break the rules and sell more cases. Attempts to monopolize supply, madcap speculation, intellectual property infringement, cancellations and nonpayments, plummeting prices—all were moves and countermoves to win, but they were coming at a cost. The Place de Bordeaux was changing.

8

Shifting Winds

The turbulence on the Place de Bordeaux created risk—and opportunity. Jean-Pierre Rousseau considered whether this might be the time to grasp the cash offer sitting before him. He was pushing sixty, and he'd made his name as a négociant since joining Diva in 1987. In the previous year, 2011, sales had shot up 73 percent, from $24 million to $42 million, with the vast majority of the firm's revenue coming from the export market. China alone accounted for $38 million of the company's 2011 sales. Diva also had significant stocks of classified growths, and a number of attractive allocations en primeur. The question was where to go from here.

Neither Rousseau nor Diva's founding partner, Pierre Beuchet, had any children who were interested in running the company, and Diva Bordeaux had gone as far as Rousseau could take it without an influx of new money. The rising prices of classified growths, the wild fluctuations in the market, and the precarious nature of doing trade in China required deep pockets and a strong distribution network. Several négociants had silent backers, but Diva was not one of them. There was, however, an entrepreneurially minded powerhouse eager to stake a position on the Place de Bordeaux: the Chinese government.

As Rousseau weighed his options, he acknowledged that selling to the Chinese might shock the Bordelais aristocracy. But he also thought that this might be where, unconsciously, they'd always been heading. Historically, every conquest of a new market brought a new breed of foreign négociants to the Place de Bordeaux. First, it was the English, then the Dutch, Germans, Scandinavians, and Americans. It was inevitable that the Chinese would acquire an established négociant firm. He just happened to be in a position to profit from the event.

On June 27, 2012, Rousseau and Beuchet signed the final papers transferring a 70 percent stake in Diva Bordeaux to Shanghai Sugar Cigarette and Wine, a subsidiary of the Bright Food Company, Shanghai's largest state-run food company. Like COFCO, Bright Food had been founded in the early days of Communist China, in 1951. "The investment in Diva has inaugurated a new business model for the Chinese enterprises to invest in Bordeaux wine industry," Bright Food announced in the official press release. "This will lay a foundation for the cooperation with local wine industry and promote a rapid expansion for the Group in the wine industry."

Bright Food had in place time-tested distribution channels that covered sixty thousand retail outlets, including China's supermarkets. It was easy enough for Bright Food to introduce a foreign-made product to the market—only now, that foreign product would be owned by the Chinese government. At the same time, Bright Food got to introduce its own portfolio of products and gain an understanding of foreign distribution networks.

Though Bright Food was not known on the Place de Bordeaux, it was a familiar presence elsewhere in Europe and in the United States, yet another Chinese industrial giant operating with public money as it pursued lucrative assets overseas. Many Chinese consumers were so afraid of being poisoned by domestic food products that they were willing to pay a premium for imported goods. Bright Food targeted companies that met Beijing's goal of wielding international influence but also of providing safe food sources for the country's 1.35 billion citizens.

The parent company's chairman, Wang Zongnan, was a powerful Communist Party official, respected for his aggressive acquisition of big foreign brands. The month before it bought Diva, Bright Food had taken a 60 percent stake in Weetabix, the popular British breakfast cereal. It had also tried to buy Yoplait yogurt and the American vitamin retailer GNC, but those efforts had been thwarted.

In Bordeaux, Bright Food met with more success. It had cut out one of the system's immovable middlemen by becoming the middleman instead, in the process gaining access to a supply of France's most prestigious wines, as well as marketing expertise, management skills, and winemaking savoir faire. According to Bright Food's chairman, the stake in Diva "laid down a solid foundation for the Group to integrate more international wine resources and brands."

From Rousseau's perspective, the offer to team with the Shanghai government was too attractive to turn down. "The Chinese offer was of cash as well as a new customer base in the world's most spectacular market in terms of progression for all luxury items, such as fine Bordeaux wine," he said.

As part of the deal, Rousseau agreed to stay on as president and CEO for five years, navigating the intricacies of the Place de Bordeaux on behalf of the conglomerate's managers and advising them on how to sell the firm's wine stocks around the world. In return, the chairman of Shanghai Sugar Cigarette and Wine, Ge Junjie, promised to support Diva's growth financially and with what he called "soft power," first and foremost by promoting fine wine culture on the mainland. He planned to launch a wine school in Shanghai before the end of the year in order to help teach the new Chinese middle class how to drink wine. It would be a Chinese branch of Cafa Formations, the sommelier school in Bordeaux.

As was the case in the deal between Philippe Raoux and COFCO, Diva would create a Bordeaux wine specifically for the Chinese palate and packaged to attract Chinese consumers. It was smart move for Bright Food. The company could buy bulk wine from local growers, determine its own blend of grape varieties, control the brand, and determine its price, volume, and distribution.

Ge claimed that by owning its own brand wine to be sold directly to consumers, Bright Food would be able to guarantee that every bottle of wine with its label was genuine. He was either the victim of wishful thinking or a master of public relations. Counterfeiters had faked Castel, and Castel controlled the entire production and distribution process, from winery to store shelf, for millions of bottles annually. If Castel couldn't stop counterfeiters, how could Bright Food? The only effective strategy against fake wine was to make your wine so difficult or costly to fake that the counterfeiters chose another target. What Ge had actually bought by acquiring a majority stake in Diva was a generation of expertise and a direct supply of classified growths as well as more modest wines.

By the time the deal was signed, the campaign to sell the 2011 vintage had stumbled to a close, and the decision to sell Diva Bordeaux to the Chinese government looked even shrewder.

❋

Every négociant on the Place de Bordeaux knew that the best card in their hand was the en primeur system. It was the fastest, most efficient method available for distributing estate-bottled wines around the globe. The négociants, as well as the courtiers and châteaux, relied on the profits made by selling and buying early, en primeur, to ensure their annual cash flow. But the high prices for Bordeaux's 2009 and 2010 vintages had put the wines beyond the pocketbooks of many of the Place's traditional customers. Once-reliable customers in America and Europe were fuming over the prices, and the value of classified growths was falling on resale markets such as Liv-ex. Unless the prices for the 2011 vintage were set low and the campaign was quick, it seemed likely that no one was going to buy this year's Bordeaux. More and more, customers were expressing disgust and looking elsewhere—to Spain, Italy, and South America.

China remained the best bet for classified growths and Bordeaux's medium-range estate-bottled wines—it was, after all, the biggest luxury goods market on the planet. The Shanghai-based Hurun Research Institute's annual report said there were more than a million "dollar millionaires" in the country. These were private business owners, professional stock market investors, real estate investors, and high-salaried executives, and the number of private business owners amassing such wealth was growing by 5 percent each year. The Bordelais had not even begun to tap into China's third-tier cities, places such as Dongguan, Foshan, Ningbo, and Suzhou, which the *Hurun Report* said boasted more than eighty thousand millionaires among them. Inner Mongolia had 12,300 millionaires. *Inner Mongolia.* Of course, these tallies of millionaires slyly didn't include government officials.

So when the courtiers relayed the message to the châteaux that prices needed to come down, it crossed more than a few minds that perhaps the négociants should stop whining about prices and get on a plane to Inner Mongolia. Regardless, the pressure on the châteaux was mounting. The argument boiled down to a few salient points: Everyone had made a lot of money on the 2009 vintage, but only the châteaux had made money on the 2010. Chinese buyers were still smarting over the falling resale value of that vintage. There had been the rash of canceled orders from capricious Chinese traders, and Château Latour's vote of no confidence in the en primeur system. An increasing percentage of the négociants' funds were tied up in a relatively small number of wines—those that had the best chance of selling. The négociants had limited budgets, reasoned the courtiers, who themselves had an interest in bringing prices down to meet demand. And the courtiers received their 2 percent commission only when a wine was sold.

The campaign would be especially challenging in the spring of 2012. After the past two years of shocks, the prices for the 2011 vintage could very well decide the fate of Bordeaux. If something didn't change soon, there wouldn't be any money left to buy wine, not just the First Growths but the hundreds of reasonably priced, family-made wines that were the soul of the region. "The Bordelais learned from their arrogance and incompetence last year, ourselves included," said Jean-Guillaume Prats of Château Cos d'Estournel. "The wines will be released early this year, and I think we will have some real interest from the U.S. if the prices come down. There has to be a substantial price reduction to make it appealing to Americans." On the Place de Bordeaux, people were suggesting that the best way to recalibrate the market was an early, short, brisk campaign with prices set lower than any of the recent vintages. The 2011 vintage had to be seen as a "good deal."

On April 16, 2012, Château Lafite Rothschild sent an answer, start-ing the campaign with their first tranche release at €350 ex-cellar, which the négociants offered at €420. The 30 percent price drop hit a sweet spot. When négociants averaged the price for the three tranches released the year before, each of which had been successively more expensive, the price for the 2011 vintage was 50 percent lower. It was also less expen-sive than the 2006 vintage, which was similar in quality and currently on the market.

But what worked for Lafite wouldn't necessarily work for other estates. "The wines were overpriced in '10, so a 30 percent drop in '11 doesn't do it for me," Chris Adams, the CEO of Sherry-Lehmann, told *Wine Spectator*. "Granted the '10 was a great wine, but '11 is just 'very good.' So 30 percent down on something that was maybe 10 percent overpriced doesn't really translate well. . . . A 30 percent drop for Lafite is one thing, because they still have a presence in the Asian market. But 30 percent for the other châteaux is not going to work. So right now, the situation is not crystal clear."

True to Adams's assessment, the campaign for the 2011 vintage never gained momentum. Château Lynch-Bages and Château Pontet-Canet, both Fifth Growths, dropped their prices close to the levels they had set for the 2008 vintage, which had been released before the full brunt of the global financial crisis, and their 2011 wines sold through to end consumers. Other estates failed to hit that sweet spot.

"The courtiers told property owners that the prices needed to come down, but could be more than 2008—but not too much," Jean-Michel Cazes, the co-owner of Lynch-Bages, told *Wine Spectator* in May 2012. "But people looked at the current retail prices and didn't want to cut too much. The problem is most of those prices reflect demand from Asia, which has cooled off."

In the United States, Sherry-Lehmann's Adams took only 15 percent of the allocations he'd bought of the previous vintage. Another large U.S. retailer, the Morrell Wine Group, ordered just 5 percent of its usual allo-cations. The prices were too high, the quality average, the economy uncertain. In London, merchants had hoped the market had bottomed out, but the value of the classified growths on the secondary market continued its downward spiral.

Rousseau's friends in the wine trade quietly saluted him for making his deal with the Chinese when he had. As much as people had misgivings about the decision, it was the way of the Place de Bordeaux to embrace foreigners. But while everyone wanted a piece of China's GDP supporting their bottom lines, that didn't mean they also wanted Beijing calling the shots. They could only hope that sales the following year would be better.

They hadn't seen the worst of it yet.

❋

As it happened, the négociants had to contend with a fair share of unwelcome Chinese invaders. In the offices of Vintex et Les Vignobles Grégoire near the Bordeaux Lac, Philippe Larché sat frustrated with the Place de Bordeaux's inability to defend itself. He'd contacted his colleagues at the Bordeaux Wine Council, "sounding the alarm" that Chinese entrepreneurs were slowly taking over the Place de Bordeaux's trade, but he felt his warning was falling on deaf ears. The number of Chinese-owned wine wholesalers operating under the radar was growing exponentially. The most visible were the Chinese château owners, all of whom were establishing export businesses, intent on shipping not only their own wines directly to China, but other wines as well. Then there were the agents and small-time traders setting up shop. Some were clearly angling to find a legitimate spot on the Place de Bordeaux. In February 2012, La Cave du Dynastie opened its doors just steps away from the Bordeaux Wine Council's offices; its Mandarin-speaking staff sold modest estate-bottled wines exclusively to Chinese customers.

Larché didn't have an issue with Chinese négociants or Chinese château owners—he'd even advised a Chinese investor on a château purchase, and he sold a great deal of wine to China. Instead he was worried about another trend.

Every day, it seemed, a new Chinese trader showed up in Bordeaux masquerading as a négociant or courtier. He tapped his computer screen for emphasis. Just that morning he had received an email from a châ-teau manager, forwarding a letter sent by a Chinese woman claiming to be a *courtière*. "Courtière!" he scoffed. Even female brokers used the male form of the title—if they were legitimate. A quick call to the pres-ident of the courtiers' syndicate confirmed that the woman was not a certified broker. Larché anticipated that these upstarts would try to steal the Place's only viable customers and pollute the market with shady deals.

It was an odd development given the rumblings about luxury wine coming out of Beijing. At the annual session of the National People's Con-gress and the Chinese People's Political Consultative Conference in March 2012, a once-in-a-decade leadership transition was under way. The following year, Premier Wen Jiabao was expected to retire and Hu Jintao, the general secretary of the Communist Party and China's president, would step down. Over the coming months, significant policy changes would be announced as rival factions struggled for influence in the party.

Since the global financial crisis, Beijing's leaders had managed the economy cautiously. Despite the increasing number of millionaires, the country's massive population of migrant workers had seen their wages frozen. In 2010, a series of strikes at foreign-owned factories had dem-onstrated just how quickly the gap between China's haves and its have-nots was growing. According to Chang Kai, a professor at Renmin University, the number of strikes was up year over year by as much as 30 percent. It was especially troubling to the general public to observe government officials living large while those who worked for a private company lived on an average annual income of 28,752 yuan (approxi-mately $4,750). It didn't matter if wages had tripled in a decade; the Communist Party elite were enjoying luxuries that very few Chinese families could.

It went without saying that the purveyors of luxury goods, including classified growth wine, focused on the people with the money. In this case, it was the people with the People's money whom they targeted as their customers. That made sense: the state owned the vast majority of the country's assets and dominated the financial, agricultural, and industrial sectors. When it was convenient for Beijing, the official state media would note that 50 percent of the luxury goods business in China involved the hyper-successful state-owned companies and the government officials linked to them. Why wouldn't the people in charge of the world's fastest growing economy want to be rewarded in some way?

At the start of the fourth week of the NPC sessions in March 2012, Wen Jiabao addressed the workers' growing discontent. He admitted that there was a gap between the public's expectations and the measures taken by the Communist Party to keep its officials in check. He vowed there would be new rules enforcing transparency in government accounts. Specifically, Beijing was clamping down on expenses on the "three public consumptions"—foreign travel, cars, and banquets.

At ASC Fine Wines, Don St. Pierre Jr. read Wen's speech with little expectation of learning anything. The government had promised to clean up its act before, but officials still walked red carpets to lavish, booze-fueled banquet halls, drove German cars, and enjoyed all-expenses-paid foreign boondoggles. But buried in the speech was one line that straightened his spine: "prohibiting the use of public funds to buy cigarettes, high-end alcohol and gifts."

It was extraordinary that the premier had singled out expensive alcohol, including upscale wines, in this way. Every official would have heard the premier's message—and understood what it meant. In fact, Wen's phrasing had an unpleasant echo of a suggestion made recently by Shen Haixiong, a legislator from Shanghai, regarding Moutai, the premier version of China's fiery baijiu that was distilled from fermented sorghum. The most famous brand of the liquor was produced by the state-owned China Kweichow Moutai Distillery in the town of Moutai. Kweichow's Moutai had been named the national liquor in 1951 and had been served to Richard Nixon on his historic visit to China in 1972.

Despite this patriotic pedigree, Shen had declared that drinking Moutai at official receptions was an "abuse of public funds." A 2012 *Hurun Report* on Chinese millionaires listed Moutai as the fifth most popular brand for gift giving—the only Chinese brand to make the top ten. (Louis Vuitton, Cartier, Hermès, and Chanel took the top four slots.) Hurun estimated the brand to be worth $12 billion; its rival baijiu brand Wuliangye was worth $7 billion. A bottle of vintage Moutai had sold on auction in Guiyang the year before for $1.36 million. A bottle of Wuliangye from the 1960s sold for $155,687. The price of a bottle of Kweichow Moutai's best-selling brand, Flying Fairy, had risen from 200 yuan in 2000 to 2,100 yuan, or $332, in 2012. Not surprisingly, Moutai expected to record soaring profits year over year.

Shen was also the editor-in-chief of the Xinhua News Agency's Shanghai bureau, so he had no trouble publicizing his views. "As far as I know, the government is prohibited from luxury consumption," he told *China Daily*. Comments on the story raised the question of whether Bordeaux wine should be banned as well. One person wrote, "Last week inspection bureau inspectors came to our hotel and we had to 'offer' a dinner. They had Moutai or Château Lafite (7,000 RMB bottle) mixed with Fanta. They have really great taste." The following day, the publicly traded shares of Kweichow Moutai dropped 6.5 percent.

More than Moutai was at issue. A 2011 report exposed the staggering misuse of public funds. According to *China Daily*, statistics from China's Ministry of Finance revealed that sixty ministries and institutions under the control of the State Council, China's highest administrative body, had spent more than 3 billion yuan, or $467 million, on foreign travel, cars, and banquets in one year. An office tasked with alleviating poverty had spent 1.45 million yuan on official banquets, and the customs office had spent a whopping 503 million yuan. The administrators of the provincial region of Beijing had spent 90 million yuan on banquets and another 130 million yuan on overseas trips. While most ministry offices had reported their expenses, none of the Communist Party's organizations had.

Was this "Socialism with Chinese Characteristics"? Without an independent judicial system or media, the Communist Party was left in the position of policing itself. Laws and regulations against graft existed, but the enforcement of those restrictions was left in the hands of people who had much more to gain by not enforcing them. "What do you want us to do? They have the tanks," commented one Chinese winemaker, bitterly. The military strength of the Communist Party could not be challenged, but its moral authority—the belief that the economic strength and stability of the country was best managed by a Communist Party elite—was increasingly in question.

In July 2012, Wen ordered civil servants to adopt "a frugal working style" by October or lose their jobs. Already they had been told to slash spending on the "public consumptions," but now Wen declared an official ban on using public money for luxury goods. Some cities had anticipated that the winds were shifting in Beijing. The port of Wenzhou had sold off 215 vehicles and barred its officials from spending more than 60 yuan, or $9.40, per person for a meal. Bordeaux was, without a doubt, not on the menu.

The largest government-funded drinks tab in history was now officially closed.

❋

The en primeur sale of the 2011 vintage was a fiasco. In some cases, négociants had discounted the entire lot of allocations they had received, just to be able to sell whatever they could and hold on to their allocations for the following year. Many believed that the campaign in the spring of 2013 would again be marked by flagrant discounting. "The distribution system doesn't work without discounting. People try the recommended price, but it won't sell. People aren't stupid," said one merchant. "The négociant makes five euros, I make seven, at the château it's costing six to produce the wine and they're making ninety-four euros. Something is not working." When it came down to it, the problem was the châteaux were making by far the most money, at the expense of the rest of the Place de Bordeaux and their network of importers and retailers.

And yet there were some promising developments. In the spring of 2013, a few of the Chinese-owned châteaux put their wines back on the Place de Bordeaux. Peter Kwok, the Francophile financier who had bought three estates so that each of his children could inherit one, had tried to drum up interest among négociants for his estates' production, which totaled two hundred thousand bottles. He still planned to sell most of the wine directly in China, but he also wanted to develop a traditional distribution channel involving the courtiers and négociants. "A good wine is first recognized by its domestic market," Kwok explained. "I know that the 2012 vintage isn't perhaps the best for launching; I don't have any expectations of great success the first year. We're in for the long haul to build our brands and establish ourselves in the market."

Several months later, two wines owned by Qu Naijie of Dalian Haichang Group were returned to Vintex. "They're finding it's not so easy to sell wine," said Philippe Larché.

While that development was reassuring, it didn't amount to much wine, and it didn't begin to mitigate the damage done by the falling value of classified growths, let alone the anger among Chinese clients who had lost money on their en primeur orders. It wasn't surprising that Chinese customers were largely disenchanted by en primeur, but now they were losing interest in bottled wine, too. Yang Wenhua, the chairman of Xiamen C&D's wine division, once the most sought-after Chinese guest at the annual barrel tastings with several million dollars at his disposal, had delivered the bad news to the négociants in the spring of 2012: C&D was no longer buying the seventeen exclusivities it had arranged with classified growth estates. C&D was cutting them loose. Yang's bosses at C&D's headquarters in Fujian Province were still allowing him to come to Bordeaux, despite the losses in his division, but that was the limit; their thirst for high-priced wines had been slaked. The château managers were alarmed by C&D's reversal, but technically Yang had not canceled any orders. He had not confirmed this year's order, which meant the négociants had not officially agreed to buy any wine from the châteaux on C&D's behalf, and the négociants had no contract with the châteaux. That meant the châteaux were free to sell the wine—if they could find a willing buyer—to someone else. It was a fine line, but an important one.

It was easy to understand how Yang's circumstances were shifting. Until recently, C&D had dealt in brand wines and alcohols over which it controlled distribution. Bordeaux's wines were sold as commodities, and their prices were widely cited on the Internet. His original plan had been to buy, for example, a $20 bottle of wine, then sell it at 1,500 yuan, or about $240, in China. When that hadn't worked, he'd cut the price to 500 yuan, about $80. It was still a good profit, and he put his division's full efforts into promoting the wines. C&D tried to woo customers from all over China, inviting them to sumptuous banquets and wine tastings. It invited châteaux owners over to China to host tastings and attend still more banquets. The exclusivities protected them from parallel imports, which would necessarily have another layer of cost, so long as C&D operated with normal profit margins, which they didn't. In the end, anyone could go on the Web and type in the name of a wine and find the market price for it around the world, including in China. That transparency meant that any wine drinker with a smartphone could establish in less than a minute when they were being overcharged. As customers caught on that C&D's prices, as well as those of many traders, had been artificially jacked up, they stopped buying.

That left C&D—and Yang, most especially—in a bind. He was managing to sell Château Mouton Rothschild and Château Margaux to a stable group of clients, that much was true. One of his most popular products was an "1855 Classification six-bottle gift pack"—he offered it in two versions, one featuring wines from the 2007 vintage and the other from the 2008. But not all of it was selling, and there were warehouses full of the 2008 and 2009 vintages that could not be sold without his company taking a loss. The overpriced 2010 vintage, soon to be bottled in Bordeaux, was weighing heavily on Yang's mind. He was discounting stock, selling off as much as he could, as fast as he could. "Soon we'll be down to five hundred thousand bottles, a reasonable level for a company like ours," said Yang. He had taken nine hundred thousand bottles of Bordeaux wine, which meant he was liquidating four hundred thousand. He'd been in the wine business in China for fifteen years, and he had no qualms about dumping his stock.

"We don't want to change the long-term landscape of the Place de Bordeaux, the importers, courtiers, négociants, and châteaux," Yang insisted. His worries were closer to home. Already Chinese domestic wines dominated the market with their volume and price—the wineries didn't have to pay import duties, and most of the wines weren't taboo under Wen's new spending rules. Yang might still be able to sell the wine, but he needed to do so quickly. He was ever watchful of C&D's prospects, and most especially the value of C&D's shares on the stock market.

As a warning of what could go wrong, Yang only had to look at what had happened to Dynasty. In the first half of 2011, Dynasty reported a 54 percent drop in profits, and the company's shares on the Hong Kong stock market had plummeted. Rémy Cointreau, which owned a 27 percent stake in Dynasty, had lost a third of its investment. In February 2013, the company had warned shareholders that it was expecting a loss for the 2012 fiscal year. Then, on Friday, March 22, 2013, the stock was suspended from trading. A few days later, Dynasty's board of directors revealed that its auditor, PricewaterhouseCoopers, "had received anonymous allegations against certain transactions" at the company. In an effort to hide its disastrous sales figures in 2011, Dynasty's management had overloaded its wholesalers with so much unsellable wine that the wholesalers asked Dynasty to buy it back. Rémy Cointreau, which had stopped any direct involvement in the joint venture over two decades before, put pressure on Dynasty to explain itself publicly, but until an independent auditor looked into the allegations, Dynasty was off the stock market and the final annual financial results would be on hold. Otherwise, the company was open for business while its senior managers tried to hold on to their jobs.

In Bordeaux, Christophe Reboul Salze had watched Dynasty's implosion with grim satisfaction. The previous year, when Lu had canceled Dynasty's orders, had been quite bad for him. He had little chance of squeezing payments from a company that was suspected of accounting shenanigans—in China of all places—but he had followed Philippe Papillon's example and took his battle with Dynasty to the Tribunal de Commerce. He won, and the tribunal gave him the authority to sequester wine in lieu of the payment he was due. Before its recent difficulties, Dynasty had paid for a valuable order of the 2009 vintage of classified growths—ordered from other négociants, not Reboul Salze—which was bottled and ready for shipment. Now that wine wouldn't move until he was paid. "They will be out of the business of fine wine," Reboul Salze predicted, with the determination of a major general who had commanded a first victory against a much larger adversary.

The London wine merchant Gary Boom wasn't optimistic about the négociants' chances in the battles ahead. "It's not a healthy situation. Five years ago, 95 percent of my business was Bordeaux; now it's 50 percent," he said. Of course, he was still selling a lot of wine. Bordeaux had lost 45 percent of his market. "And that's because of price, it's price and demand."

"Bordeaux is like a herd of wildebeests going across the plain. You can't work out where the first one is and where the one is at the back," he went on. "Some châteaux, like Margaux, listen. Lafite is a world unto itself. They don't listen, but it's my biggest-selling wine. I sell £15 million of Lafite a year, and half the time, you can walk around Lafite and they don't know who you are. We have a decent relationship with them, but they don't go out of their way to help you market their wines."

Recently, the top twenty or thirty châteaux—mainly a selection of First, Second, and Third Growths—had started dictating which importers received allocations, whether or not they wanted to buy the other wines the négociants traditionally shoehorned into deals. When the merchant said no to the other wines, the négociants were forced to find new clients for them. Those wines were increasingly being sold to the public, not to distributors and importers. "Unfortunately, that's my market, so the more they go to the public, the more I go to the château," Boom said. "My argument to the château is that I'm not different than a négociant. I'm just doing a better job."

"Suddenly my big clients are saying, why should I buy en primeur from you, when I've got it from five négociants offering me a cheaper price?" said Boom. He thought about the négociants on the Place de Bordeaux. There were some, like Diva and Maison Schröder & Schÿler, who respected the chain of distribution, but this was happening less and less. "In fact, the négociants are not really my friends; they are my competitors. This is becoming very fractious, this relationship."

China, of course, was the most bitterly contested territory between the London merchants and the négociants. In the next decade, as Chinese vintners start to make quality wines for export, the négociants may find themselves with a still smaller share of the international market.

❂

As Gary Boom surveyed the likely future of Bordeaux, he did see some hope. "Saint-Émilion and Pomerol were easy to sell because of the small volumes, and there is still romance there," he observed. "The owner is still picking the grapes and tending the vines." Boom was comparing the Saint-Émilion and Pomerol estates to the Médoc, where so many of the châteaux were owned by insurance companies, luxury groups, or other absentee investors. Of course, the Médoc had nothing on China when it came to vast vineyards controlled by faceless conglomerates. Yet China's industrial approach to winemaking had competitors. There were Chinese vintners putting personality into their wines—people like Emma Gao and her father.

Silver Heights had come a long way since that day when Emma had shared a bottle of her wine with her bosses at Torres. In December 2011, Jim Boyce, the author of the long-running blog *Grape Wall of China*, had organized a head-to-head blind-tasting contest between Ningxia and Bordeaux. Five red wines from Ningxia and Shanxi were put up against five red wines from Bordeaux. All of the wines were priced between thirty dollars and seventy dollars, and all were from the 2009 vintage. Ten expert judges were selected from the wine trade, five from France and five from China.

All of the wines received good tasting notes, but four stood well above the rest, and those four were from China. First place went to Grace Vineyard's Chairman's Reserve, while Silver Heights' Summit came in second. The top French wine, DBR Lafite's brand wine Saga Médoc 2009, came in fifth. The French judges preferred Grace Vineyard's wine but the Chinese judges preferred Emma Gao's. Every way you looked at it, Ningxia won.

"For now, the big 'takeaway' for me is that Chinese wines have again—not for the first time, not for the second time, but again—shown they can compete on a global level," wrote Boyce. "The reality check: these wines represent a sliver of the China market and the industry as a whole has a long way to go. Still, for those who ask, 'Can China make good wine?' the answer is yes."

Then, in November 2012, at a Beijing salon organized by the Chinese edition of *La Revue du Vin de France*, the largest French wine magazine,

Chinese wines were given an opportunity to be tasted next to fine wines from established powers such as France and Italy. It was a small event, with no more than thirty-five tables showcasing the wines to be tasted. But the attendees—journalists, critics, and wine bloggers—had an out-sized voice. China's small population of wine lovers paid attention to how these people judged these wines.

Of course, Jim Boyce was there. He helped himself to a glass of Silver Heights Family Reserve 2010 and savored the play of aromas and flavors. "It was, for lack of a better word, brooding, which isn't surprising given the wines made by Emma Gao have been described as having personality. It had a good fruit to body balance, and I was split between wanting to savor it and to gulp it down to its spicy finish," Boyce later recounted. Emma had earned a reputation for taking exquisite care with her wines. The Old World influences shone through.

But Silver Heights was small and Emma had never been a natural promoter, so she and her father had relied on the organizers to present the wine for them. And Emma's wine didn't come off entirely well, marred as it was by the unprofessional attitude of the people pouring it; they stayed seated while serving and knew nothing about the wine, Boyce noted. "This likely had nothing to do with Silver Heights, given it is a small operation and none of its employees were on hand, but it doesn't look good for RVF," he wrote, referring to *La Revue du Vin de France*.

A nearby table hosted Pernod Ricard's Helan Mountain brand, also from Ningxia. The winery's Reserve Pinot and Reserve Merlot, both costing around 220 yuan a bottle, were resounding crowd-pleasers. Silver Heights had competition.

Marketing wasn't the only challenge. That autumn, an unusual amount of rain had spelled disaster for Ningxia's wine grapes. Emma had seen the battle against mildew and rot in Bordeaux, and she remembered that French growers waged it more years than not, but the farmers in Ningxia didn't know how to treat the vines to protect them. Most of the local farmers responded to suggestions to buy chemical sprays with suspicion, convinced that they were being hoodwinked into purchasing costly, useless products and that the wineries must be receiving kickbacks. In the end, the Ningxia growers who treated their vines did just fine. Those that didn't lost more than half of the year's crop. It confirmed what the Gaos had instinctively known: they needed to manage their own vines and not rely on local farmers for grapes, and they needed every bit of land they had under cultivation.

Gao Lin managed their little vineyard meticulously, as he always had. The original vineyard hadn't changed since their first barrel, even as Emma had massaged the wine into a finer, fuller form. The winery was still tucked into the same small, orchard-sized enclosure, with the ramshackle series of buildings that served as lounge, storage, and vat room. Emma still used the tiny underground aging cellar that her father had built for her.

The view of the future seemed limitless, if not for the jungle of highrises creeping ever closer to the vineyard's edges.

❈

If one person was committed to transforming Ningxia's burgeoning wine industry it was Rong Jian.

Rong was president and chairman of the board of the Ningxia Grape Industry Association and a former vice secretary-general of agriculture in the Ningxia government. He had been involved in Ningxia's wine industry since the mid-1990s, when Yinchuan had hosted the wine conference at which Dr. Li Hua had spoken about Ningxia's potential for growing grapes.

Rong and the other local officials had leapt on these words of encouragement. By 1997, grapes were fully integrated into the agricultural development plans for the region, and in 2001, the same year that Gao Lin extracted the first harvest from his grapes at the Shizuishan chemical factory's vineyard, Rong formed the Ningxia Grape Industry Association. Ningxia's farmers could have simply grown grapes and sold them to Great Wall or Changyu, Rong explained, but the economic benefit to the region would have been low. The benefit was significantly greater if the growers made the wine, too. A few years later, Ningxia University opened a school of viticulture and enology, paving the way for more indepth research into the composition of the desert sand. It wasn't as prestigious as the University of Agriculture in Beijing, or the College of

Enology in Shaanxi, but Rong argued that Ningxia's wine trade would suffer if it lacked local talent as well as research.

After some debate, the Ningxia Grape Industry Association decided to select a small group of students to visit France, to learn how it was done in Bordeaux. The association's investment soon paid off. When Emma Gao took her first trip to Bordeaux it was as a translator for the association's group, but then she stayed on as an enology student herself. One of the students was now the debonair general manager of the Chandon China winery in Ningxia owned by LVMH, and Emma herself was growing famous. Magazines published stories about her. Critics lauded her wine. Restaurants and collectors wanted Silver Heights on their lists.

Being famous didn't mean Emma could quit her day job, though, not just yet. Silver Heights had very little wine to sell, and to make ends meet, Emma was working as a consulting enologist for some of the big industrial vineyards. She had worked as the chief winemaker during fermentation for the Xiangdu Winery in the Xinjiang Uygur Autonomous Region, and then consulted for Kangda winery in Shandong on the Penglai peninsula.

She liked traveling, visiting the big cities, and seeing her friends in Shanghai and Beijing, but there was always the strain of being far from her daughter, who had stayed behind with Thierry in Saint-Estèphe. It was a delight, those two or three months she spent with them every year, days doing nothing but painting and playing with her daughter, reading and cooking, while Thierry manned the cellar at Château Calon-Ségur.

Though she hadn't yet found a way to work full-time at her own vineyard, she had been able to use the favorable media coverage as leverage when her father applied for a lease for ninety-nine acres southwest of Yinchuan—a massive expansion for their little winery. They planted vines there in 2012. Soon, they would grow out of being a "garage" wine and become a fully fledged boutique winery. She was hoping they'd be able to expand from fifty thousand bottles a year to two hundred thousand bottles by 2016.

❋

In Ningxia, Rong Jian also presided as general manager of the state-funded Helan Qingxue winery located west of the city of Yinchuan, at the eastern foot of the Helan Mountains. Helan Qingxue was dedicated to the science of Chinese winemaking. The left wing of the building was fitted out with a modern vat room, and visitors were greeted by a modern gray stone facade. The massive state-owned wineries built nearby in the popular "Chinese château" style ensured that Helan Qingxue was a study in understatement.

Inside, Rong's office was plainly a place for work, every surface in the room covered with evidence of some project in progress. Behind his desk hung a stunning photo of the Helan Qingxue vineyard covered in snow, the mountains towering above the plateau—white, stark, and impassable. The winery had taken the name of a poem, "He Lan Qing Xue."

"In the Ming dynasty, the ruler of Ningxia wrote a poem," Rong explained over a cup of espresso. "The title meant that in summer days, you can see the shining bright snow on the top of the Helan mountains. With global warming, we cannot see this bright snow on the mountaintops; on summer days there is no snow. But in the winter you can see it and imagine what it looked like then, in the summer."

Helan Qingxue's experimental vineyard was one part of the Ningxia Grape Industry Association's four-part program to elevate Ningxia into a premier wine region. The program included training local technicians in viticulture and winemaking, educating wine consumers, and building the winery itself. If Ningxia's wineries were to succeed, everything from the soil to the vines needed to be studied. Most of the grape varieties and clones had been introduced, blindly, from abroad. The same was true of the yeasts and oak used during the fermentation process. There was a growing awareness that China needed to cultivate its own varieties, develop a catalog of suitable yeasts, and study the interplay of different kinds of oak and Chinese-grown vines. Rather than use yeasts selected from French vineyards, could indigenous yeasts result in a better, more unique expression of fruit? Could special yeasts be selected for Ningxia? Would American or French oak develop aromas that would appeal to Chinese consumers? Rong hoped Helan Qingxue would provide the answers.

Rong had installed his protégée, an accomplished young woman named Zhang Jing, as Helan Qingxue's winemaker. Zhang was the daughter of government workers and had graduated from the Ningxia Agricultural College in 1998, earned a master's degree in agriculture in Shanxi Province, and then traveled to the Rhône to pursue her enology degree. She had learned to taste wine with Li Demei, a professor at the Beijing University of Agriculture. She trained in South Africa and Australia before returning to Ningxia, joining Helan Qingxue in 2005.

Zhang shot to stardom in 2011, when her micro-cuvée Helan Qingxue 2009 Jia Bei Lan ("Little Feet") won the Decanter World Wine Award for the best Red Bordeaux Varietal over £10—the first Chinese wine to win any award from *Decanter* magazine. She gave the wine its name because she had made it the same year she had given birth to a baby girl, and the wine had been aged in new 100 percent French oak barrels—a gift from a friend to celebrate the birth—which were stamped with her newborn's footprint for good luck. Only a thousand bottles of Little Feet had been made, and neither Zhang nor Rong had any intention of putting it on the market. The wine would primarily be used for promotional purposes, though some would be saved for Zhang's daughter.

Two years later, following a tasting at the Raffles Beijing Hotel, Zhang was named Winemaker of the Year in the Chinese edition of *La Revue du Vin de France*. She was also named Outstanding Winemaker of China in the Fine Wine Challenge. These triumphs were intoxicating, and she relished the ownership stake she held in the Jia Bei Lan brand.

Most of Zhang's success came down to the fact that she appreciated the value of good marketing as well as viticulture skills. Petite and bubbly, she was also able to speak the language of vintners, and happily explained Helan Qingxue's experimentation with sixteen varieties from France alone, and her ambition to test several varieties from Italy. She was emerging as the darling of the Chinese wine scene, a symbol of how Ningxia would take its place on the world's map of fine wine.

❋

In early November 2013, workers at the Yinchuan Forestry Bureau got word that plans had been confirmed to build a "wine route" and fifty new châteaux in the Ningxia Hui Autonomous Region. A marked wine route would make it easy for tourists to visit the area's tasting rooms. It reminded Rong Jian of his visits to Bordeaux, driving along the D2 road, the famous route des Châteaux. "One château after another," he smiled. "It wasn't just the vineyards and wine, it was the wine culture, everywhere, just for wine. There are investors who spend a lot of money in Ningxia, but they don't find a harmony or balance like in Bordeaux." Bordeaux's route des Châteaux had developed organically over centuries. Ningxia, in contrast, was governed by the Five-Year Plans handed down by Beijing.

Cao Kailong, the middle-aged, impassive deputy director general of the Forestry Bureau and director general of the Grape Flower Industry Development Bureau of Ningxia, was exasperated. He sat behind a big desk covered with papers and files, the shelves around the room lined with methodically organized volumes of promulgations and agricultural guidance. His office had recently taken over the functions of Rong Jian's wine industry association, adding to Cao's responsibilities and influence. He sighed. "In fact, this is incorrect," he said, referring to the rumors among employees about the decision to build fifty wineries. "We have plans to develop *one thousand* châteaux," Cao said with the air of a man who longed to be understood. It was a statement that only a Chinese government official with an empty desert out his back door and a nearly limitless supply of relocated labor could make.

Cao was entirely serious. Each new estate would be given a lease to develop fifty acres. The amount of land was vital. Yinchuan, Ningxia's capital, had the appearance of a midwestern American city, all flat, wide boulevards built on a grid, a concrete sprawl that disappeared into the high plains. Ningxia needed to lay claim to the desert. It was a life-and-death struggle, and thus far, the desert sands were winning. Every year, wind storms swept down from Mongolia, and one thousand wineries would hold down a lot of sand.

Cao's plans for Ningxia weren't a surprise for anyone who had enjoyed the light reading provided by the Twelfth Five-Year Plan. The central government had launched the "Open Up the West" campaign, or Western Development Strategy, in 2000 to help the outlying provinces catch up with the development in the coastal and manufacturing centers in the east. Wine had become another means for lifting the west out of poverty. The Five-Year Plan called for production of 2.2 billion liters of Chinese wine per year by 2015, with annual growth of 15 percent. This was a direct challenge to the Old World producers. In 2011, France was the world's largest wine producer, at 5.2 billion liters—but its ranking could drop precipitously in years with bad hailstorms or pests. At any rate, neither France as a country nor Europe as a whole had a wine "plan." The International Organisation of Vine and Wine expected five non-EU countries, one of which was China, to bypass the Old World by 2030. The Chinese predicted sales revenue to increase 13 percent each year and to eventually hit 60 billion yuan, double the production level in 2010. The plan also called for profits and taxes to increase 88 percent. Western China, including Ningxia, was expected to produce 20 percent of the country's wine by 2015.

Cao was determined to establish Ningxia as the driving force of the Chinese wine industry. Beijing's planners had called for strengthening cultural brand building, developing science and technology, promoting industrial restructuring, and guaranteeing raw materials. Ningxia, Cao reasoned, could easily achieve those goals, far better than other, less resourceful provinces.

It was not, Cao wanted to make clear, that the Ningxia government was investing in wine. The government was investing in infrastructure. The government would provide the electricity, roads, and business environment conducive to growing grapes, making wine, and selling wine. It would also supply the labor.

In Ningxia, the vines were widely spaced so they could be buried each winter, to protect them from the deadly cold weather. As Gao Lin and his wife had learned, it was backbreaking work to bury the vines each winter and dig them out in the spring. In Ningxia, the job was done mainly by ethnic Hui, the Muslim minority in the region who had descended from generations of Arab and Persian traders who had traveled the Silk Road. Many Hui counted among China's rural poor and led an abject existence with a yearly income below 2,300 yuan, or $365. In Xihaigu, which included a swath of central Ningxia and eight counties in the southern mountainous region, life was even worse. Centuries of farming and herding livestock had left the land barren. Little grew and water cost more than gold, or so the locals liked to say. Then a decade-long drought beginning at the turn of the millennium sucked away what little life still clung to the mountains. Annual family income fell below 2,000 yuan.

Xihaigu was a textbook case in desertification and poverty. In 2012, the government launched a project to relocate 350,000 residents from the area to working farms in Ningxia. They were a small portion of the 23 million people "moved out" of rural poverty in China that year. In 2013, the government moved another 300,000 people.

The relocations did not go as smoothly as officials planned, despite the lures of running water, a greenhouse, two cows, better education for their children, and a job in the city for one family member. Get-rich-quick promises did little to ease a migrant's worries, nor did the bottle of cooking oil, bag of rice, and a few days' supply of vegetables upon arrival. Relocation entailed an entirely different life—one that required taking out a loan to pay for their new home, as well as loans to pay for their children's education. Their only hope was that their children would eventually earn enough to pay off the debt.

In Ningxia, the Hui had heard the promises before. Family planning rules had been relaxed for the Hui, as for other ethnic minorities, and mountain couples were permitted to have three children. But as part of the Western Development campaign, Ningxia offered Hui couples with fewer children a cash reward of 2,000 to 3,000 yuan, or free insurance worth the same, in a "fewer births, quick to be rich" scheme.

In any case, when it came time to move from their mountain homes, many of the Hui resisted the relocation. In one city in southern Ningxia that planned to move 230,000 people, the mayor expected "fierce conflict." "We have fully prepared for solving every potential trouble. About ten thousand officials will be dispatched to persuade people and do related jobs," the mayor told *China Daily*.

Whether anyone suggested that the Hui would get rich picking wine grapes is unknown. But then, the Hui themselves may not have been told in advance that many of them would be hired to work in Ningxia's vineyards. "These people are used to living in the mountains. It's a difficult life, but it doesn't mean they want to work on a farm," explained Judy Chan of Grace Vineyard. As poor as they had been, they did not necessarily want the jobs they had been given.

It was one of the many challenges of making wine in China. On the one hand, the winery owners might take pride in offering jobs to people who needed the stability. They might want to help ease the families' relocation to centralized housing and go out of their way to ensure that their workers took full advantage of their access to education, communications, and health care services. But likely as not, the wineries were obliged to hire the relocated workers as part of the region's development scheme. The deal wasn't always couched in those terms. Often it was presented as a tit for tat: a discount on the lease of land in exchange for hiring a certain number of relocated workers. Many of the workers grasped the power dynamic in play, including the fact that the wineries couldn't really fire them, so motivation on the job was low. Attempts to hire other workers had sparked riots.

On top of that, vineyard labor was a rising cost. "We used to pay forty yuan a day, and now it's one hundred yuan," said Gérard Colin, who worked with Judy Chan at Grace Vineyard in the winery's early days. Unfortunately, there were few other options. Covering the vines with dirt during the winter was labor-intensive but necessary work.

❀

Ningxia's harsh winters had another impact on the vintners' ability to produce quality grapes. Grape vines require pruning, which affects the vigor of the plant and the trellising, all critical in producing ripe grapes. It was nearly impossible to accurately determine when to prune a vine when it was covered in dirt. If a vine was uncovered too early and a cold snap hit, the vine would die. "It's a lot of work and it's not easy to manage the pruning when you have to rebury and unearth the vines each year," Gérard Colin explained.

Another headache was the wear and tear on the vine itself. After fifteen years of this treatment, the vines tended to snap. At that age, a grape vine is just beginning to produce interesting wine. Ningxia was often accused of producing red wines that were too light, exhibiting grassy aromas. That was typical of grapes harvested from young vines, and it wasn't clear that the vintners in Ningxia would ever find a long-term solution to the problem.

"We can make quality wine here—this has been proven by many international experts, not just the Decanter Award, but also domestic competitions," Rong Jian insisted. So far, Merlot, Syrah, Petit Verdot, and Italian Riesling seemed to show promise. The Cabernet Sauvignon ripened late, increasing the risks that it might not ripen at all, but when it did ripen, the tannins were silky.

Of course, both Rong and Cao Kailong knew that the region's wineries needed to improve the quality of their wines. For this reason, Ningxia was creating a classification system with five levels, strikingly similar to the famous 1855 Classification hierarchy in its structure but not in its criteria. There were no courtiers involved and the price of the wine was not a consideration.

"I want to explain something, because there are some misunderstandings," Rong said. "People think we are doing this classification because we want to make money and increase the price of the wine, but that's not it. This is a way to manage the wine trade more professionally, and increase the ability of the winery managers. It's not just to copy the Bordeaux classification; it's to get the wineries to be better organized."

The requirements for châteaux hoping to win a spot in the lowest classification, the "Fifth Growths," had been announced. To qualify, a winery had to farm at least thirteen acres and produce fifty thousand bottles a year. It also had to be able to prove that 75 percent of the grapes used to make the wine had been grown in Ningxia; 85 percent had to be from the same variety and same vintage listed on the label. It was also required to offer guest rooms at the standard of a four-star hotel, a restaurant, and wine tourism activities. All styles of architecture were welcome.

Unlike Bordeaux's 1855 Classification, an opportunity to strive and improve was built into the Ningxia ratings. Rankings had to be renewed every two years. Many estates had applied for Fifth Growth standing, but in the first year, only ten would be selected. In two years' time, in 2015, these ten estates would be allowed to apply for status as a Fourth Growth, and in 2017, some might even be promoted to Third Growth. The process would be repeated until the first "Ningxia First Growths" debuted in 2021. At each subsequent ranking, the quality of the wine would play a more important role. Wineries would receive bonuses for winning international awards.

In addition, the government had launched an initiative through which each major wine region would develop two famous brands. The brands were supposed to be tied to the characteristics of the locale—perhaps to show off the environmental and national benefit of investment in the wine industry in accordance with the Five-Year Plan, and to lay the groundwork for a bigger marketing campaign. Wineries with revenues of less than 10 billion yuan in sales need not apply for the coveted two spots as state-sponsored labels. Nationally, thirty companies produced 43 percent of China's wine, and these players had a better shot at state sponsorship; neither Emma Gao's Silver Heights nor Helan Qingxue were eligible. Cao Kailong was lucky in that Ningxia boasted wineries from some of the biggest Chinese winemakers—Changyu, Dynasty, and COFCO. Dynasty owned twenty thousand acres in the Helan Mountains, and Changyu had worked with Ningxia's agricultural department to establish an eight-thousand-acre vineyard.

International recognition was vital for building the Chinese wine industry. "The channel for Ningxia's wine is the domestic market. Here, it is a luxury product, and we can sell it for more than on the export market. The Chinese can't compete in the international market," said Rong Jian. As more Chinese people became familiar with wine, embracing it as a healthy choice over rice alcohol, and as consumer spending power increased, the more Chinese will buy wine, he argued.

"The potential is huge, but to convince the Chinese that wine is good, we need international recognition," Rong continued. "We want to be as famous as Bordeaux."

Between the state-sponsored brand wines and Ningxia's classification system, Cao had what it took to build an internationally renowned wine region. It was no small undertaking, but he would find a way to do it, five years at a time.

✱

At the fourth China Wine Challenge, held in Shanghai on July 18, 2013, Silver Heights swept the awards, winning Best Chinese Wine and a silver medal for the 2011 vintage of the Summit. The Family Reserve 2011 and Emma's Reserve 2009 both won bronze medals. No other Chinese winery fared as well, and Silver Heights was the only one to bring home a trophy.

The awards were run in close association with the Wine and Spirit Education Trust, the largest wine education program in the world, and the Institute of Masters of Wine. Other sponsors included the Hurun Research Institute, the publishers of the *Hurun Report* on Chinese economic and cultural trends; Bettane & Desseauve, the wine guide company started by former wine critics for *La Revue du Vin de France*; and the high-end glass manufacturer Riedel.

Everything seemed to be going the Gaos' way. After many years apart, Thierry and the couple's daughter had joined Emma and her parents in Yinchuan. Emma had her entire family with her, and Thierry was working in Silver Heights' vat room, drawing on his years of experience at Calon-Ségur.

But even as Silver Heights triumphed at the China Wine Challenge, the Gaos received devastating news: the local government was going to confiscate their vineyard. The city of Yinchuan had grown over the years, and the tiny vineyard was entirely surrounded by development. Their land, the Gaos were told, was being rezoned under Yinchuan's construction program and was no longer approved for industrial use. Wine was considered an industry in China, so the Gaos would be forced to give up their lease. They were obliged to move their vats and barrels, but they didn't have a ready building to accommodate them. And the years they'd spent planting and managing this first generation of vines would be lost. It felt like two steps back for every step gained.

With so much at stake, Emma was not going to accept the decision without a fight. She appealed to the local governor but to no avail. She even invited the French ambassador to China to have lunch at Silver

Heights. Emma's daughter had led the ambassador by the hand as she introduced her to the many animals her grandfather had bought her. The ambassador claimed the vineyard was like paradise, and said what a good thing it would be to preserve the tiny green space. But the opinion of the diplomat had not held any sway with the Yinchuan or Ningxia officials.

When it came time in February 2014 to announce the wineries that had been elevated to Ningxia's Fifth Growth ranking, Rong Jian and Zhang Jing's Helan Qingxue made the list of ten. Silver Heights was noticeably absent. The ramshackle collection of sheds in an urban development zone, with ponies and chickens running around everywhere, was an eyesore compared to the ten wineries that had made the list. The requirement of four-star accommodation and restaurant meant that Silver Heights couldn't even apply.

The Gaos began to realize that Ningxia's local officials were not planning for a future that featured Silver Heights as a star of the local wine scene. The awards and the publicity didn't seem to matter. Nor did the quality of the wine. In the eyes of the officials who controlled the city's development, the Gaos' original vineyard wasn't worth saving. The land was needed to house Ningxia's ever-growing population.

9

Gan Bei

China's hardworking citizens didn't have to look further than their local government authority or state-owned conglomerate to understand that the socialist promise of shared wealth had fallen victim to that all-too-common human vice: greed. In the wake of China's astonishing economic growth, traditional Chinese virtues such as austerity and restraint had given way to an unseemly, frenzied acquisitiveness. The vice director of a neighborhood in Shenzhen was accused of owning eighty homes and twenty cars. There were rumors elsewhere of bribes paid in solid gold mooncakes. And, of course, there was the crazy clamor for Château Lafite.

Graft had become a regular budget line at many successful businesses. Some entrepreneurs resigned themselves to draping the wrists of officials with expensive watches bought in Paris or tucking a prepaid gift card into a *hongbao*, or red envelope. A cash delivery to the local police might spark a cursory investigation. Need a small business permit? A Rolex Oyster Perpetual might do the trick. An important lunch with the governor? Don't forget that bottle of Lafite for him and a Louis Vuitton bag for his mistress. But it wasn't just bribes. Relationships between entrepreneurs, state-owned conglomerates, and local officials were built on this caliber of gift giving.

That's why Don St. Pierre Jr. had been amazed when Wen Jiabao had pounced on expensive alcohol as a problem at the 2012 National People's Congress. St. Pierre had sold enough cases of Bordeaux to know that wine was the lubricator of choice at many business banquets. In his head, he could hear the shouts of *"Gan bei!"*—"Dry the glass!"—the toast used to encourage fellow guests to throw back a drink so that another round could be poured. The ability to drink large quantities of alcohol was quite often considered a requirement for successful job applications. Most people thought there was no way that the ban would be enforced. It seemed impossible to remove cigarettes, alcohol, and lavish banquets from the daily work of growing the GDP of the People's Republic. ASC Fine Wines had steadily expanded over the years by making sure that China's elite never went thirsty. Was it even possible to do business in China without drinking?

Wen's announcement had come at a time when St. Pierre was preparing for a major evolution in ASC's management. He recognized that, at heart, he was an entrepreneur. He liked coming up with ideas for how to sell wine and break into emerging markets. A wall in the reception room of ASC's Shanghai headquarters was paneled with the ends of wooden wine cases, each engraved with the name of a Bordeaux classified growth that ASC imported. It was an impressive display that had not gone without notice. *Decanter* magazine had selected St. Pierre for its Power List three times, and *Wine Enthusiast* magazine had named him "International Man of the Year" at its Wine Star Awards. Recently, though, he had turned his focus to new ventures. ASC had organized the first charity wine auction in China, raising more than 700,000 yuan in donations, then, just weeks after Sotheby's spectacular Lafite sale in Hong Kong, established the first professional fine-wine auction house on the mainland since the Communist Revolution.

The father-and-son start-up was now a major player; ASC had more than 1,200 employees spread across China, including regional offices in Beijing, Chengdu, Shenzhen, Xiamen, and Hong Kong. In January 2010, Suntory Holdings, the Japanese brewing company, had bought an 80 percent stake in ASC, but the firm maintained an independent corporate culture and leadership structure. Soon after the Suntory acquisition went through, St. Pierre decided that ASC needed a professional CEO at the helm, ideally an old China hand and preferably one who enjoyed superior claret. The person he had in mind—an American named John D. Watkins Jr.—was well known to him as a client. Watkins had been the St. Pierres' first home-delivery customer.

"I think I was one of the first Western businessmen to import wine for entertaining," Watkins recalled. "I was so tired of 72 percent baijiu and 'bottoms up.' I thought if I gave them really good stuff to drink, they wouldn't do the bottoms up. But they did. . . . At least it tasted better."

Like Don St. Pierre Sr., Watkins had worked in China since the early days of joint ventures. He had started with Northwest Airlines, rising to corporate vice president and general manager for China during his eighteen years there. After Northwest, he joined the heavy equipment manufacturer Cummins, where he managed seven thousand employees spread across twenty-one sites and, over six years, quadrupled the company's profits. He was then appointed as CEO and president of a fifty-fifty joint venture between General Electric and the Aviation Industry Corporation of China. Though Watkins didn't have any experience in the wine industry, he knew how to expand a business in China and navigate a regulatory environment that often changed swiftly and without warning.

Given his long history in China, Watkins felt confident that Wen Jiabao's new policy on expensive alcohol wouldn't last. Each new leadership promised to sweep out the problems left by their predecessors. Rules tightened during the transition, and then it was back to business as usual.

But this time was different.

❋

Growing numbers of Chinese citizens were convinced that government officials were gathering riches through bribes, kickbacks, and personal use of public money. The conspicuous consumption of public servants was increasingly the target of *renrou sousou yinqing*, or a "human flesh search," an investigation in which vigilantes ferreted out negative information on the Internet or posted hard-to-access documents and photographs online for others to review. The grassroots movement was focused on solving crimes and shaming bad behavior. Government and party meetings were increasingly plagued by assaults from "flesh searchers," who would snap photos of attendees wearing Hermès belts and Pucci suits as they arrived for meetings convened in service to the people. To stoke public outrage, the photos were often accompanied with captions listing the suggested retail price in renminbi of the brand-name clothing.

Most of the early flesh searches caused embarrassment for the party, but few officials lost their jobs over their excesses, and no one was quite sure how far the government would let the amateur detectives go. Then, in late August 2012, an exuberant group of researchers set into action when photos of Yang Dacai, the director of Shaanxi's work safety administration, were published alongside news coverage of a collision between a bus and a methanol tanker. Thirty-six people had died in the horrific accident, but as Yang stood next to the charred, twisted wreckage, a photographer had caught the official smiling. The flesh searchers quickly identified Yang and investigated every trace of him on the Internet. Within days they had dug up photos of Yang wearing at least eleven different luxury watches, earning him the moniker "Brother Wristwatch" on the microblogging site Weibo, a Chinese version of Twitter. Five of the watches taken together were worth $49,000. When flesh searchers submitted a request for information on Yang's annual income as a civil servant, the provincial authorities denied it on the grounds that the information was classified. But most people following the story knew that Yang was unlikely to be making more than a couple thousand yuan a month. China's president earned only 7,020 yuan, or $1,130, a month.

The controversy drew attention in the Western media, all the more so since Wen's new rules against excessive spending were set to come into full effect on October 1, 2012. Soon enough, Yang was suspended. He wasn't seen again until the next year, when he appeared in an orange prison vest at the Intermediate People's Court in Xi'an, Shaanxi's provincial capital. The court announced that an investigation had revealed $820,000 in property that Yang could not explain. His wife and son held $1.8 million in investments. He confessed to accepting a $40,000 bribe from a company in exchange for granting a business permit. The court fined Yang $8,170 and confiscated his family's property. He was sentenced to fourteen years in jail. In his final statement, he admitted that after a decade on the job, he'd fallen into an "abyss of criminality."

On October 25, three weeks after Wen Jiabao's rules went into effect, a story in the *New York Times* revealed that the family of the premier held $2.7 billion in assets. The wealth was hidden in layers of investments, partnerships, shell companies, and government-approved aliases, which the *Times*' Shanghai bureau chief, David Barboza, had painstakingly uncovered in corporate and regulatory records. "Untangling [the Wens'] financial holdings provides an unusually detailed look at how politically connected people have profited from being at the intersection of government and business as state influence and private wealth converge in China's fast-growing economy," he wrote.

To illustrate the money trail, the *Times* published a diagram, entitled "The Wen Family Empire," showing the business links between Wen's family, close colleagues, and six Chinese tycoons. Qu Naijie, the Dalian billionaire snapping up Bordeaux vineyard real estate like candy, figured in the rogue's gallery. Barboza found that Qu had invested in Union Mobile Pay, where Wen Yunsong (also known as Winston Wen), the premier's son, was a director, and that Qu's company, Dalian Haichang Group, had bought into Sheng Churui, a diamond company. Wen's wife, Zhang Beili, practically oversaw the country's diamond and gem industry and was listed as a legal representative of Sheng Churui. Through his company, Qu also held shares in Ping An Insurance worth $75 million. Ping An was China's biggest financial services company and seemed to be positioned at the center of a web of insider investments and cronyism.

In response to the story, China blocked access to both the English- and Chinese-language sites of the *New York Times*. The government also censored posts on Weibo that referred to the *Times* or to Wen Jiabao. Nonetheless, the Chinese leadership had lost face, and Beijing could not afford such a hit to its authority.

According to a 2009 cable from the U.S. embassy in Beijing, Wen was said to be "disgusted with his family's activities, but [was] either unable or unwilling to curtail them. He particularly dislike[d] his wife for her brazenness in trading on his name." So perhaps he felt he'd found a kindred spirit in Xi Jinping, the man whom everyone assumed would become China's leader in the coming months. Back in 2004, Xi had told party officials, "Rein in your spouses, children, relatives, friends, and staff, and vow not to use power for personal gain."

Xi was a princeling, the son of Xi Zhongxun, a guerrilla leader based in northwest China during the Communist Revolution who had survived Mao's early purges to rise to political power in Guangdong. Both Xi and his father had been denounced during the Cultural Revolution, but when the son was allowed to return to Beijing, he joined the party. It had been his best chance for survival.

Xi took a series of posts in several provinces, eventually landing a seat on the powerful Politburo Standing Committee in 2007. That same year, he was put in charge of the Communist Party in Shanghai. His predecessor had been ousted for corruption. An inspection of the party's records uncovered that officials had stolen 3.7 billion yuan—$483 million—from a workers' pension fund to speculate on real estate developments, road construction, and other infrastructure projects. "Xi knows how very corrupt China is and is repulsed by the all-encompassing commercialization of Chinese society, with its attendant nouveau riche, official corruption, loss of values, dignity, and self-respect, and such 'moral evils' as drugs and prostitution," reported a 2009 U.S. diplomatic cable, which was based on information from a professor, then living in America, who had grown up with Xi. The professor speculated that if Xi were to become the party's general secretary, he was likely to aggressively attack these "evils," even if it came at the expense of China's new moneyed interests.

When Xi was confirmed as general secretary of the Communist Party on November 8, 2012, Wen's rules on excessive spending grew into an earnest crackdown on graft and corruption. In December, at an official dinner in Hebei, Xi announced that he wanted only simple dishes served, and no alcoholic drinks. The government quickly recycled the edict of

"Four Simple Dishes and One Soup," first proclaimed by a fourteenth-century Ming emperor in an attempt to quash his own court's extravagances. Xi issued an "Eight-Point Code" of conduct for party and government officials, including a ban on red carpets and ostentatious floral arrangements. "Leaders must keep in close contact with the grassroots," the points said, and "people's practical problems must be tackled." When it came to party discipline, Xi promised no leniency "no matter who was involved," according to the *Financial Times*.

In January 2013, Xi tackled the tricky question of how the Communist Party might police itself: "Keep power restricted in a cage of regulations." Speaking before the plenary meeting of the Communist Party's Central Commission for Discipline Inspection (CCDI) in Beijing, Xi vowed to crack down on unsavory behavior among officials, whether they were high-level "tigers" or low-level "flies" swirling around those with more power. Xi was cleaning up the party's ranks, top to bottom. The CCDI was a shadowy enforcer; more than 73,000 people, including 4,698 cadres, had been punished by the CCDI for corruption or dereliction of duty in the previous year—and that was before Xi came to power.

Although sales of expensive spirits such as baijiu fell 30 percent over the Chinese New Year festivities compared to the year before, many officials continued to party as they always had. One local party official invited eighty guests to a seaside resort and ran up a $63,000 tab. But at the National People's Congress in March 2013, when Xi was elected as China's new president, the public dining room of the Beijing Hotel sat empty. The delegates had wisely moved banquets to the hotel's private dining rooms and to gourmet restaurants around the capital, out of the public's sight, or canceled them. Obvious displays of gluttony were a thing of the past.

While the Chinese delegates tried to maintain a low profile, back in Bordeaux the 2012 vintage was debuting with the customary fanfare. At the barrel tastings in April 2013, the tents went up, the Michelin-starred chefs flew in, and buyers snapped on their guest badges and pulled out their notebooks, as though business was proceeding just as it had in any other year.

Don St. Pierre Jr. had brought his CEO, John Watkins, with him for the annual ritual. Seated at a corner table in the lobby bar of the swank Grand Hotel, St. Pierre ordered a round of Champagne. He looked smart in a dark velvet jacket, especially next to Watkins, who had the watchful, emotionless expression of a lifer in corporate management. It wasn't Watkins's first trip to Bordeaux, but it was his first time as a wine importer. St. Pierre was showing him the ropes. Despite Watkins's inexperience in the wine trade, it was soon clear why St. Pierre had hired him.

Watkins truly understood the political complexities of doing business in China. Even if a tycoon had earned his money lawfully, he might be picked out for an anti-corruption investigation if the public called for it—or if he didn't have guanxi with those who were making the decisions these days. Officials were afraid that even legitimate business dealings held over "four simple dishes and one soup" might be investigated. "The last thing a mayor wants to do is to be seen with a real estate developer at a restaurant, have his picture taken, and have it go on Weibo," said Watkins. Anyone doing business with state-owned companies faced a radically different lifestyle, he explained. "What has been reduced significantly is the use of state funds for entertainment and gifting," he went on. "Government to government, government to state-owned enterprise, and state-owned enterprise to state-owned enterprise, all that [entertainment] has gone away."

The austerity campaign was having an impact on sales, but Watkins seemed unflappable. A crackdown was good public relations for Xi Jinping, and if the purge also eliminated his political adversaries, all the better—a stable China was better for business. Watkins gave this latest anti-corruption campaign an expiration date of twelve months. Once the new government had consolidated its position, everything would return to normal. He was sure of it.

❂

Forty minutes east of the city of Bordeaux lies Libourne, historically the commercial hub for wines produced on the Right Bank in the appellations of Saint-Émilion, Pomerol, and Fronsac. It was here, in June 2013, that another dark-suited delegation from China had come to seal a deal with the French wine community, as Libourne tried to wrest some of the spotlight from the successes of the Bordeaux Chamber of Commerce and the classified growths in the Médoc.

The previous winter, the city of Pu'er, population 2.36 million, had negotiated a bilateral agreement with Libourne, population 24,506. The government of Pu'er would help promote Right Bank wines in China, and the government of Libourne would promote Pu'er tea in France. The agreement gave the Right Bank growers access to two large commercial spaces in Yunnan Province, one in the capital of Kunming and one in Pu'er itself, as well as license to organize a large exhibit on wine at the Pu'er city museum. Given how hard it had become to sell Bordeaux wine in China, Libourne's mayor, Philippe Buisson, and the president of the Saint-Émilion-Pomerol-Fronsac winegrowers association, Jean-François Quenin, were confident they had gotten the better part of the deal.

The Pu'er tea traders knew quite a bit about outrageously priced beverages. Some of their teas sold for $800 for 3.5 ounces. A compacted *bing* of the tea, about the size of a dinner plate, cost something on the order of $275,000. Luxury teas were purchased by the same people who bought Bordeaux classified growths. Fortunes had been made in Pu'er— some of them much larger than those made in Bordeaux—and several of those rich tea growers were present.

In contrast to Qu Naijie's camera-shy appearances that had all the excitement of a board meeting, Libourne's elite guest, the tea and hotel magnate Lam Kok, was available for interviews and photo shoots with the Pu'er officials. To mark the formal signing of the agreement, a special tasting had been organized by Kok and his wife, the owners of Brilliant Group Investment. Three beautiful Chinese women presented an elaborate tea ceremony and performance, changing costumes at each stage. The teas were carefully prepared—rare vintage brews made from dark fermented leaves pressed into disk, knob, brick, and melon shapes, some aged one hundred years, their aromas and flavors gaining complexity over time, just like a fine wine. To cement the friendship between the two cities, the teas were tasted alongside glasses of Château Cheval Blanc, Château La Fleur-Pétrus, and Château Bélair-Monange.

The atmosphere was warm and respectful, and intended to promote the idea that Pu'er tea and Bordeaux wines had a lot in common. "Pu'er tea is harvested by hand each year, is labeled with a vintage, and can be aged for up to fifty years," explained Libourne's mayor. "Its taste is affected by the soil it is grown in, and the weather conditions during the year of harvest."

Most important, Mayor Buisson knew that the Chinese government had signed off on the cooperative agreement. The Pu'er officials had gone through official channels, approaching the Right Bank winegrowers via Beijing and the French Chamber of Commerce. Yet, some members of the Pu'er delegation admitted to their French hosts that tea was not all that they had on their mind. They whispered discreetly that potential investors for Bordeaux's vineyards might number among them. Would it be possible to visit a truly magnificent estate?

Calls were made, and the mayor arranged for the Pu'er group to visit Château de la Rivière in Fronsac, which dated back to Charlemagne's reign. The fairy-tale castle sat atop a hill overlooking the Dordogne River; twenty acres of subterranean caves were carved out of the limestone rock beneath the hill and used as wine cellars. The owner, James Grégoire, had purchased the estate after selling his company, a manufacturer of mechanical harvesters.

When Kok and his wife saw La Rivière, they knew they wanted to buy the château and convert it into a luxury hotel in the Brilliant Group portfolio. The previous December, they had tried to buy the elegant Château Loudenne in the Médoc, but had lost to the Kweichow Moutai Group. Kok suspected he'd been used to create a bidding war, and it still smarted. He was not going to miss out again. It didn't matter that the estate wasn't for sale: everybody had a price. He made an offer of nearly $40 million on the spot. Though his wife put up resistance, Grégoire said yes. This gave Grégoire and his two sons a chance, he reasoned, to "trade up" for a classified growth in Saint-Émilion.

A Chinese buyer was Grégoire's only bet for such a high offer. The wines of Fronsac were hard to sell in Europe and America, but in China they were fairly well known, largely due to the efforts of his own estate. Vintex, the négociant firm Grégoire backed financially, distributed La

Rivière wines on the mainland. His wine was served in business class on Air China and at in-house events by China Southern Airlines.

Lam Kok was not the only billionaire determined to acquire a Bordeaux château. Real estate agents said there was no dearth of Chinese tycoons and conglomerates hunting for châteaux, and Chinese investors owned more than 10 percent of the vineyard surface in Fronsac.

A single foreign group investing so heavily in Bordeaux's natural resources and heritage was not disturbing. What was disturbing was that the Chinese were accelerating a trend that had begun with luxury brand groups and insurance companies. Increasingly, the owner-families no longer lived in the châteaux. Prior to the arrival of the Chinese tycoons, the corporate entities had confined their bidding wars almost entirely to the most expensive estates. The Chinese, however, were importing that same investment mentality to the Entre-Deux-Mers and to the Right Bank, which for generations had been inhabited by French families. Those estates were no longer homes. Increasingly, they were sanitized, polished, dusted offices, managed by someone who imagined that purchasing a château was like picking out a new Ferrari. Or at least that was how the locals saw it.

Despite the rules against luxury consumption, Bordeaux and China were still in business together. The Bordelais interpreted the land grab as a sign of confidence in the long-term value of their properties and the cachet of the Bordeaux name.

❋

In 2013, the number one investment for Chinese tycoons was real estate outside of China. The advantages were straightforward. In China, one might acquire a fifty-year lease that could be revoked at any time, whereas France and other foreign countries offered permanent ownership. Banks were making it easier to transfer money outside of China. The Industrial and Commercial Bank of China allowed the Chinese to use assets in China against a loan in Europe, where the interest rate was lower—say 3 percent versus the Chinese rate of 7.5 percent. Don St. Pierre Jr. thought the tycoons' investments in châteaux were less about Bordeaux than about China. "The big picture is that Chinese entrepreneurs are fearful of what's going to happen in the future with their assets in China," he said. "They don't feel secure. They are looking for asset preservation." Making a short-term profit was secondary.

As more châteaux shifted into Chinese hands, the Bordelais began to note how little was known about most of their new neighbors. A few of the buyers held press conferences, but the majority hid their identities behind shell companies. Often the real estate brokers did not even know for certain who the real owner was. "Business addresses, or indeed the geographical sources of the purchase funds, are not always the same as the owners," said Michael Baynes, a partner in Maxwell-Storrie-Baynes, the broker whom Christie's International Real Estate had made an exclusive affiliate in Bordeaux when it opened the first global advisory for buyers of vineyard estates in Hong Kong in May 2013.

Baynes estimated that seventy châteaux were under Chinese ownership as of 2013. According to the Bordeaux Chamber of Commerce's China Desk, at least twenty-five estates had been bought by Chinese interests that year, 50 percent more than in 2011 or 2012. But because so many purchases were kept secret, it was impossible to know the true number.

It was understood that Qu Naijie or his family owned Châteaux Chenu-Lafitte, Grand Jour, Branda, de Hauterive, Laurette, Millaud Montlabert, Baby, l'Enclos, Grand Branet, Thebot, and Jonqueyres. It was believed, however, that these estates represented just a portion of his holdings, and that he owned twenty-seven estates—maybe a few more or a few less. It was said that Qu had spent around $100 million in three years, laying claim to nearly 1,500 acres of French real estate and securing an annual supply of five million bottles of Bordeaux wine. He had invested in a series of relatively modest châteaux, the sort of purchases that typically would not have drawn attention in Bordeaux—if it weren't for the fact that so many Chinese tycoons were doing exactly the same thing.

More than five thousand miles to the east, Qu's wine tourism park in Dalian had officially cost 3 billion yuan thus far. That sort of project did not happen in China without local government approval, and Qu had carefully included city officials in all of his public dealings with the

Bordeaux Chamber of Commerce. But as Xi Jinping's anti-corruption crackdown got into full swing, a number of people connected to Dalian were put in the spotlight.

Bo Xilai had made his name in Dalian. Bo was yet another princeling, the son of Bo Yibo, a revolutionary hero and former minister of finance, but, unlike Xi, he had participated wholeheartedly in the Cultural Revolution, at least at the beginning. Bo joined a particularly nasty faction of the Red Guard called the Liandong, which brutalized older people and teachers. During one "struggle session," he reportedly broke his own father's ribs. Not long after, Bo was sent to a labor camp. Both father and son were eventually rehabilitated, with Bo's father climbing his way to deputy premier. With his father as his example, Bo must have dreamed of taking his own place in the nine-member Central Politburo Standing Committee, from whose ranks China's president and premier were anointed.

When Bo arrived in Dalian in 1993, he found a sleepy, dusty town. Ambitious, charismatic, and movie-star handsome, Bo immediately set his sights on transforming this stepping-stone into a model city. He imported grass to spruce up public spaces, commissioned wide boulevards and monuments, including a ceremonial *huabiao* column, and recruited substantial foreign investment. But, in the midst of all the development in the city, corruption was rife. Businesses could not succeed if "high commissions" weren't paid to the government. Bo's wife, Gu Kailai, a self-promoting lawyer, was said to collect kickbacks on many of the contracts.

After seven years in Dalian, Bo was promoted to governor of Liaoning Province, and in 2004 he gained his first national post, minister of commerce. Three years later, he won a spot on the twenty-five-member Politburo, but the Standing Committee eluded him. His enemies in Beijing tried to stall his career by banishing him to the crime-ridden, polluted, second-tier city of Chongqing. As head of Chongqing's Communist Party, Bo cleaned up the city and encouraged citizens to sing Mao-era songs. He waged a zealous war on organized crime; more than five thousand people were arrested. The success of Bo's neo-Maoist "Chongqing model" gathered headlines around the world. Then, in November 2011,

Neil Heywood, a British business consultant who seemed to have known Bo and his wife since their Dalian days, was found dead in a seedy hotel on the outskirts of Chongqing. Heywood's body was quickly cremated— but not quickly enough. Bo's top police enforcer in Chongqing, a man named Wang Lijun, found evidence showing that Heywood had been poisoned. When Wang and Bo fell out in February 2012, Wang fled to an American consulate, exposing Bo's crimes and effectively ending Bo's career.

Early on, it was obvious that Bo was not going to fare well after China's latest leadership transition. On March 15, 2012, twelve days before Wen Jiabao announced the new rules on expensive gifts, he had singled out Bo for dereliction of his duties and removed him from his post as Chongqing Communist Party chief. The next month, Bo was stripped of his remaining positions, including his seats on the Central Committee and the Politburo. His wife was arrested and charged with murdering Heywood. In October 2012, Bo was jailed and expelled from parliament. That made him fair game for prosecution by the Chinese authorities. Then he disappeared.

Nine months later, in July 2013, Bo was finally charged with corruption, bribery, and abuse of power, with most of the alleged financial crimes tied to Bo's days in Dalian. Bo was accused of embezzling $800,000 from a Dalian construction project and accepting $175,000 in bribes from the head of a Dalian development company; he was also accused of accepting monies intended for public use, including the purchase price of a French villa, from Xu Ming, the youthful chairman of the Dalian Shide Group, who had won contracts to beautify Dalian and later expanded into plastics. It was estimated that Bo and his wife's family had an estimated $136 million in assets. The next month, Bo appeared for his trial in the Intermediate People's Court in Jinan. Eighteen months had passed since he'd last been seen in public. On September 22, 2013, he was found guilty on all charges and sentenced to life in prison. Two days later, Bo's disobedient "fly," the informant Wang Lijun, was convicted of defection, bribery, and abuse of power and sentenced to fifteen years.

At Bo's trial, Xu Ming testified against him. Xu was a real estate and plastics tycoon, one of the Dalian gang. He'd made his first millions quickly, his career tracking Bo's rise as mayor of the city. By 2005, Xu was listed as the eighth richest man in China. It was reported that he had bankrolled much of Bo's high-flying lifestyle, buying, among other things, a $3.2 million villa in Cannes for his politically connected friend. In exchange, it was asserted, Dalian Shide received lucrative public works contracts and business licenses. Since Bo's trial, the Dalian Shide tycoon had disappeared from the public eye.

Qu Naijie may have watched the breaking news and worried about the political realignments in China and the obvious overlap with his real estate empire. At the moment, though, he had troubles of his own to quash in Bordeaux. One of his holding companies, Lamont, was under scrutiny for illegally hiring Chinese workers to restore his châteaux. Other Chinese estate owners had also come under criticism for their management methods. One had simply not showed up, leaving the employees without direction and without pay. Another had decided the day before bottling to use only magnums, even though standard-sized bottles had already been ordered and delivered, and the bottling machine could not handle the magnums. When word of Qu's alleged misconduct got around, his man in Bordeaux, Christian Delpeuch, distanced himself, retaining only a loose consulting role in relation to the Dalian tycoon's Bordeaux enterprises.

Then, in the summer of 2013, Qu decided to sell a handful of his French estates. According to real estate agents involved in the listings, Qu had always planned to "flip" the châteaux, selling them to other Chinese investors after installing a Chinese-style management team that would be included in any sale. It was a curious twist to Chinese real estate speculation, but Qu's idea was based on insights into the way his fellow countrymen liked to operate. Many Chinese investors did not want to deal with the winemaking business that came with owning most châteaux. His preparations simplified things.

Unfortunately for Qu, his speculation in châteaux was about to become a problem. In July 2013, France's anti-money-laundering agency, Tracfin, published its annual report. The agency highlighted the increasing number of châteaux sold to Chinese, Russian, and Ukrainian interests, many of which bought properties using shell companies based in countries with advantageous tax schedules. It was often difficult, the report said, to identify the beneficial owner, let alone the origin of the funds used to buy the estates. Tracfin's investigators suspected that Chinese syndicates might be laundering money through vineyard investments.

Later that summer, the case files arrived in Bordeaux for further inspection. This was not the kind of publicity Bordeaux needed.

❋

Bordeaux's wine trade was already navigating rough water. The previous summer, several long-standing customers in China had warned some European exporters that domestic companies were angry about competition from imported wine. Dynasty Fine Wines had been particularly vocal. Through state media outlets, Dynasty announced that it had sold only 40 percent of its annual target. The company's directors didn't blame the embarrassing sales on poor quality, dubious labeling, lackluster marketing, or buying too much top-end Bordeaux instead of focusing on brands that were within the reach of the average Chinese consumer. Instead, they blamed unfair trade practices on the part of European winemakers. "Our price for a bottle of wine is 9 or 10 yuan at the least, but the CIF price for imports from the EU could be only one euro a bottle," said Wang Weihua, Dynasty's outspoken head of legal affairs, which meant that European wine was arriving in China at €1.25 or $1.50 a bottle, including cost, insurance, and freight. "We believe that there's no way for them to enter the Chinese market at such a low price without [relying on] unreasonable subsidies or dumping."

In tandem with Dynasty's allegations, the China Alcoholic Drinks Association (CADA) released data showing that wine imports from the European Union had grown 60 percent year-on-year in 2011, far outpacing the average output growth for Chinese domestic wineries. Dynasty wasn't the only Chinese winemaker grumbling. Four other domestic wineries had complained to the association about the cheap price attached to European imports. In response, CADA was filing an application for an anti-dumping probe into the imported wines. "We need fair market competition with survival of the fittest. It is necessary for achieving a win-win situation," Wang said. When domestic wine sales for 2012 were once again dismal, CADA renewed its efforts. On May 15, 2013, the association lodged a formal petition with China's Ministry of Commerce on behalf of its members.

The European Union and China were already locked in a trade dispute. In July 2012, EU ProSun, a collective of European solar energy businesses led by the Germans, had lodged a complaint of unfair dumping of solar panels on the local market by Chinese manufacturers. According to the framework agreed to by member nations of the World Trade Organization, any investigation had to prove not only that dumping had occurred, but also that native companies had been injured by the practice. Confident that the investigation would find in its favor, the European Union imposed provisional anti-dumping duties on Chinese solar products that were quite harsh—even punitive (as high as 68 percent).

On June 5, 2013, the day after the EU plan was announced, Beijing retaliated by announcing that the complaint from the Chinese wine companies was moving forward immediately. The Chinese Ministry of Commerce notified the EU delegation in China to prepare for an investigation of subsidy and dumping practices in the wine trade. It was a tactical maneuver. The value and volume of wine imports was dwarfed by the trade in solar panels, which was worth more than $20 billion to Chinese companies. The Germans had been losing support from other EU countries for their hard line on solar panels, but the French remained staunchly pro-tariff regarding Chinese solar panels, as did Spain and Italy. It was estimated that the European Union had sold $1 billion worth of wine to China the year before, and French wine accounted for $710 million of that. Tariffs on EU wine would badly hurt the French wine trade.

"A wine probe serves as a timely warning that it is not just European photovoltaic enterprises that will be the victims if the EU sticks to its protectionist stance," reported *China Daily*. "As it has become a major target of anti-dumping charges by other countries, China also needs to start showing more teeth when protecting its legitimate interests." The response in China was triumphant. Shares in Changyu's publicly traded unit, Yantai Changyu, surged to the daily limit of 10 percent within hours of the announcement of the Chinese investigation.

For the EU Trade Commission, this latest clash was one more move in a decades-long battle with Beijing. It was the commission's job to make sure things didn't escalate. Normally the preinvestigation period would drag on for weeks, as both sides prepared the documents to be filed, but the Chinese surprised the Europeans by expediting the process. The first negotiation meeting between the EU negotiators and their Chinese counterparts was set for June 17, 2013, in Beijing—the same week as the Vinexpo wine trade show in Bordeaux. Alain Castel, the CEO of Castel Frères, had realistic expectations. "The Chinese want to protect their interests. That's normal. The Europeans want to protect their interests. That's normal," he said while attending Vinexpo. "But you have to understand that the first export market for the Chinese is Europe, and the Chinese market for Europeans is very important. Obviously we need to come to an understanding."

On June 21, the European Union's negotiation team sent its defense of the winemakers' practices to the Chinese Ministry of Commerce, but few in Bordeaux believed there was any chance of reaching an agreement until after the solar panel issue was resolved. On July 1, the Chinese formally filed for an anti-dumping and anti-subsidy investigation, again stunning the Europeans. The EU Trade Commission quickly notified the national wine trade associations.

The European wine producers and exporters had until July 20, a mere twenty days, to comply "voluntarily" with the initial stage of the Chinese inquiry. It was estimated that it would cost each company more than $6,500 in staff time as well as legal and translation fees, whether it was a giant corporation such as Castel and Les Grands Chais de France or a small family-owned estate in the Entre-Deux-Mers. Any grower that did not comply was threatened with a duty so onerous as to effectively deny it access to the Chinese market. The winemakers had been conscripted into a trade war.

At the EU Trade Commission, the magnitude and complexity of the case slowly sunk in. The commissioners dealt with anti-dumping investigations all the time. Normally, however, an investigation involved fifteen companies at the most; in this case, thousands of European companies exported wine to China. Some wine was sold in bulk and some was sold in bottles. Because of the intricate networks of distribution, many growers did not even know that their wine was being exported to China. In addition, the Chinese Ministry of Commerce insisted that all pertinent files must be translated into Mandarin. If the ministry spotted a single error, the file would be tossed out, effectively classifying the company as noncompliant in the investigation.

Emmanuel Martin, the owner of La Guyennoise, wasn't taken completely by surprise by the Ministry of Commerce's action. He had been among those forewarned. The voluntary registration wasn't that big of an issue for him; what worried him was the investigation that would surely follow. A handful of companies, called a sampling, would be selected for intensive scrutiny lasting months, possibly more than a year. If it could be proved that any Chinese company had been injured by subsidies or dumping, then every European wine exporter would be hit with a punitive duty. The worst offender in the sampling would be assigned the highest duty rate, while the company with the best record of fair practices in China would be rewarded with a low duty rate, giving it a slight advantage in the market. The average of the two extreme duties would then be levied on the wines of every other producer-exporter in the European Union, including those not in the sampling. Increasing the stakes, the subsidies given to agricultural producers under Europe's Common Agricultural Policy were also coming under scrutiny.

The French media had recently exposed the subsidies given to some of the country's largest wine producers. The subsidies were intended to keep thousands of struggling winegrowers and other European farmers in business. But according to records available from France's Ministry of Agriculture, in 2011, Castel had received $4.3 million in subsidies and Les Grands Chais de France had received $2.5 million. And in 2010, the Bordeaux Wine Council had received $8.5 million and the Union des Grands Crus de Bordeaux, which organized the annual barrel tastings promoting Bordeaux's luxury wines worldwide, had received $2 million. The numbers were widely condemned as scandalous. The anti-dumping investigation threatened to pit the heavyweights of the French wine industry against Europe's small farmers.

In mid-September, the Chinese government announced the six companies that had been selected for the sampling. The wine producers had been chosen because they had reported the highest level of wine exports by volume to China in 2012. Two of the companies were Spanish—Félix Solís Avantis and Cherubino Valsangiacomo—and four were French—Castel Frères, Les Grands Chais de France, La Guyennoise, and Moncigale.

When he heard the news, Emmanuel Martin felt the responsibility for thousands of growers throughout Europe settle on his shoulders. The future of his own estate was also in jeopardy. The amount of information the Chinese requested was mind-boggling. Every aspect of his production was being put under a microscope. He had to account for the cost of every type of label, capsule, and bottle he produced; report every bulk wine transaction he had conducted; list every employee he paid; and provide the names and addresses of every client that was based in China, and the volume and value of the wine he'd sold to them. And that was merely a portion of the necessary paperwork.

La Guyennoise wasn't a multinational firm like Castel with a team of high-powered lawyers and a staff of hundreds to answer every question put to him by the Ministry of Commerce. It was a one-stop shop for wine traders, many of whom, in recent years, had been Chinese. He knew his wine competed directly with Chinese companies; he was in the bulk wine business, after all. But if the Chinese found La Guyennoise "guilty" of unfair trade, his decisions on where and how to sell his wine would partly determine the level of punitive tariffs imposed on all European wines. Worse, he would effectively be shut out of the most lucrative market he had.

❋

In Hong Kong that November, Vincent Yip tossed the depletion reports from a major five-star hotel onto his desk with a note of despair. He had read the long list of classified growths, cru bourgeois, and petits châteaux, including some of the most famous names in Bordeaux. None of them had sold for the hotel in over a year. Demand had flat-lined. Topsy Trading still had nearly all of its 2010 stock, and this hotel wasn't going to be in the market for any of it.

"It's painful, I tell you," he said, looking over the report. "This is just some of the report, I keep it to remind myself. This is 2012—August; we have five thousand euros [\$5,600] of wine there. Mostly Bordeaux. Sales were zero for [the] whole month. No sales," he said with disgust. He turned to the report for January 2013. Eighty-nine U.S. dollars in sales. March 2013—\$243. August 2013—\$119. "It's ridiculous."

The crackdown on government entertaining had wiped out much of the high-volume event business at the five-star hotels. "It affects our business . . . a lot, really. If, for example, they are entertaining the governor, they no longer go to a hotel because it's a public place," said a sommelier from a five-star hotel, the Shangri-La, in Qingdao. The sommelier was on the hunt for midpriced, round, fruity wines with soft tannins that the hotel's guests would enjoy drinking—and that they could pay for, out of their own pockets. And he was under pressure. He had to find some way to boost wine sales in the hotel now that the government was no longer buying, or he would lose his job. There was no need for a sommelier if no one was ordering wine.

In addition, most of the hotels let customers discreetly bring their own bottles of wine to their restaurants, and VIP customers never paid a corkage fee. As a result, the Yips had stopped suggesting that their restaurant clients include First Growths on wine lists. First Growths such as Lafite and Latour were almost always sold on "consignment," which meant the restaurant didn't buy the wines outright. Officially, Topsy stored the wines at the restaurant, and the restaurant paid Topsy only for those bottles that were opened, served, and paid for. If a customer opened a bottle and didn't like it, the restaurant didn't force the person to pay for it—that would be bad customer service. But once it was opened, the bottle couldn't be served to anyone else. Topsy Trading swallowed the loss.

The retail market wasn't any better. Vincent Yip had recently received a call from a friend who lived in a Beijing apartment building with a small wine shop on the ground floor that was run by Xiamen C&D. The friend reported that C&D was selling 2007 Château Pontet-Canet for seven hundred yuan. He asked Vincent if that was a fair price. "I told him, 'Very good price. It's at cost,'" Vincent recalled. "They are dumping everything everywhere, in stores, small booths." There was no way Topsy could compete with that.

The Yips had competition from other corners as well. At Hong Kong's Asia Bankers Club, the club's founder, former investment banker Kingston Lai, was organizing a trip to Bordeaux for fifteen of its fifty thousand high-net-worth members. Each person on the trip agreed to ante up $2.3 million, creating a $34 million pot for buying First and Second Growths and their Right Bank equivalents, direct from the châteaux. No courtiers or négociants were in on the deal, and the châteaux had agreed to Lai's conditions without any qualms. Such high-net-worth individuals were precisely the type of clients Topsy specialized in, and trips like this ensured that these individuals would increasingly seek to bypass the Yips as well as the négociants.

Lai had the inside track on any number of deals. He'd been serving as a broker of sorts for a Beijing billionaire who wanted to be the first Chinese person to buy a Grand Cru Classé château. He had come very close to closing a sale. The tycoon had anted up around $135 million, but the French owners had pulled out at the last minute. It was only a matter of time, Lai said, before he found a willing seller. The wine-tasting and investment panels the club organized in Hong Kong, the buying trip to Bordeaux—it was all building Lai's credibility and guanxi with the château owners. Perhaps one day he'd be able to match a Chinese buyer with a French family that had a pile of inheritance taxes coming due and no cash to pay the bill.

Topsy Trading wasn't in the business of doling out real estate advice. It wasn't going to counsel people on investment strategies. Thomas Yip had started the business back in 1983 because he loved wine. In the years since, the company's allocations had grown almost exponentially; on average, the Yips bought twenty thousand cases en primeur each year. For the 2009 and 2010 vintages, father and son reckoned they had spent $30 million, and Topsy had 1.2 million bottles in its inventory. "That's a lot to finance, a lot to risk," said Vincent Yip. The stocks they had bought as prices peaked were losing value. Of course, the Yips could sell the wine at a 30 to 40 percent loss. They weren't willing to take that step. Not yet.

But Vincent Yip couldn't help getting testy about the business's prospects. "The people who built the market are no longer making money. [The châteaux] don't care. What they think, I'm sure, is, *You already made money before, you made a lot, too much. . . .* They think, *If you made money, it's because of us, and you are lucky. If you lost money, you're stupid.*" He didn't begrudge the châteaux their greed. Like most business owners, he was greedy, too. But by cutting out the négociants, importers, and resellers who had made the châteaux famous in China, they had lost touch with the true state of the market.

Tastes hadn't changed as much as the châteaux liked to believe. The vast majority of Chinese still didn't drink wine. "How many rich Chinese will open a bottle of wine at home? Zero," Yip said. "The problem is, we need the wine to be drunk." If the new rules against luxury goods became a permanent fixture of Communist Party doctrine, the classified growths would have no customers unless the upper middle classes decided they actually *liked* the taste of Bordeaux. The main reason for someone in China to buy a case of Lafite was to impress associates. Was that worth the risk of being spotted by a human flesh searcher or a government auditor and having your whole life investigated? Better to play it safe and buy more modestly priced wines.

"We are businessmen. We buy what we can sell. We are merchants," he continued. "We are here to make money. We made money before; that's why we're in the business. Nothing more. So we will be careful. Bordeaux has the quality, the image, the history, the brand—everything. Now we need the price."

❋

Despite the virtual ban on purchases of luxury goods by Chinese officials, ASC Fine Wines posted its best year in 2012. ASC and several of its competitors had continued to import wine after dismal sales for the first half of 2013, believing that the second half of the year would see an end to the crackdown and that sales would rebound, with people buying more than usual to make up for lost time. Unfortunately, sales had been flat, and it wasn't just the expensive First Growths that were affected. Lower categories were hit, too. "This is obvious when you look at the 2012 import figures versus 2011," Don St. Pierre Jr. explained. The volume of lower-priced wines coming into China had dropped. Gifting to and between officials and banqueting had completely dried up. At the same time, there was no shortage of Bordeaux wine floating around China as many dealers tried to off-load inventory before it lost more value—or decided to leave the business entirely.

ASC had been able to improve its sales in the second half of 2013 by offering its customers a unique selling proposition: discretion. In May 2013, the month before the Chinese wine companies lodged their anti-dumping complaint with the Ministry of Commerce, ASC had opened a shrewd addition to its portfolio: the Wine Residence, a $4.5 million, five-story mansion at 55 Urumuqi South Road, a leafy boulevard in the former French Concession of Shanghai. The ground floor of the building boasted an elegant wine store; the upper floors had a series of sumptuous reception and dining rooms; the vast cellar provided space for collectors to store and view their wine. In the cellar's tasting room, ASC staff taught wine appreciation classes. Entrepreneurs might be toning down their displays of wealth, but they still wanted to buy wine and entertain—privately. With its curtained entrance, the Wine Residence was perfect.

Most Bordelais couldn't grasp the influence of Xi Jinping's pronouncements on consumer spending. No Frenchman would heed an admonition from the head of state to cut back on his First Growths. And other than the handful of négociants dealing directly with the Chinese market, few realized that a toast given at the National People's Congress had made red wine palatable to the Chinese public in the first place. But one thing was clear: the Communist Party had all but stopped the flow of expensive wine into China. Most of the wine shipped from Bordeaux was now priced under fifty dollars per bottle, and the strongest demand was for wines costing between four dollars and twenty dollars. The party's edict granted Chinese businessmen a new luxury: offering modest gifts without paying the price of losing face.

The Chinese were buying wines to drink at a price they could afford, both financially and politically. Don St. Pierre Jr. believed there had been a return to traditional frugality. "I also think prices have gotten so high that people are using this issue as an excuse to trade down," he remarked. "They say, 'Instead of the *grand vin*, let's use the second label, because we don't want to get in trouble.' But the real reason in some cases is that they don't want to spend twenty-five hundred dollars; they'd rather spend one thousand dollars." In most cases, they didn't even want to spend that.

ASC had begun selling on the Internet, using existing sites such as Tmall and Jingdong while the firm built its own e-commerce portal, ASC Wine Gallery, hoping to reach more women and younger buyers. ASC's online site sold more than just Bordeaux classified growths; it sold an entire range of fine wine at price points that matched the reduced budgets for business entertainment and the real budget of the middle class. Sales were slim—just 1 percent of ASC's total sales—and most people bought bottles costing fifteen dollars or less, but the demand was there. St. Pierre and his CEO, John D. Watkins Jr., could feel it.

After surveying the political landscape, St. Pierre had reinvented ASC's relationship with China's General Administration of Customs. His detention in 2008 had not been pleasant, and he had gone out of his way since then to ensure that ASC's dealings were above reproach. He'd also decided that it was better to build bridges than to burn them, and he offered his company's expertise to the government's customs officials. In many cases, customs didn't have the correct information on the legitimate labeling or accurate price of imported wines. He was stunned when he learned how little many officials knew about the wine import business. ASC's staff became trusted advisers on these issues, helping the agents do a better job. The knowledge sharing had gone a long way toward erasing St. Pierre's image as a rogue trader, and he was proud of the legacy he was creating for his company. He was well on his way to handing over the reins completely to John Watkins. In the spring of 2014, he would step down as chairman and sell his remaining shares in ASC to Suntory.

As wine prices in China came down, customers wanted to be assured that they were buying genuine French wines. There was no shortage of misinformation in the market, and confusion about labeling continued to be a problem. St. Pierre and Watkins decided to invest in making ASC the gold standard for authenticity.

Building on ASC's consulting work with customs and their own experience in the market, St. Pierre and Watkins had developed a great deal of expertise in how wine counterfeiters stayed one step ahead of the authorities. There had been attempts to counterfeit the Chinese-language label that ASC affixed to the bottles it handled to identify the wine's importer and distributor. By 2013, Watkins felt that the "commercial technology was available and ubiquitous enough to launch a new label that would prevent counterfeiting." If ASC could stand behind every bottle it sold, it would rise above the flood of counterfeit wine.

Their solution was a Quick Response, or QR, code tracking system that assigned a unique eight-character alphanumeric code to every bottle. The QR labels would have been all for show if ASC had not also launched three mobile applications that their customers could easily use to inspect a wine's authenticity. The apps were costly but necessary. A survey published by Wine Intelligence in 2013 indicated that 44 percent of Chinese customers worried about buying counterfeit wine. By scanning the code using ASC's mobile phone app, a customer could view the bottle's shipping history. "ASC will be able to track each bottle to the point of delivery. The system also allows us to know to which customer each bottle was sold," said Watkins.

Watkins took the extra and expensive precaution of having the hologram labels developed by an American company and printed outside of China, then shipped directly to ASC's warehouse, where they were kept under lock and key. The company it had hired had already printed QR codes for cigarettes and for NBA-branded merchandise. ASC placed an initial order for several million QR labels—a year's worth of wine. Starting in May 2014, every bottle that came through ASC got tagged.

Yet, despite these technological advances, Watkins felt he'd been slow to react to China's new normal. Government and state officials' expenses were being aggressively monitored, and the value of the imported wine was growing at a measly 2 percent annually—nothing like the 94 percent growth that ASC had seen in 2011. "My experience in China helped me, but it was also a weakness," he admitted. "I didn't think the anti-graft campaign would last, so I waited longer than I should have to make some necessary changes." Those changes involved tightening the company's operations to take into account its new client base. Watkins laid off some employees and closed some low-performing offices, investing more heavily in ASC Wine Gallery. Online sales of wine increased 50 percent in 2014, and from looking at which bottles were selling, he could tell that Chinese consumers were starting to buy wines they wanted to drink.

"Look at the U.S. as an example," he said. "In the early 1970s, there was very little domestic wine drunk and only a bit of imported wine being consumed in the big cities. Then in the 1970s, Californian wines took off and it brought average Americans into the market. As volumes grew, people became more sophisticated and wanted to try other things; they started experimenting with French, Italian, and Spanish wines. Then the growth of imported wines grew faster than domestic wines. We're hoping the same trend happens in China."

But the crackdown wasn't the only driver of change in the Chinese market. Beijing was pressuring a wide variety of industries to lower their prices to consumers. The anti-dumping investigation of the European wine industry had dampened trade. Brand squatters continued to push brand-name wines out of China. In one notable example, the Inter-Continental Hotel chain had dropped the Penfolds brand, owned by Treasury Wine Estates, from its wine lists. "I would ask you to pull your Penfolds branded wines off your menus until further notice," wrote Tim Stanhope, the company's food and beverage director, in an email to his managers. "We don't want to be involved in any further law actions." The notorious brand squatter Li Daozhi—who had forced Castel to change the Chinese name of its wine—was again in the courts fighting for his rights as the first registrant of the natural Chinese trademark. Li Daozhi and another man named Li Shen had trademarked Ben Fu, the

Chinese name for Penfolds. Li Daozhi had trademarked Ben Fu in the hotel and restaurant category, and Li Shen had trademarked two versions of Ben Fu in the wine and spirits category. Treasury Wine Estates had won the initial court case, but the Lis had appealed.

Penfolds was able to convince InterContinental to retract its decision, but the impact from brand squatting continued to reverberate. "One of our brand owners is also in dispute with a Chinese individual who registered one of the company's wine labels. As a result, we have had to de-list this specific wine label from every account across China, at considerable cost to the brand owner and ASC," said Watkins. "These trends encourage worried wine consumers to avoid purchasing unknown wines. As the market contracts, companies . . . find it harder to sell wines without brand credibility. This has led to rumors of warehouses full of dead stock throughout China."

Of special interest to Watkins were the stories of fake Lafite. They had the quality of urban myth; published accounts, impossible to verify, declared that there were two million bottles of Château Lafite sold in China every year, though only eighty thousand of those bottles could contain real Lafite. Even if a million bottles of fake Lafite were sold each year, it would be a daunting challenge to gain the trust of consumers.

Watkins's interest was not idle. When demand for Château Lafite appeared to be peaking around the Sotheby's auction in October 2010, Lafite's managing director, Christophe Salin, had decided to select ASC as the exclusive distributor for the estate's wines in China. And so, starting on January 1, 2011, ASC was the only source in China for Lafite's wines not sold through allocations on the Place de Bordeaux. Since then, ASC had provided safe storage for and wide availability of Lafite's brands. More important, it had invested heavily in the QR code apps to reassure consumers that the wine in the bottle in front of them was genuine Lafite. By working with one reliable distributor, Salin had tightened the noose on the con artists.

In 2014, Salin rewarded ASC with the exclusive distribution of ninety-six thousand bottles of Château Paradis Casseuil, a red wine made in the Entre-Deux-Mers region that was emblazoned with the quickly identifiable five-arrow symbol of DBR Lafite and priced to sell post-crackdown. It was the first time Lafite had restricted the sale of one of its wines to a single market.

John Watkins interpreted the deal as a sign of faith in both ASC and the market for wine in China, but his own tenure at ASC ended in May 2015. After his resignation, ASC hired Bruno Baudry, a former Castel executive and veteran of the Asian wine market. Suntory, ASC's parent company, was more determined than ever that ASC expand its business. But nothing spoke to a long-term commitment to China like a decision to plant vines.

10

································

Adjust Measures to Local Conditions

In the days when Chinese tycoons were openly grap-
pling for what they considered a fair share of the
world's most famous wine, DBR Lafite had decided to stake its own
claim in the Middle Kingdom. Located twenty miles southeast of the
coastal city of Penglai in Shandong Province, the lush, green valley
above the Qiushan reservoir was home to numerous farms and orchards.
It was there, on the western slope rising above the reservoir, that Lafite's
newest vineyard was taking shape. Its vines were set to produce the most
highly anticipated wine in China. Connoisseurs wondered if the wine
could ever live up to its nomenclature as the "Chinese Lafite."

The management team at Lafite had considered the possibility of
making wine in China since at least the mid-1990s, when the joint venture between Rémy Martin and the Tianjin government was expanding
into a behemoth with more than ninety wine brands. In 2005, shortly
after China joined the World Trade Organization, the timing finally
seemed right for Lafite to move forward. To launch its venture, Christophe Salin hired Gérard Colin, one of a handful of experts on Chinese
terroir, away from Grace Vineyard, and three years later, he found a com-
patible business partner: China International Trust and Investment
Corporation, or CITIC.

Unlike many of the other partners in wine joint ventures, Lafite's Chinese partner did not have deep roots in the wine or spirits trade. CITIC was China's largest financial company, a state-owned conglomerate founded by Rong Yiren, one of Deng Xiaoping's most trusted advisers on the country's transition to state capitalism. CITIC was a key tool in China's "opening up," and it made Rong a very rich and well-connected "Red Capitalist." In 1993, Rong was appointed vice president of China. By 2000, two years after he retired from business and politics, his family had amassed a fortune reportedly worth $1.9 billion. CITIC was a well-connected enterprise, to say the least.

The partnership between CITIC and Lafite was established during a period when Beijing was particularly focused on raising the country's profile and the "international recognition of its state-owned flagships." So although CITIC would have only a 30 percent stake in the vineyard, representing a relatively minuscule investment for the company, the project was approved. Lafite was, without a doubt, a prestigious name to add to CITIC's portfolio.

Of course, CITIC was in the business of making money, and its managers appreciated the value of diversifying the company's investments. The same year CITIC sealed its partnership with Lafite, a subsidiary called CITIC Guoan Wine Company bought a majority stake in Jinchuang Suntime, a 24,700-acre vineyard on the northern slopes of the Tian Shan Mountains in the Xinjiang Uygur Autonomous Region, making it the largest vineyard owner in Asia. Suntime had once been a subsidiary of Xinjiang Production and Construction Corps, owned partially by the Chinese military, which operated industrialized farms on vast tracts of the land. This industrial approach had been applied to winemaking, too. In the late 1990s, Suntime's leaders had imported immense quantities of Chardonnay, Merlot, Cabernet Sauvignon, and Riesling vines from Europe, and the wine was made in towering stainless steel tanks in an enormous factory-like cellar. When it came time to promote the wine, Suntime cleverly co-opted the area's ancient heritage as the "birthplace" of Chinese wine; archeological evidence suggested that Xinjiang, located along the Silk Road, was where *Vitis vinifera*, the common wine grape, had first been planted in China. "We . . . found many

246 | THIRSTY DRAGON

ruins of vineyards, grape pips, and even brewing equipment and alcohol containers," said Yue Feng, director of Xinjiang's Cultural Heritage Bureau. "Some wall pictures even showed the Niya [native] people were doing some grape wine–related business."

With these investments in Suntime and in the DBR-CITIC Wine Estate, CITIC's directors indicated that they believed wine had a long and bright future in China—that is, any wine that originated in the People's Republic. That was reassuring.

But CITIC's connections also meant that Lafite had found a valuable ally for the hard work of negotiating with local leaders, far from the halls of power in Beijing. In order to guarantee the quality of their grapes, Christophe Salin wanted to build an estate, which meant wresting leases from local farmers. "If you want to secure twenty-five hectares [sixty acres]," explained Salin, "you need to negotiate with seventy to eighty farmers. You need a partner." Like other astute trailblazers in China, Lafite was adopting the ancient Chinese idiom "Adjust measures to local conditions."

Once the land deals were in place, Lafite had to dig holes—many, many holes. Preliminary studies had led Colin to select the site, but deep soil pits allowed Lafite's technicians to determine the nature of the soil and subsoil down to the underlying bedrock of ancient granite and pick the best plots for building a vineyard from scratch. The pits revealed that the southward-facing slope above the reservoir, which ranged between 225 and 500 feet in altitude, exhibited little geological variability.

Together, the soil, subsoil, climate, and sunlight promised the makings of a fine wine. So, too, did the local business environment.

❊

The port of Penglai has been a popular tourist destination in Shandong for a thousand years. An eleventh-century pavilion of temples and pagodas draws more than two million visitors every year, and Gérard Colin made a strong case that the DBR-CITIC estate would benefit from being near the flow of tourists and lines of transportation. The sprawling state-owned wineries near Penglai earned a great deal of foot traffic this way.

The area also possessed a storied legacy as an important winemaking center in China. In 1892, Zhang Bishi built the Middle Kingdom's first commercial winery, Changyu Pioneer Wine Company, on the Shandong peninsula, most likely because it was one of the first and most active treaty ports, ensuring a steady influx of European traders and diplomats who were regular wine drinkers. Zhang, known as the "Rockefeller of the East," was famous for his business acumen, so much so that it was said that the emperor had once recalled him to China to devise a national development plan.

From the start, Changyu lived up to the "pioneer" spirit later enshrined in its name. To launch his vineyard, Zhang imported two thousand vines from America. These proved a disaster. Half of the vines rotted before the harvest and the other half produced a paltry yield of unripe grapes. The next year, 640,000 vines were imported from Europe, but fewer than a third survived in the local conditions. In desperation, Changyu's peasant laborers were ordered to graft the remaining European plants onto the rootstock of Chinese vines that had been found in the northeast of China. The tactic saved Zhang's vineyard.

Despite the difficult start, the winery quickly gained an international reputation, including the four gold medals it earned at the 1915 Panama-Pacific International Exposition in San Francisco. A price list from 1917 offered nine reds and nine whites, from a basic table wine to an expensive claret (the British term for a Bordeaux red). In the decades that followed, Changyu was nationalized and became a rote bulk-wine producer, and dozens of other state-owned and private wine companies joined it in the fertile landscape spreading out from Penglai into the Yantai peninsula.

The winemaking heritage of the area had been something of an inspiration to local officials. Recently, a considerable amount of effort had been expended in trying to position the area as the "Bordeaux of China," in contrast to Ningxia and other up-and-coming regions. The officials didn't understand that Bordeaux was an appellation referring to a specific geographical area, and not simply a brand that could be copied and pasted onto marketing materials. In addition, the Penglai Vine and Wine

Bureau promoted the Shandong peninsula as one of the world's "seven grape coasts," comparing it with Bordeaux, Tuscany, Cape Town, Barossa Valley (Australia), Casablanca (Chile), and the Napa Valley. The way the bureau saw it, DBR Lafite's decision to invest in Shandong and not somewhere else in China validated its claims. The bureau itself had suggested using the name "Bordeaux" locally, until a representative of the Bordeaux Wine Council gently nixed the idea. Napa had not fared so well. COFCO, the state-controlled food conglomerate, had gone so far as to call the area surrounding its Shandong wine estate "Nava Valley." When several California winemakers complained, COFCO's managers shrugged and told them that "Nava" sounded better than the original Chinese name. True to custom, the China Patent Trademark Office rejected Napa Valley's complaint, even though consumers could easily be misled: COFCO had trademarked the name first, and there was nothing the Californians could do about it.

The local officials and Penglai's wine council shared a flexible conception of the importance of geography in winemaking. It was dutifully repeated in the Chinese media that Penglai shared the same thirty-seven degrees latitude with Bordeaux and Napa. Though Penglai was indeed positioned at thirty-seven degrees north, Napa was closer to thirty-eight and Bordeaux staunchly resided at forty-five—a latitude that many said was integral to Bordeaux's terroir. Of course, the exact latitude wasn't what mattered. Fine wine was made between the thirtieth and fiftieth parallels in both hemispheres. In the Northern Hemisphere, the best wine grapes tended to be grown close to the northern geographical limit for ripening, but the climate at the forty-fifth parallel in China— say, in the remote vineyards of the Xinjiang with its bitterly cold winters—wasn't anything like the climate of Bordeaux.

"These arguments never make any sense," Gérard Colin said with a slow shake of his head. "It isn't possible to define a terroir by its geographic location, but according to its soil, climate, and altitude."

Regardless of the hype from local officials, the weather was an issue. The Shandong peninsula had a warm marine climate. Unlike in Ningxia, the grape vines did not need to be buried in a protective layer of earth during the winter, and late-ripening varieties such as Cabernet Sauvignon might mature properly. But the area's heavy autumn rains guaranteed that rot and pests would be a constant threat until harvest time finally arrived.

Colin knew all about rot. In the nineteenth century the Bordelais had invented the fungicide *la bouillie bordelaise,* a mixture of copper sulfate and lime, to protect vines from mildew and other diseases. The threat of rain during the ripening and harvest did not preclude making the best red wine in China, Colin argued, but there was a wild card. The Shandong peninsula was subject to typhoons. Lafite might lose a year's crop to the rot that came after the rains, but the winds of a typhoon could flatten the vines, forcing them to begin again.

No one really knew whether Shandong's terroir would be worthy of the Lafite name. The answer would depend on the grapes.

One of the grape varieties growing in Shandong when Lafite arrived was known as Cabernet Gernischt. A grape by the same name was planted in many of China's emerging wine regions, but experts were not sure if it was the same grape growing everywhere. Chinese technicians believed the vine was Cabernet Franc, one of the main varieties cultivated in Bordeaux and a grape admired for the silky texture and soft tannins it yielded. But the "grape DNA detective" José Vouillamoz, an exacting Swiss botanist, had a different opinion. He obtained samples of Cabernet Gernischt directly from the Changyu winery and profiled the DNA. It turned out to be "undoubtedly Carmenère," wrote Vouillamoz.

Carmenère was one of Bordeaux's original grape varieties, a natural cross between Cabernet Franc and Gros Cabernet. The grape produced deep, rich red wines, and it was plausible that Zhang Bishi would have planted Carmenère vines for Changyu's pricey claret. When grape phylloxera hit Bordeaux's vineyards in the late nineteenth century, Carmenère, with its unreliable yields, had fallen out of favor there; Merlot and Cabernet responded far more successfully when grafted onto phylloxera-resistant American rootstock. Some vines had obviously made their way to Shandong. According to Vouillamoz, the Carmenère in Changyu's vineyard differed considerably from modern French clones, so it was likely that some of the vines were descendants of an original planting of imported vines.

The idea that China might be one of the last great strongholds of Car-menère caused a stir among wine experts in China, who, not quite believ-ing Vouillamoz, launched an independent study. There were only 101 acres of Carmenère left in France and 57 acres in the United States. Many believed the variety had all but disappeared until 1994, when 26,400 acres, previously mistaken for Merlot, were discovered thriving in Chile. The Chinese team soon confirmed that the vines were Carmenère.

Was Carmenère especially well matched to the area, or could another grape variety be more suitable? In its effort to model itself on Bordeaux and its famous blend of grapes, many Chinese wineries had invested heavily in Cabernet Sauvignon; more than half of China's vineyards were planted with it. But Cabernet Sauvignon was a relatively late-ripening grape, and it was unlikely it could mature properly in China's northern regions. It simply wasn't yet known if Chinese winemaking should be modeled on Bordeaux.

DBR-CITIC decided to plant four Bordeaux varieties—Cabernet Sauvignon, Cabernet Franc, Merlot, and Petit Verdot—then, to cover all bases, added two Mediterranean varieties, Syrah and Marselan, that produced generous, fragrant, deeply colored wines. Marselan was a recent cross between Cabernet and Grenache, bred to be more resistant to rot, powdery mildew, and other blights. It might be just the grape for Shan-dong.

❋

On a late afternoon in May 2010, Gérard Colin unfurled a scroll of papers across the table on a small rooftop terrace a few miles from the DBR-CITIC vineyard. These soil and climate studies proved, he said, that the sixty-two acres Lafite had chosen for the most anticipated vine-yard in China was not just some publicity stunt.

On a map of the vineyard, he pointed to the nearly one hundred pits that had been dug to extract soil samples. He had spent two years over-seeing the studies before the crew had started planting. With CITIC's help, the winery had successfully negotiated fifty-year leaseholds to the land. Under China's leasehold system, local farmers generally were allowed to keep most of what they grew. Often, families cultivated a few crops in order to protect themselves from bad weather and pests. At first, Colin had tried working with the local farmers. "It's run like a cooperative here. They harvest as soon as possible, and you buy from the village broker, who takes a commission," he said. He'd tried running a trial with one farmer, whereby the estate would buy directly instead. "We'd more or less agreed on a price, and I said we'd wait until the grapes were ripe, the way I wanted them." When he came to collect the harvest, he discovered that the farmer had sold the grapes to someone else. Through these experiences, he had come to realize that the only way to guarantee yield and quality was through a leasehold.

It was a Herculean task to build a vineyard from scratch. A small crew of whip-thin men had been hired to clear the soil of forty tons of rock. Bulldozers and manual laborers had then flattened the land into three hundred terraced plots. The cleared rock was used to build six miles of retaining walls for the terraces, with some of the stone reserved for the construction of winery facilities and a perimeter wall. The terraces would provide a natural drainage system during Shandong's rainy season. Colin worried about water shortages; he had been in China long enough to have firsthand knowledge of how the country's rapid growth consumed massive vital resources. He proudly showed off the estate's system for recuperating water drained from the vineyard. It almost seemed as though he was more excited about it than about the multi-level winery, which would be built into the hillside so that it blended harmoniously into the landscape.

The setting was serene and beautiful. In an empty field nearby, a village shaman had claimed his spot for the day. A husband and wife puttered by in a *san lu che*, the tiny three-wheeled truck common in the countryside, filled with wood. But this was China. More building was inevitable and it was unlikely that the vineyard would remain isolated for long. With the help of its partners at CITIC, Lafite had secured a one-thousand-acre buffer zone around its land. Any development within the zone has to be approved by the DBR-CITIC Wine Estate as well as local officials. The zone was meant to protect the vineyard against cunning entrepreneurs with plans to set up "pop-up" wineries or other outfits intended to take advantage of close proximity to the Lafite name.

However, not all potential neighbors were unwelcome. A Hong Kong investor had built a villa in the valley and planted his own vineyard, and the DBR-CITIC staff had agreed to manage it for him. They would also create an exclusive "house wine made by Lafite" for the millionaire. In exchange, Lafite could use the greater portion of his grape harvest. The arrangement addressed one of the issues raised by critics of the Shandong project: the puny size of DBR-CITIC's vineyard. Many were saying that the vineyard would never be able to produce enough bottles to satisfy the thirst for a Chinese Lafite. Sixty-two acres wasn't nearly enough land. The state-owned conglomerates in the province imported bulk wine from Europe and the New World to be able to produce enough "Chinese wine" for the domestic market. Sometimes 20 percent or more of a single wine brand was of foreign origin. "Eighty percent of the domestic Chinese wines are cut with foreign wines. It's enormous," admitted Colin. What was stopping DBR-CITIC from importing some of its own foreign-made wine and doing the same thing?

Colin winced. Lafite, he insisted, had no intention of using any grapes or wine other than what came from the winery's own land in China or land fully managed by Lafite technicians. He and his team were creating a true estate, putting in all of the time, investment, and patience required. He had grown up at Château Teyssier in Saint-Émilion, where vines had been cultivated since Roman times. Every plot of land told a story in the distinctive temperament of soil and climate that brought out the best in certain varieties of grapes. At the DBR-CITIC Wine Estate, his dream was to find an elegant and distinct Chinese terroir.

He sliced some local fruit. It was ripe, succulent. The early signs were good.

❖

"If great red wine is going to come out of anywhere in China, it will come from Ningxia," said David Henderson. Despite the unpredictable market and staggering hurdles to overcome, none of his confidence in China's potential for wine had waned. He was still producing Dragon's Hollow in Ningxia, and he still owned shares in his Beijing wine retail store,

Montrose Food & Wine. He had a lease on fifty acres on the new wine route that he intended to plant one day.

When Henderson arrived in Ningxia, the domestic wine passed muster in China but it was nowhere near the quality required for export. That had changed dramatically in the past decade. With so many wineries springing up in Ningxia, he had insisted that it was to his advantage to focus on winning customers in sophisticated wine markets. His ambitions as an early pioneer in bringing wine culture to China had evolved into a mission to bring Chinese wine to Europe and America. And he wasn't content to simply export his own wine; he also wanted to export the best product coming out of neighboring wineries, such as Jia Bei Lan and Silver Heights, through his company, China Fine Wines. Henderson wanted to replicate the model of winemaking that had been such a success in Argentina, Chile, and the United States.

"We're not a 'Chinese' wine," he insisted, speaking of his own Dragon's Hollow label. He had worked closely with winemaker Craig Grafton at Pernod Ricard to blend Dragon's Hollow with Western palates specifically in mind. By 2015, he was selling 140,000 bottles to the United States. He was also trying to build interest in Chinese wine in Europe, shipping Dragon's Hollow to the United Kingdom, Belgium, Luxembourg, and Sweden.

To make the next move and begin exporting Silver Heights and Jia Bei Lan, he needed the cooperation of the power brokers in the local government. Unfortunately, the authorities didn't currently see the benefit to them of such a deal. There were also hurdles at the national level. Before he could export Silver Heights or Jia Bei Lan, the wines were required to pass Chinese health and hygiene inspections three years in a row. But the standards were always in flux. "Being China, that could change any day," commented Henderson. "There are no rules."

At least the government officials had stopped trying to evict the Gaos from their vineyard on the edge of Yinchuan's burgeoning cityscape. In 2014, Gao Lin had finally reached a compromise with the local authorities—which he hoped would hold firm. After many months of worrying, Emma Gao could almost relax. The Gaos could renew their lease to the land as long as they paid the current market price.

There were a few other conditions, of course. They could no longer produce wine at the location. So as part of their agreement with the local government, the Gaos agreed to hire an architect to design an elegant wine museum and cultural center for the site; they had chosen a man from Bordeaux named Philippe Mazières for the job. The museum would preserve their land and the original cellar, and promote wine tourism in the region, which appeared to satisfy the authorities. Despite the official support, Silver Heights would foot the entire bill. Gao Lin would be the museum's guide. The negotiation was far from over, however, and Emma hoped there would be no sudden reversals. If the next Five-Year Plan, set to be unveiled in 2016, nudged the local government to rethink the decision, the Gaos might suffer yet another reversal of fortune in Yinchuan.

It was hard to consider such a dramatic change. From Yinchuan, Gao Lin could still drive by the Luhuatai vineyard, where he had started his life as a winemaker for the Shizuishan chemical factory. "It's one of the most beautiful vineyards in the region," said Emma. Today the vineyard belongs to the agricultural school in Ningxia. The school sells the grapes and bulk wine to regional wineries. Sometimes, the Gaos even source grapes from it.

Regardless, they came to accept that their future was in Jinshan, on the new wine route along the eastern slopes of the Helan Mountains, where the Gaos were in the process building a new estate on the ninety-nine acres for which Silver Heights had acquired a leasehold. "It's near the area with the rock paintings, which is a national park. There are twenty-seven wineries, but we were there first, two years ago," said Emma. The inevitable loss of their urban cellar as well as the new Jinshan location and increased production had required a new cellar. It took two years to obtain the necessary construction permit but it was finally approved.

Eager to have a winery that reflected their modern philosophy, the Gaos hired Philippe Mazières to design their Jinshan winery, too. When the Gaos reviewed the designs, it was as if they were realizing a dream that they had not yet imagined themselves. It was contemporary, minimalist, refined—worthy of one of the best wineries in the world. But the price tag was beyond their means. "We had to abandon the project—it cost thirty million yuan," Emma reported.

Instead, starting with the 2014 harvest, they managed to make do with a temporary facility at the Jinshan vineyard. Their vineyard grew slowly. In response to his application for more vineyard land, Gao Lin had acquired thirty-three acres each year in 2012, 2013, and 2014. With the latest parcel under cultivation, Silver Heights was able to produce sixty thousand bottles of wine annually. In 2015, the Gaos gained an additional thirty-seven acres, where they wanted to plant experimental varieties of vines. "But one thousand *mǔ* is the maximum for us," said Emma.

One thousand *mǔ* is 165 acres. A state winery might have that amount of land dedicated to landscaping and parking lots. Silver Heights had no ambition to compete with Changyu or Great Wall. Such ambition was impractical. But it was also unnecessary.

Emma had only to look to the success of Grace Vineyard to see what the future might hold for a family-owned winery. Judy Chan's keen reading of the consumer market has paid off as much as her winery's expansions. Chan resisted the trend to charge higher prices for Chinese wines, even after she visited a producer in Inner Mongolia who was charging 5,000 yuan a bottle. He had tried selling wine at 200 yuan, but the bottles priced at 5,000 yuan simply sold much better, he had told her, and he sold two million bottles. "Just in Inner Mongolia," Chan emphasized. "There is that much money." But Chan didn't believe it was a strategy that would work in the long term. "I do not think that when the client says they want a more expensive bottle, they want to give you more money. They need the price tag," she said. "So if there is another way to give him the same satisfaction, the same face, without that price tag, it's the way to go. I haven't figured it out yet, but I think it's the way to go."

With her distributor, Torres China, Chan instead launched a clever and stylish new product called "People's Cabernet," which cost under 100 yuan a bottle. The wine was promoted as a high-quality, affordable choice for gatherings of friends or romantic dinners. The first year of production sold out after the anti-graft crackdown hit. Grace Vineyard was selling ten thousand bottles a year, mostly to restaurants.

"China needs more vineyards like Grace Vineyard and Silver Heights," said Gérard Colin. Judy Chan and Emma Gao had won his respect. "I hope they can find the money. . . . They're trying so hard." He was in his sixties, when most Frenchmen choose to retire, but he expected he would continue his work searching for the best place to make wine in China. He was at home in his role as a pioneer. "I am convinced there are some very, very good soils," he said with bravado. "Dynasty started with white wine. It's certain that we could make some very good white wine in China."

In early 2013, Colin left the DBR-CITIC Wine Estate to join the Puchang Vineyard, in the far northwest of Xinjiang, where the dry climate made it possible to grow organic wine. The old Suntime vineyard wasn't far away. He expected French growers would face increasing competition in supermarkets around the world from the Chinese mega-wineries, including many of the same companies that had been his neighbors in Shandong, such as COFCO and Changyu. "COFCO has bought vineyards everywhere. They blend the wines from different regions and make brand wines. In brand wines, they can compete," said Colin. Even after sourcing grapes from all over China—sometimes all over the world—the wineries were still dependent on overproduction.

Like most French vintners, he referred to this approach as *faire pisser les vignes*, which translates into English as "make the vines piss." It was not a compliment. The Chinese vineyards often produced three times the volume that the same amount of land produced in Bordeaux. The result was a thin, lightly colored, often bitter wine with little aromatic appeal, which was why it was often blended with imported bulk wine. If the mega-wineries lowered their production quotas to improve quality, Colin thought, they could produce decent wine that would be competitive internationally. Maybe Lafite would prove that it could be done.

❋

Just before the barrel tastings for the 2013 vintage began in March 2014, China dropped its investigation into European winemakers for unfair dumping and subsidies. The triumph of China's wine conglomerates had been short-lived. In January, Dynasty's chairman, Bai Zhisheng, had lost his job, replaced by Hao Feifei, general manager and executive director of the company. Its shares were still frozen on the stock exchange. And no penalty duties would be imposed on European wine imports into China.

During the negotiations between the EU Trade Commission and Beijing, representatives of the Bordeaux Wine Council agreed to provide technical support to the Chinese wine industry. The council would encourage Bordeaux's wine academies to enroll more Chinese students and facilitate the transfer of winemaking skills to the mainland, including sending French technicians to work at Chinese vineyards. Some members of the CIVB wondered if an arrangement of this sort had been the Chinese government's goal ever since the dispute over solar panels had been settled in March 2014.

For his part, Emmanuel Martin at La Guyennoise shrugged off the settlement terms. "They didn't get anything they weren't already getting," he said. "All of our technicians and consultants are already working over there." Mostly, he was relieved that his company had emerged unscathed.

The investigation had foundered when the Chinese realized that the prices in Europe for European wine were also quite low. "Dumping" implied that a company was flooding a market with goods priced lower than it could get elsewhere in order to undermine domestic producers. In many cases, the cheapest wines shipped to China were selling for more than they had in the European Union. Nor could the Chinese companies prove that they'd been injured by the wine imports.

In six short years, Martin had turned his failing prune business into one of the largest French wine exporters to China. La Guyennoise shipped fourteen million bottles a year to the mainland. The wine was always the same, but his offer of efficient and bespoke packaging, private labels, and a fast turnaround had proved popular with Chinese distributors. He had ordered an additional bottling line just to fill different-shaped bottles destined for the Chinese market—conical shapes, the elegant, sloping shoulders of a Burgundy bottle, and heavily weighted "luxury" bottles. The market was overwhelmed with suppliers, and his room full of shelves of French-themed bottle labels wasn't enough to win business anymore. To continue to grow, he had to steal business from other suppliers by providing a service no one else offered. The new bottling line could increase his annual sales by five hundred thousand to a million bottles. The market had shifted, he said, and he had every intention of keeping ahead of his competitors.

❀

In Hong Kong, Vincent Yip was typing up Topsy Trading's annual business report, as he did every year. The news was not good, but it was what he and his father had expected. The bullish market had turned bearish, and the traditional lines of distribution, in which everyone along the chain made money, had faltered. Even during the boom, Bordeaux négociants, London merchants, and Hong Kong traders had increasingly fought to claim the same clients, but with the slump margins were slim to none.

"There is no shopping list this year, there is no business analysis this year, there is not much business this year," read the first sentence of Yip's March 2014 memorandum. Instead, he related the dispiriting events of the past year. In one case, the château director of a classified growth in the Médoc had informed Topsy Trading that yet another prestigious professional club was getting into the wine game by hosting a week of tastings in Hong Kong. The château was handling the logistics directly, providing the wines and organizing the lunches and dinners. The château director would be on hand to meet the members, too. It wasn't immediately clear to Yip why the man had paid him a call. Perhaps the estate wanted Topsy to serve as the importer-supplier? No, the château had given that business to a Bordeaux-based négociant. Yip wondered where the meeting was going. Then he learned that the château director was going to refer the club's members to Topsy if any of them wanted to order a few extra bottles of the wine after the tastings, and he wanted Topsy to stock up on the château's wines, just in case.

To make matters worse, British merchants such as Gary Boom at Bordeaux Index were regularly undercutting prices, taking advantage of favorable currency fluctuations. Yip had received a call from a private client looking for a case of Château Lagrange 2009. Yip had bought

Lagrange at €37.20 en primeur back in 2010 when the exchange rate meant it cost him HK$377 per bottle. Four years later, he offered the wine at HK$450 per bottle, delivered to the client's home. As Yip recounted it, the client's response to his price had been, "Are you joking?" He was told a British merchant operating in Hong Kong was selling the same wine for the equivalent of HK$380 a bottle. Then a call came in from a private client who wanted a case of Château Mouton Rothschild 2009. The client asked if Yip could beat a British merchant's price of less than HK$65,200 for a twelve-bottle case. Yip told the person he'd sold out of the vintage. In fact, he had all of his stock of Mouton 2009 sitting in his warehouse. He had paid the equivalent of HK$67,000 to HK$88,000 a case, depending on the tranche, four years earlier, and he wasn't willing to take a loss. "For the time being, we'd dare not offer any, even at cost," wrote Yip.

It was the same situation with nearly all of the top wines of the 2010 vintage, according to Yip. And the 2010 had been an outstanding vintage.

Settling on the right prices for Bordeaux's wines remained a challenge. Somehow, Bordeaux's global sales had slipped less than 2 percent in 2013, with more than 742 million bottles, worth $5.84 billion, shipped worldwide. But the numbers out of China were disheartening. Chinese exports had dropped 16 percent in volume and 18 percent in value. As a result, there was $83 million less going into Bordeaux's coffers for the year.

Despite the downward trend, there was no question of replacing the Chinese market. Not yet. No other market in the world could absorb the seventy-one million bottles that were shipped to China each year. Combined, Hong Kong and China still accounted for one quarter of Bordeaux's exports. Négociants had been prospecting in Brazil, India, and Russia, but each of those countries had a unique set of obstacles. Bordeaux needed China. It was still largely a taboo to drink alcohol in India, and wine faced exorbitant taxes there; the Brazilian wine market was tiny; Russia was unstable.

Once again, the négociant Yann Schÿler insisted to anyone who would listen that what Bordeaux needed was a "liquid" vintage, something that would sell through quickly. This en primeur campaign wasn't about making money; it was about saving Bordeaux's unique way of doing business.

❋

Another outstanding vintage might revive the Place de Bordeaux, but, alas, the 2013 vintage was not to be listed among the greats. The growing season began with a wet, cold May, with more rain in June, resulting in a late, uneven flowering and grapes of varying size, some of which never ripened. Then a freak hailstorm in August wiped out a tenth of the region's crop. Many of the growers convinced themselves that an Indian summer would arrive and allow the grapes to ripen until late into October. Then, toward the end of September, the wet weather returned. The intermittent rainfall and warm days created the perfect conditions for rot. The châteaux doubled and tripled their usual ranks of pickers to sort out the surviving clusters of half-ripe, half-rotten grapes. At Château Mouton Rothschild, general manager Philippe Dhalluin conscripted the entire staff, from administrative assistants to executives, to join the pickers in the vineyards and save what they could, meticulously sorting out the healthy grapes to make Philippine de Rothschild's First Growth wine.

Despite these heroic efforts, 2013 saw the smallest harvest since 1991, when an April frost had destroyed most of Bordeaux's crops and bankrupted several growers. With the small yield, the prices of bulk wine were sure to rise, but only slightly—not enough to make up for the growers' losses. This would squeeze the négociants further, as many of the firms bought bulk wine to blend into their brand wines sold for everyday drinking as a hedge against their high-end business in classified growths. Now they would have less wine to sell at less profit per bottle.

In an ideal world, the en primeur campaign might have infused some much-needed cash into the Place de Bordeaux. Unfortunately, the vintage had already suffered from horrendous press, so most of the visitors descending on Bordeaux for the annual barrel tastings in the spring of 2014 weren't expecting much. Still, the négociants tried to convey self-assurance. "There is no greenness in most of the fine wines I have tasted," said Christophe Reboul Salze of The Wine Merchant in the lead-up to the barrel tastings. "Bordeaux is going to show the world that, despite difficult weather, we can achieve great things."

The response, however, was mixed, and no one showered accolades on the vintage. The challenge for every buyer was to find the success story. As usual, Gary Boom sent his sales team to taste their way through the vintage after the official circus of barrel tastings had closed. Over four days, they had to take in as much Bordeaux wine as they could. In the staff's assessment, the wines were as uneven as the ripeness of the berries that had gone into the vats. "The best have very pretty aromatics, elegance, freshness and attractive, linear palates," Bordeaux Index reported of the Left Bank contenders, while "the worst have rough, unwieldy tannins, hollow middles and a surplus acidity." And on the Right Bank, fortunes were no better.

And this time there would be no help from China.

Earlier in the year, Yang Wenhua, the chairman of C&D Wines, announced that Bordeaux's en primeur system had lost its appeal. He would not, he stoically explained to the négociants, be buying any of the 2013 vintage en primeur, nor did he have any regrets about dumping C&D's exclusive private labels with a variety of estates. There was no getting around it: the massive investment he had made in classified growths looked like nothing more than a bad bet to his bosses in Xiamen. He had taken a tiny subsidiary and turned it into a showpiece, and several people were angling for his job. Any misstep, he knew, could be fatal to his career.

The magnitude of the speculative bubble had escaped him until it was too late. While the value of some of the wines had increased slightly, the prices of the First Growths had fluctuated a lot—far, far more than he'd anticipated. Now all Yang could do was cut his losses. Bordeaux's 2009 and 2010 vintages had been priced based on demand in one country—China—and now his countrymen did not want those wines at those prices. "We bought too much of the 2010, so now we buy only a little," he said.

This was not to say that Yang had abandoned wine. He still had faith in the Chinese wine market, and he still had faith in Bordeaux. But he was no longer sure that classified growths, sold as commodities and vulnerable to speculation, were a good fit for China. Instead, he was looking for more partnerships like the one that C&D had with Castel.

C&D was one of ten distributors chosen to work with the French giant, and Yang had never regretted the arrangement. "From 2006 to 2013, Castel sold millions of bottles in China. We sold one-third of that. In all, we've imported fifteen million bottles of wine—sixty percent was from France. We have one thousand sub-distributors for Roche Mazet, and fifteen Roche Mazet franchises. We want to be the biggest wine importer in China," Yang said. To extend its reach, C&D had recently been named as the sole distributor for a Gallo brand wine in China.

According to Yang, the key was to control the distribution and source the wine directly from the producers. "Our plan is to sell directly to final clients. We will work with Castel and our distributors [on] our boutiques Roche Mazet, only selling good ones from France at a good price and quality," he explained.

Wines that were priced between thirty and fifty dollars were selling well, Yang noted, but he wondered if the Bordelais realized that China was too vast and too complex for generalities. In Beijing and Shanghai, he had customers with cellars worth several million renminbi. These cities were more sophisticated than second-tier cities such as Xi'an or third-tier cities such as Dalian, but there was also a seemingly infinite potential for growth in China's hinterlands. In western China, which had lagged behind the economic performance of the eastern and coastal provinces, he had heard that workers were serving dry red wine at wedding banquets. This was not wine being given to improve guanxi or gei mianzi; this was wine being uncorked, consumed, and savored. It was a fascinating development. Fashions that had been adopted in Hong Kong, Guangzhou, Shanghai, and Beijing were spreading.

Of course, the volume of consumption was still lower in these more remote regions, but the new rules on frugality were not having the same impact on wine sales there. The reason, said Yang, was that people in these regions typically consumed copious amounts of baijiu, which in many cases was as expensive as quality red wine. He knew this because C&D distributed the second most popular brand of baijiu. He also knew that the Communist Party and central government had not backpedaled on their policy of promoting red wine as a healthy alternative to hard liquor or as the better option for the country's food security. Red wine provided the politically correct alcoholic choice—as long as the price was right.

Despite his own heavy losses with classified growths, Yang conceded that Bordeaux had a future in China. It continued to be the most famous wine region, and that was a draw for those Chinese consumers who had some extra income to spend. What C&D needed, he said, was a reliable supply of good Bordeaux wines at prices that were within reach of the country's professionals rather than its tycoons.

Yang wouldn't get a chance to see if his strategy would work for C&D. In May 2014, he received the bad news he had been dreading: even though he'd managed to sell forty million bottles of Castel, he had been fired.

There was no question of not landing on his feet. He weighed his misfortune against the goodwill he had earned as a regular customer in Bordeaux over the previous years and his knowledge of his country's wine market. He immediately formed a company, LK Wine, to import low-priced, quality wines to China. He hired a staff of fifteen to work in the company's headquarters in Shanghai. He courted the big négociants in Bordeaux and attended Vinexpo Hong Kong looking for suppliers willing to work with a start-up. He felt particularly welcome at Producta, a Bordeaux cooperative specializing in inexpensive wines. Producta was peddling two unused labels: Arnozan, named after an illustrious street in the Chartrons, and the more generic Le Parlement. Yang secured the exclusive Chinese distribution rights for both brands. Within six months, he had lined up more than one hundred sub-distributors in China, and he'd sold two hundred thousand bottles of Arnozan. "The négociants are always worrying about their margins," Yang said. "They need to focus on volume. Without volume you don't have a market in China."

His goal was to sell one million bottles during his first full calendar year in business for himself. Eventually, he hoped to own the largest chain of wine stores in China. At the Twelfth National People's Congress in March 2015, President Xi Jinping spoke of China's "new normal": slower growth with deeper reforms and less corruption. A few months earlier, Premier Li Keqiang had said the country would "foster a new engine of growth by encouraging mass entrepreneurship and innovation." Despite the austerity campaign, Yang believed his country was still a land of opportunity for purveyors of imported wine.

Yang sold his wines at prices ranging from one hundred to three hundred yuan—about fifteen to fifty dollars. Cautiously, he was adding a few château wines and a selection of classified growths to his offerings. Bordeaux remained synonymous with quality in China, and a display of the wines of the 1855 Classification signaled an impeccable knowledge of fine wine, even if they largely remained on the shelf, nothing more than a prop.

❂

Despite orders from Yang Wenhua and other scrappy importers who were adapting to the changing market, the Chinese government's crackdown was being felt across Bordeaux. Chinese deals had collapsed everywhere. When Philippe Raoux sold his business, La Winery, to Chinese conglomerate COFCO, he'd had high hopes about the opportunities presented by working for the Chinese, but the promises he'd heard had come to nothing. There were no brand wines, no massive deals. And his other big customer, Wang Quan, a Chinese industrialist and the chairman of Hebei Xinda Group, who had bought the Saint-Émilion classified growth Château Bellefont-Belcier and launched a chain of wine stores, had slashed his orders from $12.8 million to $1.3 million. Customers weren't coming into the stores to buy wine; they came in to taste—it was a form of entertainment, like spending the evening at the opera. Wang had closed the stores and opened tasting salons instead, with his employees diligently collecting contact information from every visitor so that they might be contacted privately about buying wine when no one was looking.

On the cours du Médoc, Philippe Papillon had taken over a nineteenth-century townhouse to serve as the new headquarters for Ipso Facto, his struggling négociant firm, and his wife's expanding legal practice. Farther down the street, toward the quai de Bacalan, DBR Lafite and several other négociants, including Maison Schröder & Schÿler, had offices.

Papillon was closer than he'd ever been to the center of the Place de Bordeaux, yet the heady days of big deals were over for him.

At the height of his business, he had obtained allocations for ten thousand cases of classified growths worth $8 million each year. Now he sold a handful of Second Growths worth $100,000. His lawsuit against USA Piilii Jepen remained in limbo. On the last court date, Piilii hadn't bothered to send an attorney, though the directors later appealed the decision, which had gone against the company. Even if he won, Papillon feared he'd never collect the $10 million that Piilii now owed him. The cases of classified growths that the Tribunal du Commerce had let him seize as collateral against Piilii's unpaid bills had not moved an inch; the court still would not allow him to take or sell the wine to settle the debt. To Papillon's chagrin, it had turned out that Jenny Chen—the charming Jenny C.—had pulled twelve négociants into Piilii's business scheme. But none had joined forces with Papillon in his case against Piilii, preferring to hide their involvement in the debacle from the public eye. After his bruising experience with the Yu brothers, Papillon had wiped his hands clean of the volatile Chinese market. He was selling to the United Kingdom, Japan, and the United States instead.

The Dalian tycoon Qu Naijie was also feeling the effects of the Chinese hangover. His wine company had shuttered its grand plan to circumvent the Place de Bordeaux. All but a small portion of the wine from his collection of French châteaux was now being offered in bulk to négociants.

Few in Bordeaux understood the true extent of Qu's wealth—the cash reserves, the personal stock portfolios, or the true number of châteaux he owned, since most had been bought in his wife's name or his son's name. He was a mystery, impenetrable to almost everyone—except the National Audit Office in Beijing. Indeed, Qu's fortunes changed overnight on June 24, 2014, when the NAO delivered a damning report to the National People's Congress. It was the latest in an avalanche of reports issued as part of Xi Jinping's crackdown on government corruption.

The NAO report listed 314 cases involving 1,100 people who were being investigated for "major violations of laws and disciplines." The government auditors accused the Haichang Group and another Dalian firm, Rui Yang Investment Management Company, of misusing 268 million yuan, or $43 million, in public funds that were earmarked for acquiring foreign technology. With outrage, the report's authors noted that Haichang and Rui Yang had allegedly bought fourteen châteaux with the cash instead.

As the Haichang Group's founder and biggest shareholder—he owned 2.2 billion shares—Qu could not easily claim that he was unaware of the company's dealings; very few important decisions would have been made without his involvement. Furthermore, he'd been seen attending conferences at the Bordeaux Chamber of Commerce, and his name was linked to château purchases in several Western media outlets.

The news of Qu's apparent fall from grace spread through Bordeaux like a shock wave. Emails and calls to Haichang and Qu's main Bordeaux subsidiary, Lamont, based at Château Branda in Fronsac, went unanswered. Many Bordelais wondered how Qu's guanxi had failed him so utterly. Maybe some connection to Bo Xilai had caught up with him. Would Qu be yet another tycoon to disappear with terrifying finality, a casualty of his profligate wealth?

Another Chinese owner, a steel tycoon, was also said to be under scrutiny by the anti-graft authorities for undisclosed transgressions. In France, the money-laundering cases first reported by Tracfin in 2013 had been transferred to Bordeaux, where the *police judiciaire*'s financial crime unit were working to peel back the layers of holding companies to uncover who was behind the flow of money. It seemed possible that a few châteaux had been used as cover to launder dirty money, but prosecutors had yet to formally pursue any case.

Weeks passed but Qu failed to surface. His employees in France did not know his whereabouts. Estates refused to authorize the publication of any photographs of Qu taken on their premises. His history of working with local businesses was scrubbed from websites. He seemed to have disappeared from Bordeaux as furtively as he had arrived.

When the third Dalian Wine and Dine Festival opened in July 2014, representatives from the Haichang Group and the Bordeaux Chamber of Commerce were noticeably absent. It wasn't just that the trade war between the European winemakers and China was under way. Earlier in the year, the chamber had declined to organize the participation of Bordeaux's négociants and winegrowers when impractical deadlines promised to create more stress than profits. Bordeaux, at its heart, was pragmatic, not political.

By the end of the year, a dead calm had settled over the Place de Bordeaux, particularly among those trading in classified growths. Bordeaux's exports had dropped another 17 percent in value. "At the moment, the fine wine market is completely stuck. Prices have collapsed," said Yann Schÿler.

Many négociants had stocks of four unsold vintages lining the walls of their cellars and weighing on their books. Others were hurting from the repercussions of the small crops in 2012 and '13. The cost of producing everyday Bordeaux had gone up, but the négociants who blended brand wines couldn't raise prices enough to maintain a tolerable profit margin. The international market was too cutthroat.

In the wake of the volatility in China, the Place de Bordeaux was increasingly trying to develop markets in India, Brazil, Africa, and Russia, and many négociants hoped they could revive business by cozying up to old friends in America. At Schröder & Schÿler, Yann Schÿler was selling his négociant brand wines in the United States for twelve dollars a bottle and doing well.

"We are selling and shipping wine at the entry level and medium range every day. When it's difficult, it's the négociant with a wide portfolio who survives. We can survive," said Schÿler. Then he shrugged matter-of-factly. "The fine wine market has always been a yo-yo."

That volatility was evident in the Chinese customs records that showed that the volume of imported French wine in 2014 had fallen to less than fourteen million cases, a decline of 26 percent from the previous year. The market for classified growths had disappeared, just like the party and government officials being rounded up in Beijing. The only good news was that, during the frenzy for Château Lafite and other First Growths, the consumer market for wine had actually expanded. As of 2015, forty million Chinese were buying imported wine with the intention of drinking it.

❋

During his years hunting for China's most promising terroir, Gérard Colin had crossed paths with a young French agronomic engineer named Stanislas Basquin, who was conducting a wine-climate study in Asia. The results, according to Colin, had been intriguing.

Basquin had utilized six indices to calculate the climate of 247 European wine regions, then mapped the profiles to potential wine regions in Asia. The indices measured the heat produced by the sun, the mean temperature at night during ripening, the regional dryness, winter and spring frosts, and the typical heat stress experienced by grape vines in the region. Not surprisingly, given the size of the country, China had the most land in Asia suitable for growing wine grapes.

The surprise came when Basquin reviewed the characteristics of each Chinese province and compared them to the major European wine regions. A small strip of southern Gansu Province, well to the south of Ningxia, was the only part of China with a climate anything like Bordeaux. The only other area in Asia that resembled Bordeaux was in the contested state of Kashmir.

Basquin's climate study confirmed what Judy Chan and Emma Gao had shown through hard work and instinctive winemaking skills: China's main wine provinces, including Ningxia, Shaanxi, and Shanxi, had great potential, but they weren't Bordeaux. According to Basquin, the climate in these provinces was more similar to that of eastern Europe, particularly Hungary, Romania, and Slovenia, and many of the areas where wineries had clustered matched the profile for the Hungarian wine-producing region of Tokaj. Choosing grape varieties native to eastern Europe rather than Bordeaux's Cabernet or Merlot would likely produce the best wines, he concluded.

There was one other good match to China—the Friuli–Venezia Giulia wine region in Italy. In fact, it was the only European region that lined up with the usual conditions found on the Shandong peninsula. Yet, Basquin's study also suggested that the best geographical areas to make European-style wine in Shandong were not near the ports, where most of the wineries had settled over the decades. "None of these areas are located in the region of Yantai and Penglai, on the coast of the Bohai Sea, where Chinese viticulture has developed historically," said Basquin. He had identified two promising spots, one around the Dazeshan Hills, about eighty miles southwest of the port of Penglai, and the other much farther inland, almost three hundred miles from Penglai, near the sacred mountain of Tai Shan, a UNESCO World Heritage Site. Both areas seemed almost a world away from the DBR-CITIC Wine Estate.

This did not mean Lafite would not rise above the obstacles and produce a wine worthy of its name in what might someday be the suburbs of Penglai. Nor did it mean good wine couldn't be made in China, let alone in Shandong. "It is possible that other regions of China [where the] climate does not correspond to European wine climates could also produce wines," Basquin argued. "These wines would then be truly Chinese and their merit would be to help build an identity for the Chinese wine culture."

Was it time for China to stop copying Bordeaux? Certainly, Basquin's study showed it was not enough to plant Bordeaux grape varieties and pray for a wine of similar style and quality to come out of the harvest. And without a doubt, his study showed that a magical terroir *did exist* in China.

....

Shangri-La

The most beguiling spot revealed in Stanislas Basquin's study was a small, remote area on the border between Tibet, Sichuan, and Yunnan that exhibited many of the features of Europe's finest wine regions. Tibetan farmers in the area around the city of Zhongdian in northwest Yunnan Province were already growing wine grapes. Could this be the Shangri-La for Chinese wine?

Characteristically for the new China, Zhongdian had renamed itself Shangri-La after the fictional Himalayan utopia portrayed in the 1930s novel *Lost Horizon*, in an unabashed move to attract tourists. The region's commercial logging industry had collapsed in 1998 after a tragic flood (partially caused by overlogging), and the local government had scrambled to find another path to economic growth. After beating out competitors for the right to rename itself Shangri-La, Zhongdian covered its logging losses with tourist revenue, offering millions of Chinese sightseers the chance to drink yak butter tea, admire Tibetan architecture, and hike in the spectacular natural surroundings.

In addition to tourism, the local economic initiative to diversify the economy strongly encouraged local Tibetan farmers to switch from their traditional crops to red wine grapes. The Tibetans were largely subsistence farmers, growing barley and corn, raising pigs, and herding yaks.

Despite the colorful clothing and picturesque hamlets, their daily life was grueling. Few had indoor plumbing or running water. Most cooked over a fire. Other than foraged medicinal plants and wild mushrooms, they had no cash crop until the Shangri-La Winery Company came to town. Shangri-La was owned by the Beijing-based liquor conglomerate VATS Group and controlled by Wu Xiangdong, a member of the National Party Congress. With the exception of a recently established winery run by a mining tycoon, Shangri-La held a monopoly on the local grape supply.

Understandably, the Tibetans were eager for a chance to earn money they could use to buy previously unattainable items and send their children to school. But a visiting anthropologist, who spent a year in the region, worried that the farmers no longer planted food among the rows of Cabernet Sauvignon vines, because they were worried about the pesticides they had to use in cultivating the grapes. They now relied on the income from selling grapes to buy food for their families, and variations in yield from vine to vine and from harvest to harvest made their livelihood unstable.

In late 2009, the winemaker Dr. Tony Jordan arrived in the region, where he was startled to see entire villages turning their energies to the cultivation of Cabernet Sauvignon grapes. He was on an assignment for Moët Hennessy, the wine and spirits arm of Bernard Arnault's luxury group LVMH. Moët Hennessy already had a successful track record as an early mover in the wine regions of Argentina, California, and Australia. Now it wanted a stake in Asia.

From the outset, the goal was to produce in Asia a world-class red wine made of Bordeaux grape varieties that would stand up to scrutiny when measured against the best wines from California, Australia, and Bordeaux. LVMH also owned two of the best properties in Bordeaux, Château Cheval Blanc in Saint-Émilion and Château d'Yquem in Sauternes. Standards were high. As part of the brief, Jordan was also tasked with finding the ideal place to make two Asian sparkling wines, one in India and one in China.

His superiors estimated the project would take eighteen months. It took five years.

✻

Like Basquin, Jordan began by studying weather maps that showed mean temperatures in July, the daily average temperature during the growing season, and rain patterns.

Kashmir looked interesting, but the political situation ruled it out. That left him with China, where he saw potential in the north from Beijing straight across to the border with Kazakhstan. He had already eliminated the entire east coast. He'd made wine in Qingdao in 1994 and remembered all too well how the harvest date had been determined by the point when vine disease was so bad, they had no choice but to pick.

Inland was more arid, lessening the risk of heavy pressure from vine disease. A handful of regions stood out: Xinjiang, Shanxi, Huailai, Gansu, and Ningxia.

Then the adventure really began, crisscrossing the vast country by plane and all-terrain vehicle. In the most promising regions, Jordan set up weather monitors and spoke to local farmers to get anecdotal evidence. He scrutinized existing vineyards for potential, undeterred by the high-cropping, low-quality industrial production.

"I just see that as a phase rather than a decision for some companies to go one way and others to go the fine wine route," said Jordan. "The industrial production will slide across to fine wine when they have an educated consumer base and when the pressure is on them to produce fine wine. The main thing they have to learn is that everything starts in the vineyards."

In many cases, Jordan figured that Moët Hennessy's team could improve the quality of the grapes fairly quickly, just by taking over the crop management. In other cases, the vineyards were plagued with virus-ridden plants, evident by the rolled-up purple leaves in the autumn. The plants had been cloned from infected vines, and propagated over and over again. "You can still produce high-quality wine with some virus, but there comes a point when the virus load is so heavy that it detracts from the vine's ability to ripen," he said. COFCO had established giant professional nurseries capable of using the latest technology to rid the plants of viruses, but the replanting effort would be massive.

Jordan decided on Ningxia for Moët Hennessy's sparkling wine, and sourced virus-free plants from a Chinese university. But for their Bordeaux blend, the research pointed him to a relatively small area in the southwest of China, in the rain shadows of the monsoons.

Chinese wine scientists confirmed his intuition. Jordan asked Li Demei, from the University of Agriculture in Beijing, for his opinion on the matter. Li told him that, when it came to commercial and logistical issues, Ningxia was the frontrunner. "People know how to produce wine, there is basic labor, and the local government is welcoming," Li said. But when Jordan pushed him to take political and economic considerations out of the equation, he changed his answer. "He asked me, 'If you don't think about anything but making a quality wine, what do you think?' I said, 'Shangri-La,'" Li recalled. "But Shangri-La is quite difficult. No one knows how to make it work."

For at least 150 years, a tiny village on the banks of the Mekong River in northwest Yunnan Province has cultivated wine grapes, a culture introduced and maintained by French Catholic priests on a mission to spiritually conquer the kingdom of Tibet. The Tibetans violently rebuked the effort, but the missionaries had stubbornly lingered at the kingdom's doorstep. One missionary founded a church in the village of Cizhong, along the ancient trade route to Lhasa.

In the Cizhong churchyard, the missionary planted French grape vines so he could produce wine for mass. The grapes growing today are said to be Rose Honey, a variety lost in Europe during the phylloxera infestation, but to modern winemakers the grapes appeared to be a hybrid, a hardy disease-resistant cross between two species, *Vitis vinifera* and *Vitis labrusca*. Gérard Colin had sampled the wines of Cizhong to see if they might augur the ideal Chinese terroir.

"The wine at the chapel vineyard is good but it doesn't age well. It lacks finesse. It's good, though. I taste it every now and then," said Colin. "But it would interest me to recuperate those vines planted two centuries ago."

It was inevitable that the pedigree of the vines would entice wine growers. The Communists had evicted the last missionary in 1952, but the villagers continued to attend mass and tend a small plot of six hundred vines in the manner the French had instructed.

When Jordan arrived in the village, he admired the well-managed vines, where the farmers had also planted Cabernet Sauvignon. They could make some nice wines there, but Jordan was put off by Cizhong's proximity to the Mekong River and its warmer, more humid weather. He wanted to go to a higher elevation. "We looked at villages from one end of the valley to the other," he said. "We had to rule out some absolutely amazing spots—totally amazing, but totally impractical."

After scouting the valleys, Jordan chose several promising vineyard plots in villages just below the Meli Snow Mountain, a sacred place in Tibetan Buddhism. He placed climate sensors nearby, and when he returned to taste the grapes at harvest time, the sensors' data confirmed that it would be warm enough to ripen the grapes and dry enough to achieve the best quality. But the weather alone would not guarantee a world-class wine; the soil had to be right as well. Jordan and his team dug more than three hundred holes, extracting deep soil profiles. They discovered uniform river-gravel soil and ancient weathered soils from the mountains. This was the place that ticked all the boxes. This was where they would make their wine Ao Yun, "Proud Clouds" of Shangri-La.

In February 2012, Moët Hennessy entered into a joint venture with the Shangri-La Winery Company, with the French controlling 66.7 percent. Jordan settled on four villages, and negotiated with the village leaders to obtain fifty-year leases on about seventy-five acres of land spread across 320 plots worked by dozens of farmers.

A year later, Jean-Guillaume Prats left his post at Château Cos d'Estournel to become CEO of Moët Hennessy's Estates and Wines group. Never had he imagined he'd be making wine in such an astonishing place. The snowcapped mountain rose 22,000 feet, and the four vineyards were at altitudes ranging from 7,000 to 8,500 feet.

Prats was confident that Moët Hennessy would succeed in making a Bordeaux varietal that could stand shoulder to shoulder with the best the West could offer. He insisted that the Shangri-La wine was "going to be made [just] as we make the great First Growths of Bordeaux."

With all of the attention placed on Shangri-La and the arrival of Moët Hennessy, the stakes had risen for Lafite in China. For Prats, it was familiar ground to be competing with Lafite. When he was still at Cos d'Estournel, people would inevitably ask how his wine compared to that of his illustrious neighbor. He once answered, "Lafite is exceptional but I think that Cos is slightly better." His answer wasn't changing much now that it was Moët Hennessy's Shangri-La pitted against the DBR-CITIC Wine Estate in Shandong.

After Gérard Colin's departure, a Bordeaux winemaker named Olivier Richaud had taken over the day-to-day management of the DBR-CITIC estate. It was Richaud's second tour in China. He had worked at Bernard Magrez's ill-fated winery in Qingdao, trying to make wine in a charmless facility with hostile locals. Once again, he was the lone Westerner on the project, but now the mood was different. The locals were overjoyed to have Lafite in their midst, and the lush vineyards and elegant low-slung buildings promised a class act. But he still faced an unforeseen foe: pests and diseases he'd not encountered during his years making wine in Chile, the Languedoc, and Bordeaux. Even familiar nemeses, such as powdery and downy mildew, behaved differently in the warm marine climate. Then there was the shock of discovering white rot, something he'd only read about in textbooks. An entirely new strategy for managing the vineyard was necessary.

Seventeen acres had been cultivated to produce the first vintage of Lafite's Chinese wine in 2013, and another five acres came into production the following spring. The estate's cellar was still not finished, so Richaud was using a temporary facility off-site. "It's made in small containers—it is more an experiment than a real harvest," Christophe Salin explained.

The first barrels gave reason for cautious optimism, but Salin refused to commit to a public release date. The quality of the wine was an improvement on anything else produced locally, but it wasn't yet ready to stand the scrutiny of consumers and critics. Salin went on to temper expectations with a quintessentially Lafite understatement about the quality of the wine: "Not bad at all."

There was no question that Lafite's Chinese wine would be the wine against which other domestic growers would be measured, though it now faced stiff competition from Moët Hennessy. The winery was scheduled to open in 2016. Maybe Lafite's Chinese wine would take its first bow then. Maybe not. The first of the Firsts refused to be rushed, even in China.

❖

Bordeaux had used the 1855 Classification to gain entry into the Middle Kingdom, as it always did when it decided to conquer new markets. Château Lafite Rothschild, a product of humble grapes transformed into a symbol of status and luxury, became one of the top ten most coveted gifts in China. It was an astonishing success, the work of decades of plying a difficult market. When the hammer fell at Sotheby's record-breaking auction in October 2010 and Bordeaux's exports to China rose another 67 percent that same year, the vintners, négociants, and their partners in commerce felt triumph. It no longer mattered that Europe was facing years of austerity packages, or that America was still recovering from the financial crisis; China, with its vast population of "new consumers," would sustain the wine market.

Bordeaux's experience in China reinforced two ideas that the négociants knew to be true. Truth: from misery can spring wealth, and wherever there is wealth, there is a desire for luxury. Truth: nothing satisfies the ego and palate better than a bottle of Bordeaux classified growth. But a third truth caught them short: no wine is sold until it's uncorked.

Bordeaux had traditionally marketed classified growths to high-end customers in order to gain an outsized share of the larger wine shelf. But the real consumer base in China was small, and within three short years the market for classified growths had evaporated. Despite warnings, the châteaux, giddy with their singular success, had priced their wines for opportunists, not for wine drinkers. Bordeaux's triumph was undercut by its reliance on sales driven by speculation and a gifting culture, rather than by consumption and the sensual pleasure of fine wine.

The rising prices of the most coveted wines and the diminishing profit margins for established négociants, importers, and merchants coincided with the Chinese strategy to eliminate middlemen. Some châteaux began secretly selling direct to local companies, clubs, restaurants, private companies, private investors, collectors, and end consumers in Hong Kong and China. Négociants did the same thing. The merchants and traders who had forged markets for Bordeaux wines found that financial reliability, supplier connections, and customer relationships were worth naught. Their days of buying low and selling high felt like yesterday. They faced "buy high, impossible to sell," and contemplated leaving the Bordeaux market altogether. Bordeaux's time-tested commercial strategy was unraveling in its most volatile market. And here, the Place de Bordeaux painfully recalled another truth—bubbles burst.

The first realignment in expectations came after Chinese traders saw that the value of Bordeaux's most-prized wines could fall as quickly as it rose. Short-term losses were sharp, and the speculators fled the market. The Place de Bordeaux had a long history of attracting speculators, but this time was different. The number of speculators, the scale of the canceled orders, and the swiftness of the traders' departure left Bordeaux reeling.

Particularly disastrous was Bordeaux's handling of the en primeur system. En primeur had always been a gamble, but Chinese traders—including those who were buying for distribution to Chinese consumers—did not easily forgive the losses they suffered. The managers at the state-owned conglomerates were primarily concerned with two things: delivering revenues that met or exceeded the goals set out in the Five-Year Plan and, if the company was listed on the stock exchange, maintaining a strong share price. The latter was just as true for publicly listed Western companies, but the board for a government-controlled company in China was essentially the Communist Party and Beijing. There was zero tolerance for embarrassment.

Unwilling to return to pre-China prices, the châteaux expected the négociants to absorb all of the financial shock as the demand for Bordeaux's wines spiraled downward. But now the costly First Growths took up most of the négociants' treasury, and the négociants could not afford to buy a range of wines unless they sold straight through to importers. Discounting became a matter of survival. At the same time, traditional markets had cooled to en primeur sales, and without the speculation on China, the entire system hung in the balance.

The second, and more dramatic, realignment came when Xi Jinping's anti-graft campaign eliminated the official entertainment and gifting sector. The classified growths, as well as many smaller châteaux, were disastrously slow in comprehending the impact of the crackdown. No one believed that the anti-graft campaign would endure, but it did. The ban on high-end alcohol for government officials and state-owned firms could remain in place until the next transition in power in China, which would likely not occur until 2023, and might be permanent. What remains of the market for classified growths in China is difficult to ascertain. Behind closed doors, foreign and privately owned businesses entertain and enjoy themselves. Tycoons build wine collections. But the largest share of demand, funded with public coffers, has disappeared.

With the thirstiest customers gone and real consumers scarce, the Place de Bordeaux found itself in a tricky situation. China did not turn out to be, as many had hoped, the salvation of the Place de Bordeaux *at any price.* China was a rich country of poor people and a relatively small and emerging middle class. In order to maintain its hard-won position, the Place now had to turn to the much more difficult task of selling every-day wine to the cost-conscious Chinese upper middle class, which has a monthly pre-tax per capita income of about $700.

This will likely require far more attention to battling wine coun-terfeiters, including substantial investments in new technology to track provenance. Brand squatting also continues to be a significant issue. Until the Chinese government adopts and enforces intellectual property laws similar to those in the European Union and the United States, brand squatters will proliferate. Smuggling will also continue to pollute the market until China adopts import duties based on volume rather than value.

Going forward, Bordeaux's competition will grow only fiercer. China has signed or is negotiating free-trade agreements with New Zealand, Chile, Australia, and Switzerland, all of which produce wine. The wines from these countries will be subject to lower import duties—in some cases zero duty—when coming into China, making them more competi-tive. The agreements also open these markets to Chinese wines under the same conditions. With the anti-dumping investigation into European wines, Beijing has signaled that it has no qualms about engaging in a trade war to protect its domestic wineries. While the Chinese were unable to prove their complaints against French and Spanish wineries, they did wring strategic concessions, including the transfer of knowledge.

China has already indicated that it intends to be a global player. To cement Hong Kong's position as a logistics hub for wine, the government of Hong Kong has signed a "memorandum of understanding" on cooperation in wine-related businesses with fourteen wine-producing regions or countries around the world. Hong Kong wine imports for 2014 were $1.09 billion, and $313 million worth of wine was legally reexported. France accounts for more than 50 percent of the wine imports into Hong Kong, dominated by Bordeaux. It has never been more vital for the négociants to hold on to this trade.

The task before the Place de Bordeaux has been made even more difficult by China's ambition to be one of the world's largest wine producers. For two decades, the Chinese government has been building the infrastructure for industrial production of better quality wine, and, even after the anti-graft campaign, official support for domestically produced wine has been expanding, not shrinking. Wine production is an approved industrial sector. State-controlled companies such as COFCO have mandates to expand their overseas wine investments. Changyu expects to buy its first overseas winery in 2015, and plans to buy nine more. This industrial policy arises from economic necessity. Millions of Chinese still fight off starvation every day, and the pressure to supply staple grains to the population remains one of Beijing's highest priorities. Decreasing the number of individuals suffering from alcoholism and the health effects of hard liquor consumption is also a government priority. It is unlikely that the Communist leadership will abandon the country's investments in wine production in the next Five-Year Plan.

Indeed, the Ningxia wine classification system is part of a larger Chinese strategy to promote the improved quality of domestic wines, expand actual consumption, and develop China's own brand names in the world of wine. The logical next step for Chinese winegrowers is to export their wines, competing head-to-head with Old World and New World vintners. If China achieves its plan—and so far, the Chinese have proved themselves to be overachievers—then the country will become the fifth largest wine-producing nation on the planet, outpacing Australia. Even if many of those vineyards grow only table grapes, China is poised to become a wine superpower. Eventually, China will look to build export markets in the Americas, Europe, and Africa, and the expertise it has gained in acquiring Bordeaux vineyards and négociants such as Diva will be invaluable.

This should not come as a surprise. China reacted to Bordeaux's incursions with the agility of a mergers and acquisitions specialist. It bought resources of a limited supply, and it eliminated middlemen. It used government-subsidized companies to compete against outsiders, and it absorbed foreign expertise. Forgers and brand squatters operated with impunity—unless a Chinese business came under attack.

Moët Hennessy and DBR Lafite, early movers in new markets, are planting roots in China, banking on the attraction of their luxury names attached to a domestically produced wine. These are daring ventures: necessary for building a long-term relationship with Chinese consumers, but risky in a country with an unpredictable commercial and regulatory environment. Several French companies invested in early joint ventures, but the Chinese ultimately refused to hand over lucrative assets to foreigners. In less than fifty years, when China's nascent terroirs have matured, the vineyard leases of DBR Lafite and Moët Hennessy—not to mention Grace Vineyard and a host of others—will be up for renegotiation. By then, the wines may well be considered the finest in China. That won't remove the chance that, like the Gaos in Yinchuan, the wineries will be forced to parley with the government for the rights to use the land. It all depends on how the Communist Party values its ties with these relatively small but highly prestigious foreign companies. The Chinese might prefer to make the wine 100 percent Chinese.

The Place de Bordeaux set out to conquer China, which, in turn, attracted the Middle Kingdom's own expansionist ambitions. Seven years ago, there was scant Asian presence in Bordeaux, but now the Chinese presence grows every year. Many Chinese students and entrepreneurs who descended on the region during the speculative frenzy have settled there permanently, some of them marrying French nationals, others bringing their Chinese families, their dreams now woven into the local social and economic fabric. The Chinese community has changed many facets of daily life, from restaurants to art to schools, generally enriching the local culture. Nearly every négociant has at least one Chinese staff member; the châteaux have Mandarin-speaking guides.

But some of the overseas Chinese brought with them a "gray" economy of black banks and cash kickbacks. And even after the crackdown, Chinese investors are still in the market for Bordeaux estates. Despite the work of Tracfin, the French judicial system has had a poor record when it comes to investigating money laundering, and Bordeaux's vineyards have a reputation as safe havens for cash. The question is not *if* a Chinese investor will acquire a classified growth, but *when*. The French government once blocked the sale of Château Margaux to an American company. How will it react to Chinese ownership? While the United Kingdom has had a lasting historical impact on Bordeaux, in the future, China is likely to influence Bordeaux's cultural and commercial landscape more than any other nation, for good or ill.

Intuitively, négociants have doubled their efforts to rebuild old markets and conquer less explored ones. The other four BRICS economies—Brazil, Russia, India, and South Africa—beckon. But the Russian ruble crisis in 2014 all but guaranteed a deep recession in 2015. And the plunging value of the ruble left Bordeaux's Russian clients unable to pay for their orders. Russia has an unpredictable political environment and a complex set of rules for importing wine. Brazil has high duties, a protectionist government, and a daunting bureaucracy. India's middle class is growing fast, but the import duties are 150 percent. Wine consumption is growing in South Africa as well as in other African nations like Nigeria and Angola, but large portions of their populations live on less than one dollar a day. Each has risks, and none can currently replace China.

The Place de Bordeaux is left facing an uncommon challenge. Bordeaux is not in a position to produce more wine; unquestionably, its volume share in the Chinese wine market will shrink as Chinese consumers discover other regions. Nor can Bordeaux hope to compete with China's industrial production of low-end generic wines, in China or abroad. It is imperative for Bordeaux to hold on to the high ground, as it were, leaning on its reputation as the worldwide leader in quality.

Adding another layer of complexity to the challenge, millions of dollars' worth of classified growths sit in Chinese warehouses, uncorked. That wine threatens a glut that can disrupt any number of established markets. The wine can be sold at steep discounts domestically or on the international market. Or it may be kept until prices rise again, driven by real demand. But until the wine is uncorked and drunk, it is not sold, and it will hang over the market.

As always, the Place de Bordeaux faces a gamble. The future of its relationship with China is not as certain as it once seemed. As the négociant Christophe Reboul Salze once said, "You want to play the game? You can win, you can lose." The essence of Bordeaux is commerce. Triumph, failure, and adventure are never far away. China challenges the rules of the game, but the game will still be played.

Notes

....

Most of the information in this book came from personal interviews or emails with those actively involved in the events at the time. Some of those interviews were done in the course of my reporting for Agence France-Presse, *Meininger's Wine Business International*, and *Wine Spectator*. As per the custom on the Place de Bordeaux, some sources preferred to remain anonymous. Historical information came from the Jardine Matheson Archive at Cambridge University (Department of Manuscripts and University Archives, Cambridge University Library) with permission from Matheson & Company, as well as the Archives Municipales de Bordeaux, Archives Départementales de Gironde, and the archives of the Musée National des Douanes. Currency conversions are based on historical rates.

Chapter 1. First Growth

Author interviews and email exchanges with the following individuals provided background information for this chapter: Chris Adams, chief executive officer, Sherry-Lehmann Wine & Spirits; Jean-Christophe Calvet, president, Aquitaine Wine Company; Bertrand Carles, former export manager, Maison Ginestet; Pierre-Antoine Castéja, chief executive officer, Maison Joanne; Philippe Dambrine, chief executive officer, Château Greysac; Yannick Evenou, former export manager, Compagnie des Vins de Bordeaux et de la Gironde (CVBG); Christophe Grenaille, former director, Diageo Château & Estate Wines (DC&E); David Launay, general manager, Château Gruaud Larose; Dewey Markham Jr., author of *1855: A History of the Bordeaux Classification*; Zsoka McDonald, senior director, external communications, Diageo North America; Jean Merlaut, owner, Château Gruaud Larose; Jean-Guillaume Prats, former managing director, Château Cos d'Estournel; Christophe Reboul Salze, president, The Wine Merchant; Jean-Pierre Rousseau, managing director, Distribution Internationale de Vins et Alcools (Diva); Christophe

Salin, president and chief executive officer, Domaines Barons de Rothschild (Lafite); Edith Tirlemont-Imbert, former commercial director, Vignobles Internationaux; Guillaume Touton, owner, Monsieur Touton Selection; John Watkins, chief executive officer, ASC Fine Wines; Thomas Yip, owner, and Vincent Yip, manager, Topsy Trading.

2   "There is always someone trying to replace you": Author interview with Jean-Pierre Rousseau, managing director, Distribution Internationale de Vins et Alcools (Diva), September 18, 2013.

3   "I've sold 20 percent of the wine to Topsy Trading": Ibid.

4   Kadoories diversified into real estate and utilities: "Lawrence Kadoorie, 94, Is Dead: A Leader in Hong Kong's Growth," Associated Press, August 26, 1993.

5   Deng did what his predecessors never dared: Martin Jacques, *When China Rules the World: The End of the Western World and the Birth of a New Global Order*, 2nd ed. (London: Penguin Books, 2012), p. 180.

5   Per capita annual income was $182: Justin Yifu Lin, "China and the Global Economy," *China Economic Journal* 4, no. 1 (October 2011): 1–14.

5   A night at the Jianguo cost $90 to $120: Email to author from John Watkins, chief executive officer, ASC Fine Wines, November 19, 2014; Watkins stayed in the Jianguo Hotel in Beijing from soon after it first opened. When he worked for Northwest Airlines from 1986 to 1990, the company's China office was located in rooms 101 and 103 of the Jianguo.

6   the leading citizens of Bordeaux were arguing over which wines to send: Dewey Markham Jr., *1855: A History of the Bordeaux Classification* (New York: John Wiley & Sons, 1998), p. 22.

6   they had received a letter from Dijon stating that the winegrowers of Burgundy and Champagne: Ibid., p. 21.

6   labeled the bottles for public consumption: A great deal of wine at this time was also sold by the négociants in barrels or half barrels.

7   Some growers thought they could use the limelight of the exhibition: Markham, *1855*, p. 21.

7   the display at the exhibition was illustrated with a large map of the entire region: Ibid., p. 98.

8   Three red wines from the Médoc peninsula: The sweet white wines of Barsac and Sauternes were also ranked in 1855. Château d'Yquem, one of the most famous and expensive wines at the time, was listed as a Premier Grand Cru Supérieur. Historians believe that Château Haut-Brion was the first estate to sell under its château name, when it opened Pontac's Head in London after the Great London Fire.

8   "delicate thing & likely to arouse sensitivities": Markham, *1855*, p. 106.

8   Château Cantemerle was added to the list of Fifth Growths: Ibid., p. 158.

8   *gei mianzi* and *liu mianzi*: Michael Harris Bond, ed., *The Oxford Handbook of Chinese Psychology* (Oxford: Oxford University Press, 2010), pp. 492, 686–87.

10   a paltry $13.71 a bottle: Author interview with Christophe Reboul Salze, president, The Wine Merchant, January 8, 2014.

10   "Let's do it": Author interview with Thomas Yip, owner, and Vincent Yip, manager, Topsy Trading, November 15, 2013.

12   "I need to impress them. I need them to come invest": Ibid.

13   Cazes was staggered by the immensity of it: Author interview with Jean-Michel Cazes, owner, Château Lynch-Bages, September 24, 2013.

13   "We bought it at sixty French francs a bottle": Author interview with Thomas Yip and Vincent Yip.

14   Li further surprised his audience by toasting with red wine: Aryn Baker, "The Sweet Taste of Success," *China Wine News*, May 26, 2009, http://www.cnwinenews .com/html/200905/26/20090526172012.htm.

15   "I have my way. It's not quick, but it works": Author interview with Jean-Pierre Rousseau, September 18, 2013.

15   "We shipped about three hundred containers": Author interview with Yannick Evenou, former export manager, Compagnie des Vins de Bordeaux et de la Gironde (CVBG), and former director, Vignobles Fayat, March 17, 2014.

15   "Topsy had bought a lot of the 1996 en primeur": Ibid.

16   increased pressure to deliver on its reputation: The influence of Robert Parker and the success of Marvin Shanken's *Wine Spectator* magazine both played a significant role. Parker had risen to fame based on his mastery of Bordeaux, Shanken put his muscle behind his own stable of critics, and both employed with phenomenal success the 100-point rating system. Competing critics and magazines felt they, too, had to focus on Bordeaux to prove their bona fides.

19   to declare 2005 the vintage of the century: The 2005 has consistently been labeled the "vintage of the century" since its debut. See, for instance, John Lichfield, "The Best Ever? Experts Hail 2005 Vintage as a Bordeaux to Die For," *Independent*, April 8, 2006; Jeffrey T. Iverson, "Cheers Leader," *Time*, June 11, 2006; Will Lyons, "Bordeaux 2005: A Verdict on the Vintage," *Wall Street Journal*, February 2, 2015; and Jancis Robinson, "2005 Red Bordeaux," *Financial Times*, February 13, 2015.

20   Prices had increased an average of 68 percent: Mitch Frank, "The Collapse of America's Bordeaux Source," *Wine Spectator*, March 28, 2011.

20   he had spent $26 million: Vincent Yip provided this figure as €20 million; the currency conversion is based on the end-of-year exchange rate.

21   Château & Estate Wines refused its allocations: Reporting for this section on C&E, later DC&E, comes from interviews and research conducted by the author at the time while writing for Agence France-Presse and *Meininger's Wine Business International*. Suzanne Mustacich, "US Market Swamped by Discounted Bordeaux," *Meininger's Wine Business International*, January 2010.

21   The *New York Times* called him a "Superpower": William Grimes, "Ab Simon, Chairman of Seagram Wine Unit, Dies at 88," *New York Times*, January 4, 2011.

Chapter 2. No Boundaries

Author interviews and email exchanges with the following individuals provided background information for this chapter: Chris Adams, chief executive officer, Sherry-Lehmann Wine & Spirits; Dan Berger, columnist, *Napa Valley Register*; Gary Boom, managing director, Bordeaux Index; Jean-Christophe Calvet, president, Aquitaine Wine Company; Bertrand Carles, former export manager, Maison Ginestet; Pierre-Antoine Castéja, chief executive officer, Maison Joanne; Stephan Delaux, president, Bordeaux Tourism Bureau, president, Bordeaux Grands Evénements, and deputy mayor of Bordeaux; Thomas Jullien, market adviser, China, Conseil Interprofessionnel du Vin de Bordeaux (CIVB)/ Bordeaux Wine Council; David Launay, general manager, Château Gruaud Larose; Jean Merlaut, owner, Château Gruaud Larose; Philippe Roudié, historian and retired professor, University of Bordeaux; Jean-Pierre Rousseau, managing director, Distribution Internationale de Vins et Alcools (Diva); Linda Sansbury, information officer, Hong Kong Economic and Trade Office; Don St. Pierre Jr., executive chairman of the board, ASC Fine Wines; Guillaume Touton, owner, Monsieur Touton Selections; Thomas Yip, owner, and Vincent Yip, manager, Topsy Trading.

25 soon many began to trade in markets farther afield: Due to its role as a trade hub, Bordeaux has been important to international relations for centuries. The first Russian consulate in France was in Bordeaux. On November 11, 1723, Czar Peter the Great nominated Ivan Ivanovic Alekseev as consul for the Russian nation in the city of Bordeaux in order to establish direct commercial relations with the region that supplied him with wine every year. Giliane Besset, "Les Relations Commerciales Entre Bordeaux et la Russie aux XVIII Siècle," *Cahiers du monde russe et soviétique* 23, no. 2 (April–June 1982). Additional information came from lectures and discussions with the historian Philippe Roudié while studying for the Diplôme Universitaire d'Aptitude à la Dégustation des Vins (DUAD), Oenology Department, University of Bordeaux 2, academic year 2006–7 and an author interview with Roudié on September 5, 2013.

25 Joseph Fenwick, a wine merchant and partner in an international shipping firm: "To George Washington from George Mason, 19 June 1789," Founders Online, National Archives (http://founders.archives.gov/documents/Washington/05-03-02-0011), in Dorothy Twohig, ed., *The Papers of George Washington*, vol. 3, *15 June 1789–5 September 1789* (Charlottesville: University Press of Virginia, 1989), pp. 49–55.

25 Ships belonging to Fenwick and his partners: Ibid.

25 Joseph Fenwick was an inspired choice: The Fenwicks were partners with the Masons in the shipping firm Fenwick, Mason and Company. On July 16, 1789, two days after the storming of the Bastille, Thomas Jefferson wrote to John Mason, thanking him for his offer of a ship to take from France. Unfortunately, Jefferson was not yet free to leave. "From Thomas Jefferson to John Mason, 16 July 1789," Founders Online, National Archives.

26 "We had four customers. If you lost two, you were dead": Author interview with Jean-Pierre Rousseau, November 18, 2014.

26 "We were one of the first négociants to be transparent": Ibid.

27 "I invited them to private, sneak movie screenings": Ibid.

27 "Thomas was discreet, behind the scenes": Ibid.

28 "We were one of ten négociants to receive allocations": Ibid.

29 old China hand: This was a term originally used to identify the nineteenth-century merchants trading out of China's treaty ports, but it has more recently meant any foreign entrepreneur with an expertise in the language, culture, and inner workings of China.

29   "the largest ammunition seizure I've ever seen": Pamela Burdman and Charles Burress, "75 Million Ammo Rounds Seized in Santa Clara," *San Francisco Chronicle*, May 4, 1995.

30   "This is absolutely ridiculous": Ibid.

30   they used it to set up a "wholly foreign-owned enterprise": Email to author from Don St. Pierre Jr., executive chairman of the board, ASC Fine Wines, December 3, 2014.

30   "We saw a middle class coming": William C. Kirby and Erica M. Zendell, "From Beijing Jeep to ASC Fine Wines: The Story of an American Family Business in China," Harvard Business School paper 9-314-053, July 29, 2014.

31   "This had nothing to do with a handover to China": Email to author from Don St. Pierre Jr., December 3, 2014.

31   April 26, 1996: Kirby and Zendell, "From Beijing Jeep to ASC Fine Wines."

31   "He hijacked the wine!": Author interview with Don St. Pierre Jr., October 15, 2012.

32   "Selling wine in China": Ibid.

32   accounted for 80 percent of the St. Pierres' business: Kirby and Zendell, "From Beijing Jeep to ASC Fine Wines."

32   Don Sr. met the billionaire Gernot Langes-Swarovski over a cigarette: Ibid.

32   Swarovski headed his family's cut-crystal empire: Gernot Langes-Swarovski was the company's "public face" until 2002, per Tom Metcalf, "New Billionaire Swarovski Surfaces with Crystal Fortune," Bloomberg, January 25, 2013.

33   "Existing wholesalers and distributors of alcoholic beverages": Kirby and Zendell, "From Beijing Jeep to ASC Fine Wines."

33   "Honestly, if we had come to China as wine people": Author interview with Don St. Pierre Jr., October 15, 2012.

33   For every four French ships sailing: Faits commerciaux N°9, Navigation, Mouvement de la Rivière de Canton, du 1 Juillet 1842 au 30 Juin 1843, Ministère de l'Agriculture et du Commerce, Musée National des Douanes, Bordeaux.

33   the First Opium War (1839–42): The British seized Hong Kong in 1841, but the First Opium War was not formally ended until the signing of the Treaty of Nanking on August 29, 1842. The treaty formally granted Hong Kong to the British Crown.

34   "I once ordered a case of '85 Pétrus": Victoria Moore, "Bordeaux Index: Boom for Your Buck?," *Telegraph*, May 28, 2012.

35   "If you pitch up in Bordeaux without money": Author interview with Gary Boom, managing director, Bordeaux Index, November 27, 2013.

35   Bordeaux Index's six employees sat on wooden boxes: Startups Team, "Gary Boom: Bordeaux Index," March 24, 2011, www.startups.co.uk/.

36   "You're not a customer with an account": Email to author from Michelle Wilson, personal assistant to Gary Boom, Bordeaux Index, February 19, 2014.

36   "You look at wines across vintages": Moore, "Bordeaux Index."

36   "Your competition absolutely trashes you": Startups Team, "Gary Boom: Bordeaux Index."

37   he was eliminating the 40 percent duty on wine imports: Peter D. Meltzer, "Hong Kong to Become Hotspot for Fine-Wine Sales?," *Wine Spectator*, February 28, 2008.

37 Tang, a tycoon politician who styled himself as a wine collector: Te-ping Chen, "Satirists Take Aim at Hong Kong Candidate Tang," *Wall Street Journal*, February 20, 2012.

37 Hong Kong was set to become the main logistics hub: Emails to author from Linda Sansbury, information officer, Hong Kong Economic and Trade Office, Government of the Hong Kong Special Administrative Region, March 3 and 15, 2010.

37 prices slashed up to 70 percent: Mustacich, "US Market Swamped by Discounted Bordeaux"; Suzanne Mustacich, "Diageo Dumps Bordeaux," *Wine Spectator*, January 31, 2010.

37 "It's a bloodbath": Suzanne Mustacich, "US Bordeaux Prices at Risk of Bloodbath, Experts Say," Agence France-Presse, November 9, 2009; Suzanne Mustacich, "Diageo Dumps Bordeaux," *Wine Spectator*, January 31, 2010.

37 shipping the 2,700 cases back to Bordeaux: Author interview with Jean Merlaut, owner, Château Gruaud Larose, and David Launay, director, Château Gruaud Larose, December 18, 2009. See also Suzanne Mustacich, "US Market Swamped by Discounted Bordeaux."

37 worth $200 million: Email to author from Dan Berger, columnist, *Napa Valley Register*, November 27, 2009, and Dan Berger, "Diageo Abandoning Bordeaux," *Napa Valley Register*, November 27, 2009.

39 the logistics involved in freight forwarding: Author interview with Didier Bouchet, director, Asia Division, J. F. Hillebrand France, June 3, 2014.

40 inventory had been offloaded long beforehand: Ibid.

41 "The reality is that Hong Kong": Email to author from Don St. Pierre Jr., March 14, 2010.

42 There were reports of trucks going across: Author interview with Don St. Pierre Jr., November 8, 2013.

42 "Every shipment, every time, it's the same thing": Author interview with a Hong Kong importer who asked to remain anonymous due to the sensitivity of the subject, November 2014.

43 The company had grown 46 percent on average per year: Kirby and Zendell, "From Beijing Jeep to ASC Fine Wines."

43 Government departments made unannounced visits every six months or so: Ibid.

44 "I wasn't going to let them take my father": Author interview with Don St. Pierre Jr., November 8, 2013.

45 He appealed to the U.S. ambassador in China: Clark Randt, a Bush appointee, is the longest-serving U.S. ambassador to China, having served from July 2001 until January 2009. As of 2014, he is an adviser to a Chinese equity firm.

46 "I had to make peace with it": Author interview with Don St. Pierre Jr., November 8, 2013.

47 What this problem required was *guanxi*: Michael Harris Bond, ed., *The Oxford Handbook of Chinese Psychology* (Oxford: Oxford University Press, 2010), pp. 231, 492, 686.

47 "It appears to have been common practice": Simon Tam, "Customs Crackdown on Top Chinese Wine Importer," March 17, 2008, www.jancisrobinson.com/.

48 "almost solely on rumor and innuendo": Jancis Robinson, "ASC and Customs: Don St. Pierre Sr. Responds," March 20, 2008, www.jancisrobinson.com/.

48 Tam had tried and failed to compete with ASC's wine education program in China: Kirby and Zendell, "From Beijing Jeep to ASC Fine Wines."

48 "What this story ends up being": Simon Tam, "Chinese Wine Market Comes of Age," April 1, 2008, www.jancisrobinson.com/.

48 "This is no longer the wild west of wine countries": Ibid.

49 "In plain American talk that's called 'peanuts'": Jim Boyce, "China Customs Investigation: ASC Managing Partner Out of Detention," April 10, 2008, www.grape wallofchina.com/.

49 "Stepping back": Elaine Kurtenbach, "China's Customs Inspectors Target Wine Importers as Sales of Foreign Vintages Boom," Associated Press, March 31, 2008.

50 there were other attractions for the mainland Chinese: Author interview with Edward Yu, principal assistant secretary, and Gabriel Pak Chun-yin, assistant secretary, Commerce and Economic Development Bureau, Hong Kong, November 15, 2013; emails to author from Gabriel Pak, November 15 and 28, 2013.

50 "Since eliminating duties on wine": Government of Hong Kong, "Financial Secretary's Speech at Hong Kong Wine and Dine Festival 2009 Opening Ceremony," press release, October 30, 2009, http://www.info.gov.hk/gia/general/200910/30/P200910300327.htm.

51 Jullien and the other organizers: Email to author from Thomas Jullien, founder and director, Pilot Fish, and market adviser, China, Conseil Interprofessionnel du Vin de Bordeaux (CIVB), March 2, 2014.

52 "Bordeaux is definitely a brand in China": Author interview with Don St. Pierre Jr., November 8, 2013.

Chapter 3. Planting Vines

Author interviews and emails with the following individuals provided background information for this chapter: Judy Chan, president, Grace Vineyard; Gérard Colin, consulting winemaker (previously winemaker, Grace Vineyard); Thierry Courtade, Silver Heights; Alberto Fernández, managing partner, Torres China; Emma Gao Yuan, owner, Silver Heights; Craig Grafton, senior winemaker, Pernod Ricard; David Henderson, president and chief executive officer, China Fine Wines, and owner, Dragon's Hollow; Bernard Magrez, chairman, Grands Vignobles Bernard Magrez; Rong Jian, president and chairman, Ningxia Grape Industry Association, and general manager, Helan Qingxue; Jean-Pierre Rousseau, managing director, Distribution Internationale de Vins et Alcools (Diva); Christophe Salin, president and CEO, Domaines Barons de Rothschild (Lafite); David Webster, non-executive director, Fine Vintage (Far East); Harry Wu Hongda, founder and executive director, Laogai Research Foundation.

54 "My [paternal] grandfather arrived with a horse, two soldiers, and a pistol": Author interview with Emma Gao Yuan, owner, Silver Heights, November 4, 2013.

54 95 percent of the population in Ningxia was illiterate: Information Office of the State Council of the Peoples Republic of China, "National Minorities Policy and Its Practice in China: III. Regional Autonomy for Ethnic Minorities," June 2000, http://www.china.org.cn/e-white/4/4.3.htm.

55 "It causes erosion to the available space": Cheng Yingqi, "Desert Land Set to Be Reclaimed," *China Daily*, March 21, 2013.

55 5,400 acres of desert, removing 450 million cubic feet of sand: Paul White, "Ningxia Spearheads Western Development Strategy," China International Intellectech Corporation, October 9, 2000.

55 In the mid-1990s, Yinchuan had hosted a wine conference: Author interview with Rong Jian, president and chairman, Ningxia Grape Industry Association, and general manager, Helan Qingxue, November 5, 2013.

56 Li Hua, who had recently founded the College of Enology: "First Grape Wine College in Asia Established in China," *Asia Pacific Biotech News* 1, no. 5 (October 13, 1997): 131.

57 In November 1979: Author interview with François Hériard-Dubreuil, chairman, Rémy Cointreau, and vice chairman, Dynasty Fine Wines, April 21, 2015.

57 Tianjin was the closest port to Beijing: Tianjin had been a military port and trading center since the fifteenth century, but came into its own as a treaty port once international settlements were established in China after the Opium Wars.

57 planted by the Bulgarian government after the People's Liberation Army marshal Nie Rongzhen: Christopher S. Wren, "Great Wall Wins Medal for China—in Wine Contest," *New York Times* News Service, November 25, 1983.

58 A churchyard winery established in 1910 by a French priest: Beijing Municipal Commission of Tourism Development website, www.visitbeijing.com.cn.

59 Tianjin would supply the electricity, water, and workers, and Rémy Martin would supply the equipment and expertise: "Château Tianjin Begins Making Wine in China," Associated Press, September 1, 1980; email exchanges with Christina Zhao, vice general manager, Tianjin Dynasty International Winery; and author interview with François Hériard-Dubreuil, April 21, 2015.

59 The initial investment from Rémy Martin: Author interview with François Hériard-Dubreuil, April 21, 2015.

59 "since Rémy Martin was eager to gain a firm foothold": The characterization of the negotiations between Tianjin and Rémy Martin in 1979 and '80 are based on an author interview with Francois Hériard-Dubreuil, April 21, 2015; and author email exchanges with Christina Zhao, vice general manager, Tianjin Dynasty International Winery.

59 offering to pay a premium—around 1.3 yuan, or twenty-one cents, per pound: Christopher Wren, "Dynasty Without Tradition," *New York Times*, November 11, 1983.

59 produced enough wine to fill one hundred thousand bottles: "Chateau Tianjin Begins Making Wine in China," Associated Press, September 1, 1980.

59 They had arrived in sacks, filthy: Wren, "Dynasty Without Tradition."

59 China did not have the logistics industry to export wine: Author interview with David Webster, non-executive director, Fine Vintage (Far East), January 3, 2014.

60 "The TV show was the most popular": Ibid.

60 The joint venture could also buy: Author interview with Harry Wu Hongda, founder and executive director, Laogai Research Foundation, March 19, 2014; email to author from Harry Wu Hongda, April 25, 2015; and Colina McDougall, "China's Bouquet of Barbed Wire," *Financial Times*, April 4, 1990.

60 When the Chinese manager took Delair to visit Tuanhe: Author interview with Pierre Delair, winemaker, Rémy Cointreau, May 18, 2015.

61 The Laogai Research Foundation: Email to author from Harry Wu Hongda, April 23, 2015.

61 During Mao's time: Laogai Handbook, Laogai Research Foundation, 2008, pp. 7–8.

61 Since opening to the West: Ibid., p. 13.

61 the Tianjin Municipal Banqiao RTL: Ibid., p. 465.

61 Tuanhe had 824 acres of vineyards: Author interview with Harry Wu Hongda, founder and executive director, Laogai Research Foundation, March 19, 2014; Helms, "China's Bouquet of Barbed Wire"; and "Chinese Prison System, 'Laogai,'" Hearing Before the Subcommittee on International Operations and Human Rights of the Committee on International Relations, House of Representatives, One Hundred Fourth Congress, First Session, U.S. Government Printing Office, April 3, 1995, pp. 13–16, 42–43.

61 In 1990, Rémy's northeast: McDougall, "China's Bouquet of Barbed Wire."

61 in an award-winning story: Dinah Lee, Robert Neff, Amy Borrus, and Joyce Barnathan, "China's Ugly Export Secret: Prison Labor," Bloomberg Businessweek, April 21, 1991.

62 they could sell the grapes for more elsewhere: Author interview with Delair, May 18, 2015.

62 "Without our knowledge": Lee, Neff, Borrus, and Barnathan, "China's Ugly Export Secret: Prison Labor."

62 "In 1986, they brought a truck of grapes": Author interview with François Hériard-Dubreuil, April 21, 2015.

62 Pernod Ricard teamed up with the Beijing Friendship Winery: This was in 1987. The Beijing Friendship winery was what remained of the Shangyi Winery, founded in 1910 in the yard of a Catholic church in Beijing, renamed the Peking Grape Wine factory after 1949. It was originally located near the Beijing city wall, but was moved in 1957 farther outside the city. Yang Cheng-Yen, "More of the Cup That Cheers," Peking Review, no. 45 (November 10, 1961).

62 Doctors prescribed nighttime wine "tonics": The observations of Chinese soap operas and the use of wine as a health tonic come from author interviews with Thomas Jullien, market adviser, China, Conseil Interprofessionnel du Vin de Bordeaux (CIVB)/Bordeaux Wine Council, May 25–27, 2010.

63 The menu helpfully suggested pairings of fine wine and ice cream: Suzanne Mustacich, "Wine Woos China's Chic," Agence France-Presse, July 14, 2010.

63 At the company's headquarters: Dynasty's castle opened to the public in November 2010.

63 "This was a humble decision": Felicity Carter, "Dynasty's Chairman Discusses the Future of Chinese," Meininger's Wine Business International, July 14, 2011. As the head of China's second joint venture, Bai Zhisheng was an important figure in Tianjin. In addition to his roles at Dynasty and Tianjin Development Holdings, he served as general manager of the Tianjin Agricultural and Industrial and Commerce Company and the chairman of Tianjin Heavenly Palace Winery, a

subsidiary of Tianjin Development. He resigned as Dynasty's chairman on January 29, 2014.

64 The turning point came in 1999: Author interview with Emma Gao Yuan, November 4, 2013. The delegation included managers from government, banking, agriculture, and education.

65 Gao Lin and his wife carefully buried each vine: All vineyards in Ningxia must follow this practice, often requiring significant investment in labor to ensure that the vines do not die in the cold or snap while being manipulated. See also Erica Bernstein, "China: The Wine World's Waking Giant," *Wine Searcher*, September 14, 2012.

66 "At first there were two Thierrys": Author interview with Emma Gao Yuan, November 4, 2013.

66 Arbitrarily, the government levied a 365 percent duty on imported wine: Author interview with David Henderson, president and chief executive officer, China Fine Wines, and owner, Dragon's Hollow, September 24, 2013.

67 "I was losing money": Author interview with Henderson, September 24, 2013.

67 He was told to try Bordeaux: Ibid. Henderson sought advice from his friend John Schwartz Sr., vice president at Wente Brothers, based in Livermore, California. Ironically, Schwartz sent him to Bordeaux rather than suggesting California red wine.

67 Montrose was the exclusive distributor in China: In January 2011, DBR Lafite granted exclusive distribution rights to ASC Fine Wines.

69 Jiaonan, facing the Yellow Sea: In 2012, Jiaonan was merged into the Huangdao District of Qingdao.

69 "To build in China was magnificent": Author interview with Bernard Magrez, chairman, Grands Vignobles Bernard Magrez, October 11, 2012.

69 he planted a twenty-acre experimental vineyard: "Chine: la nouvelle route de la soif," June 5, 1997, www.LSA.fr/.

69 "The objective is to produce wines ready to drink": Ibid.

69 "It was a remarkable wine, which sold well": Author interview with Bernard Magrez, October 11, 2012.

69 "twelfth economic counselor": "Chine: la nouvelle route de la soif."

70 "All you have to do is give the guy three RMB": Author interview with Bernard Magrez, October 11, 2012.

70 "In that case, you need to share the profits": Ibid.

70 "We left with nothing, but we left standing up": Ibid.

70 Pernod Ricard had pulled out of Dragon Seal: Michael Belby, "Moving Upmarket: Pernod-Ricard Takes the Wine Fight to China," March 8, 2013, www.brw.com.au/.

70 "It was like any other major company": Author interview with David Henderson, September 24, 2013.

71 At Dynasty, Rémy Martin had pulled its employees out: Other joint ventures also fell apart. For instance, Seagram's pulled out of Summer Palace; Cointreau pulled out of Imperial Court; Hiram Walker Wines & Spirits (HK), a subsidiary of British Allied Domecq, pulled out of the Huadong Winery in Qingdao. Eric Chol, "On s'est trompé d'eldorado," *L'Express*, October 31, 2002.

71 "When the jet landed in Ningxia": Author interview with David Henderson, February 20, 2015.

71 "It was a huge reclamation project": Author interview with David Henderson, March 3, 2015.

71 "It was so invasive": Ibid.

71 the state-owned food conglomerate in Beijing: This was COFCO, previously CEROILS, or China National Cereals, Oils and Foodstuffs Import and Export Corporation, which had the monopoly on importing wine when China first opened to the West.

72 The first vintage debuted in 2005: When Pernod Ricard bought the Helan Mountain facility from the government, Henderson made a deal. He had wisely trademarked the Helan Mountain brand. He ceded the brand to Pernod Ricard in exchange for a winemaking partnership.

72 "We were the ones directly responsible": Author interview with David Henderson, February 20, 2015.

72 "It basically went silent": Author interview with David Henderson, March 3, 2015.

74 His 2 percent sales commission: William C. Kirby, Michael Shih-ta Chen, and Keith Chi-ho Wong, "Appellation Shanxi: Grace Vineyard," Harvard Business School case study 9-309-075, February 20, 2013, p. 2.

74 "The more I was with my business associates": Kirby, Chen, and Wong, "Appellation Shanxi," p. 2.

75 He had arrived in Hong Kong a few years: Author interview with Gérard Colin, consulting winemaker (previously winemaker, Grace Vineyard), January 7, 2014.

77 Her deputy general manager, a Chinese man with a degree in mathematics, explained that the officials were interested only in short-term results: Kirby, Chen, and Wong, "Appellation Shanxi," p. 3, and author interview with Judy Chan, president, Grace Vineyard, November 11, 2013.

77 arbitrary fines when tax revenues appeared to be running low: Kirby, Chen, and Wong, "Appellation Shanxi," p. 4.

78 picking the grapes the night before and selling them to someone else: Author interview with Ken Murchison, chief winemaker and viticulturist, Grace Vineyard, at Vinexpo Hong Kong, May 25, 2010.

79 "She didn't have a future in marketing": Interview with Alberto Fernández, managing partner, Torres China, December 10, 2014.

80 "So little, so good": Ibid.

80 It was the first "garage" wine of China: The term "garage wine" refers to a wine made in small quantity in a small winery the size of a "garage."

Chapter 4. Lucky Red

Author interviews and email exchanges with the following individuals provided background information for this chapter: Chris Adams, chief executive officer, Sherry-Lehmann Wine & Spirits; John Avery, owner, Averys of Bristol; Gary Boom, managing director, Bordeaux Index; Jean-Christophe Calvet, president, Aquitaine Wine Company; Bandy Choi, owner, Banny Wine Cellars; Xavier Coumau, president, Syndicat Régional des Courtiers de Vins et Spiritueux de Bordeaux, de la Gironde et du Sud-Ouest; Didier Coustou, Bordeaux buyer, E. Leclerc supermarket chain; Delphine de la Fouchardière, export director, Domaines Albert Bichot; Justin Gibbs, director, Liv-ex Fine Wine Exchange; Sam Gleave, sales director, Bordeaux Index; James Gunter, former senior vice president, Fine Wines, Glazers; Mr. and Mrs. Jin; Philippe Laqueche, former CEO, Yvon Mau; Antonin Michel, coordinator, Diva Network, Distribution Internationale de Vins et Alcools (Diva); Jean-Guillaume Prats, former managing director, Château Cos d'Estournel; Jean-Pierre Rousseau, managing director, Distribution Internationale de Vins et Alcools (Diva); Doug Rumsam, managing director, Bordeaux Index Asia Pacific; Christophe Salin, president and CEO, Domaines Barons de Rothschild (Lafite); Christophe Reboul Salze, president, The Wine Merchant; Simon Staples, sales and marketing director, Berry Bros. & Rudd; Don St. Pierre Jr., executive chairman of the board, ASC Fine Wines; George Tong, vice president, Wong Hau Plastic Works & Trading Company; K. K. Wong, general manager, Rare & Fine Wines; Edward Yu, principal assistant secretary, and Gabriel Pak Chun-yin, assistant secretary, Commerce and Economic Development Bureau, Hong Kong; Zhou Jing, China manager, Producta.

Information from this chapter includes my own observations while reporting on a continuous basis during this time period, including the annual Bordeaux barrel tastings.

81 "It was absolutely madness": Author interview with Christophe Reboul Salze, January 8, 2014.

82 prices quoted by the *tonneau*: Originally, the barrels used for storing and transporting a variety of products by ship were the unit of sale, and ships were measured by how many of these 900-liter tonneau barrels they could carry. By the eighteenth century, the coopers in Bordeaux downsized their containers to 225 liters, or three hundred bottles of wine, but bulk wine trades continue to be measured by the old standard, the tonneau.

83 €950 per tonneau: Julie Fraysee, "Les vendanges 2009 dans le Bordelais s'annoncent sous de très bons auspices," Agence France-Presse, September 4, 2009. Also based on author reporting at the CIVB press conference.

83 generic wine was selling for €650 per tonneau: Based on author reporting at the time and attendance at the CIVB press conference and email to author from Xavier Coumau, president, Syndicat Régional des Courtiers de Vins et Spiritueux de Bordeaux, de la Gironde et du Sud-Ouest, March 6, 2015.

83 First Growths could expect 1,800 people: César Compadre, "Futures Fever: Live from the Bordeaux 2009 'en primeurs' week," *Sudouest*, March 31, 2010.

84 Wing Lung Bank: Elin McCoy, "Chinese Bank Loans to Bank Investors Say 'Drink Now, Pay Later,'" Bloomberg, November 27, 2011.

86 1996 National People's Congress: The congress approved the Ninth Five-Year Plan, which covered the period 1996–2000.

87 Lu had placed Dynasty's first order from Bordeaux: Email exchanges with Christina Zhao, vice general manager, Tianjin Dynasty International Winery, February 17 and 20, 2014, and with Lu Ming, general manager, Tianjin Dynasty International Winery (translated and sent by Angelina Li, Brand Department, Tianjin Dynasty International Winery), March 11, 2014.

88 Xiamen C&D's supply-chain and real estate business was worth $115 billion: C&D Wine website, http://www.cndwine.com/en/AboutUsManage/aboutUsIndex.aspx.

88 "second tier": The classification of Chinese cities as "second tier," "third tier," and so on is more an art than a science. For instance, some listings put all twenty-one provincial capitals in the second tier, regardless of the city's population and development. Xiamen is identified as an "emerging second-tier city" by the *China Business Review*. Richard Craig and Jacqueline Qiang, "China's Emerging Tier 2 Cities: Opportunities for U.S. Companies," *China Business Review*, November 1, 2010.

88 When C&D's parent company diversified into spirits in 1998: Author interview with Yang Wenhua, chairman, C&D Wine, February 12, 2014.

88 The deal was finalized in 2006: Ibid.

88 The following year, Yang met Baron Frédéric de Luze: Author interview with Frédéric de Luze, LD Vins, September 5, 2013.

89 C&D had been named as the exclusive Chinese distributor: C&D Wine website, http://www.cndwine.com/en/AboutUsManage/aboutUsIndex.aspx.

90 Mr. and Mrs. Jin: Author interviews with the Jins on multiple occasions, over the period from 2010 to 2014. Mr. and Mrs. Jin asked to be identified only with their last name.

92 Grand Duke Konstantin Nikolayevich: Markham, *1855*, p. 174.

92 Château Margaux sold its 1847 vintage at 2,100 francs: Ibid., Annex no. 3, pp. 380–81.

95 shrewd upstart traders were seeking an exclusivity: Author interview with Emmanuel Martin, chief executive officer, La Guyennoise Propriétaires et Négociants, April 9, 2014.

96 she'd opened the school in July 2009: Email to author from Ma Lin, director, Cafa Formations, March 14, 2010.

98 His sales director in Hong Kong, Sam Gleave: Author email exchange with Sam Gleave, sales director, Bordeaux Index, April 26, 2010, and Bordeaux Index press release, sent by email from Lauren Shalson, head of marketing, Bordeaux Index, to author, "Bordeaux Index Issues Warning over Chinese Bordeaux 2009 Frauds," April 26, 2010.

99 châteaux had not officially priced or released the wines for sale: Author interview with Gary Boom, November 27, 2013.

99 Liv-ex defended the sales: Adam Lechmere, "Liv-ex Lafite 09 Trade Causes Outrage—and Acceptance," *Decanter*, June 1, 2010.

99 "The whole circus surrounding": Ibid.

99 Haut-Brion and Latour released their first tranche at €500 a bottle wholesale: Ben O'Donnell, "Despite Record Prices, Bordeaux 2009s Are Selling," *Wine Spectator*, June 24, 2010.

99 Lafite offered Carruades de Lafite at 89 percent over the price of the 2005: Lechmere, "Liv-ex Lafite 09 Trade Causes Outrage—and Acceptance."

99 Reputable merchants: Ibid.

99 "If they aim to give their customers": Jane Anson, "Bordeaux 2009: Flood of Releases as L'Evangile, Malescot Triple '08 Prices," *Decanter*, June 17, 2010.

101 "You don't have Bordeaux": Author interview with Edith Tirlemont-Imbert, Commercial Director, Vignobles Internationaux, October 17, 2013.

101 "I told him I don't sell wine at one euro a bottle": The export director for the Beaune négociant asked to remain anonymous. Author email with the export director reconfirmed the earlier conversation in 2010 regarding the requests from Chinese buyers, March 11, 2015.

Chapter 5. Château Mania

The characterization of the Sotheby's auctions, Château Lafite Ex-Cellars, and SK Networks is based on interviews with Jamie Ritchie, chief executive officer and president, Americas and Asia, and Robert Sleigh, senior director, head of department, Asia Wine, Sotheby's Wine; Christophe Salin, chief executive officer and president, Domaines Barons de Rothschild (Lafite); and Philippe Papillon, chief executive officer, Ipso Facto.

Other sources of information for this chapter include Michael Baynes, executive partner, Maxwell-Storrie-Baynes; Thierry Charpentier, deputy manager, international tourism development, Bordeaux Chamber of Commerce and Industry (CCIB); Gregory De'eb, general manager, Crown Wine Cellars; Frédéric de Luze, owner, Château Paveil de Luze, and chief executive officer, LD Vins; Hao Ping, vice minister of education, People's Republic of China, and president, UNESCO; Peter Kwok, owner, Château Tour Saint-Christophe; Philippe Larché, partner, Vintex; Li Lijuan, China desk, Maxwell Storrie Baynes, formerly assisting Zhang Jinshan in the acquisition of a château; John Lin, deputy general manager, Haichang; Karin Maxwell, executive partner, Maxwell-Storrie-Baynes; Philippe Massol, director, Centre Culturel du Vin; Hervé Olivier, director, Gironde Department, Safer Aquitaine Atlantique; Christophe Reboul Salze, president, The Wine Merchant; Jean-Pierre Rousseau, managing director, Distribution Internationale de Vins et Alcools (Diva); Shen Dongjun, president, Tesiro; Yang Wenhua, chairman, C&D Wine.

104 Both men shared the conviction that the global wine market was now driven by Asia: The characterization of the auctions is based on an author interview with Jamie Ritchie, chief executive officer and president, Americas and Asia, Sotheby's Wine, May 5, 2014, and an author interview with Robert Sleigh, senior director, head of department, Asia Wine, Sotheby's Wine, April 22, 2014.

104 Sleigh had first learned about wine: Author interview with Robert Sleigh.

104 2007 Bordeaux ex-cellar auction for Château Mouton: Aulden Cellars–Sotheby's, "Sotheby's Historic Auction of Wines, Château Mouton Rothschild: Treasures from the Private Cellar of Baroness Philippine, Brings $2,223,417, Far Exceeding High Estimate," press release, February 28, 2007.

105 Lafite's wine had been shipped to Tuen Mun in Hong Kong's New Territories: Author interview with Jamie Ritchie.

105 It had the feeling of a five-star gala: The characterization of the auctions is based on author interviews with Jamie Ritchie and Robert Sleigh.

106 A year later: Author interview with Christophe Salin, July 2, 2014.

107 It sold for $171,579: All prices and currency conversions taken from Sothebys.com and the Sotheby's catalog *Lafite Ex-Cellars*, Hong Kong, October 29, 2010.

108 The auction had moved so swiftly: Email to author from Robert Sleigh, April 1, 2015.

109 Haichang's ambitious founder had noticed the success of the Hong Kong Wine and Dine Festival: Author interview with Thierry Charpentier, deputy manager, International Tourism Development, Bordeaux Chamber of Commerce and Industry (CCIB), January 23, 2014.

109 The company had built several more theme parks: "Dalian Discoveryland Theme Park," China Jinshitan National Holiday Resort website, accessed March 8, 2015, http://english.jinshitan.com/picture/show/96.aspx; and Discoveryland English-language website, accessed March 8, 2015, http://www.discoveryland.cn.

110 one hundred bottles of wine from 1,200 châteaux: Information gathered by author at press conference held at Bordeaux Chamber of Commerce and Industry (CCIB) on June 18, 2011; and author interview with Thierry Charpentier.

110 Qu Naijie, the founder, controlling shareholder: Dalian Haichang, "History, Reorganization, and Corporate Structure," HKExnews.hk, February 28, 2014, http://www.hkexnews.hk/listedco/listconews/SEHK/2014/0228/02255_1853474/E116.pdf.

110 Qu had invited the chamber's president: Author interview with Thierry Charpentier.

111 He was ranked by Forbes: Russell Flannery, "A New No. 1 on the Forbes China Rich List," Forbes, September 13, 2011. Qu Naijie was listed by Forbes at number 114 in 2009, number 189 in 2010, and number 216 in 2011, but most fortunes were estimated and many tycoons were closely ranked or tied.

111 France's highest appeals court sided with Château Lafitte: Alexandre Abellan, "A Vos Marques: Lafitte Contre Lafite (Rothschild), La Guerre des Châteaux Continue," Vitisphere, February 7, 2014.

111 "First, the English, Dutch, Irish came": Author interview with Georges Haushalter, CEO of Compagnie Médocaine des Grands Crus and former president of the Bordeaux Wine Council, March 1, 2011; and Suzanne Mustacich, "Amid Wine Boom, Chinese Buy Up Bordeaux Châteaux," Agence France-Presse, March 3, 2011.

112 Bordeaux Chamber of Commerce's leaders had looked into Haichang: Author interview with Thierry Charpentier.

112 Qu hired him as his managing director: Author interview with Thierry Charpentier and author reporting at the June 2011 press conference at CCIB.

112 Philippe Raoux walked into La Winery: The characterization of the sale to COFCO is based on an author interview with Philippe Raoux, owner of Château d'Arsac and former owner of La Winery, October 17, 2013; Suzanne Mustacich, "China Bets Big on Bordeaux," Wine Spectator, February 7, 2011.

113 Wu Fei, was the head of COFCO's wine and spirits division: Author interview with Philippe Raoux.

114 Great Wall Wines, which sold 120 million bottles each year: Lan Lan and Ben Yue, "COFCO to Buy More Overseas Vineyards," China Daily, April 28, 2011.

114 $60 billion: Richard Silk and Chuin-wei Yap, "Chinese Grain Firm Sees IPO in Future," Wall Street Journal, October 28, 2014.

114 started buying soybeans, grain, and other food resources overseas: Dexter Roberts, "The Chinese Want Their Own Cargill," Bloomberg Businessweek, March 20, 2014.

114 Lalande-de-Pomerol cost $184,000: Multiple author interviews with Hervé Olivier, director, Gironde Department, Safer Aquitaine Atlantique, discussing transaction

and the price of vineyard real estate, over a period of several years, including specific discussions on June 27, 2011, and September 26, 2012.

115 "We have a strategy": Chi Jingtao, vice chairman, COFCO, speech given at press conference held at La Winery, February 16, 2011.

116 "I've been thinking about the same question": Author interviews with Shen Dongjun, president, Tesiro, and Zhou Linjun, marketing executive, Tesiro, February 2, 2012.

116 "Increasing numbers of Chinese consumers are learning to drink French wine": Ibid.

116 "beat us by two weeks": Author interviews with Shen Dongjun and Zhou Linjun, March 1, 2011.

117 take his wine off the Place de Bordeaux: Author interviews with Shen Dongjun and Zhou Linjun, February 2, 2012.

117 Shen invited his new contacts: Author interview with Shen Dongjun, February 2, 2012.

117 The 2003 classification was banned: The 2003 Cru Bourgeois Classification, which included only 247 estates, was annulled in 2007, after several appeals, by the French courts.

118 he contentedly took an oath: Based on author's reporting at the event and interview with Shen Dongjun, February 2, 2012.

118 "There are loads of examples": Mustacich, "Amid Wine Boom, Chinese Buy Up Bordeaux Châteaux."

119 "The Chinese owners represent an extremely small part": Kim Willsher, "Chinese Buyers Snapped Up French Vineyards," Telegraph, March 20, 2011.

119 Chinese investors purchased at least thirty estates: The Bordeaux Chamber of Commerce and Industry keeps track of Chinese acquisitions that have been publicly announced. Their figures do not include discreet or confidential acquisitions. Emails to author from Emmanuelle Fragnaud, project manager, Food and Wine Industry, Chinese Market, Bordeaux Chamber of Commerce and Industry, May 24, 2011, December 2, 2011; interview with Thierry Charpentier; and Laurence Lemaire, "Le Vin, le Rouge, la Chine," Sirène Production Edition, published February 19, 2014, updated online weekly.

119 "The biggest difference is that, in China": Author interview with Shen Dongjun, president, Tesiro, and Zhou Linjun, marketing executive, Tesiro, March 1, 2011.

121 buy two more châteaux so that his three children: Peter Kwok bought the seven-acre La Patache in Pomerol and Château Tour Saint-Christophe in Saint-Christophe-des-Bardes. Author interview with Peter Kwok, April 10, 2014.

121 The land itself had been a steal at $27,000 for two and a half acres: Thiébault Dromard, "Une groupe chinoise s'empare du vignoble du château Latour-Laguens," Le Figaro, January 30, 2008. As throughout the book, for the ease of American readers, currencies have been converted to U.S. dollars at historical exchange rates.

121 Latour-Laguens brand, starting around $40 a bottle and climbing to $500: Elin McCoy, "Oenophile Chinese Purchase Bordeaux for $470 Mainland Bottles," Bloomberg News, February 24, 2012; and Thiébault Dromard, "Une groupe chinoise."

122 "I knew for years": Author interview with Michel Rolland, consulting winemaker and co-owner, Rolland Oenologie, May 31, 2013; and Lucy Shaw, "Rolland 'Sad' to Sell Le Bon Pasteur," *The Drinks Business*, June 12, 2013.

123 changed the name from L'Angélus to Angélus: Several people, including Dewey Markham Jr. and Pétrus Desbois, offered accounts of this event.

123 Yang was on a visit: Author interview with Christophe Reboul Salze, January 8, 2014, and Yang Wenhua, chairman, C&D Wine, February 12, 2014.

124 "They don't care if we sell it": Author interview with a Bordeaux négociant who asked to remain anonymous due to the sensitivity of the relationship between châteaux and négociant, September 8, 2013.

126 "They're nervous": Claer Barrett, "'Bordeaux Bubble' Dulls Appetite for Fine Wine," *Financial Times*, June 17, 2011.

128 "One challenge will be to temper Chinese": Author interview with Philippe Larché, partner, Vintex et Les Vignobles Grégoire, September 24, 2013; and Panos Kakaviatos, "Chinese Government Approves Wine Investment Fund," *Decanter*, October 30, 2011.

128 "There is already too much water": Author interview with Zhang Jinshan, owner, Château du Grand Moueys, and Li Lijuan, manager and translator, Château du Grand Moueys, February 17, 2012; Suzanne Mustacich, "Chinese Tycoons Snap Up Bordeaux Châteaux," Agence France-Presse, February 21, 2012.

128 "We're all worried what will happen to him": Author interview with winegrower in Ningxia who asked to remain anonymous, November 4, 2013.

Chapter 6. All in a Name

The characterization of the investigation in China is based on interviews with Nick Bartman and emails exchanged between the author and Bartman, as well as the blog entries authored by Bartman and posted on Jancis Robinson's website. Other sources of information for this chapter include Hannah Agostini, Cabinet Eric Agostini et Associés; Fabien Bova, general managing director, Conseil Interprofessionnel du Vin de Bordeaux (CIVB)/Bordeaux Wine Council; Christophe Chateau, communications, CIVB; Catherine Delaud, Sodema Conseils; Bruno Finance, export manager, Yvon Mau; Charles-Henri Gonet, export manager, Michel Gonet et Fils; Thomas Jullien, market adviser, China, CIVB; Ma Lin, former director, Cafa Formations, China; Paul Ranjard, counsel, Wen Hui Da Intellectual Property Agency; Christophe Salin, chief executive officer and president, Domaines Barons de Rothschild (Lafite); Allan Sichel, chief executive officer, Maison Sichel; Jean-Baptiste Thial de Bordenave, department manager, Lex Wine, INLEX. The author attempted to contact Zhang Taiyang via email and mutual contacts, but he did not respond.

130 "Throughout all these experiences": Nick Bartman, "Counterfeiting at Street Level," *Intellectual Property*, March 2015.

132 "It could be said the further from Beijing": Ibid.

133 "If the full force of Beijing's will": Ibid.

135 "The administration authority cannot control all things": Nick Bartman, blog post, www.jancisrobinson.com, August 3, 2010.

135 "It is absolutely, positively, and hopelessly": Nick Bartman, blog post, www
.jancisrobinson.com, July 31, 2010.

136 The next day, Bartman finally got a paying client: Nick Bartman did not at any
time identify his client as the Bordeaux Wine Council (CIVB), but other sources
at the CIVB confirmed this fact on background.

136 More recently, they had concentrated on putting fake French labels on Chinese wine
in Chinese bottles: Other countries faced counterfeiting as well, but Bartman was
investigating on the behalf of a French client.

136 "It's a myth that counterfeiters fake paperwork": Author interview with Nick Bartman, January 17, 2014.

138 He worried that his photo would be posted on QQ: Tait Lawton, "QQ Microblog
Users Exceed 80 Million," Nanjing Marketing Group, January 17, 2011, http://www
.nanjingmarketinggroup.com/blog/microblogs/qq-microblog-users-exceed-80
-million.

138 the CCTV program had shown footage of a sales manager admitting: Du Xiaodan,
ed., "Chinese Gov't Shuts Down Wineries After Adulterated Wines Exposed,"
CCTV, Xinhua News Agency, December 24, 2010.

138 linked to headaches, irregular heartbeat, and cancer: Liu Linlin, "Fake Wine Stuns
Nation," *Global Times*, December 27, 2010.

139 three wineries in Changli—Jiahua, Yeli, and Genghao—were shut down: Ibid.

139 The company sold 2.4 million bottles: Ibid.

139 Five individuals were sentenced to prison: Hebei Province, "Hebei: Fake
Wine Hangover; Life in Prison," press release, August 10, 2011, reproduced at
Intellectual Property Protection in China website, http://www.chinaipr.gov.cn
/newsarticle/news/local/201108/1244817_1.html.

139 Wang Chunping, was sentenced to life in prison: Ibid.

139 Wang and the winemakers had earned more than 28 million yuan: Ibid.

139 Bright Sword, launched by the Ministry of Public Security in November 2010: Sun
Luying, ed., "Counterfeit Products Hit by Raids," *China Daily*, April 13, 2011.

139 the police had so far confiscated more than 30 tons of bulk wines: Ibid.

141 Megara now owned the right in China: On September 30, 2011, the American Grenada Holdings (Megara Holdings) registered a slew of brands. The holding company was domiciled at a post office box in Road Town, the capital of Tortola in the
British Virgin Islands.

143 the bell was taking over as the château's identity: The estate underwent a €10 million renovation, completed in 2014, and the gold carillon was put front and center as
a form of homage. The château had two large bells, named Angélus and Émilion,
which were joined by an eighteen-bell carillon that would be rung three times each
day. It was operated by remote control, and could play dozens of national anthems.

143 "We're not even sure": Author interview with Stéphanie de Boüard-Rivoal, deputy managing director, Château Angélus, January 29, 2014. Angélus was alerted
to one of the brand squatters by Domaine de la Romanée-Conti, who had been targeted by the same crook.

145 securing the trademarks of Bordeaux's appellations: The CIVB began an important campaign to trademark Bordeaux's appellations and the graphic design used

on Bordeaux wines. Bordeaux was the first French appellation to get trademark protection from the State Administration for Industry and Commerce in 2012. As of April 2015, it had another trademark protection pending with the General Administration of Quality Supervision, Inspection and Quarantine.

147 the label design and shape was a copy: Author verified products sold by Mingyang on their website www.yt-mingyang.com, accessed on March 13, 2015.

148 The CIVB denied that Zhang Taiyang: Email to author from Céline Lavergne, Bordeaux Wine School, CIVB, January 28, 2014.

149 it was probably a "black bank" in China's so-called shadow-banking sector: Stephen McDonell, "China's Shadow-Banking Sector a Growing Problem for Booming Economy Facing Inevitable Slowdown," ABC Australia, January 24, 2014.

149 Some analysts feared that black banks carried so much debt: Jing Jiang, "Shadow Banking in China: Battling the Darkness," *Economist*, May 10, 2014.

153 Shandong Yantai Mingyang Wine Company, sometimes translated as Yantai Eagle or Yantai Ming, held the trademark: Author confirmed the name of the company in conversation with the Gonets' legal adviser, Hannah Agostini, on March 11, 2015. The information is also available on the China Patent Trademark Office website. Nick Bartman informed the Gonets that their wine was being counterfeited.

154 Gonets were quoted a price of $300,000: Author interview and email exchanges with Charles-Henri Gonet, export manager, Michel Gonet et Fils, January 28, 2014.

154 Yantai Mingyang had even trademarked the first name: Register number 8059221, class 33, China Patent Trademark Office, applied February 8, 2010, registered February 14, 2011, to a company in Shandong.

154 "He just needed to sell back two or three": Author interview with Celine Baillet, intellectual property attorney, INLEX, January 29, 2014.

155 A few days later, his mood brightened: Email to author from Bruno Finance, export manager, Yvon Mau, March 21, 2011.

155 Li explained that Lafite had registered its brand in China in 1996: DBR Lafite was not alone in being both an early filer and a victim of attacks. Château Cos d'Estournel registered the name "Les Pagodes de Cos" in 1996 and the name "Château Cos d'Estournel" in 1998, and Château Mouton Rothschild registered its name in 1997. Neither escaped unscathed.

155 On February 28, 2011, the court decided: Kevin Nie, "Lafite Wins IP Suit in China," *China IP Magazine*, undated, accessed March 10, 2015, http://www.chinaipmagazine.com/en/journal-show.asp?id=722.

155 China Central Television network ran an exposé on its program *Focus*: Ibid.

156 "If things go well": "French Wine Maker Toasts 6 Court Wins in China," China .org.cn, *Shanghai Daily*, March 16, 2012.

156 "Counterfeit control is a mental game": Suzanne Mustacich, "Counterfeit Wine Investigator Has an Idea for Fighting Fakes," *Wine Spectator*, January 21, 2015.

Chapter 7. Standoff

Author interviews and email exchanges with the following individuals provided background information for this chapter: Chris Adams, chief executive officer, Sherry-Lehmann

Wine & Spirits; Gerda Béziade, export director, Duclot Export; Stéphanie de Boüard-Rivoal, deputy managing director, Château Angélus; Dan Chen, public relations manager, Castel Frères Greater China; Barbara Hermann, wine buyer, Binny's Beverage Depot; Huang Belle, marketing director, Castel Frères Greater China; Angelina Li, Brand Department, Tianjin Dynasty International Wine Company, served as translator; Lu Ming, general manager, Tianjin Dynasty International Wine Company; Xavier Pignel-Dupont, Asia Pacific director, Castel Frères Greater China; Jean-Pierre Rousseau, managing director, Distribution Internationale de Vins et Alcools (Diva); Christophe Salin, CEO and president, Domaines Barons de Rothschild (Lafite); Alain Sichel, chief executive officer, Maison Sichel; George Tong, vice president, Wong Hau Plastic Works & Trading Company; Teresa Wang, corporate communications, Dynasty Fine Wines Group; and Christina Zhao, vice general manager, Tianjin Dynasty International Wine Company.

The characterization of events regarding USA Piilii Jepen is based on author interviews with Philippe Papillon, founder and chief executive officer, Ipso Facto, on February 21, 2014, and February 9, 2015, as well as emails exchanged with Papillon, and court documents provided by Papillon's lawyer Nathalie Castagnon.

157 "I believe the high price of Bordeaux": Email to author from George Tong, vice president, Wong Hau Plastic Works & Trading Company, July 19, 2011.

157 "You Name It, We Make It": Wong Hau Plastic Works & Trading Company website, http://www.wonghau.com/.

157 *Asia Tatler*'s "500 List": "500 List: The List of Hong Kong's Power Elite," *Hong Kong Tatler*, http://hk.asiatatler.com/500list.

158 "Berry Bros. & Rudd had six hundred cases": Email to author from George Tong, July 19, 2011. See also Suzanne Mustacich, "Has Bordeaux's Bubble Burst?," *Wine Spectator*, January 18, 2012.

158 Investors feared: Château Cos d'Estournel released its 2007 and 2008 vintages en primeur at €65, then released the 2009 vintage at €210 and the 2010 at €198. The 2011 was released at €108.

158 Quite a few of the tycoons who were buying classified growths: Author interview with Don St. Pierre Jr., executive chairman of the board, ASC Fine Wines, January 9, 2012. See also Mustacich, "Has Bordeaux's Bubble Burst?"

158 A 2010 audit revealed that approximately ten thousand: Jonathan Fenby, *Tiger Head, Snake Tails: China Today, How It Got There, and Where It Is Heading* (London: Simon and Schuster, 2013), p. 350.

159 Moody's had found an additional 3.5 trillion yuan: Koh Gui Qing and Kim Coghill, "Chinese Local Debt Understated by $540 Billion: Moody's," Reuters, July 5, 2011.

159 local authorities and businesses turned to the unregulated "shadow banking" sector: Fenby, *Tiger Head, Snake Tails*, pp. 349–51.

159 They were forced to transfer money from Hong Kong to China to repay loans: Email to author from George Tong, January 10, 2012.

159 "There is a panic among the speculators": Mustacich, "Has Bordeaux's Bubble Burst?"; and author interview with Don St. Pierre Jr., January 9, 2012.

159 SK had been Papillon's only major client then: The former sommelier Jung Hoon Kim worked at SK and helped with the Ipso Facto deals.

160 "This is the time when the machine started working": Author interview with Philippe Papillon, founder and chief executive officer, Ipso Facto, February 21, 2014.

160 "They always added or subtracted a few zeroes": Ibid.

161 "They invested too much on crazy vintages": Email to author from Philippe Papillon, March 17, 2015.

161 Now they were dumping the wine: Philippe Papillon's decision was prescient. After Papillon parted ways with SK, the company's wine distribution business collapsed, and the value of its wine funds plummeted. SK closed its wine-focused offices in Shenzhen and Hong Kong. When the wine funds became liquid again in 2015, SK announced that it wanted out of the wine business permanently. "They'll lose millions, but they don't care," said Papillon. In 2003, Chey Tae-Won, the chairman of SK Corporation, had been convicted of embezzling $43.5 million from his own company. Author interview with Philippe Papillon, February 21, 2014.

161 There was no trace of Piilii on the Internet: According to the *Hong Kong Companies Registry*, company number 1225036 was incorporated on April 9, 2008, as Win City International Holdings, changing the name to USA Piilii Jepen International Group on June 24, 2010. The company name also appeared under a listing for Paule Jepen at the address Flat/RM 1505 15/F, World-Wide House, 19 Des Voeux Road, Central Hong Kong, at the trademark search site www.searchtmr.com.

162 the total value of the four contracts he entered with Piilii topped €17 million: The exact amount was €17,236,869, per the "Summons to Appear Before Bordeaux Commercial Court," October 5, 2011.

162 Papillon scheduled eight payments from Piilii: The exact amount of the first payment was €2,800,596.30, per the "Summons to Appear Before Bordeaux Commercial Court," October 5, 2011.

162 Piilii's en primeur tab ran to approximately $30 million for the 2010 vintage: Email to author from Philippe Papillon, March 3, 2014.

162 "At that time, it was crazy in Bordeaux": Author interview with Philippe Papillon, February 21, 2014.

162 Piilii now owed him $10.4 million in late payments: "Summons to Appear Before Bordeaux Commercial Court," October 5, 2011

163 three so-called emissaries: The name of Yu Kelong's brother was understood by Philippe Papillon to be Yu "Cayenne," who is possibly USA Piilii Jepen shareholder "You Cun Ju" (Cun Ju), as listed on the company's 2011 annual report available from the *Hong Kong Companies Register*, http://www.icris.cr.gov.hk.

166 she had just received authorization from the Tribunal de Commerce: The wine was held at G. R. Valade in Bruges, France, per author interview with Philippe Papillon, February 9, 2015.

166 hoping to move the wine out of reach of the French authorities: Author interview with Philippe Papillon, February 21, 2014. Papillon asked that his informant remain anonymous.

167 "You little piece of shit": Ibid.

167 "If you cancel your order with the châteaux": Ibid.

169 It was listed on the main board of the Hong Kong Stock Exchange: Trading in Dynasty shares was halted on March 22, 2013. According to reports, the company's

shares had been withdrawn from the Hong Kong Stock Exchange "pending an internal investigation by Ernst & Young." Joshua Fellman, "Tianjin Development to Sell Dynasty Fine Wines Stake to Parent," *Bloomberg Businessweek*, May 5, 2014.

169 The company's chairman, Bai Zhisheng, had announced in a 2010 interview: Wing-Gar Cheng, "Dynasty Fine Wines Seeks to Purchase Vineyards in Australia, France, Chile," Bloomberg News, May 26, 2010.

170 "We wanted to find a negotiation": Author interview with Christophe Reboul Salze, January 8, 2014.

170 Lu's response: Ibid.

170 "The day I cannot honor a commitment": Ibid.

171 "It was my job to protect the wine": Author interview with Yannick Evenou, March 17, 2014.

171 "For every canceled order": Author interview with Philippe Larché, partner, Vintex et Les Vignobles Grégoire, September 24, 2013.

171 "Our mainland Chinese customers": Author interview with Simon Staples, sales director, Asia, Berry Bros. & Rudd, January 10, 2012.

171 "There were a lot of unprofessional brokers": Author interview with Don St. Pierre Jr., January 9, 2012.

172 "The fundamental of business is that there is no future": Author interview with Vincent Yip, manager, Topsy Trading, November 15, 2013.

172 One such négociant who had a pile of unpaid contracts with Chinese clients: Author interview with a Bordeaux-based négociant in their offices, July 3, 2014. The négociant asked to remain anonymous.

173 shipments of modest Bordeaux wines had increased: Mustacich, "Has Bordeaux's Bubble Burst?"

173 "Our turnover is up almost a third on last year": "Bordeaux First Growth Prices Fall as Investors Turn to Burgundy," *Harpers Wine & Spirit*, October 14, 2011.

173 "We've seen a whole host of various DRC wines": Ibid.

173 The tasting: "Wine Future 2011: Awesome Event for All Who Are Serious About the Industry," China Wine Chick blog, November 9, 2011, http://chinawinechick .blogspot.co.uk/2011/11/wine-future-2011-awesome-event-for-all.html.

174 Pancho Campo, at the time a Master of Wine and the president of the Wine Academy of Spain: Author interview with Ezequiel Franco Lopez, Marketing, Purchasing, Sales, and Wine Education, Panati Wine and CavesMaître, February 3, 2014. Author requested to interview Li Daozhi on several occasions, but Li declined.

174 Emblazoned on the backdrop: Author first saw the photograph on Jim Budd's blog *Jim's Loire*, "WineFuture HK: CavesMaître—'One of the Most Important Importer-Distributor of Wines in China,' " December 19, 2011.

174 A native of Wenzhou: "France Castel Frères Was Sentenced to 33.73 Million Yuan Compensation," China IP News, State Intellectual Property Office of the People's Republic of China, April 19, 2012, http://english.sipo.gov.cn/news/iprspecial /201204/t20120419_673806.html.

174 In 2002, when the company was restructured, Li left: Ibid.

175 In 1999, Castel's first Chinese bottling plant: François Collombet, Jean-Luc Brigot, Christophe Menou, and Sylvain Marchand, "Castel's Setbacks in China," Dictionary of Wine, n.d., www.dico-du-vin.com/c/chine-les-desboires-de-castel/.

175 Red Castle listed its owner as "Faguo Kasite Jituan": "Fa Guo" is the phonetic representation of "France"; "Ka Si Te" is the phonetic representation of "Castel"; and "Ji Tuan" means "Group."

175 Changyu had snatched a quarter of the domestic consumer market: Changyu is often cited as the "biggest winemaker" in China based on available sales data. See, for instance, Simon Montlake, "Grape Leap: China's Biggest Winemaker," *Forbes*, July 25, 2012, and Will Lyons, "Indulge in China's Latest Export," *Wall Street Journal*, April 5, 2013.

175 Two years later, in 2003, Castel opened an office in Shanghai: The translation of "Faguo Kasite Xiongdi Gufen Youxian Gongsi Shanghai Daibiao Chu" corresponds to the English "France Castel Brothers Limited Company Shanghai Representative Office."

176 Jacubs International: According to its website, www.jacubs.com, Jacubs International imported Australian wine—a cheeky nod to Jacob's Creek Wines, Australia's largest winemaker. Accessed March 10, 2015.

177 a quiet payment to purchase the trademark was the only way to resolve the problem: Author interview with Yang Wenhua, chairman, LK Wine, and former chairman, C&D Wine, February 15, 2015.

177 In Mandarin, CavesMaître had a more direct translation: Jim Budd, "Wine Future HK: CavesMaître—'One of the Most Important Importer-Distributor of Wines in China,'" on his blog *Jim's Loire*, December 19, 2011.

177 he had registered "Kasite Jin Zhong," roughly meaning "Castle Angel Bell": This was trademark filing number 9105485, China Patent Trademark Office, http://www.chinatrademarkoffice.com/index.php/tdsearch/xbshow/9105485/33/1, accessed March 10, 2015.

177 "Château Le Vin": This was trademark filing number 5267727, China Patent Trademark Office, accessed March 10, 2015, http://www.chinatrademarkoffice.com/index.php/tdsearch/xbshow/5267727/33/1.

177 Château Mouton as "Mu Tong" and "Mu Tong Jiu Zhuang": These were trademark filing numbers 669728 and 6685751, China Patent Trademark Office.

177 he tried registering "Lafei" and "Li Zi Laei": These were trademark filing numbers 6889466 and 6889468.

177 He and another man named Li Shen: Angus Grigg, "Penfolds Suffers from China Squatters," *Australian Financial Review*, July 14, 2014.

178 "The court held that Castel Frères took advantage of the Kasite's reputation": "France Castel Frères Was Sentenced to 33.73 Million Yuan Compensation," China IP News, State Intellectual Property Office of the P.R.C., April 19, 2012, http://english.sipo.gov.cn/news/iprspecial/201204/t20120419_673806.html.

178 "Would anyone in the wine industry believe that Castel": Zhang Zhao, "Castel Trademark Dispute Not Over in Spite of Court Ruling," *China Daily*, August 28, 2013.

178 Li quietly bought three châteaux in Bordeaux for $6 million: The total purchase price for the châteaux was €4,578,000 according to the protocol of the sale, dated October 29, 2011.

179 Consumers wanted wines that cost between $25 and $50: These were wines originally listed at prices of €20 to €40 in Bordeaux.

180 "More and more producers try to eliminate us": Topsy Trading 2012 market report.

181 "It didn't seem like a good use of my company's money": Author interview with Barbara Hermann, wine buyer, Binny's Beverage Depot, April 3, 2012.

181 "It started out with him asking for the country where the wine was being shipped": The négociant quoted has since retired but asked not to be named. The information requested by Frédéric Engerer for use by Château Latour has, however, been confirmed in interviews with several négociants.

182 With some sleuthing, they found proof: "Palmarès 2010 des enterprises du commerce extèrieur" and "Palmarès 2011 des enterprises du commerce extèrieur," emailed to author from Cellule Diffusion, Département des Statistiques et des Etudes Economiques, Direction Générale des Douanes et des Droits Indirects, April 3, 2015. These documents list the "award winners" among exporters from Aquitaine. Château Latour was in the top thirty-two.

182 When Château Latour announced it was quitting the en primeur system: Elin McCoy, "Latour Takes on Lafite in China Wine Battles, Czar's Champagne," Bloomberg, May 16, 2011.

183 "It might work in some markets": Author interview with Yann Schÿler, April 13, 2012.

184 He had determined the price for Lafite's first tranche: Author interview with Christophe Salin, July 2, 2014.

184 "It's great, they came out early": Suzanne Mustacich, "Bordeaux Châteaux Shake Up Market with Rival Plans," Agence France-Presse, April 16, 2012.

184 She was equally excited when two more First Growths: The announced price was €360.

185 She and her father, Anthony Barton, had set the price: The announced price was €45.

Chapter 8. Shifting Winds

Author interviews and email exchanges with the following individuals provided background information for this chapter: Chris Adams, chief executive officer, Sherry-Lehmann Wine & Spirits; Gary Boom, managing director, Bordeaux Index; Cao Kailong, deputy director general, Forestry Bureau, and director general, Grape Flower Industry Development Bureau, Ningxia Hui Autonomous Region; Jean-Michel Cazes, owner, Château Lynch-Bages; Judy Chan, president, Grace Vineyard; Gérard Colin, consulting winemaker (previously winemaker, Grace Vineyard); Thierry Courtade, Silver Heights; Emma Gao Yuan, Silver Heights; David Henderson, president and chief executive officer, China Fine Wines, and owner, Dragon's Hollow; Philippe Larché, partner, Vintex et Les Vignobles Grégoire; Lu Ming, general manager, Tianjin Dynasty International Wine Company; Christophe Reboul Salze, president, The Wine Merchant;

Brett Richardson, national vineyard manager, Pernod Ricard; Rong Jian, president and chairman, Ningxia Grape Industry Association, and general manager, Helan Qingxue; Jean-Pierre Rousseau, managing director, Distribution Internationale de Vins et Alcools (Diva); Yann Schÿler, chief executive officer, Maison Schröder & Schÿler; Don St. Pierre Jr., executive chairman of the board, ASC Fine Wines; John D. Watkins Jr., chief executive officer, ASC Fine Wines; Nicole Wang, operation executive communications manager, China Fine Wines; Yang Wenhua, chairman, Xiamen C&D Wines, and chief executive officer, LK Wine; Vincent Yip, manager, Topsy Trading Company; Christina Zhao, vice general manager, Tianjin Dynasty International Wine Company.

187 "This will lay a foundation": Shanghai Sugar Cigarette and Wine, "The Ceremony of 70% Diva Stock Shares Transfer Was Successfully Held," press release, Shanghai, July 5, 2012, http://www.sscw.com.cn/news_newsContent_en.action?id =16702.

187 pursued lucrative assets overseas: Denny Thomas, "China Bright Food to Buy Manassen for Over $516 Million," Reuters, August 14, 2011.

187 Beijing's goal of wielding international influence: "Statistical Communiqué of the People's Republic of China on the 2012 National Economic and Social Development," China National Bureau of Statistics, February 22, 2013.

188 Bright Food had taken a 60 percent stake in Weetabix: Nathalie Thomas, "China's Bright Food Takes 60 Percent Stake in Weetabix," *Telegraph*, May 3, 2012. In October 2014, Bright Food announced that it would acquire the remaining 40 percent stake in Weetabix.

188 It had also tried to buy Yoplait yogurt and the American vitamin retailer GNC: Louise Lucas, "Lessons from Bright Food's Failed Bid," *Financial Times*, March 18, 2011.

188 "laid down a solid foundation": "Chairman of the Board of Supervisors Cui Zhiren Visits the French Company Diva," *People's Daily Online*, July 23, 2013.

188 "The Chinese offer was of cash": Scheherazade Daneshkhu, "China's Bright Food Buys Diva Bordeaux," *Financial Times*, June 26, 2012.

190 places such as Dongguan, Foshan, Ningbo, and Suzhou: Hurun Research Institute, *Hurun Wealth Report 2014* (Shanghai, 2014), http://www.hurun.net/EN /ArticleShow.aspx?nid=4558.

190 "The Bordelais learned from their arrogance": Suzanne Mustacich, "Bordeaux Châteaus Say They'll Lower Prices, but How Much?," *Wine Spectator*, April 10, 2012.

191 30 percent price drop: This was a 30 percent drop in the eurozone. Because of fluctuating currency exchange rates, the price reduction calculated in other currencies may have been more or less.

191 price for the 2011 vintage was 50 percent lower: James Molesworth, "Château Lafite Rothschild Releases Its 2011 Price," *Wine Spectator*, April 17, 2012. Again, fluctuating currency exchange rates means that in real terms, the changes in prices may have been more or less than 50 percent.

191 "Granted the '10 was a great wine, but '11 is just 'very good'": Molesworth, "Château Lafite Rothschild Releases Its 2011 Price."

191 "But people looked at the current retail": Mitch Frank, "Bordeaux Futures Hit the Market, but Is Anyone Buying?," *Wine Spectator*, May 25, 2012.

191 Adams took only 15 percent: Ben O'Donnell, "Bordeaux 2011 Futures Fizzle," *Wine Spectator*, July 10, 2012.

191 ordered just 5 percent: Ibid.

192 he felt his warning was falling on deaf ears: Author interview with Philippe Larché, partner, Vintex et Les Vignobles Grégoire, September 24, 2013.

193 "Courtière!": Ibid.

193 the number of strikes was up: Jonathan Watts, "Strikes in China Signal End to Era of Low-Cost Labour and Cheap Exports," *Guardian*, June 17, 2010.

193 28,752 yuan: "China Wages Jump in 2012 Despite Slowing Economy," Market-Watch, May 17, 2013.

193 wages had tripled in a decade: International Labour Organization, *Global Wage Report 2012/13: Wages and Equitable Growth* (Geneva: International Labour Organization, 2013), p. xiv.

194 50 percent of the luxury goods business in China involved the hyper-successful state-owned companies and the government officials: Cai Hong, "Public Spending Fans Luxury Prices," Xinhua News Agency, April 16, 2012.

194 "three public consumptions"—foreign travel, cars, and banquets: "New Rule Limit Chinese Government Spending," Xinhua News Agency, July 9, 2012.

194 "prohibiting the use of public funds to buy cigarettes, high-end alcohol and gifts": Qu Yunxu and Wang Chen, "End of Baijiu Binge Means Party Is Over for Producers, Dealers," Caixin Online, February 21, 2013. Premier Wen Jiabao's speech is also available in the 2012 NPC & CPPCC section of the china.org.cn website. In some translations of Premier Wen's speech, "fine wines" was used rather than "high-end alcohol." Sui-Lee Wee, "China's Wen: Corruption Could Threaten Power Structure," Reuters, March 26, 2012.

194 "abuse of public funds": Xie Yu, "Ban Moutai at Official Banquets, Says Deputy," *China Daily*, January 17, 2012.

194 Moutai as the fifth most popular brand: Hurun Research Institute and Group, *The Chinese Millionaires Wealth Report 2012: Connect with Chinese Millionaires* (Shanghai: Hurun Research Institute, 2012).

194 Hurun estimated the brand to be worth: Venessa Wong, "Luxury Chinese Liquors Become Multibillion-Dollar Brands," *Bloomberg Businessweek*, March 16, 2012.

195 A bottle of Wuliangye: Ibid.

195 "Last week inspection bureau inspectors": Xie Yu, "Ban Moutai at Official Banquets, Says Deputy."

195 publicly traded shares of Kweichow Moutai: Robert Cookson, "Wen Drink Warning Hits Moutai Shares," *Financial Times*, March 27, 2012.

195 had spent more than 3 billion yuan, or $467 million: Yan Jie, "Central Government Reveals Details on Spending," *China Daily*, July 22, 2011.

195 An office tasked with alleviating poverty: Ibid.

195 "What do you want us to do?": Author interview with confidential source, 2013.

196 In July 2012, Wen ordered civil servants: "New Rule Limit Chinese Government Spending," Xinhua News Agency, July 9, 2012.

196 Wenzhou had sold off 215 vehicles: Jason Chow, "Luxury Ban Imposed on Chinese Bureaucrats," *Wall Street Journal*, July 11, 2012.

196 "The distribution system doesn't work without discounting": Author interview with confidential source in November 2013.

196 "A good wine is first recognized by its domestic market": César Compadre, "Avec trois châteaux, Peter Kwok fait sa campagne," *Sudouest.com*, April 9, 2013.

197 "They're finding it's not so easy to sell wine": Author interview with Philippe Larché, September 24, 2013.

197 C&D was no longer buying: Author interview with Christophe Reboul Salze, January 8, 2014; author interview with Yang Wenhua, former chairman, Xiamen C&D Wines, and chief executive officer, LK Wine, February 12, 2014.

198 "We don't want to change the long-term landscape": Ibid. "They were very worried about the value of their stock on the stock market," Reboul Salze said. "They wanted to avoid the situation of Dynasty." Author interview with Christophe Reboul Salze, January 8, 2014.

199 Rémy Cointreau, which owned a 27 percent stake in Dynasty, had lost a third of its investment: Rémy Martin merged with Cointreau in 1990–91.

199 expecting a loss for the 2012 fiscal year: Dynasty Fine Wines Group, "Profit Warning," press release, Hong Kong, February 4, 2013.

199 on Friday, March 22, 2013, the stock was suspended: Dynasty Fine Wines Group, "Suspension of Trading," press release, Hong Kong, March 22, 2013.

199 "had received anonymous allegations": Dynasty Fine Wines Group, "Announcement Pursuant to Rule 13.09 of the Listing Rules and the Inside Information Provisions and Delay in Publication of 2012 Annual Results," press release, Hong Kong, March 26, 2013.

199 In an effort to hide: Author interview with François Hériard-Dubreuil, April 21, 2015.

199 The previous year, when Lu had canceled Dynasty's orders: Author interview with Christophe Reboul Salze, January 8, 2014.

199 "They will be out of the business of fine wine": Ibid.

199 "It's not a healthy situation": Author interview with Gary Boom, November 27, 2013.

200 "Bordeaux is like a herd of wildebeests": Ibid.

200 "Unfortunately, that's my market": Ibid.

201 "Saint-Émilion and Pomerol were easy to sell": Ibid.

201 "For now, the big 'takeaway' for me": Jim Boyce, "Grace Under Pressure: Ningxia Tops Bordeaux in Beijing Wine Challenge," *Grape Wall of China*, December 14, 2011, http://www.grapewallofchina.com/2011/12/14/grace-under-pressure-ningxia-tops-bordeaux-in-beijing-wine-challenge. After the results were published on Jim Boyce's blog, several commenters argued that the contest was unfair because the French wines in the showdown were all high-volume brand wines. Boyce defended the selections, arguing that most wine consumers would have assumed that the high-volume French wines would still be better than wines produced in China.

202 "It was, for lack of a better word, brooding": Jim Boyce, "RVF Beijing 'Salon': On Nubes, 1421, Helan Mountain, Silver Heights, Helan Qing Xue," *Grape Wall of*

China, January 3, 2013, http://www.grapewallofchina.com/2013/01/03/rvf
-beijing-salon-on-nubes-1421-helan-mountain-silver-heights-helan-qing-xue/.

203 wine conference at which Li Hua had spoken about Ningxia's potential for growing grapes: Author interview with Rong Jian, president and chairman, Ningxia
Grape Industry Association, and general manager, Helan Qingxue, November 5,
2013.

203 Rong formed the Ningxia Wine Grape Industry Association: Ibid.

205 "In the Ming dynasty, the ruler of Ningxia wrote a poem": Ibid.

207 "In fact, this is incorrect": Author interview with Cao Kailong, deputy director general, Forestry Bureau, and director general, Grape Flower Industry Development
Bureau, Ningxia Hui Autonomous Region, November 4, 2013.

208 Organisation of Vine and Wine expected five non-EU countries: Per Karlsson, "The
World's Wine Production, 2000–2012," *BK Wine Magazine*, June 13, 2013.

208 Western China, including Ningxia, was expected to produce 20 percent: Yao Lu,
"China Briefing," Dezan Shira & Associates, July 9, 2012.

209 Annual family income fell below 2,000 yuan: Xu Fan, "Massive Ningxia Relocation Set to Start Soon," *China Daily*, March 13, 2013.

209 the government moved another 300,000 people: Ibid.

209 "fewer births, quick to be rich": Chen Chao, "Ningxia Progress Report on Western
Development," China Internet Information Center, March 19, 2002, China.org.cn/.

209 "We have fully prepared": Xu Fan, "Massive Ningxia Relocation Set to Start Soon."

209 "These people are used to living": Author interview with Judy Chan, president,
Grace Vineyard, November 11, 2013.

211 "We can make quality wine here": Author interview with Rong Jian, November 5,
2013.

211 "I want to explain something, because there are some misunderstandings": Ibid.

212 Dynasty owned twenty thousand acres in the Helan Mountains: "Grape Expansion: Chinese Companies Move West," *China Times*, December 15, 2011.

212 "The channel for Ningxia's wine is the domestic market": Author interview with
Rong Jian, November 5, 2013.

212 "The potential is huge": Ibid.

214 the wineries that had been elevated to Ningxia's Fifth Growth ranking: The other
wineries on the list of Ningxia Fifth Growths were Xixia King, Yuanshi, Bacchus,
Yuange, Changyu Moser XV, Lanyi, Yuhuang, Leirenshou, and Chengcheng.

Chapter 9. *Gan Bei*

Author interviews and email exchanges with the following individuals provided background information for this chapter: Philippe Buisson, mayor, Libourne, France; Thierry Charpentier, deputy manager of international tourism development, Bordeaux
Chamber of Commerce and Industry (CCIB); Nicolas Grégoire, son of James Grégoire,
former owner, Château de la Rivière, Fronsac; Lam Kok, founder and owner, Brilliant
Group Investment; Philippe Larché, partner, Vintex et Les Vignobles Grégoire; Li
Lijuan, China desk, Maxwell-Storrie-Baynes Real Estate Agents; Emmanuel Martin,
chief executive officer, La Guyennoise Propriétaires et Négociants; Karen Maxwell, executive partner, Maxwell-Storrie-Baynes Real Estate Agents; Hervé Olivier, director of

property operations, Aquitaine Atlantic Region, Sociétés d'Aménagement Foncier et d'Establissment Rural (Safer); Christophe Salin, managing director, Domaines Barons de Rothschild (Lafite); and Yang Wenhua, chairman, Xiamen C&D Fine Wines.

The characterization of the Meeting of Tea and Wine Civilizations, Libourne Town Hall, June 17, 2013, is based on author's reporting at the event, including interviews with Philippe Buisson, Liu Xiangyun (wife of Lam Kok), and Yang Lin, deputy mayor of Pu'er Municipal Government.

215 eighty homes and twenty cars: "Shenzhen Village Official Accused for Bribery," *China Daily*, January 3, 2014; Fiona Tam, "Shenzhen Village Official's Accuser Taken into Custody," *South China Morning Post*, November 29, 2012.

215 solid gold mooncakes: Hu Tao and Yuan Ruting, "Gold Mooncakes Raise Suspicions of Corruption," Xinhua News Agency, September 28, 2012.

215 a *hongbao*, or red envelope: "How to Win Friends and Pass Bribes at Chinese New Year's," *China Economic Review*, January 30, 2014.

216 *Decanter* magazine had selected St. Pierre for its Power List three times: Don St. Pierre Jr. was listed on *Decanter*'s "Power List" at number 7 in 2011 and number 16 in 2009. ASC Fine Wines, "Milestones," ASC Fine Wines website, 2015, http://www.asc-wines.com/about-asc/our-leadership.

216 *Wine Enthusiast* magazine had named him "International Man of the Year": "2011 Wine Star Award Winners," *Wine Enthusiast*, January 30, 2012, http://www.winemag.com/Web-2011/2011-Wine-Star-Award-Winners.

216 ASC had organized the first charity wine auction in China: ASC Fine Wines website, www.asc-wines.com.

217 Watkins had been the St. Pierres' first home-delivery customer: Author interview with John D. Watkins Jr., February 11, 2015.

217 "I think I was one of the first Western businessmen to import wine for entertaining": Author interview with John D. Watkins Jr., February 11, 2015.

217 After Northwest, he joined the heavy equipment manufacturer Cummins: Ibid.

217 CEO and president of a fifty-fifty joint venture: "Executive Team: John D. Watkins, Jr., Executive Officer," ASC Fine Wines, http://www.asc-wines.com.

217 Each new leadership promised to sweep out: Author interview with John D. Watkins Jr., February 11, 2015.

217 *renrou sousou yinqing*, or a "human flesh search": Jessica Levine, "What Is a 'Human Flesh Search,' and How Is It Changing China?," *Atlantic*, October 5, 2012.

218 photos of attendees wearing Hermès belts and Pucci suits as they arrived for meetings: Jing Gao, "Chinese Lawmakers, Political Delegates Sporting High Fashion Draw Criticism from Netizens," *Ministry of Tofu*, March 6, 2012; Jeremy Goldkorn, "Should Chinese Political Delegates Wear $2,000 Suits?," *Danwei*, March 6, 2012.

218 "Brother Wristwatch": David Wertime, "Did a Chinese Safety Official Just Get Caught Smiling at a Horrific Accident Scene?," *Tea Leaf Nation*, August 27, 2012. In Chinese, the name given to Yang Dacai was Renda Dai Biao, which translates to "National People's Congress Member Wearing a Watch" or "Big Man Wears Watch."

218 China's president earned only 7,020 yuan, or $1,130, a month: Luo Wangshu, "Public Employees Get Salary Increase," *China Daily*, January 20, 2015.

218 His wife and son held $1.8 million in investments: Ma Lie, "'Brother Watch' Pleads Guilty to Corruption," *China Daily*, August 31, 2013; "'Brother Watch' Sentenced to 14 Years in Prison," *China Daily*, September 5, 2013.

219 "abyss of criminality": Jonathan Kaiman, "China's 'Brother Wristwatch' Yang Dacai Jailed for Fourteen Years for Corruption," *Guardian*, September 5, 2013.

219 *New York Times* revealed that the family of the premier held $2.7 billion in assets: David Barboza, "Billions in Hidden Riches for Family of Chinese Leader," *New York Times*, October 25, 2012.

219 "Untangling [the Wens'] financial holdings": Ibid.

219 China blocked access: Keith Bradsher, "China Blocks Access to *Times* After Article," *New York Times*, October 25, 2012. In June 2012, the Chinese government had also blocked access to a Bloomberg investigation of then presumed presidential successor Xi Jinping. The report uncovered assets worth $367 million that could be traced to members of Xi's extended family. While none of the suspicious assets were tied directly to Xi, his wife, or their daughter, the article was off-limits to IP addresses on the mainland; the Chinese government blocked access to the Bloomberg site as well as to any Internet searches related to the topic.

220 "disgusted with his family's activities": U.S. Embassy Beijing, "From American Embassy Beijing to China All China Posts/National Security Council/Secretary of State," diplomatic cable, November 16, 2009, as reproduced at Wikileaks.org, canonical ID 09Beijing3128a.

220 "Rein in your spouses, children, relatives": Michael Forsythe, Shai Oster, Natasha Khan, and Dune Lawrence, "Xi Jingping Millionaire Relations Reveal Fortunes of Elite," Bloomberg News, June 29, 2012.

220 party's records uncovered that officials had stolen 3.7 billion yuan: "Xi Jinping Elected Party Chief of Shanghai," Xinhua News Agency, May 29, 2007.

220 "Xi knows how very corrupt China is": U.S. Embassy Beijing, "From American Embassy Beijing to China" diplomatic cable.

220 In December, at an official dinner in Hebei: Brian Spegele, "Xi Eats Plainly Amid Focus on Official Waistlines," *Wall Street Journal*, December 31, 2012.

221 "Four Simple Dishes and One Soup": Australian Centre on China in the World, "China's Luxury Fever and Curbing Official Ostentation," 2013, www.thechina story.org/.

221 "Leaders must keep in close contact with the grassroots": Official English translation of the "Eight-Point Code," available at Australian Centre on China in the World, "China's Luxury Fever and Curbing Official Ostentation," 2013, www .thechinastory.org/.

221 "no matter who was involved": Kathrin Hille and Simon Rabinovitch, "China Rulers Struggle with Corruption Culture," *Financial Times*, February 17, 2013.

221 "Keep power restricted in a cage of regulations": An Baijie, "Xi Jinping Vows 'Power with Cage of Regulations,'" *China Daily*, January 23, 2013. Intriguingly, this story also reveals that the discipline commission had read Alexis de Tocqueville

and learned that the French Revolution was caused by the "collapse of public trust." A longer version of the story is "Xi Jinping Vows 'Power Within Cage of Regulations,'" Xinhua News Agency, January 22, 2013.

221 Xi vowed to crack down: "Xi Jinping Vows 'Power Within Cage of Regulations,'" Xinhua News Agency, January 22, 2013.

221 more than 73,000 people, including 4,698 cadres, had been punished: Ibid.

221 sales of expensive spirits like baijiu fell 30 percent: Liza Lin, "Mao's $300 Red Army Liquor Suffers Before China Congress," Bloomberg, February 27, 2013.

221 One local party official invited eighty guests: Andrew Jacobs, "Elite in China Face Austerity Under Xi's Rule," New York Times, March 27, 2013.

221 But at the National People's Congress in March 2013: J.C., "Chinese Officials: Spending Less? Or Hiding It Better?," Economist, March 7, 2013.

222 "The last thing a mayor wants to do": Author interview with John D. Watkins Jr., March 24, 2013.

223 Some of their teas sold for $800 for 3.5 ounces: Author reporting at Meeting of Tea and Wine Civilizations, Libourne Town Hall, June 17, 2013.

224 "Pu'er tea is harvested by hand": Author reporting of speech given by Philippe Buisson, mayor, city of Libourne, at the Meeting of Tea and Wine Civilizations, Libourne Town Hall, June 17, 2013.

224 The previous December: Author interview with Philippe Larché, December 19, 2013.

225 Chinese investors owned more than 10 percent of the vineyard surface in Fronsac: Tragically, Lam Kok died in a helicopter accident, along with his eleven-year-old son, the new Chinese manager of the estates, and the seller, James Grégoire, the day Kok took ownership of Château La Rivière.

225 The Industrial and Commercial Bank of China: Author interview with Li Lijuan, China desk, Maxwell-Storrie-Baynes, January 12, 2015.

225 "The big picture is that Chinese entrepreneurs": Author interview with Don St. Pierre Jr., March 24, 2013.

226 "Business addresses, or indeed the geographical": Suzanne Mustacich, "China Buys Big in Bordeaux Wineries," Wine Spectator, December 20, 2013.

226 It was understood that Qu Naijie or his family owned: "Is Bordeaux Becoming France's New Chinatown?," Unfiltered, Wine Spectator, December 8, 2011. See also Suzanne Mustacich, "Chinese Tycoons Snap up Bordeaux Châteaux," Agence France-Presse, February 22, 2012. Additional information came from the China desk, Bordeaux Chamber of Commerce and Industry (CCIB). Qu did his best to keep his acquisitions out of the public eye.

226 cost 3 billion yuan thus far: Yang Cheng, "Bordeaux Looks to China Amid Slump," China Daily, April 10, 2012.

227 During one "struggle session": Jamil Anderlini, "Bo Xilai: Power, Death and Politics," FT Magazine, July 20, 2012.

227 Bo must have dreamed of taking his own place: Erich Follath and Wieland Wagner, "Murder, Sex and Corruption: The Battle for China's Most Powerful Office," Der Spiegel, October 18, 2012.

227 He imported grass to spruce up public spaces: Ibid.

227 Businesses could not succeed if "high commissions": Hou Qiang, "China Focus: Bo Xilai Sentenced to Life in Prison for Bribery, Embezzlement, Power Abuse," Xinhua News Agency, September 22, 2013.

228 he had singled out Bo for dereliction of his duties: Jamie A. FlorCruz and Peter Shadbolt, "China's Bo Xilai: From Rising Star to Scandal," CNN.com, September 23, 2013; Brian Rhoads and Benjamin Kang Lim, "With Bo Xilai Down, Nine Leaders Who May Soon Run China," Reuters, March 16, 2012.

228 That made him fair game for prosecution: William Wan, "Bo's Family Complains of Chinese Government Obstacles to His Defense," *Washington Post*, October 24, 2012.

228 Then he disappeared: "Bo Xilai Scandal: Timeline," BBC News, November 11, 2013.

228 Bo was accused of embezzling $800,000: "Bo Xilai Embezzlement Charge Linked to Jiang Jemin Holiday Home: Sources," *South China Morning Post*, September 7, 2013.

228 accepting $175,000 in bribes: Hou Qiang, "China Focus: Bo Xilai Sentenced to Life in Prison for Bribery, Embezzlement, Power Abuse."

228 purchase price of a French villa, from Xu Ming: Nectar Gan, Laura Zhou, and Angela Meng, "Luxury French Villa of Jailed Chinese Politician Bo Xilai 'Up for Sale at HK$66 Million,'" *South China Morning Post*, December 22, 2014.

228 Bo's disobedient "fly," the informant Wang Lijun: "Bo Xilai Scandal: Timeline."

229 By 2005, Xu was listed as the eighth richest: "The 400 Richest Chinese," *Forbes*, http://www.forbes .com/lists/2005/74/Rank_1.html.

229 It was reported that he had bankrolled much of Bo's high-flying lifestyle: Gan, Zhou, and Meng, "Luxury French Villa of Jailed Chinese Politician Bo Xilai 'Up for Sale at HK$66 Million.'"

229 the Dalian Shide tycoon had disappeared: Yu Ning, Wen Xiu, and Jin Qing, "Dalian Businessman Who Built an Empire Vanishes," Caixin Online, April 9, 2012.

229 One of his holding companies, Lamont: This information was based on discussions with several sources in Bordeaux.

229 Qu had always planned to "flip" the châteaux: This information was confirmed by two real estate agents, who asked to remain anonymous.

230 It was often difficult: Traitement du Renseignement et Action contre Les Circuits Financiers Clandestins (Tracfin), "Rapport Annuel d'Analyse et d'Activité 2012," Ministère de l'Economie et des Finances (France), July 2013, p. 27.

230 Dynasty announced that it had sold only 40 percent of its annual target: Qin Xue, "Chinese Wineries Back Anti-Dumping Probe on EU Wines," CCTV.com, August 24, 2012.

230 "We believe that there's no way": Ibid.

230 wine imports from the European Union had grown 60 percent year-on-year in 2011: Ibid.

231 "We need fair market competition": Ibid.

231 the association lodged a formal petition: "China's Wine Industry Supports Investigation into EU Dumping," CCTV.com, July 3, 2013.

231 In July 2012, EU ProSun: "Notice of Initiation of an Anti-Dumping Proceeding Concerning Imports of Crystalline Silicon Photovoltaic Modules and Key Compo-

nents (i.e., Cells and Wafers) Originating in the People's Republic of China," document number 2012/C 269/04, *Official Journal of the European Union*, September
6, 2012.

231 On June 5, 2013: "Official from Bureau of Fair Trade or Imports and Exports of
MOFCOM Commented on China's Initiation of Anti-Dumping and Countervail-
ing Investigations Against Imports of Wines Originated in the EU," China Ministry of Commerce website, July 4, 2013, http://english.mofcom.gov.cn/article
/newsrelease/significantnews/201307/20130700186535.shtml.

231 It was a tactical maneuver: Editorial, "Negotiation Is the Best Solution to Solar
Panel Dispute," *South China Morning Post*, June 8, 2013.

231 The value and volume of wine imports was dwarfed: Li Jiabao, "EU Warned About
Solar Dispute," *China Daily*, April 5, 2013.

231 It was estimated that the European Union had sold $1 billion worth of wine: "Nego-
tiation Is the Best Solution to Solar Panel Dispute."

231 "A wine probe serves as a timely warning": "EU Action Hurts Trade," *China Daily*,
June 6, 2013.

232 Shares in Changyu's publicly traded unit, Yantai Changyu, surged: Darren Boey,
"Most Chinese Stocks Rise, Led by Winemakers; Sany Drops," Bloomberg, June
5, 2013.

232 "The Chinese want to protect their interests": Suzanne Mustacich, "Trade Dispute
Threatens European Wine Sales to China," *Wine Spectator*, July 24, 2013.

232 Any grower that did not comply: The level of the duty to be levied on noncompliant winegrowers was not specified, but in several interviews with a negotiator familiar with the talks as well as producer-exporters, the duty was characterized as
being so high that it would make it impossible for a company to sell wine in China
without posting a loss.

233 The French media had recently exposed the subsidies: Antonin Iommi-Amunategui,
"Politique agricole commune: ces géants du vin qui touchent le pactole," *Nouvel
Obs*, December 10, 2012.

233 in 2011 Castel had received $4.3 million in subsidies: Ibid.

234 The wine producers had been chosen: Author interview with Emmanuel Martin,
January 7, 2015.

234 Worse, he would effectively be shut out of the most lucrative market he had: Ibid.

235 "It's ridiculous": Author interview with Vincent Yip, November 15, 2013.

235 "It affects our business": Author interview with Steven Yin, sommelier, Shangri-
La Hotel, Qingdao, at Château Pavie-Macquin, Saint-Émilion, April 6, 2013.

236 "I told him, 'Very good price. It's at cost'": Author interview with Vincent Yip,
November 15, 2013.

236 The tycoon had transferred around $135 million, but the French owners had
pulled out at the last minute: Author interview with Kingston Lai, founder and
CEO, Asia Bankers Club, November 15, 2013.

236 "That's a lot to finance, a lot to risk": Author interview with Vincent Yip, November 15, 2013.

237 "The people who built the market are no longer making money": Ibid.

237 "How many rich Chinese will open a bottle of wine": Ibid.

237 "We are businessmen": Ibid.

238 Lower categories were hit: Suzanne Mustacich, "China Cuts Back on Big Buck Bordeaux," *Wine Spectator*, April 12, 2013.

238 "This is obvious when you look at the 2012 import figures": Author interview with Don St. Pierre Jr., March 24, 2013.

238 the Wine Residence: Characterization based on author's visit to ASC's Wine Residence on November 8, 2013.

239 "I also think prices have gotten so high": Author interview with Don St. Pierre Jr., March 24, 2013.

239 In the spring of 2014: Kirby and Zendell, "From Beijing Jeep to ASC Fine Wines."

240 "commercial technology was available": Email to author from John D. Watkins Jr., February 11, 2015.

240 A survey published by Wine Intelligence: Rui Su et al., *China Wine Market Landscape Report: Wine Consumption Behavior in China* (London: Wine Intelligence, January 2013).

240 "ASC will be able to track each bottle": Email to author from John D. Watkins Jr., February 11, 2015.

241 nothing like the 94 percent growth that ASC: The figures were no better when wine imports were measured by volume. The volume of imported wine had grown 65 percent in 2011 versus 10 percent in 2012 and 4 percent in 2014. Author interview with John D. Watkins Jr., February 11, 2015.

241 "My experience in China helped me": Ibid.

241 Online sales of wine increased 50 percent in 2014: Ibid.

241 "Look at the U.S. as an example": Ibid.

241 Beijing was pressuring a wide variety of industries to lower their prices to consumers: John D. Watkins Jr., "ASC Annual Letter to Supplier Partners 2013," ASC Fine Wines, Shanghai, China, January 2014.

241 "I would ask you to pull your Penfolds": "Chinese Hotel Chain Pulls Penfolds," *Australian Business Review*, August 6, 2014.

241 Li Daozhi and another man: Patrick Boehler, "Winemaker Penfolds in Legal Battle with 'Trademark Squatters' over Right to Use Its Chinese Name," *South China Morning Post*, July 14, 2014.

242 "One of our brand owners is also in dispute": Watkins, "ASC Annual Letter to Supplier Partners 2013."

242 two million bottles of Château Lafite sold in China every year: "The Chinese Wine Market, Both Promising and Difficult," Daxue Consulting, September 22, 2014, http://daxueconsulting.com/chinese-red-wine-market/.

Chapter 10. Adjust Measures to Local Conditions

Author interviews and email exchanges with the following individuals provided background information for this chapter: Stanislas Basquin, agronomic engineer; Gérard Colin, consulting winemaker; Craig Grafton, senior winemaker, Pernod Ricard; Philippe Papillon, CEO, Ipso Facto; Carlo Pinto, head of sector, Directorate General for Trade, European Commission; Jean-Guillaume Prats, chief executive officer, Estates and Wines, LVMH; Olivier Richaud, technical director, DBR-CITIC Wine Estate; Nicole Wang, operation executive communications manager, China Fine Wines; Yang Wenhua, chairman, LK Wine; Zhou Jing, China manager, Producta.

245 his family had amassed a fortune: "Rong Yiren, a Chinese Billionaire, Died on October 26, Age 89," *Economist*, November 3, 2005.

245 "international recognition of its state-owned flagships": Donny Kwok, "CITIC Group Eyes $12 Billion HK IPO Next Year: Report," Reuters, July 23, 2010.

245 CITIC Guoan Wine Company bought a majority stake in Jinchuang Suntime: Minnie Chan, "Xinjiang Taps into Booming Red Wine Market," *South China Morning Post*, November 28, 2010. CITIC Guoan Wine Company hired a French winemaker, Fred Nauleau, to oversee production.

245 "We . . . found many ruins of vineyards": Ibid.

246 "If you want to secure twenty-five hectares": Mitch Frank, "Lafite Rothschild Owners Launch Wine Project in China," *Wine Spectator*, June 15, 2009.

246 "Adjust measures to local conditions": This is a common translation of the Chinese idiom *Yindizhiyi*. The concept is usually interpreted to mean that one must adapt to the given natural, social, and economic situation in order to obtain the best results. In agriculture, the idiom encompasses climate, geographical position, and human support.

246 An eleventh-century pavilion of temples and pagodas draws more than two million visitors: "Yantai: A Beautiful Coastal City of Tourist Attraction," China Internet Information Center, China.org.cn/.

247 "Rockefeller of the East": Cheong Fatt Tze Mansion website, www.cheongfatttze mansion.com. Additional information came from "Employment Contract" in English, dated July 18, 1896, made in Singapore between Baron Max von Babo and Thio Tiauw Siat (Zhang Bishi) of Changyu Pioneer Wine Company, for Von Babo to supervise Changyu in Shantung (Shandong). Christie's sale 5074, lot 52.

247 A price list from 1917 offered nine reds and nine whites: "Printed Price List in Chinese and English, Chang Yu Pioneer Wine Company, Ltd.," exact date unknown, but likely prior to 1917, Christie's sale 5074, lot 52.

247 "Bordeaux of China": Chris Bayley, *PanVenture, Inc., Market Intelligence Report* (Yantai, China: PanVenture, June 19, 2008).

248 "seven grape coasts": Author visit to the Penglai Vine and Wine Council, Penglai, China, June 2010.

248 "Nava" sounded better than the original Chinese name: Email from J. Scott Gerian, Dickenson, Peatman & Fogarty, a law firm representing several Napa Valley vintners, June 6, 2014.

248 Penglai shared the same thirty-seven degrees latitude with Bordeaux: Author visit to Penglai Vine and Wine Council, June 2010.

248 "These arguments never make any sense": Email to author from Gérard Colin, consulting winemaker (previously technical director, DBR-CITIC Wine Estate), June 8, 2014.

249 Cabernet Gernischt: Gernischt was possibly a misspelling of *gemischt*, the German word for "mixed."

249 "undoubtedly Carmenère": Email to author from José Vouillamoz, coauthor with Julia Harding and Jancis Robinson of *Wine Grapes: A Complete Guide to 1,368 Vine Varieties, Including Their Origins and Flavours* (New York: Ecco, 2012), June 6, 2014.

249 Carmenère was one of Bordeaux's original grape varieties: Carmenère was first mentioned in the Gironde in 1783–84, according to Vouillamoz, Harding, and Robinson, *Wine Grapes*. It is the progeny and great-grandchild of Cabernet Franc, and half-sibling to Merlot and Cabernet Sauvignon. For this reason, it is often confused with its close relatives.

249 a natural cross between Cabernet Franc and Gros Cabernet: Email to author from José Vouillamoz, June 6, 2014.

249 the Carmenère in Changyu's vineyard differed considerably from modern French clones: Ibid.

250 There were only 101 acres of Carmenère left in France and 57 acres in the United States: Patrick Schmitt, "China: More Carmenère Than Chile?," *Drinks Business*, December 5, 2014.

250 until 1994, when 26,400 acres, previously mistaken for Merlot: Ibid.

250 Chinese team soon confirmed: Email to author from José Vouillamoz, June 6, 2014.

250 many Chinese wineries had invested heavily in Cabernet Sauvignon: Li Demei, "Great Cabernets from China at the Decanter Shanghai Fine Wine Encounter," December 9, 2014, Decanterchina.com/.

250 Gérard Colin unfurled a scroll of papers: Author visit to DBR-CITIC Wine Estate and interview with Gérard Colin, technical director, DBR-CITIC Wine Estate, June 2–3, 2010.

251 "It's run like a cooperative here": Author interview with Gérard Colin, June 2–3, 2010.

251 the only way to guarantee yield and quality was through a leasehold: Ibid. They first planted in 2011 and the first small crop was in 2014.

252 Sometimes 20 percent or more of a single wine brand was of foreign origin: Author interview with Gérard Colin, January 7, 2014.

252 "Eighty percent of the domestic Chinese wines": Ibid.

252 "If great red wine is going to come out of anywhere in China, it will come from Ningxia": Email to author from David Henderson, chief executive officer, Dragon's Hollow, and president, China Fine Wines, February 20, 2015.

253 "We're not a 'Chinese' wine": Ibid.

253 "Being China, that could change any day": Ibid.

254 "It's one of the most beautiful vineyards in the region": Email to author from Emma Gao Yuan, owner, Silver Heights, February 13, 2015.

254 "It's near the area with the rock paintings": Author interview with Emma Gao Yuan, November 2013.

255 "We had to abandon the project": Email to author from Emma Gao Yuan, February 5, 2015.

255 "But one thousand *mǔ* is the maximum for us": Email to author from Emma Gao Yuan, February 13, 2015.

255 "I do not think that when the client says": Author interview with Judy Chan, president, Grace Vineyard, November 11, 2013.

255 Grace Vineyard was selling ten thousand bottles a year: Email to author from Alberto Fernández, managing partner, Torres China, February 20, 2015.

256 "I am convinced there are some very, very good soils": Author interview with Gérard Colin, January 7, 2014.

256 "COFCO has bought vineyards everywhere": Ibid.

257 facilitate the transfer of winemaking skills to the mainland: Author interview with Fabien Bova, director, Conseil Interprofessionnel du Vins de Bordeaux (CIVB)/ Bordeaux Wine Council, July 1, 2014.

257 Some members of the CIVB wondered if an arrangement: Ibid.

257 "They didn't get anything they weren't already getting": Author interview with Emmanuel Martin, chief executive officer, La Guyennoise Propriétaires et Négociants, January 27, 2015.

258 "There is no shopping list this year, there is no business analysis this year, there is not much business this year": Vincent Yip, Business Update, Hong Kong, March 2014.

259 more than 742 million bottles, worth $5.84 billion, shipped worldwide: CIVB.

259 Combined, Hong Kong and China still accounted for one-quarter of Bordeaux's exports: Ibid.

260 The growing season began with a wet, cold May: When blooms do not develop normally, it is referred to as "poor fruit set." Entire flower clusters or individual flowers may be affected; some flowers may never form fruit while others may form small, green "shot berries" that never ripen.

260 general manager Philippe Dhalluin conscripted the entire staff: Author interview with Philippe Dhalluin, executive director, Châteaux Wines, Baron Philippe de Rothschild, September 26, 2014, during a harvest lunch at Château d'Armailhac.

260 "There is no greenness in most of the fine wines I have tasted": Email to author from Christophe Reboul Salze, March 27, 2014.

261 "The best have very pretty aromatics, elegance, freshness and attractive, linear palates": Giles Cooper, "Bordeaux En Primeur 2013: Day One," Bordeaux Index blog, April 1, 2014.

261 "We bought too much of the 2010": Author interview with Yang Wenhua, chairman, Xiamen C&D Fine Wines, February 12, 2014.

262 "From 2006 to 2013, Castel sold millions of bottles in China": Ibid.

262 "Our plan is to sell directly to final clients": Ibid.

263 What C&D needed: Ibid.

263 "The négociants are always worrying about their margins": Author interview with Yang Wenhua, chief executive officer, LK Wine, February 15, 2015.

263 China's "new normal," slower growth with deeper reforms and less corruption: "Xi in Spotlight at 'Two Sessions,'" China Daily, March 15, 2015.

264 "foster a new engine of growth by encouraging mass entrepreneurship and innovation": "China Focus: A–Z of 'Two Sessions' Talking Points," National People's Congress of the People's Republic of China, March 3, 2015, http://www.npc.gov.cn/englishnpc/Special_12_3/2015-03/03/content_1907901.htm.

264 he'd had high hopes about the opportunities presented by working for the Chinese:

Author interview with Philippe Raoux, owner of Château d'Arsac and former owner of La Winery, October 17, 2013.

264 And his other big customer: Author interview with Philippe Raoux, May 21, 2015. Wang Quan acquired the château through his company, Hebei Xinda Group, and listed his son, Wang Songwei, as the owner.

265 At the height of his business: Author interview with Philippe Papillon and Nathalie Castagnon, February 10, 2015.

265 his collection of French châteaux was now being offered in bulk to négociants: Author interview with Chinese export manager for Bordeaux négociant, February 15, 2015.

265 "major violations of laws and disciplines": Suzanne Mustacich, "Chinese Corruption Probe Targets Firms That Bought Bordeaux Wineries," *Wine Spectator*, July 1, 2014.

266 Another Chinese owner, a steel tycoon: Author interview with a Bordeaux négociant on January 27, 2015, who confirmed the information, while author was present, with a broker in recent business dealings with the tycoon.

266 In France, the money-laundering cases first reported by Tracfin in 2013 had been transferred to Bordeaux: Author confirmed by phone with Tracfin on February 20, 2015. This is the normal procedure.

266 When the third Dalian Wine and Dine Festival opened in July 2014: Author interview with Thierry Charpentier, deputy manager of international tourism development, Bordeaux Chamber of Commerce and Industry (CCIB), January 23, 2014.

267 Bordeaux's exports had dropped another 17 percent in value: CIVB.

267 "At the moment, the fine wine market is completely stuck. Prices have collapsed": Suzanne Mustacich, "Can Bordeaux Bounce Back?," *Wine Spectator*, November 14, 2014.

267 "We are selling and shipping wine at the entry level": Ibid.

267 volume of imported French wine in 2014: CIVB.

268 China had the most land in Asia suitable for growing wine grapes: Stanislas Basquin, "Study of the Viticultural Agro-Climatic Potentialities of China," (master's diss., University of Burgundy, Montpellier SupAgro, and Paris Institute of Technology for Life, Food and Environmental Studies, 2012).

268 A small strip of southern Gansu Province: Ibid.

268 Friuli–Venezia Giulia wine region: Basquin also found that the Xinxiang Uygur Autonomous Region, with its cold winters and sizzling hot summers, most resembled La Mancha in Spain or the Douro region of Portugal, where port is made. Author interview with Stanislas Basquin, consulting agronomic engineer, March 6, 2014.

268 "None of these areas are located in the region of Yantai and Penglai, on the coast of the Bohai Sea": Ibid.

269 "It is possible that other regions of China": Ibid.

Epilogue: Shangri-La

Author interviews and email exchanges with the following individuals provided background information for this chapter: Stanislas Basquin, agronomic engineer; Gérard Colin, consulting winemaker and former managing director, DBR-CITIC Wine Estate;

Maxence Dulou, estate manager, Estates and Wines, LVMH; Dr. Tony Jordan, chief executive officer, Oenotec Pty, and former chief executive officer, Domaine Chandon Australia, Cape Mentelle, and Cloudy Bay; Philippe Papillon, CEO, Ipso Facto; Carlo Pinto, head of sector, Directorate General for Trade, European Commission; Jean-Guillaume Prats, chief executive officer, Estates and Wines, LVMH; Olivier Richaud, technical director, DBR-CITIC Wine Estate; Linda Sansbury, information officer, Hong Kong Economic and Trade Office, Brussels; Christophe Salin, CEO and president, Domaines Barons de Rothschild (Lafite); Shen Yang, general manager, Domaine Chandon China, Ningxia; Nicole Wang, operation executive communications manager, China Fine Wines; Yang Wenhua, chairman, LK Wine; Zhou Jing, China manager, Producta.

270 commercial logging industry had collapsed in 1998: Mark Jenkins, "Parallel Rivers," *National Geographic*, May 2009.

270 the local economic initiative to diversify the economy: Author interview with Dr. Tony Jordan, chief executive officer, Oenotec Pty, and former chief executive officer, Domaine Chandon Australia, Cape Mentelle, and Cloudy Bay, March 25, 2015.

271 Shangri-La held a monopoly: Jancis Robinson and Nicholas Lander, "Finding Shangri-La in Yunnan, China," *Financial Times*, June 20, 2014. Sunspirit Wines invested $4.74 million to set up a winery in 2007, according to Xiao Xiangyi and Li Yingqing, "High Ambitions," *China Daily*, August 31, 2012.

271 They now relied on the income from selling grapes to buy food: Brendan Galipeau, "Tibetan Wine Boom Threatens Food Security," *East by Southeast*, October 24, 2013.

273 "He asked me": Author interview with Li Demei, associate professor, Wine Tasting and Enology, Beijing University of Agriculture, November 13, 2013, at ProWein in Shanghai.

273 the grapes appeared to be a hybrid: Author interview with Dr. Tony Jordan, March 25, 2015. Additional information came from Vouillamoz, Harding, and Robinson, *Wine Grapes*.

273 "The wine at the chapel vineyard is good": Author interview with Gérard Colin, January 7, 2014.

274 Moët Hennessy entered into a joint venture: Jinliufu Enterprises was founded in 1996 in Beijing. It was renamed VATS Group in 2006. LVMH and VATS entered into their wine joint venture in 2012. Terril Yue Jones, "Moët Hennessy Aims for Super-Premium Red Wine from China," Reuters, February 23, 2012.

274 fifty-year leases on about seventy-five acres: Email to author from Jean-Guillaume Prats, chief executive officer, Estates and Wines, a subsidiary of LVMH, February 23, 2015; and author interview with Dr. Tony Jordan, March 25, 2015.

274 Never had he imagined he'd be making wine in such an astonishing place: Suzanne Mustacich, "Why Would Jean-Guillaume Prats Leave Cos d'Estournel?," *Wine Spectator*, April 3, 2013.

274 was "going to be made [just] as we make the great First Growths of Bordeaux": Ibid.

275 "Lafite is exceptional but I think that Cos is slightly better": Email to author from Jean-Guillaume Prats, February 23, 2015.

275 He had worked at Bernard Magrez's: Author interview with Olivier Richaud, technical director, DBR-CITIC Wine Estate, January 26, 2014.

275 Then there was the shock of discovering white rot: Ibid.

275 "It's made in small containers": Email to author from Christophe Salin, February 16, 2015.

275 "Not bad at all": Ibid. This assessment was similar to one given by Salin at the Institute of Masters of Wine symposium in Florence, Italy, in May 2014: "Last year was the first crop and the wine is not bad, not yet good, but not bad compared to everything drunk locally—which was bad." Patrick Schmitt, "Lafite China's First Wine Declared 'Not Bad,'" *Drinks Business*, July 2, 2014.

277 "buy high, impossible to sell": Vincent Yip, manager, Topsy Trading, Business Update, Hong Kong, March 2015.

278 monthly pre-tax per capita income of about $700: Rui Su and Chuan Zhou, *China Internet and Social Media 2014* (London: Wine Intelligence, June 2014).

279 the government of Hong Kong has signed a "memorandum of understanding": Since August 2008, Hong Kong has signed MOUs or wine cooperation agreements with Australia, Chile, France (including Bordeaux and Burgundy), Germany, Hungary, Italy, New Zealand, Portugal, Spain, and the United States (including Oregon and Washington State). Email to author from Linda Sansbury, information officer, Hong Kong Economic and Trade Office, Brussels, on March 27, 2015, plus numerous emails over the course of several years.

279 Hong Kong wine imports for 2014 were $1.09 billion: Commerce and Economic Development Bureau, Government of the Hong Kong Special Administrative Region, www.cedb.gov.hk.

279 Changyu expects to buy its first overseas winery in 2015, and plans to buy nine more: Robert Joseph, "Spectacular Sales Growth," *Meininger's Wine Business International*, February 2015.

282 "You want to play the game? You can win, you can lose": Author interview with Christophe Reboul Salze, January 8, 2014.

Acknowledgments

....

From the moment I decided to write a book about Bordeaux, I knew my starting point was the Place de Bordeaux, a source of fascination for me. When China appeared on the horizon, the story I had been looking for unfolded before my eyes.

Over the past fifteen years in Bordeaux, I have enjoyed countless conversations with acquaintances, sources, and friends in the wine business. Many live and work in Bordeaux; others are based in the United States, Great Britain, or other countries. All of their insight and information has been invaluable.

Of course, this kind of book would not be possible without the stories shared, often with refreshing frankness, by so many people. Some of those people prefer to remain anonymous.

I'm grateful for the people who took the time to speak to me and assist me in my research: Chris Adams, Nick Bartman, Lilian Barton-Sartorius, Stanislas Basquin, Gary Boom, Didier Bouchet, Fabien Bova, Sara Briot-Lesage, Grace Cai, Bertrand Carles, Jean-Michel Cazes, Sylvie Cazes, Judy Chan, Thierry Charpentier, Bandy Choi, Gérard Colin, César Compadre, Michael Corso, Xavier Coumau, Philippe Dambrine, Stephan Delaux, Frédéric de Luze, Pétrus Desbois, Alberto Fernandez, Emma Gao Yuan, James Gunter, David Henderson, François Hériard-Dubreuil,

Denis Johnston, Dr. Tony Jordan, Philippe Laqueche, Philippe Larché, Brice Leboucq, François Lévêque, Li Demei, Li Lijuan, Ma Lin, Ma Qingyun, Bernard Magrez, Emmanuel Martin, Jean-Christophe Mau, Antonin Michel, Hervé Olivier, Philippe Papillon, Jean-Guillaume Prats, Jamie Ritchie, Michel Rolland, Philippe Roudié, Jean-Pierre Rousseau, Doug Rumsam, Christophe Salin, Sophie Schÿler, Yann Schÿler, Shen Dongjun, Shen Yang, Allan Sichel, Robert Sleigh, Simon Staples, Don St. Pierre Jr., George Tong, Dr. José Vouillamoz, Wang Zhang, John D. Watkins Jr., David Webster, Harry Wu Hongda, Yang Wenhua, Vincent Yip, Zhou Jing, and Zhou Linjun.

My travels in greater China, and the exchanges with those sources over the years, have been a marvelous part of writing this book. I also owe a debt to the incisive reporting done by the many journalists based in China and Hong Kong whose work I have relied on to further understand the complexities of this country.

Regarding archival research, I would like to thank Matheson & Company for access to the Jardine Matheson Archive (Department of Manuscripts and University Archives, Cambridge University Library); the Conseil Interprofessionnel du Vin de Bordeaux (CIVB)/Bordeaux Wine Council; Erik Samazeuilh at Tastet-Lawton; and Sandrine Faure at the Musée National des Douanes.

My work as a journalist in Bordeaux would not have been possible without the support of *Wine Spectator, Meininger's Wine Business International*, and Agence France-Presse. I am especially grateful to my editors at *Wine Spectator*, Thomas Matthews, Dana Nigro, and Mitch Frank. At AFP, I would not have been able to cover the exciting stories I did without the support of Dave Clark, Hugh Dent, the late Bernard Estrade, Angus MacKinnon, Bernard Pellegrin, and Claire Rosemberg. And a special thanks goes to Felicity Carter, who sat me down in the pressroom at Vinexpo and encouraged me to write a book about Bordeaux. Those were my marching orders.

At Henry Holt, executive editor Paul Golob offered his unflappable professionalism and encouragement. Thanks to the design and marketing team for their enthusiasm for this book, executive managing editor Kenn Russell for his keen eye, associate publicity director Carolyn

O'Keefe for her support, associate editor Emi Ikkanda for her terrific organization, and my editor, Robin Dennis, for her insight and guidance. All writers need a good agent, and I was lucky to have Michelle Tessler.

Writing is a lonely business without friends, and Valentina Britten, Maria Burton, Colleen Carbery, Phyllis Housen, Billy Kolber, Peter Meech, and Elle Triedman have never failed to inspire me. Dewey Markham Jr. generously agreed to cast his keen eye over the manuscript. My father paid for a superb education, my mother encouraged me to explore foreign countries, my sister stood by me, always, and my brother kept my ego in check. And finally, the two who did not choose the writing life, but live it just the same, Pétrus and Pétrus: without them, there would be no book.

Index

Accenture, 109
Adams, Chris, 37, 191
Africa, 25, 267
Air China, 225
Alexander II, Czar of Russia, 92
allocations
    competition for, 19–20
    defined, 2–3
Alsace, 35
Aman resorts, 53
American Bar Association (ABA), 62
American Grenada Holdings, 141.
    See also Megara
American market, 21, 25, 28, 82,
    180–81, 189–92, 241, 253,
    267
American Motors Corp., 29
American Revolutionary War, 25
Angélus, Château, 123–25, 143, 174,
    177
Ao Yun, "Proud Clouds" of Shangri-La,
    274
Aquitaine, 98
Argentina, 32, 253, 271
Arnault, Bernard, 92, 271
ASC Wine Gallery, 239, 241
Asia Bankers Club, 236
Asian financial crisis of 1990s, 2, 15

Asia Solutions Corporation (ASC) Fine
    Wines, 31–32, 36, 43–49, 159, 194,
    216–17, 237–43
    Wine Residence, 238
Asia Tatler, 157
Ausone, Château, 123
Australia, 30, 65, 71, 87, 271, 278

Baby, Château, 226
Bacardi Greater China, 47
baijiu, 5, 14, 194–95, 221, 262
Baillet, Celine, 154
Bai Yin, 58–59
Bai Zhisheng, 63, 169, 256–57
Banqiao Farm Machinery Parts Factory
    RTL, 61
Banque de France de Commerce
    d'Extérieur, 12
Barboza, David, 219
Barrière Frères, 99
Bartman, Nick, 130–41, 143–53, 156
Barton, Anthony, 185
Barton-Sartorius, Lilian, 184
Basquin, Stanislas, 268–70
Baudry, Bruno, 243
Baynes, Michael, 226
Beijing Automobile Works, 29
Beijing churchyard winery, 58

Beijing Friendship Winery, 62
Bellefont-Belcier, Château, 264
Beringer, 30
Berry Bros. & Rudd, 36, 126, 158
Bettane & Desseauve, 213
Beuchet, Pierre, 24, 26–27, 186
Beychevelle, Château, 12, 27
Billot-Grima, Nicolas, 56
Binny's, 181
black banks, 149–50, 281
Blaye, 119, 169
Bollinger, 30
Boom, Gary, 34–38, 97–98, 126, 173,
    199–201, 258, 261
Bordeaux. *See also* Bordeaux vintages;
    *and specific appellations, châteaux,
    firms, and individuals*
  annual barrel tastings, 43, 83–88,
    90–99, 161, 178–81, 183, 197,
    221–22, 233, 260–61
  bogus futures and, 98
  brand squatting and, 141–43, 147–48,
    153–56, 174–78, 241–42, 278, 280
  cancelled orders and, 157–74, 180
  Chinese châteaux purchases and,
    110–23, 128–29, 178, 196–97,
    224–26, 229–30, 236, 265–66, 281
  Chinese corruption crackdown and,
    194–96, 215–22, 225, 227–29,
    235–39, 241, 243, 263–66, 278,
    281–82
  Chinese customs charges and, 40–47,
    66–67, 75, 144, 239, 278
  Chinese demand grows, 38–39, 84–87
  Chinese tourism in, 64–65, 78–79,
    280–81
  Chinese vs. middlemen in, 115–18,
    187–88, 192–93, 236–27
  classification system and, 6–8, 19, 92,
    117, 127, 142, 182, 276
  competition from Chinese vintners
    and, 201–3
  counterfeiting and, 106, 130–56, 189,
    240, 280
  critics and, 16–18
  discounting and, 99, 125–27, 196, 198,
    236–37, 277
  en primeur system and, 9–11, 18, 23,
    84–85, 89–90, 98–99, 106, 124, 160,
    171–72, 179–84, 189–90, 196–97,
    260–61, 277

ex-cellar sales and, 32, 102–9, 124
exclusivity and, 89–91, 95, 122–23,
    168, 197–98, 261
lessons of Chinese trade and, 276–82
generic wines, 20, 83, 100–101, 121
history of, 6–8, 23–28
imports to China begun, 5–6, 11–15,
    21, 29–35, 52, 67–69
money laundering and, 150, 165,
    229–30, 266, 281
négociant and courtier system in, 1–2,
    200
pricing and, 1–3, 10–12, 16, 20–22,
    26–27, 81–82, 99, 124–26, 157, 179,
    190, 196, 267, 276–77
quality and methods in, 16–18, 118
small vineyards and, 81–83
smuggling and, 41–43, 46, 51, 143, 157,
    278
speculation and, 18–20, 39, 125, 128,
    157, 159–60, 179, 261, 277
trade dispute with China and, 230–34,
    238, 241, 256–57, 266, 278–79
tranche system and, 87–88, 99
wine tourism and, 50, 207
Bordeaux Chamber of Commerce, 109–12,
    117, 155, 165, 223, 226–27, 266–67
Bordeaux Grands Evénements, 49–51
Bordeaux Grand Théâtre (opera house),
    91, 92, 116
Bordeaux Index, 34–38, 97, 173, 258, 261
Bordeaux Tourism Bureau, 49
Bordeaux Tribunal de Commerce, 164,
    166–67, 199, 265
Bordeaux vintages
  1785, 25
  1847, 92
  1982, 9
  1993, 10
  1995, 11, 15
  1996, 15
  1997, 15–16, 21
  1998, 21, 133
  2000, 19, 160
  2001, 22
  2003, 19, 160
  2005, 19–20, 92, 98–100, 160
  2006, 20, 22, 160, 179, 191
  2007, 20, 160, 179, 198
  2008, 1, 22, 23, 38–39, 81, 84, 87–88,
    103, 126, 191, 198

2009, 51, 84, 92–101, 126, 158, 179, 189–90, 198, 261
2010, 125–27, 158, 162, 168, 171–72, 179–80, 189–91, 198, 259, 261
2011, 171, 180–81, 184, 189–92, 196
2012, 197, 221–21, 267
2013, 260–61, 267
Bordeaux Wine Council (CIVB), 51, 83, 112, 135–37, 141, 145, 148, 151–53, 156, 192, 233, 248, 257
Botrytis cinerea (noble rot), 92
Boüard, Hubert de, 123–25, 143
Boüard-Rivoal, Stéphanie de, 143
Boubals, Denis, 75
Bo Xilai, 227–29, 266
Boyce, Jim, 201, 202
Bo Yibo, 227
Branda, Château, 226, 266
Brazil, 267, 281
Bright Food Company, 187–89
Bright Sword campaign, 139
Brilliant Group Investment, 223, 224
Britain, 33–37, 57. *See also* London merchants; United Kingdom
British Virgin Islands, 160
Buisson, Philippe, 223, 224
Bulgaria, 57–58
Burgundy, 6, 24, 26–27, 35, 101, 158, 173
BusinessWeek, 61

Cabernet Franc, 17, 65, 76, 249, 250
Cabernet Gernischt, 65, 249
Cabernet Sauvignon, 17, 65, 69, 71, 76, 80, 211, 245, 248–50, 271, 274
Cafa Formations, 95, 148, 188
Café Lavinal, 43
Caldbeck MacGregor & Company, 4, 59
California, 29, 71, 158, 271
Calon-Ségur, Château, 66, 204
Calvet, 67
Campo, Pancho, 174
C&D Grand Cru Union, 122. *See also* Xiamen C&D
Cantemerle, Château, 8
Cao Kailong, 207–8, 211–12
Carignan, 58, 60
Carles, Bertrand, 31–32
Carmenère, 63, 249–50
Carruades de Lafite (*formerly* Moulin de Carruades), 13, 20, 98–99, 108, 122–23, 132

Carthusian monks, 24
Casino Royale (film), 123
Castagnon, Nathalie, 159, 163–66
Castel, Alain, 232
Castel Frères, 88, 122, 174–78, 189, 232–34, 241, 262–63
Cathay Pacific, 12–13, 43
CavesMaître France (Kasite), 175, 177–78
Cazes, Jean-Michel, 12–13, 50, 191
Central Commission for Discipline Inspection (CCDI), 221
Certain de May de Certan, Château, 142
Champagne, 6, 24, 27, 35
Chan, Chun-Keung "C.K.," 73–77, 79
Chan, Judy, 74, 76–79, 210, 255–56, 268
Chandon China winery, 204
Chang Kai, 193
Changli, 137–40, 145
Changsha Intermediate People's Court, 155
Changyu Pioneer Wine Company, 247
Changyu winery, 57–58, 87, 132, 175, 203, 212, 232, 249, 255, 279
Chardonnay, 65, 69, 76, 245
Château & Estate Wines (C&E), 3, 21–22, 37, 101
Château Changyu-Castel, 175
Château de Bordeaux (Chinese winery), 110–12
Château Junding (Chinese winery), 132
Chen, Jenny "Jenny C.," 161–63, 165–67, 265
Chengdu wine fair, 106, 156
Cheng Haiyan, Daisy, 121
Chenin Blanc, 76
Chenu-Lafitte, Château, 111, 226
Cherubino Valsangiacomo, 234
Cheung, Benny, 57
Cheval Blanc, Château, 27, 223, 271
Chevallier, Charles, 16
Chianti, 67
Chi Jingtao, 114–15
Chile, 40, 87, 135, 253, 275, 278
China. *See also* Bordeaux; *and specific agencies; importers; regions; and wineries*
 Communist takeover of, 3–4, 54, 57, 113–14, 220
 corruption crackdown in, 194–96, 215–22, 225, 227–29, 235–39, 241, 243, 263–66, 278, 281–82

China (*cont'd*)
customs charges and, 40–47, 66–67, 75, 144, 239, 278
as first-to-file nation, 141–42, 176
GDP of, 5, 14
wine market, 5–6, 11–15, 21, 29–35, 52, 67–69
wineries, 201–14, 230, 246–56, 268–76, 279–80
China Alcoholic Drinks Association (CADA), 230–31
China Central Television (CCTV), 138–39, 155–56
China Court Network, 155
China Daily, 195, 209, 231–32
China Fine Wines, 253
China International Trust and Investment Corporation (CITIC), 244–46
China Light & Power Company Syndicate, 4
China National Cereals, Oils and Foodstuffs Corporation (COFCO), 113–16, 118, 125, 132, 138, 188, 212, 248, 256, 264, 272, 279
China Southern Airlines, 225
China Sugar and Wine Fair (Chengdu), 106, 156
China Wine Challenge (Shanghai), 213
Chinese Communist Party, 54, 113–14, 158, 188, 193–96, 198, 220–21, 238–39
Politburo, 57
Politburo Standing Committee, 220, 227
Chinese Customs Service, 43–47, 239
Chinese Department of Investment Fund Supervision, 127
Chinese Evangelical Baptist church (Paris), 149–50
Chinese General Administration of Quality Supervision, Inspection and Quarantine, 151–52
Chinese Health and Hygiene Department, 42
Chinese Intellectual Property Office, 142, 178
Chinese Ministry of Agriculture, 72
Chinese Ministry of Commerce, 231–33, 234, 238
Chinese Ministry of Finance, 195
Chinese Ministry of Public Security, 139
Chinese National Audit Office, 265

Chinese National People's Congress, 265
1984, 109
1996, 14, 29, 56, 86–87
2012, 193–94, 216
2013, 221
2015, 263–64
Chinese New Year, 85, 151, 221
Chinese Patent Trademark Office, 141, 176, 248
Chinese People's Liberation Army, 54, 57
Chinese People's Political Consultative Conference (2012), 193
Chinese Smuggling Prevention Department, 43, 46, 51
Chinese State Council, 195
Chinese State Forestry Administration, 55
Chongqing Communist Party, 227–28
Christie's International Real Estate, 226
Cité des Civilisations du Vin, 110
Citibank, 109
CIVB. *See* Bordeaux Wine Council
Cizhong village, 273–74
1855 Classification, Medoc and Graves, 6–8, 19, 92, 117, 127, 142, 182, 276. *See also specific growths*
Clément-Fayat, Château, 170–71
Clinton, Bill, 29
Cognac, 27
Col d'Orcia, 30
Colin, Gérard, 75–76, 78, 210, 244, 246, 248–51, 256, 268, 273, 275
College of Enology, Northwest Agriculture and Forestry University (Yangling), 56
Commanderie du Bontemps, 118
Compagnie des Vins de Bordeaux et de la Gironde (CVBG), 2, 9–10, 13, 15, 171
Compagnie Française d'Assurance pour le Commerce Extérieur (Coface), 112
Concha y Toro, 28
Connétable Talbot, Château, 142
Conseil des Vins du Médoc, 96
Cordier, Jean, 68
Cos d'Estournel, Château, 18–20, 31, 99, 127, 158, 165, 174, 190, 274–75
Côte de Nuits, 173
Côtes de Bourg, 111
Cottin, Philippe, 26–27
Courtade, Thierry, 66, 72, 204, 213
courtiers, 2, 7, 10, 24–25, 85, 115, 118, 124, 173, 184, 190, 193

Crook, Carl (Ke Lu), 66, 67
Crown Cellars, 105–6
cru bourgeois (Médoc), 117–18
Cultural Revolution, 54, 62, 67, 73, 175, 220, 227
currency hedging, 46–47, 49, 51

Dalian, 109–11, 119, 226–29, 265–66
Dalian Haichang, 110, 197, 219
Dalian Shide, 228–29
Dalian Tiger Beach Ocean Park, 109, 226
Dalian Wine & Dine Festival, 110, 266–67
DBR-CITIC Wine Estate, 246–52, 256, 269, 274–76, 280
Decanter, 36, 206, 216
Delair, Pierre, 59–60, 62
Delaux, Stephan, 49–50
Delpeuch, Christian, 112, 129, 229
Deng Xiaoping, 5, 14, 41, 57, 114, 175, 245
Depardieu, Gérard, 27
Dhalluin, Philippe, 260
Diageo, 21–22, 37
Dimyat, 58, 60
Dinghong Fund, 127–28
Discoveryland theme park, 109
Distribution Internationale de Vins et Alcools (Diva), 2, 3, 24, 26–28, 180, 183, 186–89, 200, 280
Dongguan R&O Sovilong Trading Company, 143
Domaine de Baron'arques, 142
Domaine de la Romanée Conti (DRC), 35, 173
Domaines Barons de Rothschild (Lafite) (DBR Lafite), 10, 16, 67, 78, 98, 102–9, 111, 155, 161, 183, 201, 243–49, 264, 276
Dourthe, Pierre, 15
Dragon Seal, 62, 70–71
Dragon's Eye, 58, 60, 71
Dragon's Hollow, 72, 252–53
Duclot Export, 183
Duhart-Milon, Château, 108
Duprat Frères, 135
Dynasty, 56–64, 71, 73, 87, 90, 95, 168–70, 175, 199, 212, 230, 244, 256–57

Ehrmann, Laurent, 99
Engerer, Frédéric, 181–83

Enoteca (Japan), 27
en primeur sales, 9–11, 18, 23, 84, 89–90, 124, 160, 179–84, 189, 196–97, 260–61, 277
    fraud and, 98–99
    Hong Kong auction and, 106
    Latour and, 171–72, 181–84, 190
    tranche system, 87
Entre-Deux-Mers, 92, 98, 120–22, 225, 242–43
EU ProSun, 231
European Union, 100
    Trade Commission, 231–34, 238, 256–57
Evenou, Yannick, 15, 170–71

Faculté d'Oenologie, Bordeaux University, 56, 64–65
Farr Vintners, 28
Félix Solís Avantis, 234
Fenwick, Joseph, 25
Fernández, Alberto, 72, 79–80
Fifth Growths, 8, 12, 162, 191
Figeac, Château, 27
Finance, Bruno, 155
financial crisis of 2008–10, 2–3, 22, 81, 100, 158–59, 191, 193
Financial Times, 61, 221
First Growths, 1, 3, 7–8, 12, 16, 20–21, 26–27, 34, 40, 81, 83, 89, 123, 126, 159, 162, 173, 179, 183, 200, 261
Five-Year Plans, 14, 55, 86–87, 113–14, 207–8
flesh searches, 217–18, 237
Focus (Chinese TV program), 156
Forbes, 111
"Four Simple Dishes and One Soup" edict, 221
Fourth Growths, 162
French Ministry of Agriculture, 233
Friendship Vineyard of Bulgaria and China, 57–59
Friuli-Venezia Giulia, 268
Fronsac, 222, 224, 266
Fujian Province, 88
Fuzhou, 39

Gallo, 262
Gansu Province, 268, 272
Gao Lin, 53–56, 64–66, 72, 80, 87, 201, 203, 208, 253–55, 280

Gao Yuan, Emma,, 53–55, 64–66, 72–73, 76–77, 79–80, 201–4, 212–14, 253–56, 268, 280
Gapenne, Laurent, 83
gei mianzi (give face or show respect), 8, 158
Ge Junjie, 188–189
Genghao winery, 139
Gleave, Sam, 98
Goldin Group, 122
Gonet
    Charles-Henri, 154
    Michel Gonet et Fils, 147, 148, 153
Grace Vineyard, 73, 75–80, 210, 244, 255–56, 280
    Chairman's Reserve, 73, 201
    People's Cabernet, 255
    Symphony, 79
Grafton, Craig, 253
Grand Branet, Château de, 129, 226
Grand Cru Classé ranking, 123
Grand Jour, Château, 226
Grand Mouëys, Château du, 128
Grands Chais de France, 87, 170, 177, 232–34
Grape Flower Industry Development Bureau of Ningxia, 207
phylloxera, 107, 249, 273
Grape Wall of China blog, 201
Graves, 8, 68
Great Famine, 14, 62
Great Wall wine, 62, 87, 114, 138–39, 175, 203, 255
Grégoire, James, 224
Greloud, Henri, 68
Grenache, 250
Gros Cabernet, 249
GSI identification system, 144
Guangdong Province, 132
Guangzhou, 132
guanxi (personal connections), 47, 54, 73, 75
Guillard, Christine, 119
Gu Kailai, 227–28

Haichang Group, 109–12, 265–67
Hao Feifei, 257
Haushalter, Georges, 111–112
Haut-Brion, Château, 8, 28, 96, 99, 179
    Haut-Brisson, Château, 121
Hauterive, Château de, 226

Hebei Province, 137, 220
Hebei Xinda Group, 264
Helan Mountain winery (Ningxia and later Pernod Ricard), 71, 202
Helan Mountains, 55, 56, 72, 80, 205, 212, 254
Helan Qingxue winery, 205–6, 212, 214
    Jia Bei Lan (Little Feet), 206, 253
Henderson, David, 66, 68, 70–71, 252–53
Hériard-Dubreuil, François, 57–60, 62
Hermann, Barbara, 181
Heywood, Neil, 228
Hillebrand France, J. F., 39
Hinton, Bill, 67
Hong Kong, 3–4, 15, 27–28, 31, 33–34, 36, 59, 74, 279
    Lafite ex-cellar auction, 104–9, 126, 161
    zero-duty, 37–41, 45, 50–51, 130
Hong Kong International Wine and Spirits Fair, 130
Hong Kong Stock Exchange, 169, 199
Hong Kong Wine and Dine Festival, 49–52, 83, 109, 144
Hôtel de Fenwick, 25
House of Flying Daggers (film), 117
Huailai, 272
Hui Muslim minority, 208–10
Hu Jintao, 193
Hungary, 61, 268
Hurun Research Institute, 189, 194–95, 213
    Report, 190, 194, 213

Indian market, 267, 281
Indonesia, 74
Industrial and Commercial Bank of China, 225
Inner Mongolia, 142, 190, 255
Institute of Master of Wine, 213
InterContinental Hotels, 241–42
International Herald Tribune, 48
International Monetary Fund, 100
International Organisation of Vine and Wine, 208
Internet, 16, 124–25, 197, 239
Ipso Facto, 159–68, 171, 264
Italy, 30, 67, 82, 189, 268

Jackson, Jess, 71
Jacubs International, 176
Janvier, Sylvain, 74–75

Japan, 4, 27–28, 57, 105
Jauffret, Jean-Paul, 10
Jefferson, Thomas, 25
Jiahua winery, 139
Jin, Mr. and Mrs., 90–92, 95–97, 100–102
Jinan Intermediate People's Court, 228
Jinchuang Suntime, 245–46, 256
Jinghongde Corporation, 155
Jin Shi Tan (development in Dalian), 110
Jiuhang website, 98
Jonqueyres, Château, 226
Jordan, Dr. Tony, 271–75
Jullien, Thomas, 51

Kadoorie family, 4–5
Kangda winery, 204
Kashmir, 268, 272
Kasite trademark, 174–78
Kasmire, Robert, 62
Kendall-Jackson, 71
Kirwan, Château, 183
Kok, Lam, 223–25
Konstantin Nikolayevich, Grand Duke of Russia, 92
Kunming, 223
Kweichow Moutai Distillery, 194–95, 224
Kwok, Peter, 121, 196–97

La Cave du Dynastie, 192
"Lafite" or "Lafitte," as name, 111
Lafite Rothschild, Château, 3, 5, 10–12, 13–14, 16–21, 28, 42, 81, 83, 98–99, 103, 105–7, 179, 195, 200, 215, 235, 276
  brand squatting and, 177
  counterfeiting and, 106, 132–34, 143–44, 155–56, 242
  ex-cellar auction of 2010, 102–9
Lafleur, Château, 68
Lafleur Chevalier, Château, 142
La Fleur de Boüard, 143
La Fleur-Pétrus, Château, 9, 223
Lagrange, Château, 258–59
La Guyennoise, 94–95, 120, 233–34, 257–58
Lai, Kingston, 236
Lalande-de-Pomerol, 113, 114
Lambrusco, 67
La Mission Haut-Brion, Château, 96
Lam Kok, 223

Lamont holding company, 229, 266
Lamour, Château, 178
Langfang Winery Château Rouge, 175
Langoa-Barton, Château, 184
Languedoc, 135, 275
Laogai Research Foundation, 61
La Pagode de l'Amitié, 69–70
Larché, Philippe, 118, 127–28, 171, 192–93, 197
La Rivière, Château de, 224–25
la Salle, Château de, 119
Latour, Château, 8, 21, 29, 49, 68, 121, 142, 181–84, 99, 190, 235
Latour á Pomerol, Château, 142
Latour-Laguens, Château, 121
Laulan Ducos, Château, 116–17, 119
Laulan French Wine, 117
Laurette, Château, 226
La Winery, 112–13, 264
LD Vins, 89, 148
Le Bon Pasteur, Château, 122
Le Carillon de l'Angélus, 143
Lehman Brothers, 81
L'Enclos, Château, 226
Léoville-Barton, Château, 184
Les Brulières de Beychevelle, Château, 142
Les Carmes Haut-Brion, Château, 142
Les Pagodes de Cos, 165
"Lesparre" wines, 153
L'Évangile, Château, 108
Liaoning Province, 109, 227
Libourne, 26, 222–25
Li Daozhi, 143, 174–78, 241–42
Li Demei, 206, 273
Li Hua, Dr. 56, 203
Li Keqiang, 264
Li Lijuan, 128
Ling Zhijun, Christie, 127
Li Peng, 14, 29, 56
Li Shen, 177, 241–42
liu mianzi, (save or gain face), 8, 101
Li Yonbo, 155
LK Wine, 263
  Le Parlement brand wine, 263
  Arnozan brand wine, 263
London International Vintners Exchange (Liv-ex), 98–99, 106, 126, 179, 189
London International Wine Fair, 134
London merchants, 126, 192, 200
Longhai Investment Group, 121

Loudenne, Château, 224
Louis Latour, 27
Louis XVI, King of France, 164
Louis Roederer, 12
Lucullus, 4
Luhuatai state farm, 55, 64–65, 254
Lu Ming, 87–88, 95, 168–71, 199
Lurton, Pierre, 92
Luze, Frédéric de, 88–89, 117–18
LVMH, 92, 204, 271
Lynch-Bages, Château, 12–13, 29, 43, 50, 174, 191

Magrez, Bernard, 67–70, 275
Maison Bouey, 147–48
Maison Ginestet, 2, 31, 112
Maison Joanne, 2
Maison Schröder & Schÿler, 2, 183, 200, 264–65, 267
Malesan, 68
Ma Lin, 95–96
Mao Zedong, 4, 14, 54, 61, 149
Margaux, Château, 8, 25, 28, 83, 92, 99, 158, 184, 198, 200, 281
Margaux region, 117, 162
Marselan, 250
Martin, Emmanuel, 94, 233–34, 257–58
Martin, Michel, 94, 120
Mau, Yvon, 155
Mazières, Philippe, 254
Médoc, 6, 8, 75, 120, 142, 201
Megara, 141–43
Merlot, 17, 65, 69, 76, 211, 245, 249–50
Mid-Autumn (Moon) Festival, 60, 85
Mido Trading, 142
Millaud Montlabert, Château, 226
Millésima, 183
Moët Hennessy, 271–74, 276, 280
Moncigale, 234
Montaigne, Michel de, 63
Montrose Food & Wine, 66–68, 253
Moody's, 159
Morrell Wine Group, 191
Moueix, Jean-Pierre, 27, 127
Moutai baijiu, 194–95
Mouton Cadet, 27
"Mouton Latour," 142
Mouton Rothschild, Château, 8, 26–28, 50, 99, 179, 184, 198, 259, 260
    brand squatting and, 142, 177
    ex-cellar auction of 2007, 104

Murchison, Ken, 78–79
Muscat
    Hamburg, 57–58, 60
    Russian, 69

Napa Valley, 30, 122, 248
Nationalist Chinese, 57
"Nava Valley," 140, 248
négociants, 1–3, 6–8, 12, 16–17, 21, 24–27, 38–39, 67–68, 82, 84–85, 91, 115, 118, 124–27, 135, 153, 155, 172–73, 180–84, 189–90, 192–93, 196, 200, 277
New York Times, 21, 219
New Zealand, 278
Niagara Icewine, 134
Nie Rongzhen, 57
'98' trade, 74
Ningxia Grape Industry Association, 203–5
Ningxiahong, 128
Ningxia Hui Autonomous Region, 53–56, 64–66, 201–14, 247, 248, 252–54, 268, 272, 273
    appellation in, 71–72
    classification and, 211–12, 214, 279
    wine route, 206–9, 254
Ningxia University, 203–4
Nixon, Richard, 194

Olivier, Hervé, 120–21
Opium Wars
    First, 33–34
    Second, 57
Opus One, 72

Pacific Asset Management, 127
Panama-Pacific International Exposition (1915), 57–58, 247
Panati Wine, 174, 176
Pan Sutong, 122
Pape Clément, Château, 68
Papillon, Philippe, 108, 159–68, 170, 173, 199, 264–65
Paradis Casseuil, Château, 242–43
Parker, Robert, 173–74
Pauillac, 10, 102
Paveil de Luze, Château, 88, 117
Pavie, Château, 142
Pei, I. M., 63
Penfolds, 177–78, 241–42

Penglai, 132, 134, 137, 140–41, 145–46, 151–52, 175, 244, 246–49, 268
Penglai Vine and Wine Bureau, 247–48
Peninsula Hotels, 4, 9
Pernod Ricard, 55, 62, 70–71, 202, 253
Petaluma, 30
Petit Verdot, 17, 211, 250
Pétrus, Château, 9, 39, 114
Pichon Baron, Château, 185
Pichon Longueville Comtesse de Lalande, Château, 10, 41, 185
Piilii. *See* USA Piilii Jepen International Group
Pinault, François, 68, 181
Ping An, 219
Place de Bordeaux, 1–2, 7, 10–12, 14–16, 21, 25–26, 28, 32, 35, 81–82, 87, 89, 91, 99, 117–18, 125, 148, 160, 167, 171–72, 182–84, 187–88, 192–93, 196, 267, 281–82
Pomerol, 114, 122, 142, 201, 222
Pontet-Canet, Château, 99, 158, 191, 236
Prats, Jean-Guillaume, 19, 31, 43, 127, 190, 274–75
Premier Cru Superieur, 92
prison labor, 60–62
Producta, 148, 263
Puchang Vineyard, 256
Pu'er, 223–25

Qingdao, 68–70, 133, 149, 153, 272, 275
QQ online service, 138
Quantum of Solace (film), 123
Qu Cheng, 111
Quenin, Jean-François, 223
Qu Naijie, 110–12, 118, 129, 197, 219, 223, 226–27, 229–30, 265–66

Raoux, Philippe, 112–16, 121, 188, 264
Reboul Salze, Christophe, 9–10, 12, 13, 81, 89, 123–25, 168–71, 199, 261, 282
Red Guard, 227
Rémy Cointreau (formerly Rémy Martin), 27, 57–62, 71, 90, 169, 199, 244
Revue du Vin de France, La, 201–2, 206, 213
Reybier, Michel, 19, 127
Richaud, Olivier, 275
Riesling, 65, 69, 76, 211, 245
Rieussec, Château, 1967, 108
Ritchie, Jamie, 104–8

Riunite, 67
Robinson, Jancis, 47–48, 135
Roche Mazet, 176, 262
Rolland, Dany, 121–22
Rolland, Michel, 121–22
Rong Jian, 203–7, 211–12, 214
Rong Yiren, 245
Rose Honey, 273
Rothschild, Edmond de, 75
Rothschild, Eric de, 16, 102
Rothschild, James de, 107
Rothschild, Philippe de, 8, 27, 50, 72, 260
Rousseau, Jean-Pierre, 1–3, 11, 15, 22–24, 26–29, 38, 180, 186–88, 192
Rouzaud, Jean-Claude, 12
RTL (reform through labor) camps, 60–61
Ruian, 161
Rui Yang Investment Management Company, 266
Russia
    Imperial, 25
    post-Soviet, 30, 53–54, 164, 267, 281

Saga , 93, 201
Saint-Émilion, 91–92, 118, 120–21, 123, 178, 201, 222, 252, 264, 271
    Classification of, 123, 125, 142
Saint-Émilion-Pomerol-Fronsac winegrowers association, 223
Saint-Estèphe, 18–19, 66, 116, 162
Saint-Julien, 162
Salin, Christophe, 10, 16, 67, 78, 102–3, 105–8, 156, 183–84, 242, 244, 246, 275
Sauternes, 92, 108, 271
Sauveterre-de-Guyenne, 98–99
Sauvignon Blanc, 92
Schÿler, Yann, 183, 259–60, 267
Seagram, 21–22, 62, 114
secondary market, 126, 192
Second Growths, 8, 18–19, 20, 40, 41, 162, 184–85, 200, 183
Sémillon, 69, 92
Shaanxi Province, 54, 56, 67, 218, 268
Shandong Province, 68, 72, 132, 137, 175, 244, 246–52, 256, 268–69, 275
Shandong Yantai Mingyang, 146, 152–54
Shanghai, 4, 39, 72
Shanghai Castel, 174, 176
Shanghai Detention Center, 45
Shanghai Panati, 176

Shanghai Prison No. 1, 62
Shanghai Sugar Cigarette and Wine,
    187–88
Shangri-La (formerly Zhongdian), 270–75
Shangri-La Winery, 271, 273–75
Shanxi Province, 73–75, 77, 79, 268, 272
Shen Dongjun, 116–19
Sheng Churui, 219
Shen Haixiong, 194–95
Shenzhen, 57, 160, 215
    counterfeit wine and, 135, 143–44, 155
Shenzhen Panati, 176
Sherry-Lehmann, 37, 100, 191
Shizuishan, 55, 254
Sichuan, 270
Silver Heights, 80, 201, 204, 212–14,
    253–56
    Emma's Reserve, 80, 213
    Family Reserve, 80, 202, 213
    Summit, 80, 201, 213
Simon, Abdallah "Ab," 21
Sino-French Demonstration Vineyard, 56
SK Group, 108, 159–61
Skyfall (film), 123–24
Sleigh, Robert, 104–5, 107–8
Sociétés d'Aménagement Foncier et
    d'Établissement Rural (Safer), 120
Sotheby's, 102–9, 126, 161, 216, 242, 276
South Africa, 74, 281
Spain, 82, 94, 100, 189, 234
special economic zones (SEZ), defined, 109
Stanhope, Tim, 241
Staples, Simon, 126
St. Pierre, Don, Jr., 29–32, 38, 41–49,
    51–52, 82–83, 159, 171–72, 194,
    216–17, 222, 225–26, 238–40
St. Pierre, Don, Sr., 29–32, 38, 42–45,
    47–49
Suntory, 49, 216–17, 240, 243
Sutcliffe, Serena, 102
Swarovski, Gernot Langes-, 32, 49
Syrah, 211, 250

Taittinger, 27, 72
Taiwan, 15
Taiyuan Institute of Technology, 73
Talbot, Château, 12
Tam, Simon, 47–49
Tang, Henry, 37
Terra Burdigala,142
terroir, 26, 56, 65, 75, 268–69

Tesiro, 116–17, 119
Teyssier, Château, 252
Thebot, Château, 226
The Wine Merchant, 81, 123, 168, 261
Third Growths, 66, 162, 183, 200
Tianjin, 59, 113, 56–64
Tianjin Agribusiness Group, 57
Tianjin Development Holdings, 63
Tianjin Farm Bureau, 58
Tianjin Food Import and Export Stock
    Company, 143
Tianjin Municipal Banqiao RTL, 61
Tianjin Yiqing Group, 57
Tian Shan Mountains, 245
Tibet, 270–71, 273
Tirlemont-Imbert, Edith, 101
Tokaj, 268
Tong, George, 157–59
Tong, Kathy, 157
Topsy Trading, 3–4, 9, 12–15, 20, 22, 28,
    125–26, 172, 178–80, 235–37, 258
Torres China, 72–73, 79–80, 255
Touton, Guillaume, 37
Tracfin, 230, 266, 281
trademarks, 150, 155–56, 174–78
Treasury Wine Estates, 177, 241–42
Tsang, John, 49–51
Tuanhe Farms, 60–62
Tuen Mun, Hong Kong, 105

Union des Grands Crus de Bordeaux
    (UGC), 83, 233–34
Union des Maisons de Bordeaux, 119
Union Mobile Pay, 219
United Kingdom, 69, 82. See also
    Britain; London merchants
United States. See also American market
    ambassador to China, 45, 47
    foreign consulate, Bordeaux, 25
U.S. Bureau of Alcohol, Tobacco, and
    Firearms (ATF), 29
Universal Exhibition (Paris, 1844), 6–7
USA Piilii Jepen International Group
    (Piilii), 161–68, 171–72, 265

VASF, 175
VATS Group, 271
Viaud, Château de, 114–16
Vignobles & Traditions, 26
Vignobles Internationaux, 21–22, 101
vin de négoce (brand wine), 82

vine diseases (mildew, rot, etc.), 17, 56, 58, 202, 249–50, 275
Vinexpo Asia-Pacific, 171
Vinexpo Bordeaux, 68, 232
Vinexpo Hong Kong, 110, 263
Vintex et Les Vignobles Grégoire, 118, 127–28, 192, 197, 224–25
Vitis labrusca, 273
Vitis vineifera, 65, 245, 273
Vouillamoz, Dr. José, 249–50

Wang Chunping, 139
Wang Lijun, 228
Wang Quan, 264
Wang Weihua, 230
Wang Zongnan, 188
Washington, George, 25
Watkins, John D., Jr., 217, 222, 239–43
Watson, A. S., 59
Webster, David, 27, 59–60
Weibo, 218–19
Wen Jiabao, 56, 193–94, 196, 198, 216–20, 228
Wen Yunsong (Winston Wen), 219
Wenzhou, 90–91, 161, 174–75, 196
Wenzhou Hardware and Electric Material Chemical Corporation, 174
Wenzhou Intermediate People's Court, 177–78
Wenzhou Panati, 176
WFOE (wholly-foreign-owned enterprise), 30–31, 44, 109
White Feather, 58
William Peel, 68
William Pitters, 68, 69
Wine and Spirit Education Trust, 213
Wine Enthusiast, 216
Wine Future Hong Kong, 173–74
Wine Intelligence (market analysts), 240
Wine Spectator, 191
Wing Lung Bank, 84
Wong, John, 61
Wong Hau Plastic Works & Trading, 157
World Economic Forum, 57
World Trade Organization, 231, 244
World War II, 4
Wu Fei, 113
Wu Hongda, Harry, 61
Wuliangye baijiu, 195
Wu Xiangdong, 271

Xiamen C&D, 88–90, 95, 117, 122–23, 125, 168, 176–77, 197–99, 236, 261–63
Xiangdu Winery, 204
Xi'an Intermediate People's Court, 218
Xihaigu, 208–9
Xi Jinping, 220–22, 227, 238, 263–65, 278
Xinhua News Agency, 195
Xinjiang Production and Construction, 245
Xinjiang Uygur Autonomous Region, 72, 245, 256, 272
Xi Xia wine, 71
Xi Zhongxun, 220
Xu, Monica, 44
Xuan, Carrie, 45, 49
Xu Ming, 228–29

Yang Dacai, 218–19
Yang Wenhua, 88–89, 95, 122–25, 176–77, 197–99, 261–64
Yantai, 132, 134, 137, 142, 151–52, 175, 268
Yeli winery, 139
Yinchuan, 53, 55–56, 79, 128, 213–14, 254
Yinchuan Forestry Bureau, 206
Yin Kai, 178
Yip, Thomas, 3–6, 8–15, 27–29, 38, 236
Yip, Vincent, 10–11, 13, 19–20, 28–29, 38, 125–26, 172, 178–80, 234–37, 258–59
Yquem, Château d', 91–93, 116, 271
Yue Feng, 246
Yu Kelong, 161–68, 171, 265
Yunnan Province, 223, 270, 273

Zhang Beili, 219
Zhang Bishi, 57, 132, 175, 247, 249
Zhang Hao, 47
Zhang Jing, 206, 214
Zhang Jinshan, 128–29
Zhang Quang Ming, 146–50, 152
Zhang Taiyang, 147–50, 153
Zhang Yanzhi, 127
Zhang Yongli, 55
Zhang Ziyi, 117
Zhao Ziyang, 29
Zhejiang Province, 90, 142, 156, 161
Zhongai, 119
Zhou Linjun, 119

ABOUT THE AUTHOR

SUZANNE MUSTACICH is a contributing editor at *Wine Specta-tor*. She was previously a Bordeaux correspondent for Agence France-Presse, a columnist for the Chinese magazine *Wine Life*, a contributor to *Meininger's Wine Business Interna-tional*, and a television producer for NBC News and several production companies. She holds a bachelor's degree from Yale University and an enology diploma from the University of Bordeaux. She lives in Bordeaux with her family.